THE WESTERN
MEDITERRANEAN
AND THE WORLD

THE BLACKWELL HISTORY OF THE WORLD

General Editor: **R.I. Moore**

A History of Latin America
Available in third edition as 'A
History of Latin America to 1825'
Peter Bakewell

The Birth of the Modern World
C.A. Bayly

The Origins of Human Society
Peter Bogucki

A History of Russia, Central Asia
and Mongolia: Volume I
David Christian

A History of Australia, New Zealand
and the Pacific
*Donald Denoon, Philippa Mein-Smith
& Marivic Wyndham*

A History of South-East Asia
Anthony Reid

A History of China
Morris Rossabi

The Western Mediterranean and the
World
Teofilo F. Ruiz

A History of India
Second Edition
Burton Stein

A History of Japan
Second Edition
Conrad Totman

THE WESTERN MEDITERRANEAN AND THE WORLD

400 CE to the Present

Teofilo F. Ruiz

WILEY Blackwell

This edition first published 2018
© 2018 John Wiley & Sons, Ltd.

The right of Teofilo F. Ruiz to be identified as the author of this work has been asserted in accordance with law.

Registered Office(s)
John Wiley & Sons, Inc., 111 River Street, Hoboken, NJ 07030, USA
John Wiley & Sons Ltd, The Atrium, Southern Gate, Chichester, West Sussex, PO19 8SQ, UK

Editorial Office
350 Main Street, Malden, MA 02148–5020, USA

For details of our global editorial offices, customer services, and more information about Wiley products visit us at www.wiley.com.

Wiley also publishes its books in a variety of electronic formats and by print-on-demand. Some content that appears in standard print versions of this book may not be available in other formats.

Library of Congress Cataloging-in-Publication Data
Names: Ruiz, Teofilo F., 1943- author.
Title: Western Mediterranean and the world : 400 CE to the Present / Teofilo F. Ruiz.
Description: 1 | Hoboken, NJ : Wiley-Blackwell, 2017. | Series: Blackwell
   history of the world ; 2331 | Includes bibliographical references and index. |
Identifiers: LCCN 2017013708 (print) | LCCN 2017019348 (ebook) |
   ISBN 9781118871423 (pdf) | ISBN 9781118871430 (epub) |
   ISBN 9781405188173 (hardback) | ISBN 9781405188166 (paper)
Subjects: LCSH: Western Mediterranean–History. | BISAC: HISTORY / Europe /
   General.
Classification: LCC DE80 (ebook) | LCC DE80 .R86 2017 (print) | DDC
   909/.09822–dc23
LC record available at https://lccn.loc.gov/2017013708

Cover image: Iryna1/Gettyimages
Cover design by Wiley

Set in 10/12 pt PlantinStd by Thomson Digital, Noida, India
Printed and bound in Malaysia by Vivar Printing Sdn Bhd

1   2018

To my sons
Daniel F. Ruiz,
David F. Ruiz, 1966–2016

CONTENTS

SERIES EDITOR'S PREFACE

THERE is nothing new in the attempt to grasp history as a whole. To understand how humanity began and how it has come to its present condition is one of the oldest and most universal of human needs, expressed in the religious and philosophical systems of every civilization. But only in the last few decades has it begun to appear both necessary and possible to meet that need by means of a rational and systematic appraisal of current historical knowledge. Until the middle of the nineteenth century, history itself was generally treated as a subordinate branch of other fields of thought and learning – of literature, rhetoric, law, philosophy, or religion. When historians began at that time to establish its independence as a field of scholarship in its own right, with its own subject matter and its own rules and methods, they made it in practice not the attempt to achieve a comprehensive account of the human past, but the history of Western Europe and of the societies created by European expansion and colonization. In laying the scholarly foundations of their discipline they also reinforced the Enlightenment's belief in the advance of "civilization" (and, more recently, of "western civilization"), and made it in this form, with relatively minor regional variations, the basis of the teaching of history almost everywhere for most of the twentieth century. Research and teaching of the histories of other parts of the world developed mainly in the context of area studies like those of ancient Greece and Rome, rooted in philology, and conducted through the exposition of the canonical texts of their respective languages.

While those approaches prevailed, world history as such remained largely the province of thinkers and writers principally interested in constructing theoretical or metaphysical systems. Only towards the end of the twentieth century did the community of academic historians begin to recognize it as a proper and even urgent field for the application of their knowledge and skills. The inadequacy of the traditional parameters of the discipline is now widely acknowledged, and the sense is growing that a world facing a common future of headlong and potentially catastrophic transformation needs its common history. The realization of such a history has been delayed, however, by simple ignorance on the one hand – for the history of enormous stretches of space and time has until very recently been known not at all, or so patchily and superficially as not to be worth revisiting – and on the other by the lack of a widely acceptable basis upon which to organize and discuss what is nevertheless the enormous and enormously diverse knowledge that we have.

The first of those obstacles is now being rapidly overcome. There is almost no part of the world or period of its history that is not the object of energetic and sophisticated investigation by archaeologists and historians. The expansion of the horizons of academic history since the 1980s has been dramatic. The quality and quantity of historical research and writing have risen exponentially in each decade, and the advances have been most spectacular in some of the areas previously most neglected. The academics have not failed to share the results of their labors. Reliable and accessible, often brilliant accounts are now readily available of regions, periods, and topics that even 20 years ago were obscure to everyone but a handful of specialists. In particular, collaborative publication, in the form of volumes or sets of volumes in which teams of authors set forth, in more or less detail, their expert and up-to-date conclusions in the field of their research, has been a natural and necessary response to the growth of knowledge. Only in that way can non-specialists, at any level, be kept even approximately in touch with the constantly accelerating accumulation of information about the past.

Yet the amelioration of one problem exacerbates the other. It is truer than it has ever been that knowledge is growing and perspectives multiplying more quickly than they can be assimilated and recorded in synthetic form. We can now describe a great many more trees in a great deal more detail than we could before. It does not always follow that we have a better view of the wood. Collaboration has many strengths, but clarity, still less originality of vision, is rarely among them. History acquires shape, structure, relevance – becomes, in the fashionable catchphrase, something for thinking with – by advancing and debating new suggestions about what past societies were like, how they worked and why they changed over long periods of time, how they resembled and why they differed from contemporaneous societies in other parts of the world, and how they interacted with one another. Such insights, like the sympathetic understanding without which the past is dead, are almost always born of individual creativity and imagination. That is why each volume in this series embodies the work and vision of a single author. Synthesis on such a scale demands learning, resolution, and, not least, intellectual and professional courage of no ordinary degree. We have been singularly fortunate in finding scholars of great distinction who are willing to undertake it.

There is a wealth of ways in which world history can be written. The oldest and simplest view, that it is best understood as the history of contacts between peoples previously isolated from one another, from which (as some think) all change arises, is now seen to be capable of application since the earliest times. An influential alternative focuses upon the tendency of economic exchange to create self-sufficient but ever expanding "worlds" which sustain successive systems of power and culture. Another seeks to understand the differences between societies and cultures, and therefore the particular character of each, by comparing the ways in which their values, social relationships, and structures of power have developed. The rapidly emerging field of ecological history returns to a very ancient tradition of seeing interaction with the physical environment, and with other animals, at the center of the human predicament, while insisting that its understanding demands an approach which is culturally, chronologically, and geographically comprehensive. More recently still, "Big History," led by a contributor to this series, has begun to show how human history can be integrated with that not only of the natural, but of the cosmic environment, and better understood in consequence.

The Blackwell History of the World seeks not to embody any single approach, but to support them all, as it will use them all, by providing a modern, comprehensive, and accessible account of the entire human past. Each volume offers a substantial overview of a portion of world history large enough to permit, and indeed demand, the reappraisal of customary boundaries of regions, periods, and topics, and in doing so reflects the idiosyncrasies of its sources and its subjects, as well as the vision and judgment of its author. The series as a whole combines the indispensable narratives of very long-term regional development with global surveys of developments across the world, and of interaction between regions and what they have experienced in common, or visited upon one another, at particular times. Together these volumes will provide a framework in which the history of every part of the world can be viewed, and a basis upon which most aspects of human activity can be compared across both time and space. A frame offers perspective. Comparison implies respect for difference. That is the beginning of what the past has to offer the future.

R.I. Moore

SERIES EDITOR'S ACKNOWLEDGMENTS

The editor is grateful to all the contributors for advise and assistance on the design and contents of the series as a whole, as well as on individual volumes. Both editor and contributors wish to place on record their immense debt, individually and collectively, to John Davey, formerly of Blackwell publishers, without whose vision and enthusiasm the series could not have been initiated, and to his successor Tessa Harvey, without whose energy, skill, and diplomacy, sustained over many years, it could not have been realized.

ACKNOWLEDGMENTS

Writing this brief acknowledgment while visiting Cuba in late November 2016 – the day after Fidel Castro's death marked the passing of a towering historical figure (regardless of one's ideological point of view) and preceded by the incongruous election of Donald Trump as president of the United States – I was struck by the connections between my concluding remarks in this book on the significance of present-day migration in the western Mediterranean as one of the key issue of the early twenty-first century and the concomitant vicious anti-immigrant discourse from many western powers and from Trump and his followers. Brexit and the rise of white nationalist and/or populist parties and sentiments in the United States and in Europe has unleashed something quite sinister and troubling on the world. Our children and grandchildren will suffer the consequences of fear-mongering discourse and racial hatred. They will need to struggle mightily to recover the social and political gains made in the western Mediterranean and elsewhere in the world over the last six or seven decades.

While the Mediterranean has been historically a place of conflict – ethnic, religious, political – it has also been a site of cultural, linguistic, and religious plurality and of productive encounters. These encounters and conflicts have yielded seminal cultural achievements and a way of life conducive to positive human experiences. Let's hope against hope that in the lands around the Middle Sea, in the United States, and in Europe the free movement of diverse people and their enduring encounters lead to novel hybrid cultural production and mutual understanding.

I apologize for beginning my acknowledgments in such a somber manner. Far more pleasant is to acknowledge here those colleagues and friends whose scholarly example, suggestions, and friendship have helped shape my academic life in general and this book in particular. First and foremost is Robert I. Moore, the general editor of the series in which this book appears. His wise counsel, profound erudition, generosity, and, most of all, his kind guidance and good humor have been inspiring and helpful. As with everything I have ever published, in France I owe a great debt of gratitude to the late Jacques Le Goff and to Denis Menjot, Jacques Revel, Adeline Rucquoi, Abraham Udovitch, and Lucette Valensi. In Spain, I have benefitted from the enduring support and friendship of James Amelang, Hilario Casado, Francisco García Serrano, Xavier Gil Pujol, Manuel González Jiménez, Jorge Ortuño, and Jesús Solórzano Telechea.

In England, Sir John H. Elliott has been a sustaining influence in my personal and academic life, as have been Judith Herrin and Peter Linehan's exemplary scholarly life and friendship. In the United States, I have learned a great deal from the late and much missed Olivia Remie Constable, and from Paul Freedman, Brian Catlos, William Jordan, Richard Kagan, Marie Keheller, Yuan Gen Liang, David Nirenberg, Jarbel Rodríguez, Núria Silleras Fernández, and my graduate and undergraduate students. At UCLA, Lynn Hunt and Margaret Jacob have been both colleagues and a true emotional family. Similarly, Stephen Aron, Ali Behdad, Arch Getty, Efrain Kristal, Ron Mellor, David Myers, Jesús Torrecilla, Joan Waugh, Juliet Williams, and many others have made our life at UCLA a most rewarding one. Janani Govindankutty, Wiley-India, by her selfless work and constant attentiveness, has had an important role in bringing this book into print. I owe a great debt to Giles Flitney, who has copy-edited the entire manuscript and saved me from endless grammatical infelicities, inconsistences, and other sins. Truly, his work here has been remarkable while allowing my voice and idiosyncrasies to remain. I feel as if this book would not be possible without Giles's work. Although I am not T.S. Eliot, he truly is, as Eliot wrote of Pound's editorial work, *il miglior fabbro*. I am grateful to Giles, to Janani, and to all my friends. My wife and comrade, Scarlett Freund, has always sailed the Mediterranean, both physically and metaphorically, with me. She does so in this book as well.

On August 15, 2016, my son David died suddenly. A selfless human being and indefatigable traveler, his death was a wrenching blow, the kind from which one never fully recovers. My oldest son, Daniel, has proven a tower of strength keeping the family afloat during these difficult times. It is to my two sons, one no longer here, the other very much so, that I dedicate this book, a token of my paternal love.

Los Angeles, Paris, La Habana, 2017

[1] THE WESTERN MEDITERRANEAN: SITES OF ENCOUNTER AND CULTURAL PRODUCTION

Mediterráneo

Lyrics of a song by Joan Manuel Serrat

Quizá porque mi niñez sigue jugando en tu playa
y escondido tras las cañas duerme mi primer amor
llevo tu luz y tu olor por donde quiera que vaya
y amontonado en tu arena guardo amor, juegos y penas.

Yo que en la piel tengo el sabor amargo del llanto eterno
que han vertido en ti cien pueblos de Algeciras a Estambul
para que pintes de azul sus largas noches de invierno
a fuerza de desventuras tu alma es profunda y oscura.

A tus atardeceres rojos se acostumbraron mis ojos como el recodo al camino
soy cantor, soy embustero, me gusta el juego y el vino, tengo alma de marinero.
¡Qué le voy hacer! si yo nací en el Mediterráneo.

Y te acercas y te vas después de besar mi aldea
jugando con la marea te vas pensando en volver
eres como una mujer perfumadita de brea
que se añora y que se quiere, que se conoce y se teme.

¡Ay!, si un día para mi mal viene a buscarme la parca
empujad al mar mi barca con un levante otoñal
y dejad que el temporal desguace sus alas blancas
y a mi enterradme sin duelo entre la playa y el cielo.

The Western Mediterranean and the World: 400 CE to the Present, First Edition. Teofilo F. Ruiz.
© 2018 John Wiley & Sons, Ltd. Published 2018 by John Wiley & Sons, Ltd.

En la ladera de un monte más alto que el horizonte quiero
tener buena vista mi cuerpo será camino, le daré verde a los pinos
y amarillo a la. . . . Cerca del mar porque yo nací en el Mediterráneo.

Source: http://fotos.euroresidentes.com/fotos/postales_Alicante/Mar_Mediterraneo_Azul/
imagepages/image22.html. The song, as written and performed by Joan Manuel Serrat, may
be found on youtube.com or on Google under "Yo nací en el Mediterráneo."

In Joan Manuel Serrat's extraordinarily lyrical song "Mediterráneo" (1970), the gifted Catalan singer presents us with a moving vision of the Mediterranean Sea. His song captures the sea's essence far more compellingly than historiographical debates or scholarly works may do. In its moving lyrics, Serrat packs an emotional and psychological punch that goes to the very heart of the issues this book seeks to address. The portrait of the Mediterranean that emerges from his well-crafted song is a complex one, aiming to grasp and explain what it means to be born and to grow by the shores of a sea or an ocean, and, in Serrat's case, to be born by the shores of the Mediterranean. Perhaps because I too was born and grew up by the shores of a sea (the Caribbean) – a different sea indeed but as beguiling nonetheless – the song speaks to me in ways that it may not do to someone bound to the land and not to the ocean.

In Serrat's song, the protagonist carries the "light and smell of the Mediterranean on his skin," but also the "bitter taste of the tears shed by a hundred different people [nations] from Algeciras to Istanbul." We gaze therefore on the whole span of the Middle Sea: from one of its most westernmost towns, Algeciras, a town redolent with its Muslim past and Arabic name, to the magical city of Istanbul with its Roman, Greek, and Ottoman overlapping histories. "Mediterranean" evokes the love dreams of childhood and adolescence, but also the accumulated bitter memories of many generations. The sea, compared in a song to a woman – and in several Romance languages the sea is either feminine, as in *la mer* in French, or has changing gender registers, either masculine: *el mar es azul* (the sea is blue), or feminine: *echar un barco a la mar* (to sail a boat in the sea) in Spanish – is longed for, loved, known and unknown, feared. The Mediterranean is a space of storms, long winter nights – something that we seldom associate with the Mediterranean, but which is another of its realities. But the Mediterranean is also is a sea of crystalline blue.

Nothing, however, is more telling about the relations of people to the sea than the song's reoccurring phrase: "yo nací en el Mediterráneo." I was born, Serrat insists, not in Spain, not in Catalonia. I was born, he reminds us throughout the song, on the shores of a sea that has shaped my identity, my memories, my hopes, and my sadness. And seas truly shape one's identity – whether Serrat's, mine, or those of others born by the shores of a sea – in ways not very different but far more intense than the identities shaped by nations. The fluid and constructed way in which Serrat identifies himself is not very different from the manner in which I have often, through my very long life, identified myself as "having been born in the Caribbean." That is, not born in Cuba itself, but born by the shores of a sea that gives me a shared culture, language, music, and identity with all those who came from the collection of islands that dot the Caribbean Sea. Thus, my Caribbean identity remains the constant in the long list of all other sorts of identities gained and lost over the decades of my life. And, yet, my connection with the sea remains stronger than identities constructed by political jurisdictions, ideological loyalties, and the like. Written in 1970, Serrat's wonderful song reached out to a world outside Franco's repressive Spain (especially towards the Catalans) and pledged allegiance to something older, broader, and far more enduring than the demands of the nation-state.

This overlapping set of identities, this sense of belonging to an ancestral sea that is our home, can also be found in the Mediterranean Sea's quintessential novel, Alexander Dumas's enchanting *The Count of Monte Cristo*. Although the late chapters of the novel have Paris as a setting, far away from the warm shores of the Mediterranean, the site for its early dramatic developments that power the entire novel are firmly bound with the history of the sea. From the ship, the *Pharaon*, that brought Edmund Dantès from Smyrna, Trieste, Naples, Civitavecchia, and the island of Elba to Marseille and his cruel destiny, from the fears about the fate of the *Pharaon* in a later voyage and thus the threat to the financial fate of the Morrell family, to the Catalan community on the fringes of Marseille, the Mediterranean Sea is ever present, as are its uncertainty, passionless cruelties, and rewards. In *The Count of Monte Cristo* we also meet those sailors – a mysterious and heterogeneous crew in the service of the Count. Their places of origin were to be found in many different towns and islands dotting the Mediterranean. They spoke a *lingua franca*, understood only by those who lived *in* the sea; they had no home or loyalty to any nation, except to their calling, to their master, to their sea. We also meet bandits on the outskirts of Rome, a reminder of Braudel's description of violence and banditry as resistance to the state in his study of the Mediterranean in the age of Philip II (see below). In Dumas's fictional work, bandits remained a fixture of the nineteenth-century Mediterranean landscape.

In a lesser key, Pérez Reverte's entertaining novel, *La reina del sur* (*The Queen of the South*), a novel inspired loosely by *The Count of Monte Cristo*, presents us, once again, with a group of men carrying drugs between North Africa and Spain. Their allegiances, diverse places of origin, and identities are erased by their illicit activities and by the brotherhood of the sea. That the protagonist of the novel is a Mexican woman, fleeing to Spain away from the violence and vengeance of drug lords, serves only as a reminder, though a fictional one, of the manner in which the Mediterranean, ancient or present, has always been connected to a broader world beyond its shores.

There were of course earlier fictional histories spanning the Mediterranean and bringing into focus the transnational character of the Sea. Storytelling describing the links that bound the Middle Sea is also an important part of this book. These stories often glossed the inextricable relations between Muslims and Christians along the shores of the Mediterranean, or the movement from one shore to another. In Johanot Martorell's *Tirant lo Blanch* (late fifteenth century), for example, the hero, born in Brittany, travels (and fights) in France, England, and the eastern Mediterranean. Serving the Byzantine emperor in his campaigns against the Ottoman Turks, Tirant, one of Cervantes's most beloved characters and mentioned most lovingly in *Don Quixote*, is a very different knight from the usual preposterous and hard-to-believe warriors of late medieval romances. Through Tirant's deeds, we see a portrait of the diversity and "connectivity" of the entire sea.

Flores y Blancaflor, a medieval text I will revisit in greater detail in Chapter 9, was also a Mediterranean romance (most likely of southern French origin), with versions in several languages. The entire fictional story was integrated as historical fact into one of Alfonso X of Castile's (1252–1284) works. As was often the case, it told the story of a romance between a Muslim and a Christian, alerting us to the porous sexual frontiers, notwithstanding the strict rules governing interfaith sexual liaisons that existed along the shores of the Mediterranean. In Chapter 9, I will discuss Simon Barton's remarkable recent book on the subject of interfaith sexual and romantic liaisons, but we must now move from fiction to history and what it tells us about the Mediterranean.

WRITING THE HISTORY OF THE MEDITERRANEAN

All who attempt such an enterprise as writing the history of the Mediterranean do so in the considerable shadow cast by Fernand Braudel's monumental *The Mediterranean and the Mediterranean World in the Age of Philip II*. Any serious attempt to capture the history of that sea and of the people who lived along its shores needs to be located, first and foremost, in Braudel's paradigmatic and ambitious efforts. But Braudel has been followed, altered, and refined by the efforts of subsequent historians. Over the more than a half-century since the original publication, in French, of *The Mediterranean* in 1949, these scholarly works have helped to fill some of the gaps in Braudel's narrative or to mildly and diplomatically critique some of his findings.[1] In many ways, more than a thoughtful and superbly researched history book, *The Mediterranean* is also a heartfelt declaration of Braudel's emotional involvement with the Middle Sea. The first lines of his preface to the first edition (in French) are articulated in a language not far removed from that of Serrat's song with which this introduction begins. Braudel writes: "I have loved the Mediterranean with passion, no doubt because I am a northerner like so many others in whose footsteps I have followed. I have joyfully dedicated long years of study to it – much more than all my youth. In return, I hope that a little of this joy and great deal of Mediterranean sunlight will shine from the pages of this book."[2]

Braudel sets his monumental work within the context of passion and sunlight. His work is imbued with both: by his obvious relish in his task and by the manner in which he captured the light and spirit of the Mediterranean. Although much has been done over the last three decades to cover some of the gaps left by Braudel and to formulate new conceptual and methodological ways of doing this history, *The Mediterranean* remains the paradigmatic treatment of seas in general and of the Middle Sea in particular. More to the point, the attempts to fill some of the gaps in Braudel's formulations have also coincided with growing interest in the Mediterranean, its religious and linguistic plurality, and its role as a site of encounter and boundary crossings. These interests have led to vigorous historiographical debates. But all begins with, and stems from, Braudel's legacy. As important as the topic is, however, this book is not about the historiography of the Mediterranean or about Braudel's achievements or faults. This book is about some very specific themes in the western Mediterranean over *la longue durée* (another one of Braudel's contributions to the way in which we do history). Nonetheless, I would be remiss were I not to mention briefly some of the most salient recent contributions to Mediterranean studies. The chapters that follow are of course deeply indebted to them.

MEDITERRANEAN HISTORIOGRAPHY

Braudel's *The Mediterranean* deployed some formidable and innovative approaches to regional history. Focusing, as he did, on the early modern Mediterranean – though he had written a counterpart for the ancient Mediterranean that has come to light only recently[3] – his work was propelled by three significant methodological innovations, emerging, as they did, from the influential *École des Annales*. One was the idea of *histoire totale* or "total history," that is, a history that examines historical processes and changes as a whole, with attention to geography, climate, economic exchanges, and other historical factors without reifying traditional political narratives. The other significant contribution was to see these historical processes and changes over a long period of time (*la longue durée*). This long perspective allowed Braudel, as it does other historians committed to this methodological project, to see the development and transformations of social, economic, and political structures (Braudel did not always fully address topics such as culture and religion) over time.

His other significant methodological stance had to do with *conjoncture*. This is a difficult term to translate. Its literal meaning is conjuncture, by which Braudel meant the combination of circumstances that propelled historical change and events, or conjuncture between things happening on each different timescale. The third aspect of Braudel's work has often been neglected. Because his *The Mediterranean* is written with such compelling vigor and because the book (two volumes) begins with a long, expansive, and extraordinarily engaging geographical study of the sea and of Mediterranean lands, scholars often fail to pay enough attention to the second part of the book. It contains a detailed account of political events: what he called "*histoire évén-ementielle*," that is, the history of events. All three elements of this ambitious novel way of writing history offered, or Braudel hoped it would do, a total history of the sea and of its main political protagonists, Philip II and the Sublime Porte or Ottoman Empire.

Placing the sea, geography, and the economy at the center of his account, Braudel promoted an awareness of the environment and the relationship between landmass and sea that forcefully reversed long traditions of historical writing. Although privileging the environment was not new – there is the remarkable description of the *sertão* or barren lands in Bahia's (Brazil) interior in Euclides da Cunha's late nineteenth-century description of the Canudos rebellion – Braudel's book shook traditional historiography with its bold call to a different kind of history. Still very much read and assigned in graduate courses (I do so even in undergraduate courses) as a model of historical excellence, Braudel has had critics over the years. His "total history" has been found not to be all-inclusive, as critics have noted his neglect or underestimation of the roles of religion and culture in historical processes. Others, such as the noted Mediterranean historian David Abulafia, have questioned the uniqueness of the Mediterranean while engaging in broad comparative approaches to Middle Seas in Europe and elsewhere, though, to be fair, Braudel himself also raised some of the same questions.

Although many historians have sought to modify or challenge specific aspects of Braudel's magnum opus, the most salient additions or critiques have come from several Anglo-American scholars who have redrawn and notably expanded the boundaries of Mediterranean studies. Yet, if I may be bold enough to say this, without lessening the value of Braudel's original contribution, we see further than Braudel because we still sit, paraphrasing Bernard de Chartres's comments about medieval use of classical knowledge, on the shoulders of a giant.

David Abulafia, a distinguished medievalist at Cambridge and one of the foremost scholars of the western Mediterranean, has published numerous works on the topic, ranging from a remarkable study of Frederick II (1212–1250), the Hohenstaufen ruler of Sicily and Imperial Germany, to a series of valuable studies of the western Mediterranean, above all, of the medieval kingdom of Majorca (Mallorca) – which also encompassed areas of what is now southern France. Abulafia has recently defined the Mediterranean as a heuristic category within a global framework. Rather than privileging Mediterranean uniqueness, as has been done traditionally since Late Antiquity, Abulafia posits it as a "Middle Sea," sharing with other "middle seas" throughout the world their role as sites for cultural and economic exchanges. Although Braudel had already described the Mediterranean's role in broader patterns of commercial and cultural exchanges, Abulafia, by decentering the Mediterranean, locates his studies of the sea within a methodological approach in which specific geographical location becomes less important than shared historical processes of material culture and commercial links.

Abulafia's critique of Braudel's preference for structures rather than for human beings may be perhaps a bit unfair. Braudel did indeed conceive his work in a structuralist framework, but he peppered his narrative – even his descriptions of the landscape – with vivid vignettes, showing the interaction between humans and the environment. Nonetheless, Abulafia's emphasis on a comparative analysis and on exchanges and cultural transmissions beyond the narrow geographical borders of the Middle Sea locates human experiences at the center of his inquiry. Braudel, for all my defense of his examples and vignettes, clearly placed the Mediterranean physical space – here understood as a broad geographical region with the sea as its center – as the driving locomotive for his broad understanding of the Mediterranean world.[4]

Peregrine Horden and Nicholas Purcell's influential study, *The Corrupting Sea: A Study of Mediterranean History*, a book that will invoked in one of my notes since it provides a thoughtful and expansive historiographical introduction to the study of the Mediterranean, is the first volume of a projected two-volume work. The planned follow-up to Horden and Purcell's ambitious first volume is entitled *The Liquid Sea*. In these two volumes, Horden (a medievalist) and Purcell (an ancient historian) seek to explore those periods of Mediterranean history, ancient and medieval, not examined by Braudel. Although we now know, as noted earlier, that Braudel had written a study of the ancient Mediterranean, it was not published until one year after (2001) the publication of *The Corrupting Sea*. The latter book offers readers and scholars something approaching Braudel's *histoire totale* but in a very different methodological key. Covering a period of more than two millennia, *The Corrupting Sea* defines what the Mediterranean meant to those who have written, lived, or sought to historicize the sea as a category of knowledge. Here also, the historical ecology of the sea trumps the history of nations and lands that surrounded (and surround) the Mediterranean. Horden and Purcell make the critical distinction between the history *of* the Mediterranean, that is, the history of the sea itself, and history *in* the Mediterranean, that is, the history not of the sea itself but of the region's polities and geographical features.[5]

Emphasizing, in Part II of *The Corrupting Sea*, the ecological features of the sea and of Mediterranean lands, Horden and Purcell turn their attention from the broad expanses of the Middle Sea to what they describe as "micro ecologies," narrowing their focus to overlapping "connectivities." Horden and Purcell's eye for detail, their liberal borrowing of a diversity of methodological approaches and ancillary disciplines, and, most of all, the remarkable ambitious breadth of their enterprise makes *The Corrupting Sea* a landmark of historical research and writing. I will come back to some of the most significant features of this book in subsequent chapters, but for now it may be useful to engage the distinction its two authors make between history *of* and history *in* the Mediterranean.

Whether one may agree or not with the usefulness of defining the history *of/in* the Mediterranean, the reality is that Horden and Purcell posit two distinct ways of doing that history. At the simplest level, history *in* the Mediterranean addresses historical developments taking place within specific geographical or ecological contexts. For all practical purposes, these histories are written with little regard to the history of the sea. History *of* the Mediterranean, on the other hand, blends the history of the sea itself, its geography and ecology, with the history of events, the rise and fall of polities along the Mediterranean shores, that is, what happened in the Mediterranean and adjacent lands. In that sense, their critique of Braudel for neglecting, as noted above in the case of Abulafia, human agency is also not fully grounded in the reality of Braudel's contributions.

There have been numerous histories in the Mediterranean that focus on the narrative of battles, piracy, political developments, and the like. John Julius Norwich's *The Middle Sea: A History of the Mediterranean* (2006) is a very good example of a cultural and political narrative with little or next to nothing about the sea itself. At the same time, one could not write a history *of* the Mediterranean that is not at the same time also a history that takes place *in* that sea and its adjacent landmasses. Beyond Abulafia, Horden, and Purcell's signal interventions into Mediterranean historiographical debates, Herzfeld and others have in turn criticized Horden, Purcell, and other historians for artificially constructing the Mediterranean as a category that, according to Herzfeld, may approach the same standing as Edward Said's "Orientalism," that is, a cultural construction of a model that reflects the ideological and methodological proclivities of specific scholars, rather than the reality of the Mediterranean's historical and anthropological structures.[6]

How Then to Write a History of the Mediterranean?

Perhaps one way to escape the essentializing of the Mediterranean as a heuristic or epistemological category (to adopt Herzfeld's ironic trope) is to place the sea, as Abulafia and Bresson have suggested, in a comparative global framework, emphasizing common themes rather than unique aspects. It may also be worth highlighting something that Horden and Purcell's *The Corrupting Sea* already does so well: the varieties of Mediterraneans (within the Mediterranean itself). The sea must be understood in its totality while, at the same time, the geographical, topographical, and historical differences of its various regions must be noted. In writing a history *of* the sea and the history of each region *on* the shores of the Mediterranean and of the lands beyond the sea – areas that were connected to it by trade and culture – we may end of with a plurality of histories. As Sharon Farmer discusses in a recent book on the silk industry in thirteenth- and fourteenth-century Paris, to give just one example, immigrants from the Mediterranean and silk cocoons from Persia were at the heart of silk production in Paris.[7] Once again, we see the circulation of people and commodities from the Mediterranean into Northern Europe and back, or the "connectivity" of the Middle Sea with a world beyond. Only if we consider all these links between the sea and other parts of the world may we have a more sensible view of the complexities, difficulties, and romance of Mediterranean history.

The task at hand is therefore challenging indeed. To begin, this volume addresses the history of the western Mediterranean – one of those many seas within the larger sea. There are many excellent reasons to think of the Mediterranean as a whole, and to write its history not piecemeal but as an integrated scholarly enterprise: à la Braudel, Horden, Purcell, and Abulafia. The sea of course knows no boundaries, and the many different subdivisions imposed on the Mediterranean – the Aegean Sea, the Adriatic, the Alboran Basin, the Algerian Basin, and so forth – are the result as much of the geographers' and historians' appetite for creating taxonomies of knowledge as they are the result of specific historically lived experiences.

Nonetheless, the western Mediterranean basin is indeed a recognizable and separate entity within the entire span of the whole Mediterranean. It is clearly and sharply different in terms of its geography and climate from the eastern Mediterranean (see Chapter 2). It is also distinct in terms of its history after the demise of the Roman Empire in the West. In chapters 2, 3, and 4, I attempt to make a far more elaborate argument of why topographically and historically the western Mediterranean was indeed a discrete and recognizable subject for our inquiry. A companion volume in this series addresses the eastern Mediterranean. These works will, I hope, complement each other and provide a comprehensive portrait of different facets of the entire Mediterranean and Mediterranean society in the context of world history.

In examining history *in* the Mediterranean (a necessary concomitant to the history *of* the Sea) there are powerful incentives to focus on one particular region of the sea and to do so within specific points of departure and conclusion for our story. Circa 400 CE witnessed the progressive disruption of the political, religious, and linguistic unity of the Roman Mediterranean world. Such fractures resulted from the division of the Roman Empire (the prodigious builder of Mediterranean civilization) into distinctive eastern and western parts – a process institutionally started by Diocletian and Constantine in the late third and early fourth century. The further collapse of the empire in the West and its replacement by a variety of Germanic kingdoms in the fifth century, on the one hand, and the emergence of Byzantium in the East, on the other, accelerated the process of fragmentation of the unity of the Roman world. The rise of Islam and its rapid spread throughout the southern shores of the Mediterranean, and eventually into Iberia and Sicily, further helped to create the social, political, linguistic, religious, and cultural context for the emergence of new Mediterranean societies. I will have a great deal more to say about the historical developments of polities in the western Mediterranean in Chapter 3, but for now it suffices to acknowledge the geographical and temporal limits of this book. Succeeding chapters seek to provide, through the use of case studies, vignettes, and a thematic approach, a view of the western Mediterranean. Our story focuses on the sea and the lands adjacent to the sea from the Straits of Gibraltar to Sicily, from the European northern Mediterranean lands – what eventually became Spain, France, and Italy – to the shores of North Africa. Islands also play an important role in Mediterranean history – the Balearic Islands, Corsica, Sardinia, and Sicily – so do the smaller islands that dot the western sea. Equally important for this inquiry is the Mediterranean southern coast in North Africa and the narrow strip of lands between the sea and the Atlas and Riff Mountains. The latter served as pathways into the Sahara and into a very different sea of sand.

But as Braudel and others have taught us, the impact of the Mediterranean, whether climatic, economic, political, or cultural, extended far inland into the heart of the continental masses that bounded the sea and beyond the region, as the Mediterranean became an integral part of a global community. Unless this is to become a brief synopsis of historical developments in the Mediterranean, the only possible way to approach the Mediterranean's long history is, as noted earlier, to do so thematically and to illustrate these varied themes with examples that, though necessarily arranged in chronological fashion, attempt to provide the experience of what the Mediterranean meant for those who lived and died in its waters, for those who traveled, traded, were sold into slavery and redeemed, produced and carried cultural artifacts from one part of the sea to the other, waged war, and loved there. What I wish to do here is to approximate the complex range of experiences of those people who, like Joan Manuel Serrat, were born in the Mediterranean, or who, as Fernand Braudel wrote in the introduction to his great book, "loved the Mediterranean with passion, no doubt because I am a northerner like so many others in whose footsteps I have followed," in the centuries between the waning of Rome in the West and our modern global world.

OVERVIEW AND CONTENTS

As noted before, while one cannot easily escape the methodological questions and issues raised by Braudel's great book more than half a century ago, this volume of Blackwell's *History of the World* seeks to place the Mediterranean within a broader geographical and chronological context and to address questions about culture, language, and religion partially neglected by Braudel's rightly famous work. Parting from a not so veiled geographical and climatic determinism, Braudel emphasized the unity of the Mediterranean world. Although the political axis of his book was located in Madrid and centered chronologically on the long and complex reign of Philip II (1556–1598), *The Mediterranean* could have been also titled *The Mediterranean in the Age of Suleiman I, the Magnificent (1520–66)*. The historical reality of what the Romans called "Mare Nostrum" and recent historiography has described as the "corrupting sea" is that one cannot examine one part of the Mediterranean, as this volume may do in emphasizing the Western Mediterranean, without reference to the entire sea. One should also accept the links that bound, in spite of seemingly cultural, political, and religious differences, the Mediterranean world into a coherent or "connected" whole.

Nonetheless, I do not wish to mislead the reader by stressing the unity of the Mediterranean or the continuity of specific structures. One of the most attractive aspects of attempting to write a history of the Mediterranean from the waning of Late Antiquity in the West to the present is the possibility of exploring in some detail the tensions between continuity and discontinuity in the region, between unity and fragmentation. For example, Braudel pointed to the ease of communication provided by the sea as an important factor in making the region a coherent whole (though he pointed to the difficulties of travel as well); yet, recent research has shown that sailing the Mediterranean was not always easy or fast (see Chapter 2 et passim). Calm winds, corsair activity, storms, and the like – which seem to have been rather frequent – could make travel between the Spanish coast and Oran, a Spanish outpost on the North African coast, to give just one example, a very difficult and lengthy enterprise indeed in the sixteenth century.

In facing the challenges of this project, I am conscious of its great difficulties and of the vast literature that needs to be mastered to achieve an acceptable outcome. Any expectation of the most perfunctory chronological coverage must be immediately abandoned. Even a thematic approach would have to occasionally neglect entire regions and/or chronological periods. The sources extant will also determine what can or cannot be covered in some detail. Perhaps, it may be best to spell out what kind of contributions this volume can make to our understanding of the Mediterranean and to locate the sea and its surrounding lands in the larger context of world history.

THEMES AND CHAPTERS

After this preliminary and introductory chapter, Part I includes six distinct chapters or discussions of different but interrelated topics. These chapters seek to provide geographical, historical, and cultural contexts to the themes subsequently explored throughout the book. Part I, Geography, History, and Cultural Contexts, Chapter 2 explores the geography and climate of the western Mediterranean region. Moving clockwise from Sicily to continental Italy, this chapter offers a summary of our present knowledge of the geography and climate of the region and the role of the environment on the historical development of the Mediterranean world. While I do not think geography solely determines historical developments, it is clear that geographical and climatic features have a great deal to do with historical development, patterns of trade, linguistic transmission, and the like. It is important to note that geographical conditions changed due to diverse historical developments and climatic changes. The coast of North Africa, one of the largest grain-producing regions of the ancient world, to give just one example, has a very different climate today and a very different economic structure.

In Chapter 2 (and in subsequent chapters), I deploy archival information, gathered at the Archivo de la Corona de Aragón (specifically documents from the Consulado de Comercio, 1766–1868). This approach allows for archival-based case studies that illuminate specific moments or issues in the history of the sea. These case studies, in Chapter 2 and in other chapters, add, I hope, to our understanding of the Mediterranean climate and economy. They serve to emphasize the real difficulties found by sailors and sea captains as they plied the waters of the western Mediterranean in pursuit of knowledge, profits, and prey. Since these "protests against the sea," as these documents are known, will be cited elsewhere throughout this book, I offer here a full reference to these materials, as well as a short explanation of the archive.[8]

In Part I, chapters 3 and 4, I wish to present a brief outline of the political history of the region from around 400 CE to the late twentieth century. While eschewing any hope of providing an extensive political narrative, it is important to establish a political context against which we may explore other themes in the history of the region. My brief historical narrative is told with emphasis on geographical regions – certainly in Chapter 3 – rather than on the world of present-day nations. As I have done with geography, I have attempted to trace the political developments of Sicily, North Africa, Mediterranean Iberia, Mediterranean France, and western Italy, before exploring the well-known world of nations in Chapter 4. Thematically, I am interested here in the swings from unity to fragmentation, that is, the end of the Roman Mediterranean world, the rise of fragmented political entities, and the eventual reshaping of these polities on the shores of the western Mediterranean around national identities. Emphasis is placed on the medieval and early modern period when the political identities of these different political entities began to be set in permanent patterns of political organization. Only a brief description of modern political developments has been included in Chapter 4. It would take another volume just to list the complex politics of the western Mediterranean in the twentieth century alone.

This does not mean, of course, that political developments in the contemporary world are not important. In many respects, important topics, explored along the course of the book, such as immigration, warfare, standardization of language, religious forms, the transmission of cultural forms, and others resulted from, or were deeply influenced by, the rise of nations. My own sense of this is that, while we should not neglect contemporary events – and I try to comment on them elsewhere – the Late Middle Ages and the early modern period were significant moments in the construction of Mediterranean societies. As I will argue later, increase in corsair activity and naval conflicts between Christian powers, corsairs, and the Sublime Porte radically rearranged the economic structures that had long defined Mediterranean society.

In Part I, chapters 5, 6, and 7, I turn to questions of religious culture and language, and the move from a theoretical religious and linguistic unity in the ancient western Mediterranean to the fragmented religious and linguistic landscape that has existed since the eighth century. For religion, I do so by tracing the development of religious affiliation, or lack of it, over time. Chapter 5 examines not only the diverse religions that to this day divide the western Mediterranean, but also those heterodox movements that challenged the hegemony of some of the religions that had established their systems of beliefs in the western Mediterranean basin. Emphasis is placed on the role of religion in creating regional and national identities; thus, my approach here is less on questions of spirituality, though I briefly examine them, as it is on the function of religion as a cultural factor in the emergence of regional and national identities.

Chapter 6 focuses on the question of individual conversions from one religious culture to another and the role of renegades in the religious, cultural, and political life of the western Mediterranean, while chapter 7 explores the relationship of language, culture, and place. I focus on language formation and linguistic identity. In many respects, the emergence of new languages was closely related to the emergence of national communities. In this chapter, as in other chapters, I seek to address the same issues of unity and fragmentation raised earlier. I do so by following the development of different linguistic communities in the region from the demise of Rome to the present. Language is of course deeply bound to other topics explored in this book. Mediterranean languages, derived as they were from classical languages – Latin, Hebrew, and Arabic – played a significant role in the articulation of distinct forms of spirituality, cultural production, and political life. They did so throughout the slow evolution of the Mediterranean from the demise of Rome and the coming of Islam onward. They do so today.

In Part II, Mediterranean Encounters, chapters 8 and 9, I turn from a narrative of the geography, history, religion, and languages of the western Mediterranean to the issues of encounters. These first two chapters of Part II explore the issues of encounters, that is, the movement of people from areas dominated by one religion to another, as a part of the physical encounter with new geographical, cultural, and political realities. In these two chapters, I turn to the questions of representation, that is, of how Muslims voyagers and thinkers described their own lands, Dar al-Islam, and their encounters with Christian or modern Europe. Thus, I seek to describe and interpret the encounters of Muslims with the Christian western Mediterranean. Selecting a few case studies, I follow the travels and geographical works of some well-known Muslim medieval and early modern writers. Each of the examples provides a different perspective on Muslim perception of the Mediterranean. These include Muslims who worked for a Christian ruler but never converted to Christianity, and others who traveled exclusively in Dar al-Islam. Still others converted to Christianity and embraced Renaissance culture before returning home and reconverting back to Islam. Travel literature, such as the great and numerous examples produced by Muslim writers or converts, among them Ibn Battūta and Leo Africanus, offer particular visions of the Mediterranean world at a moment in time when that world was dramatically changing. Clearly, the vision of these travelers and geographers does not represent the sum total of how specific people from one side of the western Mediterranean looked on the other half. These representations, of course, are grounded in temporal and geographical contexts that help shape the manner in which travelers and scholars from one religion looked on the other side. This has been felicitously described as the "image on the mirror," that is, that when we look at others in the Mediterranean, we are looking at a reflected image of ourselves. Other more recent Muslim travelers, from immigrants to ambassadors, also make brief appearances throughout this chapter.

The theme of encounters is further explored from Christian and Jewish perspectives in these two chapters. Pilgrims, merchants, diplomats, corsairs, settler colonists (as was the case with Spanish and French colonists in North Africa) populate the pages of chapters 8 and 9. It is not a comprehensive study of all those who journeyed to the lands of Islam (how could it be?), or who encountered Islam, but the chapters seek to provide a taste of what it was like to move across the sea to a world, a faith, a language, and a culture that were different from one's own. Other themes to be examined in as much detail as possible and to be illustrated by vignettes and narrative accounts are the topics of seafaring, travel narratives, pilgrimage, and contacts within the Mediterranean world (with emphasis on the western Mediterranean) and between the Mediterranean and other regions of the world. Along these lines, even though I do not include him in my discussion in this particular chapter, Ramón Muntaner's description of the adventures of Catalan soldiers and merchants in the conquests of Majorca and Minorca (Menorca) and in the eastern Mediterranean is a very good example of the sources that are available to tell this story. Along those lines, and perhaps as a possible line of inquiry for a future work, there is the extensive collection of European material (mostly of

Italian provenance) on the early modern Ottoman Empire, which is far more revealing of western attitudes towards the Sublime Porte than these writings are about life in Ottoman lands. Literary works also provide a veritable trove of engaging information as to what the movement of people may have been like in the Mediterranean. Think, for example, of Cervantes's *Don Quixote*, an important section of which (to be cited throughout this book) tells, in fictionalized fashion, the history of his own captivity in North Africa. In fact, the issue is not the paucity of material. Rather, the question is how to select judiciously from these vast arrays of texts to create a comprehensive description (both geographical and chronological) of human movement within and outward from the Mediterranean.

In this vein, hospitality (as described in Olivia Constable's book on the *funduq*), captivity, and ransoming of captives can contribute to a complex depiction of travel, whether voluntary or forced, that would engage the reader with these narratives of movement, dislocation, and identity. Along the same lines, one should make a reference to the role of ambassadors. Often, as was the case of Italian legates, their observations on the countries they visited provide us with the most perceptive account of life along the shores of the Mediterranean. The theme of ambassadors links these initial chapters with the larger issue of Mediterranean contacts with the world beyond. It may be useful to remember that Italians penned most of the first accounts of the New World in the service of Spain. Trade, considered from the perspective of a case study of the protests against the sea and for a period usually neglected in the descriptions of the Mediterranean, is a topic discussed here as well, as are the links between the western Mediterranean and other parts of the world. Migration, a significant issue throughout the long history of the western Mediterranean, is also explored, as are the consequences of the large movement of what are, essentially, mostly Mediterranean people to northern Western Europe.

In Part II, chapters 10 and 11, we turn to a more focused perception of what the relationship between place and cultural encounters was all about. Chapter 10 examines in some detail specific regions of the western Mediterranean that functioned as places or sites of encounter in the medieval, early modern, and contemporary worlds. Sites such as the Iberian Peninsula, Sicily, Marseille, Tunis, and other urban centers around the western Mediterranean served as meeting points for different cultures. Their interaction led to new cultural products and artifacts that integrated a plurality of cultures. This is most obvious in architectural projects that borrowed aesthetic sensibilities from different groups to create unique artistic monuments. In Chapter 10, my approach has been to provide succinct descriptions of each of these sites of encounter at particular points in time, while also providing a perspective on change.

In Chapter 11, however, I reverse the approach of the previous chapter by tracing the evolution of a discrete number of small towns, cities, their hinterlands, and islands as representative examples for the tenor of life in certain localities in the western Mediterranean. The chapter compares a few selected port cities such as Oran with small locations such as Vernazza, Sète, and other small ports. Such an approach may yield a far more satisfying vision of the development of the western sea than simply focusing on the history of major settlements along the shores of the Mediterranean. Similarly, islands can be explored from a comparative perspective, assessing their role in the development of trade networks, warfare, and culture throughout the long span of time covered by this book. Some of the islands, such as Elba, Montecristo, or Sardinia, provide excellent comparisons with the quintessential western Mediterranean islands of Sicily and Majorca (Sicily is examined in detail elsewhere). A final chapter and conclusion focuses on the historical circumstances that led to the decline of the Mediterranean in the Late Middle Ages and at the onset of the early modern period. Here I wish to examine not only how the western Mediterranean became somewhat relegated to a secondary role in the Western European economy and political culture, but also how the Middle Sea became linked to an expansive world economic order. The final chapter also considers briefly how the Mediterranean has regained, although in an unfortunate fashion, some of its centrality. The present-day Mediterranean has become the main gateway, a bridge in fact, for people from Africa and the Middle East, seeking frantically to reach the European Union in general and Northern European industrial nations in particular. Escaping civil war and misery, they ventured into the waters of the Middle Sea, often paying with their lives for their wishes to reach, as Thomas Friedman wrote recently, places of order. It is the movement into and across and out of the Middle Sea that this chapter in particular and this book in general has sought to capture. Not unlike the Mediterranean waves and currents, always in movement, we must also pay attention to the enduring movement of people along its shores and across its waters. But now, it is time to begin.

NOTES

1 The book was first published in French in 1949. The first English translation appeared in 1972, translated by Siân Reynolds and published by Harper and Row. I refer here to the reprinting of the 1972 edition, Fernand Braudel, *The Mediterranean and the Mediterranean World in the Age of Philip II*, 2 vols, trans. Siân Reynolds (Berkeley and Los Angeles: University of California Press, 1995).

2 Braudel, *The Mediterranean and the Mediterranean World in the Age of Philip II*, vol. 1: 17. See also Lucette Valensi, "The Problem of Unbelief in Braudel's *Mediterranean*," in Gabriel Piterberg, Teofilo F. Ruiz, and Geoffrey Symcox, *Braudel Revisited. The Mediterranean World 1600–1800* (Toronto: University of Toronto Press, 2010), 17–34.

3 Fernand Braudel, *Les mémoires de la Méditerranée: préhistoire et antiquité*, eds. Roselyne de Ayala, Paule Braudel. Preface and notes by Jean Guilaine et Pierre Rouillard (Paris: Editions de Fallois, 1998).

4 See Abulafia's article, "Mediterraneans," in W.V. Harris, ed. *Rethinking the Mediterranean* (Oxford: Oxford University Press, 2005); also his collections of essays, *Commerce and Conquest in the Mediterranean* (Aldershot, UK: Variorum, 1993); *The Mediterranean in History* (London: Thames & Hudson, 2003); his *A Mediterranean Emporium: The Catalan Kingdom of Majorca* (Cambridge: Cambridge University Press, 1994), and his superb *Frederick II. A Medieval Emperor* (London: Penguin,

1988), plus numerous other books on the western Mediterranean. Most of all, Abulafia's monumental book *The Great Sea. A Human History of the Mediterranean* (Oxford: Oxford University press, 2011) seeks to address Braudel's neglect of humans along the shores of the sea.

5   Peregrine Horden and Nicholas Purcell, *The Corrupting Sea. A Study of Mediterranean History* (Oxford: Blackwell Publishing, 2000), 7–49 for the historical and geographical contexts to the book. See also their individual articles in W.V. Harris, ed. *Rethinking the Mediterranean*: Peregrine Horden, "Travel Sickness: Medicine and Mobility in the Mediterranean from Antiquity to the Renaissance," 179–200 and Nicholas Purcell, "The Ancient Mediterranean: The View from the Customs House," 200–232.

6   Michael Herzfeld, "Practical Mediterraneanism: Excuses for Everything, from Epistemology to Eating," in W.V. Harris, ed. *Rethinking the Mediterranean*, 45–63.

7   Sharon Farmer, *The Silk Industries of Medieval Paris: Artisanal Migration, Technological Innovation, and Gendered Experience* (Philadelphia: University of Pennsylvania Press, 2016).

8   On the Barcelona Consulate of Commerce there has been little written. See María Jesús Espuny Tomás, "El Real Consulado de Comercio del Principado de Cataluña (1758–1829)." PhD diss., Universitat Autònoma de Barcelona, 1992). Available on line at http://www.tdx.cat/TDX-0630109-121322. The Consulates of Commerce were the heirs to the medieval Consulates of the Sea on which there is an extensive bibliography. See, for example, Román Piña Homs, *El Consolat de Mar, Mallorca, 1326–1800* (Palma de Mallorca: Institut d'Estudis Baleàrics, 1985); *Consulado del mar de Barcelona: nuevamente traducido de cathalan en castellano*, trans. Don Cayetano de Pallejá (Barcelona: J. Piferrer, 1732). This title is available on line (though with restricted access). Also Stanley S. Jados, *Consolat de Mar, and related documents* (University, AL: University of Alabama Press, 1975). These holdings in the Arxiu de la Corona d'Aragó contain a series of diverse holdings that deal with maritime trade in and out of Barcelona. The holdings are overwhelming. They are organized as follows: there is an inventory of registers and volumes for the Consulate of the Sea (1715–1761) and another register for the Royal Consulate of Commerce (1762–1829) with an additional register for the tribunal of Commerce (1830–1868), plus additional inventories and an index of litigation carried out under the jurisdiction of these bodies. I have focused on the register of protests against the sea. There is an index (that allows for the gathering of information and data speedily: *Indice de los registros de protestas de mar (1766–1868)*, which I have used in the preparation of this book and *Registros de protestas de mar. 1766–1868* in 33 vols. (All of them now gathered in one enormous volume and including close to 25,000 such protests.)

PART I *GEOGRAPHY, HISTORY, AND CULTURAL CONTEXTS*

[2] THE IMPERATIVES OF GEOGRAPHY AND CLIMATE: SEA AND LAND IN THE WESTERN MEDITERRANEAN

THE Mediterranean Sea existed long before humans walked upon its shores or sailed its waters. It had, as Daniel Lord Smail has so persuasively shown us when arguing about deep time, a geological and physical history that preceded humans and human writing.[1] That story of the Mediterranean is written in the slow erosion of its shores, in the abrupt and deadly eruptions of its fiery volcanoes, in the ebb and rise of its sea level; in its salinity, smells, storms, and windless days. It is written in the hot winds that blow in summer from Africa, turning the northern shores of the sea into furnaces. It is written in its cold winters, thin soils, and other such topographical features that dominate Mediterranean landscapes. It can be read in the elegant cypresses that crowd the hills around its shores. It can be felt in the olive trees and vineyards that grow along its shores.

But the Mediterranean cannot be understood fully without humans.[2] They recorded, painted, wrote songs and poems about its physical aspects, measured its temperature, the strength of its winds, the movements of its currents. A sea, once thriving with marine life, has been polluted and overfished over the centuries. New crops, livestock, and agricultural technologies have altered the lands around its shores. Rivers have silted its coasts. Sometimes, as was the case of Aigues-Mortes, the sea would have its revenge, leaving the French medieval opening to the Mediterranean far from the sea. Wars have been waged for millennia on its surface, littering the bottom of the sea with the wreckage of thousands of battles, the bodies of thousands of men and women. It still does so with the bodies of immigrants who have lost (and continue to lose) their lives as they have sought to reach the European shores, fleeing misery and violence.

The sea's geographical contours invited specific forms of sailing that came, from Roman times to the onset of the modern period, to depend on prisoners or slaves to power Roman ships or early modern galleys. Though in this chapter and succeeding ones I discuss geography and history as discrete categories, one

The Western Mediterranean and the World: 400 CE to the Present, First Edition. Teofilo F. Ruiz.
© 2018 John Wiley & Sons, Ltd. Published 2018 by John Wiley & Sons, Ltd.

must remember that they are inexorably linked and impossible to separate one from the other.

THE MEDITERRANEAN WORLD: THE WESTERN MEDITERRANEAN

It would be useless to reproduce here the moving and detailed opening sections of Braudel's *The Mediterranean and the Mediterranean World in the Age of Philip II* or the carefully crafted discussions of the sea's characteristics found in Horden and Purcell's *The Corrupting Sea*.[3] These histories of the Mediterranean and its adjacent land masses provide more than wonderful entry points to an understanding of the sea as a distinct geographical entity, to its diverse landscapes, microclimates, and micro-ecologies. Yet, while not wishing to recreate such extensive and well-crafted descriptions, one cannot proceed without some attention to the sea itself, to its natural history, and to its role in and impact on the history of Mediterranean people through time.

A relatively young sea as things go in geological time, the Mediterranean was formed by the collision of the land masses that today correspond to Africa and Europe and by the subsequent geological elevations and subsidences, creating the space for the formation of the sea. These geological processes were not uniform throughout the entire extent of the ocean. As there would be historical reasons to argue for a distinct history of the western Mediterranean (see the introduction to this book), there are also geological ones. The west basin, quite distinct from its eastern counterpart, is bound by young mountain ranges, yielding specific types of land and seascapes. But, above all, whether we are describing the western or eastern section of the Mediterranean Sea, the Middle Sea, as this body of water has often been described, is an interior sea, bound by land everywhere, except in its narrow westernmost opening at the Gulf of Cádiz or Straits of Gibraltar, the fabled ancient Pillars of Hercules. Alexander Dumas described it as a lake in his quintessential Mediterranean novel, *The Count of Monte Cristo*. He describes the sea as a "huge lake that extends from Gibraltar to the Dardanelles and from Tunis to Venice."[4]

This sense of a sea without outlets is even more pronounced if we consider the Black Sea as an eastern extension of the Mediterranean, described, as it has been in an early geography book, as "a vast alcove of the Mediterranean." Only in recent times has human activity, the building of the Suez Canal, linked the Mediterranean to other bodies of water on its eastern terminus. Yet, because of the topography of the lands, peninsulas, and islands of the Middle Sea, the people who had lived upon its shores, and those who have described the sea, have fragmented the intrinsic unity of the Mediterranean into a sense of overlapping and interlocking smaller seas. These are easily identifiable to us by their peculiar geographical features, but most of all by their place and role in the long historical renderings of life along the Mediterranean shores. Thus, we speak of the Adriatic, Tyrrhenian, and Aegean Seas less because of their unique geographical features – though they are real enough – than because of the history imbedded in these specific geographical locations.

Extending on its east-west axis for almost 2,800 miles, the width of the Mediterranean on its north-south axis varies widely, with an average of 500 miles. This is a deceiving figure since the Straits of Gibraltar are only around 8 miles wide and the coasts of Africa and Europe are easily visible from each other's shores or from inland, and from islands at specific locations throughout the sea. Having sailed almost the entirety of the Mediterranean in 2010 and 2014, I was, once again, struck by the narrow openings of the Straits of Gibraltar and the view from the ship's deck of both continents linked to each other by proximity and yet separated by the sea. Equally striking was the unique experience that I had of standing on a high point in Erice (Sicily) and seeing, barely through the morning mist, the coast of Africa.

The other significant measure is that of the Mediterranean's depth. It varies as well. It has a maximum depth of around 16,000 feet or almost 5,000 meters. Yet, the sea ridges or sills that effectively divide the Mediterranean into different regions could range from an average of a bit over 1,000 feet in the sill dividing the Atlantic from the Mediterranean to a mere 230–300 feet in the sills in the Dardanelles and the Bosporus, dividing the Mediterranean from the Black Sea. An underwater mountain range running from Sicily to the North African coast (at an average depth of 1,200 feet) sharply divides the Mediterranean into a western and eastern section. Geologically the western part, that is, the maritime region with its boundaries in the West at the Straits of Gibraltar, the East at Sicily, the North at Europe, and the South at North Africa, is itself divided into three basins or geographical and geological sub-regions: the Alboran Basin, east of the Straits of Gibraltar and flanked by what is today Spain and Morocco; the Algerian Basin, bound by the coasts of Algeria, Sardinia, and Corsica; and, finally, the Tyrrhenian Basin, a region encompassed by Italy, Sardinia, and Corsica. The latter, because of its association with Rome, is laden with

Figure 2.1 The Straits of Gibraltar as the ship sailed into Europe. Source: Courtesy of Scarlett Freund.

historical significance and remained so through the centuries-long struggle between the Crown of Aragon and its Italian and French rivals for control of Sicily, Naples, and most of southern Italy.[5]

TIDE, STORMS, AND WINDLESS DAYS IN THE WESTERN MEDITERRANEAN

Having grown up in the Caribbean and living now on the shores of the endless Pacific, I often tend to think of the Mediterranean, following Dumas's description, as a large lake, with placid and azure water. The almost complete absence of sea tides adds to this vision. A vision, I should add, that has been assiduously conjured and lovingly nurtured by tourist enclaves along its shores. We do not portray the Mediterranean as an angry ocean, nor do we see often its turbulence. Unlike the Atlantic and the Pacific, the Mediterranean Sea barely responds to the gravitational pull of Sun and Moon. The absence of tides or their meager impact throughout most of the Mediterranean, measured in centimeters as opposed to meters, also affects the safety of navigation and the stability of tidal land areas. Growing up by the sea in Cuba, I was always keenly aware of the difference between low and high tide and of the impact of these two different faces of the ocean on safety, the force and sequence of waves, swimming, and sailing conditions.

The western Mediterranean, however, has significant tide activity in the Straits of Gibraltar and its environs, as the Atlantic tidal patterns intrude into Mediterranean waters. Similar activity (but for very different oceanic reasons) occurs in Venice. In both Gibraltar and Venice, tides of 1 meter are regular features of the seascape. If I have digressed to this discussion of the absence or presence of tides in the western Mediterranean, it is because ecological phenomena have to be measured in relation to their impact on the human population and polities that crowded the shores of the sea. Venice's famous or infamous Aqua Alta, the high tides that inundate the city almost every year, results from a combination of factors not all related to tide activity. In the western gate to the Mediterranean Sea, the flow of Atlantic Sea water into the Mediterranean basin created conditions that served, when accompanied by other specific political factors (piracy, conflicts between Muslims and Christians in the area), to thwart navigation by certain types of vessels out into the open waters of the Atlantic.

Such flow of water created great difficulty for trade in and out of the Mediterranean until the Late Middle Ages. Many years ago, Archibald R. Lewis described the particular navigational difficulties of the Straits of Gibraltar with reference to two distinct currents flowing in and out of the western Mediterranean. "The upper one flows from the Atlantic into the Mediterranean [at a speed of] over four to six knots. And there is a corresponding lower countercurrent which carries the heavier, more saline Mediterranean water into the Atlantic and runs under the upper one."[6] If one adds the westerly winds blowing into the Mediterranean, as Lewis explains, the difficulties in sailing *out* of the Mediterranean into the Atlantic were significant. To that, for most of the Middle Ages and almost into the nineteenth century, one most add the additional threat of corsairs, either from Atlantic and Mediterranean Moroccan ports or from Atlantic Iberian ports, waiting to pounce on vessels laboring against current and wind. And even the French, as mentioned in Cervantes's narrative of the Christian captive's escape from imprisonment in Algiers in *Don Quixote*, also took their turn in tormenting merchants in the waters near the opening of the Mediterranean into the Atlantic. Lewis notes that as late as the mid-nineteenth century, ships sailing into the Atlantic had to wait for months at ports, such as Algeciras, for an occasional easterly to ease their way out of the western Mediterranean and into the Atlantic. Anyone who has spent time in Algeciras would object to such a long stay.[7]

Northern European and Atlantic ships sailing into the Mediterranean did not meet such difficulties; yet, as Lewis also points out, in the Central Middle Ages these voyages were often one-way affairs, with those who returned home often making their way back over land routes, their ships scuttled. But Lewis's article is really about how, through a combination of changing political circumstances, new ship technology and seafaring, and strategically located friendly ports on both shores of the western Mediterranean adjacent to the Straits of Gibraltar, merchants from Genoa, Pisa, Barcelona, and elsewhere began to make regular runs out of the Mediterranean into northern parts. This lively trade in and out the Mediterranean connected both northern and southern markets – a global Mediterranean – and rang the death toll for the ancient fairs of Champagne that depended on the road traffic up the natural byways created by the Rhône valley. Although geography and ecology played an important role, they cannot ever be divorced from the impact that history had, and still has, on our perception and construction of lived environments. Nor should we discount the impact of human agency in transforming what may seem to be the limitations of geography, or in this instance, those of maritime currents as found in the Straits of Gibraltar.

A Cruel and Unpredictable Sea (at times)

If one returns to the postcard images of the western Mediterranean, one ought to remember that the beautiful weather depicted in tourist brochures was not consistently so. The fabled Mediterranean climate and its azure waters are a reality. But that reality has to be tempered at times by adverse conditions of weather and sea. Tempestuous weather, coastal people profiting from naval disasters, or hostile humans' piratical deeds could and did wreak havoc on the best laid plans. Sailing the Mediterranean in the pre-modern world, or even today, was (and is), at times, full of dangers. In the Strait of Messina, between Sicily and the tip of Italy, reefs and shoals were well-known destroyers of ships and killers of men and women. Very early in the western imaginary, Scylla and Charybdis, the two sea monsters or sirens that guarded the strait, stood as metaphors for the dangers of such crossing. Odysseus tempted such danger as he sailed into the West and escaped. I sailed through the Strait of Messina in

2014, saw something that looked like a whirlpool, but made my way to Amalfi with little trouble. I must note that our large cruise ship depended on a local pilot to navigate from the city of Messina to the opening of the strait near the Sorrento coast. Others, in an earlier period, did not. And today, illegal immigrants from North Africa, sailing small boats across the sea, meet with disasters and death. As to the past, the literary imaginings of the ancient, and even more recent, world serve as bitter reminders of the dangers involved in crossing from the eastern to the western Mediterranean. As already noted, in the *Count of Monte Cristo*, a work invoked earlier in this book and referred to throughout, Dumas built a great deal of its dramatic expectations on the arrival or not of the *Pharaon*, the ship once captained by Edmund Dantès, at its Marseille home port. The absence of means of communication, which we all take for granted today, made life at sea, even in the nineteenth century, one in which the outcome was always uncertain. Only because of the truth of such an assertion could Dumas make the survival of the Morrell family fortune so unpredictable.

Earlier than Dumas, Cervantes, whose stories in *Don Quixote* have often such a strong resemblance to reality, captures the uncertainty of sailing the western Mediterranean. In the "Captive's Tale" (Part I, chapters 39–80), we have the conflation of several narrative tropes deeply connected to the Mediterranean. The tale narrates a history of Christian captivity in North Africa, one with which Cervantes was deeply familiar, having spent time in Argel (Algiers) as a captive (a story that will be revisited in a later chapter). The story within the larger story of Don Quixote also recounts the ebb and flow of individuals along the boundaries of religion and language. We meet renegades and other characters with which we will become better acquainted later. But the story is also about the peril and uncertainty of sailing the relatively short distance between the coast of northern Africa and Islam and the Mediterranean shores of Spain and Christianity.

Even in a world of compasses, agile ships, and the like, it was still not easy to make such a crossing: "a moderate northwestern was blowing and the sea was choppy, it was impossible to keep a straight course for Majorca, and we had to tack [westward] in the direction of Oran" (386). All of this additional sailing they did because of their fear of running into Muslim ships. But, more was still to come. On their way to Spain, the captive, Zoraida (the Muslim woman who had paid for his escape and had fled with him), and the rest of fleeing company fell into the hands of French privateers or corsairs. Cervantes makes the French captain generous enough to release the captives after he has taken most of their wealth. In the real world of early modern conflicts in the western Mediterranean, such courtesy would have been rarely the case. They would most probably have been sold into slavery or killed outright, and Zoraida raped.

As they approached the Spanish coast, they did so with great caution for fear of foundering on the rocky shore. Leaving his Algerian slavery, it took the captive and his companions days to make the crossing. And it meant perilous encounters and constant fear. And upon landing on Spanish soil, they were met with the hue and cry of a population consistently afraid of pirate landings, and not knowing precisely where in Spain their landfall had taken place.[8] If

Cervantes could build such an elaborate narrative, it was because part of the history was autobiographical and because his account rang true to those who sailed in and lived close to the western Mediterranean.

Literary examples do not fully capture the drama that may be found in such seafaring. Although most travel went on with little or no problem, there were enough mishaps to make a sea voyage always dangerous. It may be useful to turn to a few examples and reports of localized rough seas as garnered from the "protests against the sea," found in the Consulate of Commerce's documentation (extant in the Archivo de la Corona de Aragón) for the period between 1766 and 1868. Although these reports, essentially preventive insurance claims, provide only a partial view of the weather and of seafaring mishaps, these protests against the sea offer a window into weather conditions in the western Mediterranean and the consequences of rough seas and high winds.

THE PROTESTS AGAINST THE SEA

On January 7, 1766, Gabriel Carreras, a citizen of Gibraltar and captain of the English registered ship the *Cathalina*, appeared in front of the officials (*consuls*) of Barcelona's recently founded (1763) Consulate of Commerce (*Consulado de Comercio*).[9] In his deposition to the Consulado's authorities, Carreras stated that he had left Genoa on January 1, 1766, with a shipment of wheat and other merchandise bound for Málaga; his ship was, he stated, "well fit for sailing." Along his sea voyage, Carreras told the consuls, his ship met bad weather and high seas that did or may have damaged his cargo; thus, he "wished to protest and protested against the sea and the bad weather."[10]

Over the next century – the years between 1766 and 1868 for which we have extant protests in the Consulate's registers – captains of merchant ships flocked in the thousands to the Consulate's offices to lodge similar protests against the sea and against inclement weather. That same January 1766, French, English, Dutch, Spanish, and other sea captains complained of tempestuous weather, voicing their fears (duly recorded by the Consulate's clerks in Barcelona) that their merchandise may have been damaged or lost. For the next century, all these depositions, around 25,000 altogether, closed with the formulaic sentence: "I wish to protest and I protest against the sea, bad weather, high seas . . ."[11] and possible – and in many cases real – damages to their ships and cargo.

Although the highly formulaic nature of these depositions alerts us to the fact that these were the equivalent of insurance claims (some of them obviously filled preemptively before a real assessment of the damage could be made), there were nonetheless slight but noticeable changes over time in the information found in these protests against the sea. As much as I love Barcelona (and I truly do), I would require another lifetime to examine each one of these documents individually. My approach to the Consulado de Comercio's registers has been dictated by the sheer volume of the extant records and by the limitations imposed by a short research trip. What I have attempted to do is to sample different years in succeeding decades, attempting to construct case studies and vignettes of maritime disasters and what they tell us about life, weather conditions, and commerce in the western Mediterranean (see Chapter 9) over slightly more than a century. This was a period of rapid social, economic, and political change both in Mediterranean Europe and beyond the shores of the Middle Sea. These changes were particularly vivid for Barcelona. In 1766, the city still languished somewhat under the centralizing policies of its Bourbon rulers and neglect from Madrid. By 1868, when the last entry was recorded, Barcelona's industrial revival was already well under way.

A CRUEL SEA REVISITED

On my arrival in Barcelona on March 6, 2010, to continue my research for this chapter in the extraordinary holdings of the Arxiu de la Corona d'Aragó, newspapers and TV reports still resonated with the tragedy that had taken place two days before. A cruise ship had been battered by high winds and high waves in the Gulf of Lion (Golfo de León) with loss of lives and damage to the vessel. The Mediterranean Sea had delivered a grim reminder that even in the twenty-first century one always sails its waters at one's peril. The Gulf of Lion was quite familiar to earlier travelers in the Mediterranean and the site of numerous maritime disasters. Extending from the Catalan shores to the port of Toulon in southern France, the gulf was often the site for tempestuous weather and the home of the Mistral and the Tramontane winds.

Although not all the depositions made by merchant captains to the consuls at the Consulate of Commerce in Barcelona focused on the Gulf of Lion, a large number of the most dramatic ones reported difficulties in sailing through the area. And it was not as if one could go around the region. Most of the trade between Italy and Spain and between southern France and Spain and Italy has had to go through the Gulf of Lion until recent times. Sailing south of it placed the ships in the open waters of the Mediterranean, still vulnerable to heavy winds, and even more vulnerable still to corsair activity from North Africa, a problem in the western Mediterranean until the nineteenth century. It was, after all, bad weather in the Gulf of Lion that kept the young Philip (later to become Philip II of Spain) grounded for many days in Catalonia, delaying his voyage to Genoa, and pushing him into Marseille, a city under the rule of French enemies in 1548.[12]

The unpredictable fury of the western Mediterranean in general, and of the Gulf of Lion in particular, is a constant reminder that sailing the western Mediterranean was not an easy task in Antiquity, nor is it in the present. The complaints about rough seas and high winds (notwithstanding the insurance-inflicted nature of these protests) for the port of Barcelona alone in over a century tell us that it was never safe to travel from one part of the Mediterranean to another, even if most of the sailing was done close to the coast.

We will have an opportunity below to review in greater detail Philip's sea voyage from Catalonia to Italy in 1548. The threats of the sea were, however, not confined to royal princes or the early modern period. In the late twentieth and early twenty-first centuries, untold numbers of illegal immigrants have lost their lives as they have attempted to make their way from North Africa to countries in the European community or from Albania and other parts of Eastern Europe to Italy. The newspapers, daily TV, and radio news, and most recently a grim account in the *New York Times* Sunday magazine in early September 2015, have been filled with tragic accounts of disaster at sea, of sinking or intercepted ships. Not unlike the exodus of Haitians and Cubans to Florida, some make it and disappear into the mass of illegal immigrants flocking to Europe in spite of the economic crisis; others are intercepted and returned to their homelands or placed in detention camps, such as those on the Italian island of Lampedusa and at Mineo in Sicily. Some unfortunate ones perish at sea. The Mediterranean is indeed beautiful, but its beauty can, at times, be fatal.

The vagaries of the weather in the western Mediterranean did not only punish merchants and sea captains sailing in the eighteenth and nineteenth centuries, fearful captives (such as Cervantes's fictional characters) fleeing to freedom, or illegal immigrants risking everything in the hope of better lives. Affairs of state and princely travel often fell victim to an unyielding sea. Hannibal's daring invasion of Italy from Spain and his arduous crossing of the Alps may have been prompted by the Romans' superior naval strength, but it also reflected the uncertainty of a sea voyage with such a large army. Even though Hannibal's Phoenician ancestors had long mastered Mediterranean seafaring, after the destruction of Carthage the western Mediterranean had become a Roman lake. Many centuries after Hannibal's bold attack on Roman Italy, the young Philip – soon to become the king of Spain as Philip II and the eventual protagonist of Braudel's great book – would also have to swallow the bitter consequences of an uncertain sea.

Philip of Spain, the young heir to Charles V's sprawling empire, began a grand tour to become acquainted with his soon-to-be Habsburg inheritance and for his subjects to know their king-in-waiting. In 1548, he traveled overland from Madrid to the Crown of Aragon to a lavish princely entry into Girona and an indifferent one into Barcelona. On October 19, 1548, he reached Castellón de Empurias to review the fleet (composed mostly of galleys) that would convey him to Italy. Juan Cristóbal Calvete de Estrella, an eyewitness who narrated Philip's voyage with utmost care, reports on the violent rainstorm that plagued the princely cortège. Because of the inclement weather, Philip remained in Castellón for another 12 days. Only on November 2 did the prince seize a window of good weather to sail from Rosas into the Mediterranean. Yet, after sailing for around eight leagues, "the weather turned so bad [that] it forced a return to the port of Colibris" (22) with Philip, who must have been by now exceedingly frustrated, traveling to Perpignan to put his idle time to good use. And then they tried again, only to be driven back ashore once more. This time, however, instead of tempest and high seas, the winds died out and the galleys had to be powered entirely by oar. The conditions were such that there was a discussion on whether to postpone the young prince's trip until the spring. Philip or his advisors persevered. On November 11 the Spanish fleet reached Aigues-Mortes and from there proceeded, in what must have been coastal seafaring, to Marseille. In spite of a cordial reception at Marseille, Phillip and his formidable father, Charles V, must have been quite upset to have to seek the hospitality and help of their erstwhile enemy, the French. Yet, they were not finished with bad weather. The wind (or lack of it) and stormy conditions kept impeding their princely progress to such an extent that supplies began to run out, and they had to land on the island of Marguerite to be re-provisioned from Genoa.

The unfortunate voyage continued along the shore of the Mediterranean, past Nice and Monaco on the way to Genoa, but not before one of Phillip's galleys ran into a bark and large quantities of supplies and other goods were lost at sea. Finally, Philip arrived in Genoa, though the tempestuous sea marred his planned dramatic progression from his ceremonial galley to land across an artificial bridge. Later on, a full riot exploded throughout the city in response to Spanish violence against the Genoese. It had to be quelled before Philip's official ceremonial entry into the city took place. It was a fitting conclusion to what had been a disastrous sojourn.

The soon-to-be king of Spain could command the vast resources of his sprawling empire, but he could not command the Mediterranean in the fall of 1548, any more that he could command the waters of the English Channel in 1588. Of course, not every Mediterranean crossing met the inauspicious weather that Philip's fleet did in late October and November. Most ships' sailing across the western Mediterranean took place during summer. Most of these voyages went smoothly, and without all the angst that Philip and his retinue faced. Even though his galleys – the Spanish Mediterranean fleet – were among the best in the region, his voyage was thwarted again and again. When he was finally able to sail from Spain to Genoa, he had to undergo the humiliating experience of seeking refuge in French ports, wait for provisions from his Genoese allies, and take the risky route of coastal sailing. The lesson to be learned from this long vignette is that, until the advent of steamships and modern vessels, the Mediterranean Sea could always surprise seafarers, impede their progress, and even end their lives. Philip had waited and waited in Catalonia for good weather to sail to Genoa in what was to be a triumphal (and by now delayed) tour of the Habsburg lands. He sat powerless in front of the rough sea. He had no choice.[13] In the sixteenth century, to provide just another example, official correspondence, troops, and supplies sent from the Spanish mainland to the Spanish outpost in Oran (North Africa), a voyage that could be done today in a day or so, could be delayed for months. Currents, adverse winds, storms, and the constant threat of North African pirates made the trip always a perilous and unpredictable affair.

A PEACEFUL SEA (AT TIMES)

Two kind readers of this book at the manuscript stage pointed out that I may have overdone the "cruelty" side of the Mediterranean Sea. They are correct, and I am guilty of perhaps overdramatizing the difficulties without noting that these were exceptional circumstances. My intent all along was to dispel that common notion of the Mediterranean as an inland sea of calm waters, where safe navigation was always possible. Indeed, as I will note in another chapter, the thousands of protests against the sea represented only a small percentage of crossings and stood in contrast to the many more thousands of Mediterranean crossing that did not meet with storms, bad weather, or maritime disasters. The very frequency of these reports is convincing evidence that the sea remained, certainly until the development of railroads, the fastest, most economical, and safest way to transport people and commodities from one region to another within the Middle Sea. The lively north-south commercial exchanges across the sea from the end of the Roman Empire in the West to the present are ample testimony to those many days (especially in summer months) when the sea was easily navigable.

As far as we know, the western Mediterranean did not undergo the environmental crisis experienced in the eastern parts of the sea during the eleventh and twelfth centuries, well illustrated by Roni Ellenblum's book. Strikingly, those same centuries (and the succeeding ones) witness a dramatic increase in trade in the western Mediterranean. These commercial exchanges – once described as the "commercial revolution" – led to enduring trade patterns after the demise of Roman power in the West. In the eleventh and twelfth centuries, Genoese and other Italian merchants from Piacenza, Lucca, and elsewhere led naval activities. Moreover, the period also witnessed the high point of the Muslim world's enduring trade connections between Fustat (in Egypt), North Africa, and Sicily. Such continued activities provide a correction to my depiction of the Mediterranean as a cruel sea, though the Mediterranean surprised merchants with unexpected storms and bad weather at times.[14]

CLIMATE

In summer 1990, I drove from Madrid to Rome at the end of June and returned a month later following more or less the same route. Driving a small, non-air-conditioned car and avoiding as much as possible the expensive toll roads while hugging the Mediterranean coast, I was struck by the two very different temperatures I encountered in my travels only a month apart. If in late June it was warn and pleasant, on the return voyage, this time accompanied by my wife, Provence was a veritable furnace, as hot winds and sand blew across the Mediterranean from the Sahara Desert: the dreadful Sirocco.

The climate of the Mediterranean region – one that has given the name to climatic ecosystems throughout the world, including the shores of Southern California (which we often call Mediterranean plus) – is marked by hot and dry summers and mild and rainy winters. Yet, as is well known and certainly even more so in the age of global warming, the weather is fairly unpredictable. Although there is a basic constant range – obvious when examining average temperature around port cities on the western Mediterranean – departures from the norm were, and are, not unusual. This range of temperatures – the lifeblood of Mediterranean cruises and tourism – may be best rendered in a table (Table 2.1), although those of you who have been to Europe recently know that summer may bring very high temperatures.

It is important to note that these are *average* temperatures from a selected number of port cities around the western Mediterranean. Inland temperatures,

Table 2.1 Temperature in Selected Cities in the Western Mediterranean: Average Temperature by Season (F).

	January	March	May	July	September	November	December
Barcelona	55.4	59	73.4	84.2	78.8	57.2	57.2
Genoa	49	60	67	82	77	62	51
Marseille	45	51	64	75	70	52	46
Naples	48	53	64	76	71	55	49
Oran	57	56	65	77	74	59	54
Palermo	55	56	65	78	76	63	57
Palma de Majorca	50	53	62	75	62	56	52
Tunis	53	56	66	80	76	60	55
Valencia	48	55	64	75	72	55	50
Gibraltar	56	59	65	75	74	62	58

away from the sea, could be much higher or lower, belying the impression one receives from these average temperatures of a fairly constant climate throughout the seashores. Nothing could be farther from the truth. Even close to the sea, the summer heat could be suffocating with high levels of humidity. Winters could be harsh. In March 2010, I was caught in the midst of a storm in Barcelona with low temperatures and even some snow. I have also experienced extreme heat in Málaga during the summer of 2005. What these anecdotic accounts reveal is the uncertainty of the weather from month to month and even day to day, or the ebb and flow of climatic cycles in the region. In another chapter, we will also see how storms and rough seas in the Mediterranean were quite unpredictable. Although following a rough pattern (summer weather was usually calm; winter was usually the period of storms), each year, each season was *sui generis*.

The eighteenth- and nineteenth-century protests against the sea provide a rough portrait of weather patterns at sea, as reflected in the depositions or claims for lost or damaged cargo and ships. The number of protests registered changed from month to month and from year to year, offering some clue as to when one may reasonably expect bad weather. These figures also give a sense of the proportion of intra-Mediterranean movement, as opposed to ships that came into the western Mediterranean from the Atlantic through the Straits of Gibraltar. Information about the weather is perhaps best rendered in a table (Table 2.2) that shows examples from different decades. Of course, not all of the evidence is presented here, and weather was often unpredictable. Nonetheless, the data may provide a preliminary glance at weather patterns in the late eighteenth and early nineteenth centuries.

Table 2.1 indicates that, in terms of weather patterns, each year was *sui generis*. It is difficult therefore to make assumptions as to weather conditions

Table 2.2 Weather and Trade Patterns in the Western Mediterranean, 1766–1868. Number of Protests Against the Sea and Inclement Weather (A Sample).

	1766	1776	1777	1785	1786	1866	1868
January	7	17	20	13	29	18	28
February	20	13	22	13	14	5	22
March	15	25	13	24	28	28	17
April	12	30	10	20	15	10	20
May	8	24	7	23	13	28	20
June	2	14	4	14	8	13	22
July	12	16	7	14	9	13	16
August	1	4	2	20	10	10	35
September	3	20	3	16	13	14	51
October	3	14	14	16	23	8	41
November	7	20	5	24	41	32	28
December	32	11	18	41	11	11	23

Total number of protests: 1766: 122; 1776: 208; 1777: 125; 1785: 128; 1786: 214; 1866: 170; 1868: 323.
Total number of protests from sea captains whose voyages began and ended in the Mediterranean: 1766: 18; 1776: 110; 1777: 61; 1785: 74; 1786: 80; 1866: 19; 1868: 118.
Source: From ACA, *Indice los registros de las protestas de mar (1766–1868)*.

from year to year or even from month to month. Nonetheless, summer months appear to have elicited far fewer protests against rough seas and high winds than winter months did, though in August 1868, there were 35 depositions or protests against the sea, only surpassed that year by 51 such protests for September. Otherwise, from May to August the western Mediterranean seemed to have been fairly navigable and peaceful. The breakdown of protests also offers a glimpse at the importance of trade in and out of the Mediterranean, and how it compared to intra-Mediterranean commerce. By the late eighteenth and nineteenth century, the western Mediterranean in general, and Barcelona in particular, was already linked to a global economy, though the number of protests against the sea varied randomly according to the particular year's weather conditions and the vagaries of who was entering a complaint and when.

It is also not always clear whether rough seas and high winds had really damaged the cargo. Furthermore, the depositions do not always state the precise location of high winds and rough seas. The area around the Straits of Gibraltar, with all the difficulties for navigating in and out of the Mediterranean, was clearly one of the rough spots, whether on the Atlantic or the Mediterranean side.[15] The Gulf of Lion was also, as already noted, a frequent focus of complaints. Since there was little evidence of commerce with North African ports or markets (at least in the Barcelona evidence and before the beginnings of European colonial ventures in the region), the reports of bad weather and turbulent seas tended to concentrate on the western Mediterranean northern shores or along the coastal byways of the Iberian Peninsula. This discussion confirms Braudel's observations that summer sailing was preferred in the Mediterranean over winter sailing. Yet, commercial needs trumped the uncertainty of the climate, of storms and rain. Sailors and sea captains had to brave the elements and probably pay with their cargo, and sometimes even their lives, for doing so.

Discussion of the climate needs, of course, to be contextualized within reliable recorded information about temperatures, rainfall, and other markers of weather patterns. Verifiable and sustained information on these different climatological components – unlike the evidence from the protests against the sea, which is circumstantial and addresses only maritime disasters – dates back only to the nineteenth century and does not reflect long-term changes or cyclical climate shifts. For the weather a millennium ago or 400 years ago, we have some textual information and the evidence from tree rings and other botanical and archeological sources. We also know from textual sources that the western Mediterranean climate was not the same in the third century as it would have been earlier or would be later, and that economic developments triggered by climatic changes led to a reorganization (and the eventual demise) of the Roman Empire in the West. We know that most of Western Europe underwent a Little Ice Age in the Late Middle Ages, but the exact temperature for a variety of locations, so easily accessible today through a Google search, was just not available. While most self-respecting Romans today know that July, and certainly August, are unbearable months in the city (because of the heat), and its monuments and beauties are best left to dehydrated tourists, it has not always been the case. Human intervention, the rapid deforestation of the shores of the western Mediterranean, the advance of the Sahara, a mini ice age around the thirteenth century, and myriad other ecological factors – some human-induced and others part of normal climate shifts – have shaped the changing weather patterns of the region.

CLIMATE: RAIN AND WINDS

The shifting direction of westerly winds, bringing moisture from the Atlantic into Europe, north and south, also creates fairly recognizable weather patterns. The western region of any area associated with the Mediterranean receives more rainfall on average than the eastern shores. That is, Lisbon, facing the Atlantic, may see as much as 25 to 48 inches of rain annually whereas Barcelona and its hinterland would get less than half of that: 15 to 19 inches of rainfall as an annual average. The differences are even more striking between cities on the Italian Tyrrhenian Sea (Italy's west coast) and some interior or Adriatic (Italy's east coast) locations. Genoa, for example, receives from around 4 inches of rain in January to a high of 6.74 in October and to a low of 0.95 in July, the average driest month of the year. Naples, further south and more open to the westerly winds blowing into the Mediterranean, receives an average of 4.11 inches in January, 6.38 in November, the rainiest month, and 0.95 in July, the driest month. These monthly averages are not very different from those of Genoa. On the other hand, if we turn to the city of Ravenna on the Adriatic coast, the average rainfall is noticeably lower. January and February have the lowest monthly rainfall averages with less than 2 inches per month, with July showing a similar amount of around 2 inches. November, the rainiest month, registers a monthly average of only around 3 inches. Venice, a city we associate with water and flooding, receives 3.5 inches less on average in November (also the rainiest month) than do Naples or Genoa.

A similar distinction follows between the northern shores of the western Mediterranean (Europe) and the southern shores (Africa), the north receiving considerably more rainfall and being cooler than the southern shores. Yet, as was the case with earlier examples, climatic conditions have changed over time, reflecting historical contexts. The western Mediterranean coast of North Africa was not always as we experience it today. Ancient Carthage is a very good example. Its Phoenician (and later Carthaginian) masters made it a prosperous trading depot, channeling products from the African interior to Western Europe. Rome, once it had conquered all of northern Africa, turned it into one of the important grain-producing regions of the Empire. Augustine (St Augustine), growing up in Thagaste (today in modern Algeria) and spending some of his adolescent years in Carthage (Tunis), not only benefitted from the rich and complex cultural inheritance of Roman civilization in provincial North Africa, but was also shaped, as shown in such dramatic and brilliant detail by the great Peter Brown, by the strange beauty of his homeland. Although he could have remained in Italy and prospered greatly from the patronage of Ambrose and other influential Church leaders, he went home to write, to engage heretics in bitter polemics, and to die at his post as bishop of Hippo as the city was besieged by Vandal invaders. And home was a land on the shores of the western Mediterranean Sea. Augustine's life and philosophical reflections are punctuated by references to the sea. From his discussion on the Trinity by the analogy of a child trying to fill the sea into a beach cavity to the heart-rending encounter with his mother, Monica, at Ostia (Rome's port into the Mediterranean), the sea was everywhere in his work. And North Africa sent not only grain to feed Rome's multitudes, philosophers, and others, but, as late as the fifth century, most of the fish and fish sauce consumed in large quantities by Rome's and Ostia's citizens came from North Africa.[16]

CLIMATE AND HISTORY

There was a medieval saying in Spain, cited by Braudel in his *The Mediterranean*, that the peripatetic Castilian kings preferred to spend winters in forbiddingly cold Burgos, smack in the middle of the northern plain, and summers in torrid Seville. This saying was followed by the acknowledgment that northern Castile's harsh winters had led to a series of measures – fireplaces, the use of furs for clothing, and the like – to withstand the cold. In Seville, inner courtyards in most houses, fountains, and the type of materials used in, and the design of, construction helped weather the heat. But anyone who has ever lived on the shores of the Mediterranean will know that winters can be unpleasant indeed, or as Californians may say – California being another one of those regions described as having "a Mediterranean climate" – one has never been as cold as when spending a summer in San Francisco.

The point, of course, is that the balmy temperatures and benign climatic patterns we associate with the Mediterranean are often a reality, but not always. In the western Mediterranean the range of climatic possibilities has always been broad and contingent on wind patterns and other such climatic factors. Moreover, while in some regions the benefits of proximity to the sea reach deep inland, in others geological factors neutralize or alter the influence of the sea. The Sahara Desert looms closer to the Mediterranean shores than one may imagine. The spurs of the Pyrenees and the high country of Old Catalonia are within easy reach from Barcelona, one of the paradigmatic western Mediterranean cities. Yet, in Provence and the Languedoc, the Mediterranean climate extends far inland, made most obvious by the presence of olive trees and viticulture. Thus, climate shaped the nature of cultivation, types of landholdings, and other factors that fashioned the unique history of each Mediterranean region. As Horden and Purcell have correctly insisted, the Mediterranean Sea has to be seen as a juxtaposition of micro-ecological niches and what gives the entire sea – or in this case what gives the western Mediterranean – unity is the links that connect one region to another (thus connectivity). Most of those places of economic connectivity were found where the sea met the land.

SHORES, MOUNTAINS, AND PLAINS

The Mediterranean is more than the sea. Sitting at the center of the Afro-Eurasian landmasses, sea and land are part of a larger geographical, historical, and cultural exchange system, sites of encounter that constituted the "Mediterranean world," in Braudel's formulation. Anyone sailing through the western Mediterranean and coming ashore, whether in North Africa, Spain, Italy, or on any of the many islands dotting the western sea, would not have far to travel inland before moving into rugged country. This is not the case everywhere in the eastern portions of the sea (think of Egypt or Libya), providing further evidence as to the distinct character of the western Mediterranean as compared to the eastern part.

This topographical reality was already foreshadowed in the previous section on climate. Mountains rising from the shore impacted climate patterns, as they did the social, economic, and political structures of the regions around the western Mediterranean basin. But before reaching the mountains or the high inland plains, such as those of Old and New Castile, our imaginary traveler would come to those coastal or alluvial plains that played such a significant role in the historical life of the western Mediterranean. Along these shores rose some of the most significant players in the urban history of the Mediterranean: Marseille, Barcelona, Valencia, Málaga, Tunis, Tangier (on the Atlantic opening of the Sea), Oran, Venice, Rome (open to the sea through its Mediterranean port at Ostia and now through Civitavecchia), Genoa, and

Naples among others. The Rhône's great river plain represented a deep wedge into the North, pushing the ecological boundaries of the Mediterranean into Northern Europe. Valencia's fabled *huerta*, tilled by Muslims, Mudejares (Muslims under Christian rule), Moriscos (Muslims nominally converted to Christianity in the early sixteenth century), and Christians from the Middle Ages until today, is just an example of how topography could shape economic destinies. But such schemes and destinies did not always work as planned.

Aigues-Mortes (dead waters) is a very good example of how historical circumstances, climate, and topography shape the contours of landscape. In the mid-thirteenth century, the French kings had only a tenuous grip on the southern areas of what is France today. Marseille, one of the great Mediterranean ports and a quintessential Mediterranean city, was then beyond French royal jurisdiction. The shores of the Languedoc region did not provide a suitable port from which to launch ambitious expeditions into the Mediterranean. The French king, Louis IX (1226–1227), rebuilt Aigues-Mortes and refurbished its port as a point of departure for his failed Second Crusade. He had conceived a bizarre plan to invade North Africa and then to proceed overland to the Holy Land. But Aigues-Mortes soon ceased to play a role in the maritime ambitions of French kings (see Chapter 11). The silting of the fluvial plain around Aigues-Mortes (part of the Camargue region) cut its access to the sea and relegated it to one of these cities preserved in time by its impractical location and failed vocation as a Mediterranean port.[17]

A comparison between Valencia, a city and region mentioned above briefly, and Murcia provides another example of the manner in which history impacted agriculture and later development. Valencia was a rich agricultural region that had been wisely cultivated by the Muslims from the eighth century onwards. The region prospered from the judicious Muslim adaptation of Roman irrigation technology. Arago-Catalan armies, led by Jaume I (1213–1276), conquered the city in 1238. When the Christian rulers of Valencia faced a Mudejar uprising in the 1260s, they did not expel the Muslims from their land, as had been done throughout most of western Andalusia. Instead, they turned the Muslim population into a semi-servile agricultural workforce. Valencia became one of the richest agricultural regions in late medieval Iberia. Murcia, captured by the Castilian armies in 1266, also faced a Mudejar uprising. After the Mudejares were expelled from the region, the gardens went to waste, the irrigation works suffered, and the now sparsely populated region became one of the destinations of the transhumance. Here is an example of where similar Muslim husbandry, climate, and geography yielded very different results because of momentous decisions on whether or not to exile the Muslim population.[18]

MOUNTAINS AND MOVEMENT

In the North African shores bordering the western Mediterranean, rugged mountains and, south of them, the Sahara created a fairly effective barrier to movement. Although an ancient link existed between the African

Mediterranean coast and the interior – with the fabled Timbuktu as one of the main entrepôts or places for exchange of goods between the Mediterranean, sub-Saharan, and West African markets – this was a specialized trade network, controlled by Berbers and other desert people and not easily accessible to all. Along the northern African coast a few coves and ports – most of them with limited harborage – provided the settings for urban centers that would come to play a significant role in the history of the western Mediterranean from Classical Antiquity until the present: Carthage, Oran, Algiers, Bougie, Tétouan, and others. Although we may think of this North African coastal plain as not as attractive in terms of climate, topography, and rainfall as its better known counterpart in Europe, that was not the case in Antiquity or even into the early modern period. Specific regions in North Africa, such as the Tell in the eastern spurs of the Riff Mountains, were places well irrigated by mountain streams, with abundant rain and fertile and productive soils, the so-called gardens of North Africa. And North Africa had been a flourishing economic center under successive Carthaginian, Roman, and Fatimid rulers.

The same pattern of coastal plains is often replicated on the northern Mediterranean shores. Most of the northern coast of Catalonia rises sharply into the eastern spurs of the Pyrenees. This is also the case in the areas around Málaga and Alicante where a short car drive marks the transition between the coast and the rugged mountain range of the Alpujarras. Not unlike the Tell in North Africa, the valleys of the Alpujarras sustained important agricultural production, most notably mulberry trees and silk-producing worms in the Late Middle Ages and the early modern period. Yet, as we have seen, history also shaped the productivity of these regions. After the Moriscos rose up in arms in the Alpujarras Mountains in response to punitive legislation against their language, culinary practices, faithfulness to Islam, and forms of dress in 1568, their bitter defeat in 1570–1571 led to the dispersal of the local population throughout Castile, with others sold into slavery or killed. With the prosperous Alpujarras valleys bereft of their almost millennium-long occupation by Muslims and their careful husbandry, the Spanish Crown sought to resettle the region with Christian immigrants. The result was the collapse of the silk industry and a long period of adjustment and poverty.

Further west, the fertile river plain of the Guadalquivir is encircled by a complex mountain system: the Sierra Morena. It acts as a barrier between western Andalusia and the plains of New Castile. In Italy, one cannot roam too far off the coast, whether from the Tyrrhenian or the Adriatic shores, before running into coastal hills or the Apennines when traveling east or west, or the imposing barrier of the Alps. Cinque Terre is a very good example of those small coastal towns or villages (Vernazza, Riomaggiore, and others), with their small coves open to the sea but so difficult to access that communication between each other was mostly carried out by boat until the building of the railroad and a pathway for tourists within recent history.

Sicily, Sardinia, and Corsica provide similar experiences in their swift transition between sea and mountain. The flow from sea to mountain is less abrupt only in the southern French Mediterranean coast, roughly between Perpignan, Sète, and the new tourist town of La Grande Motte (see

Chapter 11), before high hills to the east (spurs of the Alps), along which the fabled *corniches* run east-west, hug coastal towns: Cannes, Nice, Monte Carlo, and others, providing a spectacular backdrop to these tourist destinations. The Camargue and the great alluvial plain of the Rhône offer sweeping landscapes seldom found anywhere else in the western Mediterranean. Yet, the geological features of these regions seem also to preclude the spacious harbors that became sites for commercial and human exchanges, the entry and departure points for cultural transmission. (See chapters 10 and 11 for coastal towns.)

If we imagine the Mediterranean as a sea encircled by mountains with gaps opening into surrounding lands, we ought also to expand this portrait of the western Mediterranean world – in fact, of the whole of the Mediterranean – as a series of concentric circles that girdled the sea with imposing mountain frames. South of the Atlas Mountains and the Riff was the barrier of the Sahara Desert. Northwest of the Alpujarras one would run into the Central Sierras (north of Madrid). North of that and, in dramatic succession, one would encounter the high plains of Old Castile, the Picos de Europa, and the Pyrenees. Traveling northwards from the Camargue or the Languedoc, one meets the Dordogne mountain range, not as imposing as all those topographical features listed above, but still an impediment to travel. Beyond the Alps lies the Jura and southern German rough country. All these barriers had gaps or natural byways that, following river valley or mountain passes, allowed the free flow of travelers, commerce, and armies from the Mediterranean basin to the world beyond, or, as was most often the case after the demise of Rome, from the north into the Mediterranean.

This is most certainly the case of the Lake region in the southern spurs of the Italian Alps. Lakes Como, Maggiore, and the other substantial Alpine bodies of water were byways through which commerce, ideas, and, unfortunately, armies moved north and south. And, in the particular case of the Lake Como region, the combination of abundant water and the protection provided by the mountains from northern winds created yet another ecosystem or habitat. Silk production in Como, olive trees, and viticulture provide abundant evidence of the uniqueness of these transitional areas, which, by the fortuitous combination of climate, soil, and the protection given by the imposing Alps, thrived in what were most certainly Mediterranean economic endeavors. The Rhône valley connected France, Italy, and the Mediterranean with the great medieval fairs in Champagne. In the early modern period, it became the "Spanish Road to Flanders," a thoroughfare for Spanish military deployments from Italy to the Low Countries.

The Alps were, as multiple Germanic, Carthaginian, and Napoleonic military excursions proved, not much of a barrier after all. Whether German emperors, savants (think of Buridan or Petrarch traveling from Paris or Avignon to Italy, respectively), or modern tourists, there was a continuous circulation between the Mediterranean shores and the North. On the southern shores of the sea, caravans crossed the Sahara on regular schedules that were as old as history itself, human bridges across the vastness of the desert. Yet, for all these gaps and openings in the barriers surrounding the western sea, one must be also impressed by the resourcefulness of Mediterranean people in seeking access to the world beyond their own habitats on the shores of the Middle Sea. Conversely, northerners, as was the case with Goethe in his old age or Keats as a dying young man, yearned for the warmth and sunlight that was also part of the shimmering sea.

MOUNTAINS

Away from the sea but not too far away, the mountains were, and remain, impressive topological features encircling, and encompassing, the Mediterranean sea in walls of stone. While this is not a book on the geography of the Mediterranean world, my climatic and geographical introduction represents a gesture and acknowledgment to Braudel, Horden, Purcell, and others for their contributions to our sense of geography as an important category of knowledge. It is also a statement as to the importance of climatic and geographical contexts in the making of Mediterranean history. This is certainly the case when dealing with mountains. Geographical features in the first line of mountains hugging the western Mediterranean coast shaped social structures, patterns of human settlement, agricultural and pastoral economies, and other such factors that constitute the region's total history.

Where were mountain passes located? How did access to a certain mountain region shape the political contours of historical periods? The Val d'Aran, to give just one example here, remained a bone of contention between the Crown of Aragon and France throughout the Middle Ages. It had its own identity and its own dialect that was neither Catalan nor French. The Val d'Aran was one of those liminal spaces that could be found abundantly on the high ground above the western Mediterranean. Some of them have resisted the onslaught of centralizing modern nations to this day. San Marino, located on the northeast corner of the Apennines, is an example. Andorra is yet another of those peculiar regions, surviving precisely because of their rugged topography and the presence of more powerful adjacent nation-states or ecclesiastical lords that, as was the case in Andorra, canceled each other out. Switzerland is perhaps the best and most successful example of what geography and peculiar historical circumstances may be able to create out of the political uncertainties of the Late Middle Ages. The Berbers' fierce independence and sense of unique identity against waves of outsiders was deeply centered in the abrupt Atlas and Riff Mountains and, of course, in the desert. Diverse linguistic communities – the Berbers, the Basques, the Sardinians with their various dialects – prospered in the mountainous regions around the Mediterranean Sea. Each of these examples, and there are many others, bespeaks of the diversity of ecological niches proliferating on the shores and inland from the western sea. Each of them had a peculiar history. Each of them had their own distinct social structures. Each of them followed a different path from Late Antiquity into the contemporary world. But what can one say of the mountains themselves?

I have already referred to these mountains in a previous section, but it may be useful to include here a brief description of each of these individual mountain regions – though their distinct geological history emerges from a common origin. One must always begin where humanity began, that is, in Africa. The southern shores of the western Mediterranean give way quite quickly to fairly high and abrupt mountain ranges in what is today northern Morocco. On its Mediterranean coast rose the Riff Mountains. Although the Riff mountain range did not reach on average the height of other mountain ranges, and while its highest peak (around 2,450 meters high) did not come close to the Atlas mountain formations further south or to those of its northern counterparts in Europe, its proximity to the coast shaped the commercial history of western Morocco with, as noted earlier, few spacious harbors or great trading stations. The Riff was also a world of small settlements, not easily tamed politically. In the Central Middle Ages, the Riff and Atlas mountains would provide most of the manpower for the Almoravid and Almohad invasions of southern Spain and the latter's aspirations to a western Mediterranean Empire. The ascetical and fundamentalist beliefs of mountain and desert people would then shape the history of late medieval Spain and North Africa.

Although the Riff Mountains were not strictly part of the Atlas mountain range, they also shaped the turbulent history of North Africa, from the Vandal invasion in the early fifth century to the settler colonialism of recent centuries. And yet the Riff are meager mountains when compared to the Atlas mountain range. For more than 2,500 kilometers, the Atlas range parallels the Mediterranean from western Morocco into modern Tunisia. Although divided into a series of sub ranges and not always as rugged or as high everywhere – remember the example of the Tell Atlas given earlier – the Jbel Toubkat in southwestern Morocco rises to as high as 4,167 meters. One also tends to forget that the Atlas mountain range sharply divides modern Morocco, and that most of their most important urban centers, such as ancient inland Marrakesh, Salé, Tangier, Casablanca, and others, are located either on the Atlantic or close to it. Moreover, the ancient ties that these locations had with Europe – through the Iberian Peninsula – occurred frequently through Atlantic routes. Only inland and coastal Oran, Fez, and Tétouan had full Mediterranean vocations.[19]

Moving clockwise across the Straits of Gibraltar, one immediately runs into the rising hills of the Betic system (*sistema Bético*), running from Gibraltar eastward to the abrupt Alpujarras Mountains and the Sierra Nevada (with heights over 3,000 meters). These were the sites of Mudejar and Morisco rebellion against the Spanish Crown in 1499 and 1568. North and east of Granada, alluvial plains in Murcia, Valencia, and the delta of the Ebro River, south of Tarragona, provide a transitional rising ground before the Montsagre de Paüls. From there, one could follow the coastal roads northwards to the easternmost spurs of the Pyrenees.

The eastern part of the Pyrenees does not reach the heights found in the central and western part of the range. Mountain passes are high and few, winter average temperatures are usually below freezing. Precipitation levels are lower in the eastern Pyrenees than in the West towards the Basque homeland. Traveling, as I did in 2005, from southern France into Andorra and from there to La Seu d'Urgell, an ancient episcopal center, onwards to Figueres (the home of Salvador Dalí), and, finally, to the Mediterranean shore north of Barcelona, I was struck, in spite of the modern roads and tunnels that breach high mountains, by the extraordinary difficulties one finds – notwithstanding the striking scenery – in driving from mountain to sea. How difficult would this have been in a world before paved roads and cars?

In Braudel's formulation, the mountains, the Pyrenees in particular, have been seen as sites of freedom, the independent hill people at war with the civilized plain. Throughout history this has not always been so. The mountains have also been, above all the high country sloping from the eastern Pyrenees or Old Catalonia, sites of harsh servitude, as was the case with the *remença* peasants (servile peasantry that had to pay for emancipation, a remença) in Old Catalonia in the Late Middle Ages.[20]

In the past, similar to most rugged and hilly regions in the Mediterranean basin, the Pyrenees Mountains were infested with bandits and resistance. The county of Ribagorza, covering most of the Central Pyrenees in the Aragonese region and extending into the Catalonian eastern Pyrenean spurs, was plagued by violent civil strife from the Late Middle Ages into the late sixteenth century. Under Philip II, the Spanish Crown bribed rebellious lords into a peaceful agreement. Bandits, often led by the infamous Lupercio Latrás in the late sixteenth century, descended from the mountains to scourge Morisco villages in the Ebro river valley. The mountains thus became bandit lairs, embellished in the literary and popular imagination, and the bandits – from Roca (or Roque) Guinart (an actual bandit who entered into fable, appearing in the pages of *Don Quixote* as an early modern Robin Hood) to Salvatore Giuliani, the real-life twentieth-century Sicilian who was often represented as yet another Robin Hood, operating throughout Sicily's rugged terrain (see below) – became popular figures among those at the bottom of society. Think of the story within the story in Dumas's *The Count of Monte Cristo* and the sympathetic representation of Luigi Vampa, the archetypical Mediterranean bandit.

Beyond bandits and rebels, the Pyrenees – as was the case in the Riff and Atlas ranges, and similar to the Ardeche, the Alps, the Apennines, and other mountain areas encircling the Mediterranean Sea – fostered small village communities, pastoral economies, and specific social networks distinct from those of plain people. Popular culture was also different, and it would not be amiss to think, along with Carlo Ginzburg, Hugh Trevor-Roper, the authors of the *Malleus Maleficarum,* and Primo Levi, that mountain regions created peculiar conditions that fostered archaic beliefs, such as those of the *Benandanti,* so elegantly and persuasively described by Carlo Ginzburg for the early modern Friuli. I apologize for digressing from a brief look at the Pyrenees to reflections on popular culture, freedom, and banditry. In many respects, these questions attest to the variety of Mediterranean experiences but also to the importance of topography and location in the forging of a history *of* (and *in*) the Mediterranean.

Traveling eastward across the geographical and political frontiers shaped by the Pyrenees from the Middle Ages onwards, one reaches the alluvial plains and marshlands of southern France. North from the Mediterranean shores, directly northwards as the crow flies from Narbonne, one runs into the hilly country that was the geographical heart of the so-called Cathar heresy at Albi (see Chapter 5) and elsewhere in the twelfth and early thirteenth century. It is only further north that the Massif Central provides a mountain barrier. Eastwards, the Rhône valley eventually gives way to the western spurs of the imposing Alpine range. With a rugged topography, this high hilly country hugs the sea around Cannes, Nice, and Monte Carlo. These mountains and hills, the fabled *corniches*, provide a dramatic backdrop to fashionable seaside resorts that have prospered in the region since the modern period.

THE ALPS

The Alps are imposing mountains. Anyone who has seen them or flown over them cannot but be impressed by their extent and high snow-covered peaks. I was just in Lugano and was, once again, enchanted by the topography and views from up high of beautiful Lake Maggiore. The Alps are fairly young mountains, geologically connected to the Apennines, the Sicilian mountain system, and the Atlas range in North Africa. Some of their high peaks rise over 4,000 meters, such as the Gran Paradiso, Mont Blanc, and others; many Alpine peaks exceed 3,000 meters. Others, although not as high, such as, for example, Mont Ventoux (the site, as the name indicates, of ferocious winds), though on the fringes of the Alps, have played an important role in the western imaginary. The latter became Petrarch's chosen place for his meditations and reflections that would change the cultural history of Western Europe. Today, Mont Ventoux is well known as one of the most arduous climbs in the Tour de France.

As impenetrable as the Alps seem to be, there are openings and mountain passes that have allowed for commerce and invaders to move in and out of the Italian Peninsula. A coastal route allows for transit from Provence and the Rhône Valley to Genoa, the Cinque Terre region, and, eventually, the heart of the Italian Peninsula. The very high mountain passes of Mons Matrona or Montgenèvre (1,853 meters high) and the even higher and fabled Saint Bernard Mountain pass (over 2,000 meters), though not always easy to negotiate (especially in winter), have allowed for a succession of invaders since the Classical period. The Brenner Pass (1,362 meters) in the Central Alps served also as a gate for Germanic invaders into Italy. The Alps, not unlike the Atlas and Pyrenees mountains, constitute their own peculiar ecological system, or, to be more precise, an overlapping and complementary set of ecological niches. Their rich forests became the main source for the Mediterranean lumber trade, though in Antiquity the most important source of timber for Roman Italy remained the Apennines and the plains adjacent to the mountains.

The mountains girdling western Mediterranean countries continue almost uninterrupted and are replicated in the central mountainous spines of Sicily, Sardinia, and Corsica. To a far less extent, this extension of mountain ranges also is present in Majorca, the largest of the Balearic Islands. Sicily's rugged interior connects, through an underwater ridge, with the Apennines and with Africa. And, as noted earlier, mountain and plains yield different ecological niches, economies, forms of organizing space, types of land tenure, and sizes of village. The ability to impose order and gain political control, opposing banditry, also differs, as does the fierce independence of mountain people compared to those of the plains. Each of these topics would require a separate chapter to do justice to their importance in a social and economic history of the Mediterranean and its people. I fear that generalizations about such geographically dictated ecological structures do not fully capture the micro-ecological niches that abounded and are still present along the shores of the western Mediterranean.

Yet, human activity and human culture have, after all, also shaped and reshaped these ecologies over the long span of historical time. The burning of forests, something that is still going on in the twenty-first century, whether by accident or with malice, affected, and still shapes, the landscape and climate of the Mediterranean. Types of cultivation, irrigation or lack of it, and the extension of central authority from cities on the plain into the mountains have also transformed the dynamics of each location. Religion – from the fundamentalist waves that swept the Riff and Atlas mountains and translated into invasions of Iberia in the eleventh, twelfth, and fourteenth centuries (the Almoravids, Almohads, and Marinids) to the heretics who gave up their lives at Montségur (the last bastion of the Albigensian heresy) in the fourteenth – also shaped the social life of Mediterranean lands.

Taking all these factors into consideration and remaining cautious as to the perils of any such broad generalization, one could posit, once again, that numerous but small villages were often a feature of mountain societies. Large village and towns could be found on the coastal plains and river valleys. Pastoral economies, livestock, fruit trees (but not citrus fruits) were more often found in high places than by the seashore, though the transhumance, whether in Spain or Italy, connected both ecologies. Fishing and other seafaring activities, including, of course, long-distance trade, could be found along the shores of the western sea, though, as shall be seen later, the sinews of trade linked mountain, plain, coast, and the world beyond the Mediterranean into complex networks of interdependency.

And then, of course, there were the traditional and millennial-long basic staples of the Mediterranean diet and economy: bread, wine, olive oil, fish, and others. We have long understood the boundaries of the Roman world at its peak to be the limits imposed by geography and climate. Where could one cultivate the vine? Where would olive trees thrive? But such assumptions may be deceiving. Each chronological period was *sui generis* and the political, cultural, and economic realities attached to those periods dictated what was grown and why. Wine, for example, was produced in places such as England in the twelfth century, a place that had ceased to be a wine producer for a long while. Today, climatic change and national pride have fostered a renewed wine production in England, but it was not so for many centuries before our own. Olive trees, that quintessential staple of the Mediterranean, could be found in the Middle Ages in small ecological niches north of the Central Sierras in Spain, surrounded by places either too high or too cold to foster the cultivation of olives. They are also found in the microclimate around Lake Como in the shadows of the Alps. All these staples, including the bread (in its many variations of barley, wheat, rye, etc.) that was so necessary for the people of the area for their nutrition and liturgical needs (the host), dictated forms of cultivating and tending of the soil that would be revolutionized in recent times by economies of scale, ease of transportation, and the like. Thus, even though we still associate the long row of olive orchards or the hills covered with rows of grapes with Mediterranean landscapes, it has always been a changing landscape, adapting and being transformed by climatic change and human necessity.

In spite of my wish to complicate and problematize the story I am describing here, one fairly constant element, however, remains as part of the topographical reality of the western Mediterranean. That is the presence of thin soils around the shores of the western sea. Although here and there irrigation and careful husbandry could yield plentiful crops – for example in Valencia, or the Tell valley in the Riff – the reality was that throughout its history the lands around the Mediterranean faced the disadvantage of thin soils that needed – in a world before the availability of chemical fertilizers – considerable fallow time and biannual rotation of crops. The deep and fertile soils of most of Northern Europe would foster in time a three field system, new crops, heavy and often wheeled plows that dug deep into the soil bringing nutrients to the surface. In the Mediterranean world, the enduring presence of the Roman plow that merely scratched the surface of its thin soils serves as a tell-tale sign of the essential differences between the Mediterranean and the North. In many respects, thin soils, as opposed to deep ones, determined the manner in which rural space was organized. There were none of those long open fields on the shores of the Mediterranean. Fences, small plots, specific types of agricultural utensils, and animals to pull the plough, remain fairly unchanged almost to this day, reflecting the unique peculiarities of Mediterranean life.

CONCLUSION

Geography, climate, topography, and types of soil do not make for inexorable destinies. Human activity did, either by adaptation to, or transformation of, the landscape – irrigation being a good example – lead to the continuous and enduring change of the lands around the Middle Sea. These transformations may be slight and only perceptible over a long span of time, but those intrepid peasants, merchants, and lords who toiled and ruled around the European and African shores of the western Mediterranean did change their habits. The history of mankind – from our hominid ancestors long ago to the present – is the long and arduous process of adapting to, and transforming, our lived environment. So it was in the Mediterranean, where, in spite of mountains, suffocating hot winds, and unpredictable seas, human agency built great civilizations along its shores. These civilizations provide the context for our stories. To them, we turn now.

NOTES

1 Daniel Smail, *On Deep History and the Brain* (Berkeley: University of California Press, 2008).

2 This is the point made in David Abulafia's wonderful recent book, *The Great Sea. A Human History of the Mediterranean* (Oxford: Oxford University Press, 2011).

3 Fernand Braudel, *The Mediterranean and the Mediterranean World in the Age of Philip II*, 2 vols, trans. Siân Reynolds (Berkeley: University of California Press, 1995). This is a reprinting of the first English edition in 1972. See Chapter 1. Peregrine Horden and Nicholas Purcell, *The Corrupting Sea. A Study of Mediterranean History* (Oxford: Blackwell, 2000), 9–25 et passim.

4 Alexander Dumas, *The Count of Monte Cristo* (London & New York: Penguin, 2003), 1230.

5 See the massive geographical study by James M. Houston, *The Western Mediterranean World: An Introduction to its Regional Landscapes*, with sections by J. Roglic and J.I. Clarke (New York: Praeger, 1967); see also earlier references to Braudel and Horden and Purcell, as well as Faruk Tabak, *The Waning of the Mediterranean, 1550–1870: A Geohistorical Approach* (Baltimore: Johns Hopkins University Press, 2008).

6 Archibald R. Lewis, "Northern European Sea Power and the Straits of Gibraltar, 1031–1350 A.D.," in *Order and Innovation in the Middle Ages. Essays in Honor of Joseph R. Strayer*, edited by William C. Jordan, Bruce McNab, and Teofilo F. Ruiz (Princeton: Princeton University Press, 1976), 139–164.

7 Lewis, 140.

8 Cervantes, 394. They had landed in Vélez-Málaga even though they had originally aimed for Majorca.

9 Although I provide this bibliographical information elsewhere, I have reproduced it here for easier reference, since this is the first full use of the protests against the sea in this book. On the Barcelona Consulate of Commerce there has been little written. See María Jesús Espuny Tomás, "El Real Consulado de Comercio del Principado de Cataluña (1758–1829)." PhD diss., Universitat Autònoma de Barcelona, 1992). Available online at http://www.tdx.cat/TDX-0630109-121322. The Consulates of Commerce were the heirs to the medieval Consulates of the Sea on which there is an extensive bibliography. See, for example, Román Piña Homs, *El Consolat de Mar, Mallorca, 1326–1800* (Palma de Mallorca: Institut d'Estudis Baleàrics, 1985); *Consulado del mar de Barcelona: nuevamente traducido de cathalan en castellano*, trans. Don Cayetano de Palleja (Barcelona: J. Piferrer, 1732). This title is available online (though with restricted access). Also Stanley S. Jados, *Consolat de Mar, and Related Documents* (University, AL: University of Alabama Press, 1975).

10 Arxiu de la Corona d'Aragó (Archivo de la Corona de Aragón). Hereafter ACA, Consulado de Comercio. *Registro de protestas de mar*, 4/1 (129), fol. 1. These holdings in the Arxiu de la Corona d'Aragó contain a series of diverse holdings that deal with maritime trade in and out of Barcelona. The holdings are overwhelming. They are organized as follows: there is an inventory of registers and volumes for the Consulate of the Sea (1715–1761) and another register for the Royal Consulate of Commerce (1762–1829) with an additional register for the tribunal of Commerce (1830–1868), plus additional inventories and an index of litigation carried out under the jurisdiction of these bodies. I have focused on the register of protests against the sea. There is an index (that allows for the gathering of information and data speedily: *Indice de los registros de protestas de mar (1766–1868)*, which I have used in the preparation of this chapter and *Registros de protestas de mar. 1766–1868* in 33 vols. (All of them now gathered in one enormous volume and including over 25,000 such protests.)

11 ACA, Consulado de Comercio. *Registro de protestas de mar*, 4/1 (129), fols. 1–3. Some examples will suffice. In January 1766, besides Carreras, the following

protests were recorded at the Consulado de Comercio in Barcelona: M. Hange, captain of the ship *Our Lady of Mercy*, a citizen of Carnet with his ship registered in Spain, carried diverse merchandise from Cádiz (probably coming from Atlantic markets and transferred to his ship outside the Straits of Gibraltar) to Alicante and Barcelona. His ship met bad weather that damaged some of his cargo. He protested against the sea and against bad weather. On January 1, 1766, the Dutch captain Sepher de Wilder (the scribes in the Consulate of Commerce tried to render foreign names as accurately as they could but often failed to do so), master of the ship *Liberty*, registered in the Netherlands, stated through an interpreter (Juan Bautista Cabanyes, vice consul of the Netherlands in Barcelona) that on his voyage from Amsterdam, from where he was bringing grain, he met bad weather that may have damaged his cargo. He wished to protest against the sea. On January 15, 1766, Robert Hogg, the English captain of the ship *King George*, sailed from New York to Barcelona carrying wheat. He also met bad weather and rough seas that damaged his cargo and wished, therefore, to protest against the sea and against the intemperate weather. Two other protests were registered that day through two different interpreters. One came from another Dutch captain, and the other from an English one. Both ships carried wheat from the Netherlands and England. Both claimed to have had their cargo damaged by tempests at sea. Both used translators who served as consuls or vice consuls for their respective countries.

12   Juan Cristóbal Calvete de Estrella, *El felicísimo viaje del muy alto y poderoso príncipe Don Felipe . . . desde España a sus tierras de la baja Alemania*, 2 vols (Antwerp, 1562; Madrid: Sociedad de bibliófilos españoles, vols 7 & 8, 1930), I: 14–66.

13   Calvete de Estrella, I: 2–43 et passim. See also, Teofilo F. Ruiz, *A King Travels. Festive Traditions in Late Medieval and Early Modern Spain* (Princeton: Princeton University Press, 2012), chapter 5 et passim.

14   For environmental changes in the eastern Mediterranean, see Roni Ellenblum, *The Collapse of the Eastern Mediterranean: Climate Change and the Decline of the East, 950–1072* (Cambridge: Cambridge University Press, 2012); for trade in the Western part of the sea throughout this period see Paul Reynolds' massive documentary evidence for the trade in ceramics in the western Mediterranean *after* the collapse of the Roman empire in the West, *Trade in the Western Mediterranean, AD 400–700: The Ceramic Evidence* (Oxford: Tempus Reparatum, 1995); see also the work of Jessica Goldberg, often quoted throughout this book, on Geniza merchants trading between the region of Tunis (today) and Sicily.

15   On the difficulties of sailing in and out of the Mediterranean and on seafaring in general in the Mediterranean, see Fernand Braudel, *The Mediterranean and the Mediterranean World in the Age of Philip II*, trans. Siân Reynolds, 2 vols (Berkeley and Los Angeles: University of California Press, 1995.), I:103–138; 168–230. See also Archibald R. Lewis, "Northern European Sea Power and the Straits of Gibraltar, 1031–1350 A.D.," in William C. Jordan, Bruce McNab, and Teofilo F. Ruiz, eds., *Order and Innovation in the Middle Ages. Essays in Honor of Joseph R. Strayer* (Princeton: Princeton University Press, 1976), 139–141.

16   See Peter Brown, *Augustine of Hippo: A Biography*, new. ed. (London: Faber and Faber, 2000); and his new and striking descriptions of the lands around the Mediterranean, *Through the Eye of a Needle: Wealth, the Fall of Rome, and the Making of Christianity in the West, 350–550 AD* (Princeton: Princeton University Press, 2012).

17   See William C. Jordan, "Supplying Aigues-Mortes for the Crusade of 1248: The Problem of Restructuring Trade," in William C. Jordan, Bruce McNab, and

Teofilo F. Ruiz, eds. *Order and Innovation in the Middle Ages. Essays in Honor of Joseph R. Strayer* (Princeton: Princeton University Press, 1976), 165–172. See also Georges Jehel, *Aigues-Mortes, un port pour un roi: les capétiens et la Méditerranée* (Roanne, Le Coteau: Horvath, 1985).

18 For the critical period for the transition between Islamic to Christian rule in Valencia, see Robert I. Burns, *The Crusader Kingdom of Valencia (1238–1276): A Study in the Organization of the Mediaeval Frontier* (Baltimore: Johns Hopkins University Press, 1958). On the transfer of technology between Muslims and Christians in medieval Iberia, see Thomas F. Glick, *Islamic and Christian Spain in the Early Middle Ages. Comparative Perspectives on Social and Cultural Formation* (Princeton: Princeton University Press, 1979). For Murcia in the thirteenth century, see Juan Torres Fontes, *Repartimiento de la huerta y campo de Murcia en el siglo XIII* (Murcia: Consejo Superior de Investigaciones Científicas, 1971).

19 On the geological evolution of the Atlas Mountains, see Voleker H. Jacobshagen, ed., *The Atlas System of Morocco: Studies on its Geodynamic Evolution* (Berlin & New York: Springer-Verlag, 1988). We have numerous travel accounts in the Atlas, which will be examined in a different chapter. For a glimpse of traveling in the Atlas region in the nineteenth century, see James Grey Jackson, *An Account of Timbuctoo and Housa, territories in the interior of Africa, by El Hage Abd Salam Shabeeny ...* (London: Longman, Hurst, Rees, Orme and Brown, 1820).

20 For the mountains and freedom in Braudel, see Vol. I, 38–41. On the remença peasantry and their servitude, see Paul H. Freedman, *The Origins of Peasant Servitude in Medieval Catalonia* (Cambridge: Cambridge University Press, 1991).

[3] History in the Mediterranean: From Unity to Fragmentation, circa 450 CE until the Early Modern World

ALTHOUGH this is not a political history of the western Mediter-ranean polities – that is, not a history *in* the Mediterranean – travel, encounters, transmissions of new and hybrid culture forms, and the dynamic exchanges that propelled Mediterranean history took place in the context of the rise and fall of large and small political entities along the shores of the western sea.

In this and the next chapter, I wish to provide a brief account of those polities that, through their social, political, economic, and cultural structures, whether successful or not, shaped the historical development of Mediterranean lands between the waning of Roman imperial power in the West and the present. Much is neglected in these pages. For example, in this chapter I have sought to emphasize the medieval and early modern period. The western Mediterranean, between the collapse of the Roman world in the West and the rise of nation-states throughout most of the western Mediterranean basin (but not all), was essentially a world in flux. Nonetheless, by 1600, as shall be seen in the next chapter, the political landscape of the western Mediterranean was fairly fixed until the colonial ventures of European powers into North Africa. A second chapter on the proto-states that rose and fell in the western Mediterranean follows this one and seeks to tell the story up to the present period. To provide a complete history of the societies that came into being, disappeared, or were conquered throughout the region's long history would require volumes. Here is just one brief glance at that history.

The Western Mediterranean and the World: 400 CE to the Present, First Edition. Teofilo F. Ruiz.
© 2018 John Wiley & Sons, Ltd. Published 2018 by John Wiley & Sons, Ltd.

THE WESTERN MEDITERRANEAN IN HISTORY: AN INTRODUCTION

Long before historical records would be kept, early hominids, and later present-day humans (homo sapiens), settled in the lands around the western Mediterranean. Archeology, paleontology, and other methods of studying the remote past provide us with striking accounts of human adaptability and ingenuity in meeting the challenges of a changing environment. The extraordinarily vivid cave paintings at Altamira (in northern Spain and dating to the Upper Paleolithic), Lascaux (southern France, dating back 17,000 years), and elsewhere throughout Southern Europe tell us, in striking fashion, about these early humans' sensibilities. I had the great fortune to see the Altamira cave painting more than 40 years ago, and the brilliant colors and vigorous depictions of totemic animals remain one of the most powerful aesthetic experiences of my lifetime.

In historical time, the western Mediterranean has always served as a site of encounter and cultural production. Phoenicians settled trading colonies on the northern African shore, above all at mighty Carthage, and on the Iberian and French Mediterranean coast. The Greeks sailed westward to Sicily and beyond, voyages preserved in myth and epic such as Hercules's sojourn to, and making of, the famous Pillars of Hercules (or the Straits of Gibraltar), or Odysseus's wandering on western waters in his circuitous travels back to Ithaca and faithful Penelope. And then there were others, Etruscans first and then Romans. To this very day, a traveler in Tuscany and parts of Umbria cannot but marvel at these hill towns of Etruscan origin that spectacularly dot the countryside of central Italy. These groups represented the main players in the western Mediterranean before the beginning of our story, but there were many other people in North Africa, Spain, France (Celtic people), and Italy whose cultures and languages were partly erased by the rising power, first of Carthage and then of Rome. In the end, control over the western Mediterranean became a long and deadly struggle between Carthage and Rome, a period of warfare brilliantly described by the Greek historian Polybius and the Roman historian Livy. Part of that conflict involved the struggle between Rome and Carthage's heirs in Iberia, the members of the Barca family. But even Hannibal's bold invasion (218–203 BCE) of Italy could not overcome Roman resilience and martial ability. After Carthage's final defeat in the third Punic war (203 BCE), Rome established its hegemony throughout all of the western Mediterranean and, by the beginning of the Common Era, throughout the shores of the entire sea. By the first century CE the entire Mediterranean Sea had become a Roman lake. The Sea became truly a Mare Nostrum, Rome's Sea, and over the next 300 years a dual process of Roman settlements, usually discharged soldiers establishing colonies all around the Mediterranean shores, or native populations being assimilated into *Romanitas* (the culture, language, and values of Rome), created a fairly homogeneous urban civilization throughout the region. Although linguistic and ethnic pockets of resistance to a complete assimilation to Roman cultural values endured in spite of Roman hegemony, anyone traveling along the western

Mediterranean lands today has to be impressed by the physical presence of Roman ruins from North Africa to Spain and France. In some places vivid reminders remain of the fashion in which the Romans organized urban spaces – such as in Provence and the great monuments at Arles, or at Nîmes in the Occitanie region – and impacted agricultural practices – such as the irrigation works in Valencia and elsewhere – while planting deep linguistic, political, and cultural roots throughout. Language, law, agricultural practices, educational systems, networks of roads, and urban centers were among some of the most notable legacies of Rome to the Mediterranean. The Sea, patrolled for pirates (for pirates plied the waters of the Mediterranean in spite of Roman power) by Roman triremes, was the link joining East and West, North and South, Africa and Europe, Asia and Europe.

Although local and regional differences emerged, as for example the contrast between North African Roman society in the late fourth and early fifth century and that of Rome and Milan, both worlds magisterially rendered alive in Peter Brown's marvelous biography of Saint Augustine and in his most recent book, *Through the Eye of a Needle*, enduring links remained. Augustine of Hippo, born and early educated in North Africa, could move back and forth between the two shores of the Mediterranean with intellectual ease, even if not with equal psychological assurance. He would, as I have noted already in the previous chapter, eschew brilliant prospects in Italy to return to Africa, and to die in the early fifth century as his city, Hippo, was besieged by Germanic bands. Augustine's death coincided with the demise of that Roman world in which he had grown up. By the decades following his death, the western parts of the Roman Empire became unraveled and ceased, first politically and later cultur-ally, to exist fully. This is where our story really begins.[1]

THE WESTERN MEDITERRANEAN: LATE ANTIQUITY AND THE EARLY MIDDLE AGES

Roman power in the West did not come to an end on any given date or at any particular moment, even if Gibbon's influential dating of the fall of Rome had enjoyed such a powerful hold on the popular imaginary. In many respects, Rome had been slowly coming apart from a much earlier period. The enlight-ened but tyrannical rule of the so-called Antonine emperors (95–192 BCE) – their rule described by Gibbon as the most peaceful period in mankind's history – did indeed keep the peace and kept those threatening that peace safely at bay outside the borders of the empire. But the brilliant stewardship of the Antonines also suffocated creativity and led to the stagnation of the empire. In the third century, social, political, and cultural crises threatened to topple the empire altogether. In the end, the reforms of Diocletian (285–305) and Constantine (313–332) saved the empire, but at a heavy price. The eastern portions of the empire – the region with the largest demographic resources and wealth – were renewed and given such a life that Rome would survive in the East as the Byzantine Empire until 1453. The West was semi-abandoned to its own

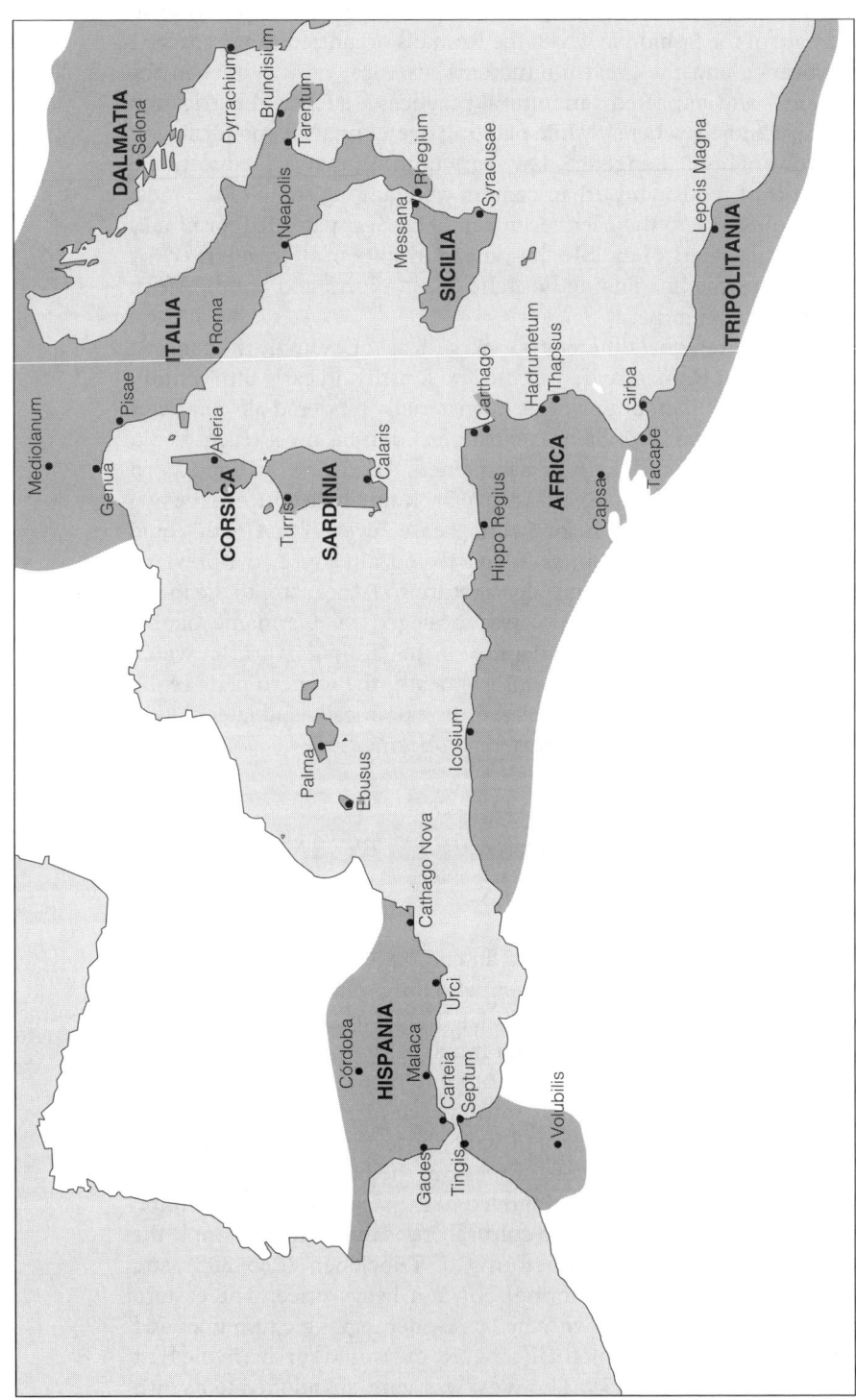

Map 3.1 A map of the major civilizations in the western Mediterranean circa 500 BCE.

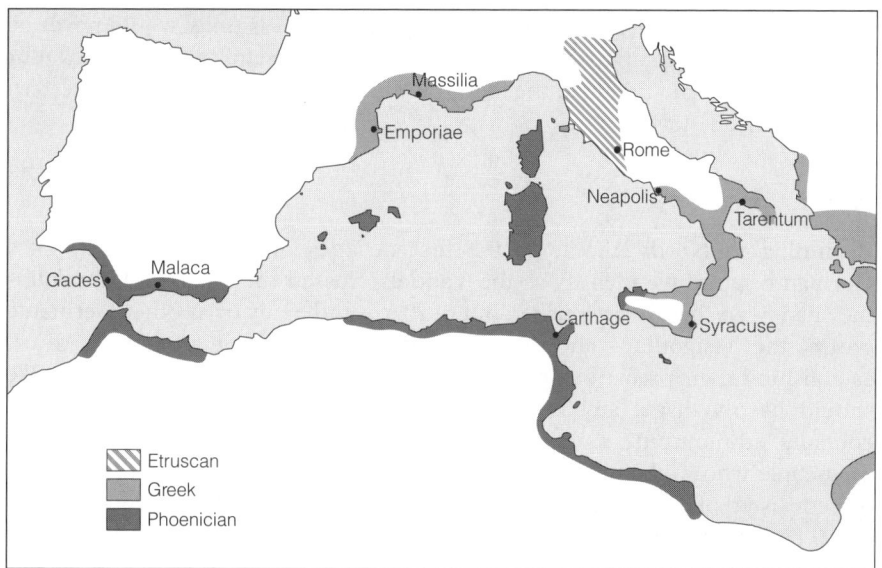

Map 3.2 Map illustrating the Byzantine Empire throughout the western Mediterranean circa 555 CE. Source: Tataryn, 2012, https://commons.wikimedia.org/wiki/File:Justinian 555AD.png. Used under CC BY-SA 3.0, https://creativecommons.org/licenses/by-sa/3.0/deed.en.

devices. Christianity became a tolerated religion under Constantine (313, Edict of Milan) and the official religion of the empire under Theodosius (395). By then, a cadre of aristocratic (and, in the case of Augustine, not so aristocratic) bishops dominated the Church's upper hierarchy. Under their rule, the Christian Church came to fill in the West the administrative vacuum left by the flight of Roman bureaucrats.

By the early fifth century, the political unity of the western Mediterranean had collapsed. Besides the internal collapse, underlined by the growing enserfment (the colonate) of the rural population in the absence of a steady supply of slaves, exhausted soils, and the lack of technological innovations, many among those left in the wake of the collapse of the empire and Germanic invasions sought refuge in transcendental religions (of which Christianity was one), magic, and astrology. The frontiers of the western empire were breached at every point by Germanic groups all at different levels of being Romanized and most of them acting, at least nominally, in the name of the Roman emperor at Constantinople, the new Christian capital built by Constantine on the Bosporus as a rival and counterpart to pagan Rome.

By 500 and for the next 100 years, new polities rose along the shores of the western Mediterranean. While still adhering to some Roman administrative practices, and living, as most people in the Middle Ages and the Renaissance did, in Rome's considerable shadow, these new political entities were not Rome. Their very existence was a sign of how the unity of the western

Mediterranean under Rome had been fragmented. This unity would never be fully recovered even up to the present day. It may be useful to take a quick tour of these lands and identify the new players who appeared on the western Mediterranean stage.

North Africa

Beginning in North Africa, by the first decades of the fifth century CE a Germanic group we identify as the Vandals crossed the straits of Gibraltar – they had been themselves pushed out of Iberia and Sicily by another Germanic group, the Visigoths – and swept through most of Roman North Africa, establishing their precarious rule for most of the remaining fifth century. We should hastily dispel any notion that these Germanic groups represented coherent ethnic units. As has been shown over the last three decades or so, the people who we know in history as Visigoths, Vandals, Ostrogoths, and the like consisted of diverse groups of people, some of whom forged an identity only in the period after the fall of Rome in the West. Nineteenth-century nationalist historians who sought to trace national identities to a mythical past also influenced this process of ethnogenesis. Such was the case, as shall be seen, later in Iberia with the appeals to Gothic blood in the Late Middle Ages and the early modern period, or, as Patrick Geary has shown in his *The Myth of Nations*, in the construction of fictitious ethnic genealogies.[2]

I apologize to the reader for the digression and beg leave to return to the Vandals who created havoc in North Africa and brought to an end more than 400 years of Roman rule in the area. For all their impact in the demise of Roman power in Africa, the Vandals did not leave any noticeable imprint on the region. Few in number, themselves displaced from their original habitats in northern and central Europe, North Africa must have been a different place for them and ecologically challenging. They left no toponyms, no monuments, or only a handful of archeological traces. Unlike other Germanic groups settling along the Mediterranean, their rule was ephemeral. Their proclivity to piracy and plunder would turn their name into a synonym for destruction, and make them a target for attacks. And indeed, the Vandals faced real threats on every front. The Visigoths who had pushed them out of Iberia had always had designs on North Africa. The closeness between the shores of southern Iberia and those of North Africa made expansion into the contiguous region always tempting. North Africa was also the terminus for important commercial exchanges and, thus, economically critical for trade in the western Mediterranean. The Vandals also had to face the unruly resistance of Berbers and other mountain people who had never been really subdued by the Carthaginians or the Romans. At most, these two powers had only kept the mountain and desert people at bay over the long period of their rule over the areas of what are today Tunisia, Algeria, and Morocco.

The Byzantine attempted reconquest of the western empire under Justinian in the 530s CE brought an end to the Vandals' rule of North Africa. For almost a century, Byzantine outposts on the North African Mediterranean coast kept a tenuous hold on the region, but the Byzantines were unable to make any significant gains inland from the coast or to subdue either the mountains or the interior. After the death of Justinian and the slow erosion of Byzantine power in the West, the Byzantine Exarch in Ravenna (the stronghold of Byzantine power in Italy) or Byzantine rulers in faraway Constantinople had their hands full with enemies on every front, whether on their eastern frontier or in the troubled and fragmented West. The period between the coming of the Vandals and the demise of Byzantine power in the region remains a fairly unexplored period and not fully charted. The difficulties of establishing an assertive rule over the local population or gaining control of its profitable trade had a great deal to do with paving the way for the dramatic transformation of the region; that came in time, but from other more agile, dynamic, and unexpected historical actors.

THE EUROPEAN WESTERN MEDITERRANEAN

Traveling clockwise and crossing the Straits of Gibraltar, we reach the Iberian Peninsula. Rome's long presence in the peninsula – more than five centuries – is evident in the network of Roman roads, languages, the myriad of monuments still standing throughout the land, and the many cities and towns that trace their genesis to original Roman settlements. Not unlike in North Africa, Roman rule did not extend evenly throughout the region. The Northern Mountains, that is the southern slope of the Pyrenees, most of the Basque homeland, and the Pyrenean western mountain spurs (the Picos de Europa) remained fairly immune to Roman civilization, and so did large portions of the countryside. As was also the case in Roman North Africa, Roman civilization was mostly an urban *and Mediterranean* phenomenon. Besides the elegant countryside villas of the Roman elites, the countryside in imperial provinces remained fairly loyal to pre-Roman language, customs, and folkways.

Iberia – Hispania, or what is today Spain and Portugal – became one of the most intensely Romanized areas of the empire. It produced emperors (such as Trajan) and philosophers (Seneca among them), and played a significant economic role as a land rich in minerals (tin, iron) and grain within the Western European Roman economy. But, as was the case elsewhere, the decline of Roman hegemony, mostly in the West, opened the door for dramatic changes. In the maelstrom that consumed the Roman world from the third century through the fifth century, Germanic groups successfully invaded Hispania. The people whom we now know as Vandals passed briefly through Spain before, as noted earlier, the Visigoths pushed them out of the peninsula and into North Africa. The Suevi, a small Germanic group, marched into Hispania and created a small kingdom in the northwest corner of Iberia (Galicia), before being overrun by the Visigoths in the fifth and sixth centuries. The Suevi play no role in this story. Facing the Atlantic and blocked from the Mediterranean by topography and other polities, they had no impact on Mediterranean life. The Visigoths were another matter altogether.

Led by their king or leader Alanc, the Visigoths, originating in Eastern and Northern Europe, sacked Rome in 410 CE (an event that resonated profoundly with Augustine of Hippo and led him the write *The City of God*) before moving westward into southern Gaul. There they remained until forced out of the region by the Franks, another one of those innumerable German groups breaching Roman borders and settling within the Roman Empire. Coming into Spain in the first half of the fifth century and received, as Orosius, an Ibero-Roman writer, reports, with relief by the local population as representatives of imperial authority, the Visigoths took little time before establishing themselves firmly on Iberian soil. Because the Visigoths were Arians, that is, Christians but followers of Arius, whose beliefs on the nature of the Trinity had been condemned as heretical, there were serious difficulties in breaching the differences between the native Ibero-Roman population and the Germanic newcomers in the first century of their rule. Nonetheless, with Toledo as their center, the Visigoths extended their rule throughout most of the peninsula. Just as the Romans did, they either neglected or failed to exert their power fully in the northern mountains, a region difficult to conquer and with no significant economic appeal. As other Germanic groups also did in Italy, the Visigoths slowly assimilated the remains of Roman fiscal and administrative practices. Their legal system, the fabled *Lex Visigothorum*, borrowed freely from Roman law, as they did in terms of organizing rural space, rural social structures, and irrigation works.

When, in 587, their king, Reccared, formally converted to Christianity, the process of integrating Roman and Germanic elements was on the way to completion. Great Church councils meeting at Toledo, Braga, and other Visigothic urban centers pronounced on important questions of Christian doctrine – their decisions still echoed in the influential IV Lateran Council (1215) and in Castilian legislation through the Central and Late Middle Ages. Although Visigothic impact, as was the case with some of the Germanic groups settling on the shores of the Mediterranean (as distinct from northern France, England, and Germany), was not substantial, their presence in the peninsula shaped the imaginary of later polities in Iberia. Although these ideological constructs were often illusory or without any real historical foundation, for those in the Late Middle Ages the Visigothic inheritance remained a powerful ideological construct. From the reconquest to the purity of descent – being a descendant of Gothic blood played a signal role in discourses of difference in late medieval and early modern Spain – idealized re-creation of Visigothic history dominated the mental landscape of later peninsular history.

The Visigoths made the conscious choice of presenting themselves as the rightful representatives of Roman authority; their determined efforts to adapt as much of Roman practices and techniques as possible to their own nascent polity had important consequences for the preservation of the unity of Mediterranean civilization. The Visigoths were not the Romans but, with Spain as a site of encounter, the meeting of the cultures produced not only remarkable examples of goldsmith work, but also architectural styles that bridged the classical and medieval art world. It imitated the past. It created new things. A polymath, such as Isidore of Seville, could create encyclopedic works that remained normative in European culture until the Renaissance of the Twelfth Century and even beyond. Yet, in spite of the Visigothic kings' sacral claims and elaborate rituals, they also suffered from serious internal instability. Unable to resolve the questions of succession to the throne in satisfactory ways – the enduring medieval political oscillation between Germanic notions of power, that is, power emerging from below, marked by the "election" of the ruler by the people (by which was meant the great men) or power descending from above (from God) as Christian clerics insisted – the Visigothic kingdom was torn by endless assassinations and fierce struggles to decide who was to be the next ruler. That political culture made the Visigoths a target for defeat. In 711, probing expeditions from North Africa carrying the banner of Islam sent the almost three-centuries-old empire tumbling down. Paradoxically, on the eve of the Muslim conquest of Iberia, the Visigoths were pushing for radical measures against the Jews, including their forced conversion or expulsion from the peninsula. Some of these edicts would be re-enacted in later centuries by Christian rulers who posed to their subjects as the heirs to Visigothic rule. As Iberia was entering a multicultural, multi-religious period, the Visigoths were moving forcibly to end that plurality that was so intrinsic to Mediterranean life.[3]

TOWARDS FRANKLAND

Moving northeast across the Pyrenees, we enter the old world of Septimania or southern Gaul, the area known in the Middle Ages as Occitania and today as parts of Languedoc and Provence. The most Romanized region outside of Italy itself, the northern shores of the Mediterranean of what is France today had long been a destination for Greek seafarers and merchants, Carthaginians, and Romans. The Visigoths occupied the region for a short span of time until pushed south – mostly across the Pyrenees – by new waves of Germanic invaders, the most important of which were the Franks in the early sixth century. The Visigoths, nonetheless, retained some control over regions north of the Pyrenees in a coastal area that coincidentally would come under the control of the Crown of Aragon 700 years later.

Although the people known as the Franks had their center in the North, around Soissons, Aix-La-Chapelle (Aächen), Paris, and other hubs in northern Gaul, the Mediterranean always held a great attraction. Much later under Charlemagne (d. 814), the Franks extended their power into Catalonia (the Spanish March) and into Italy itself with Charlemagne's becoming king of the Lombards. That, however, still lay in the future. In the sixth and seventh centuries, the Frankish Merovingian dynasty, in spite of its fratricidal wars, ruled, notwithstanding the growing power of the mayors of the palace, through-out most of Frankland. Not having come into the empire with the taint of heterodoxy (Arianism) as most other Germanic groups did, the Franks became the favorites of the Church. In turn, ecclesiastical authorities placed their considerable talents for what may be described as propaganda campaigns in the service of the Frankish kings. Along the shores of the Mediterranean, the survival of Roman culture, so evident in the dazzling output of Sidonius Apollinaris's (ca. 430–489) circle, as well as that of other Gallo-Roman members of the learned elite – Gregory of Tours comes to mind – preserved ties to the classical past in the South (Sidonius was born in Lyon, a city connected to the Mediterranean through the Rhône River) that were quite distinct from those of the North. This growing cultural divorce between North and South in Frankland, one that would be re-emphasized by linguistic and culinary differences, deeply affected the development of the Frankish Mediterranean regions in centuries to come.

In spite of a brief Ostrogothic occupation in the eastern parts of what is today Mediterranean France and an earlier Visigoths presence in the West, the Franks slowly filled that space after the final demise of Roman authority in the West. The emerging vernacular language(s), for one, retained their closeness to Latin. Roman notarial, administrative, and fiscal practices endured far better than in the northern regions of Frankland. Even today, traveling through Provence one is struck by churches, the Abbey of Saint-Gilles being one, where ancient classical columns (classical spolia) were used to reconstruct churches that, in their hybrid style, borrowed both from classical culture and from new Christian forms emerging in the wake of the demise of the Roman Empire and the coming of new Germanic settlers.

As political rule became fragmented in Frankland by internecine struggles in the seventh century, the realm was pieced together again by the dynamic actions of the early Carolingians (Pippin the Short and Charlemagne in the late eighth and early ninth centuries), and fragmented once again as independent lordship emerged in the region. It is clear that the abrupt topography of parts of what is today Mediterranean France, as well as peculiar political developments in the region, yielded power structures that were fundamentally different from those of the North. All along, Marseille, the quintessential southern Frankish Mediterranean port, remained a funnel through which waves of ideas, trade, and people – the Byzantines held it for a while in their ephemeral attempt to recover Rome's western parts of the empire – poured into the region laying the foundations for its unique cultural production in later years.[4]

ONWARDS TO ITALY

The Ostrogoths held part of what is today southeast France, with Burgundians and Alemmani holding lands somewhat north of the sea. Ostrogothic rule was always tenuous. Coming into Italy in the late fifth century led by their great king Theodoric (493–526), their successful conquests led to the emergence of an Ostrogothic kingdom that extended its jurisdiction throughout most of Italy and into areas which today form part of southeast France. The Ostrogoths delivered a fatal blow to any illusions of Roman political continuity in the West by their establishment of their own polity. Although the Ostrogoths, as the Visigoths and the Franks did elsewhere in Europe, bent backwards to preserve and adapt to Roman practices, the western Mediterranean world had changed radically. In addition, the Ostrogoths' embrace of Arianism created an enduring source of strife between Roman orthodox Christians and the newcomers. The famous affair that led to Boethius's execution marked only the high point of the conflict (Boethius, from a Roman senatorial family, one of the foremost intellectuals of the age, and the author, among many other works, of *The*

Consolation of Philosophy, was accused of treason and cooperation with Byzantium and executed). By 526, on the eve of Theodoric's death and the beginning of the Byzantines' attempts to reconquer the western part of the empire, the lands that had been the core of Rome's rise to hegemony in the western Mediterranean were fragmented among different Germanic groups. In North Africa, the Vandals held sway, as the Visigoths did in Iberia and a small region of southwest Gaul. Franks ruled in what is today southern France, and Ostrogoths controlled parts of southeast France, Italy, and Sicily.

By 565 CE, the year of Justinian's death, the Byzantines had established their rule over most of Italy, Sicily, North Africa, areas of southern Iberia, and small outposts in southern Gaul. The Ostrogoths had vanished from the scene and, in a certain limited sense, the western Mediterranean became once again a "Roman" sea. It would not last long. After Justinian's death in 565 CE, the Byzantine Empire turned its back on its Latin roots. The challenge of the Sassanid Empire in the East, the cultural and political assertion of its Greek core areas, and the lack of economic incentives in the West made the maintenance and defense of the West a burden. This was certainly the case as an even more serious threat was already in the making.[5]

THE NORTH AFRICAN WESTERN MEDITERRANEAN: THE COMING OF ISLAM

If I have included a brief outline of political developments in the western Mediterranean between the demise of Rome and the coming of Islam into the region, opening, as it were, a new chronological period with the later event, it is because the Muslim conquests of the seventh and eighth centuries dramatically transformed the political landscape of the region and impacted (and still impacts to this very day) the development of both shores of the Mediterranean. While many areas occupied by Islam on the northern shores of the Middle Sea slowly returned to Christian rule throughout the period covered by this book, the North African shores of the Middle Sea have remained Muslim, notwithstanding a period of European colonial occupation, into the present. If Roman rule on the entire Mediterranean Sea had been the most important shaping force in the historical life of the region, the Muslim conquests of the southern shores of the Mediterranean and of substantial parts of the sea's northern shores (Iberia, Sicily) were not too far behind in their historical impact. In hindsight, the administrative structures and religious patterns constructed by the Islamic invasions of the seventh, eighth, and ninth centuries have remained fairly in place in many parts of the Mediterranean world to this very day. The Middle Sea is to this day as much Muslim as it is Christian and perhaps far more the former than the latter. This is obviously the case with the growing presence of Islam – through the influx of immigrants – in areas where the Crescent once held sway (see Chapter 12).

Shortly after Muhammad's death in 632, the Arabs, galvanized by the preaching of the Prophet and by the dynamism of Islam, began their more than two-centuries-long conquest and conversion of most of the known world. Within a few decades, the Muslims (for the Arabs were themselves too few in number to impose their rule without the conversion and assimilation of conquered people into the Dar al-Islam, the world of Islam) had conquered all of North Africa from the Mediterranean shores to the edges of the Sahara, including rich Egypt. During this earlier period, all of Palestine, the Arabian Peninsula, today's Syria, Iraq, and Persia (Iran) had come under Muslim rule. The Islamic advance also pushed the Byzantine Empire out of Africa and of vital sections of the Anatolian plain. By the next century (711), the Visigothic Empire fell without much struggle, and Islamic rule extended throughout most of Iberia and parts of southern France. In the East, the Umayyad Caliphate (661–750), from its capital in Damascus, pushed into the Indus valley in the Indian subcontinent.

By the mid-ninth century, Muslim expeditions from North Africa had conquered some of the main islands of the western Mediterranean (the Balearics and Sicily among them). Their rule over these crucial and strategic links for western Mediterranean trade would leave a powerful imprint on these insular cultures. By the early to mid-eighth century, most of the Mediterranean and certainly the western Mediterranean had become a Muslim lake. At the same time, Muslim rulers in Iberia, North Africa, and Sicily firmly connected their lands and their dominion over the sea to the expansive cultural, political, and economic world of Islam. The Mediterranean thus became firmly integrated into a global economy. Muslim ships sailing the Indian Ocean, the Arabian Sea, and the Mediterranean linked the far reaches of China and the Spice Islands with Western European markets. Caravans along the ancient Silk Road, partly on a road network laid out long before by far-sighted Persian kings, brought goods from Central Asia to Western European consumers. Other caravans trekked south across the Sahara to fabled Timbuktu and Mali, the gateways to sub-Saharan products.

Muslim civilization in its first three or four centuries served also as the great bridge between the learning of the Classical past and Barbarian Europe. Greek works of philosophy and science, lost in the debacle that befell Rome in the third and fourth centuries, found once again their way into the West. And these works came back to the West with the added commentaries and questioning of Muslim philosophers such as Avicenna, al-Kindi, Averroes, and others. Not without reason, Dante, more than seven centuries after the Muslims broke into the western sea, paired Averroes, the Commentator, with Aristotle, the Philosopher. Perhaps, the reader may think that my depiction of Mediterranean Islamic civilization is too glowing. Indeed, the acceptance of Jews and Christians as People of the Book (Chapter 5) ebbed and flowed from one period to another. That toleration was, of course, anchored in the recognition of Islam and Muslims as the superior religion and hegemonic political power, as well as in the obligation of fiscal contributions to the Muslim state.

As Christians, Jews, and even Muslims found out in Spain, the successive invasions of Almoravids (1086) and Almohads (late twelfth century) from North Africa meant a return to more fundamentalist religious practices from the lax behavior of early Muslim rulers. Both of these Berber groups also enacted harsh policies, especially against the Jews, when compared to the rather tolerant practices of earlier Islamic rulers in al-Andalus. The fall of Baghdad in 1258 to the Mongol onslaught also had a deleterious impact on the evolution of Islamic civilization. Nonetheless, the point I wished to bring home with my previous remarks is the complex nature of the western (and eastern as well) Mediterranean from the seventh century until today. It was both Muslim and Christian. And this dual identity *was not*, in spite of frequent conflict, a "clash of civilizations."

Rather, it was an uneasy symbiosis, a give and take, a continuous process of adaptation, borrowing, and rejection.[6] Long before the voyages of discovery across the Atlantic, Muslim polities along the shores of western Mediterranean were firmly connected by trade, knowledge, religion, and the *Qur'an* to the world beyond Europe and to the expansive Dar al-Islam. And through the Islamic civilizations that prospered on the shores of the western Mediterranean, the rest of Western Europe benefitted mightily economically and intellectually.

More than eight decades ago, Henri Pirenne, in his seminal *Mahomet et Charlemagne*, famously argued for a break in the continuity of western and Roman civilization as the consequence of the Muslims' capture of the Mediterranean, bringing to an end the commercial transfers between western Mediterranean Europe and the North. For a long while we have known that such was not the case and that Pirenne, erudite and as formidable a historian as he was, failed to see the continuity of pre-Muslim exchanges even during a period of Islamic hegemony. But Pirenne was perhaps correct in positing a historiographical break or historical myth: one perpetuated by endless textbooks, monographs, and our own teaching. That break or myth is that of the sharp distinction between the northern and southern shores of the Mediterranean in that period. That break or myth has more to do with the neglect of Mediterranean history in this period and the privileging of Frankland and Charlemagne over the heirs of Muhammad. And this historical choice probably had more to do with the hegemony of certain powers, England, France, and Germany in the modern period, than with actual historical events. The myth still pervades European political discourse to this very day as politicians in and out of power assert "the Christian" nature of European civilization, or trace the true roots of their particular communities to the Carolingian Empire – what Patrick Geary has described, as noted earlier, as "the myth of nations." This occurs in the face of, and in response to, massive Muslim migrations into Western Europe from North Africa, sub-Saharan Africa, and Turkey. I will have more to say about this later in this book, but for now, let's remember that a break occurs only in the representations of the slow transformation of the western Mediterranean world, not on its day-to-day realities.

THE WESTERN MEDITERRANEAN: BETWEEN ISLAM AND CHRISTIANITY, 660s–1492

What did indeed happen to the western Mediterranean world between the 660s and the early eight century, when Islam swept across North Africa, and 1492, when the last Muslim enclave in Western Europe fell to the armies of Ferdinand and Isabella? The history of Islam in Western Europe is indeed a complex one. Many books have been written on the topic, and here we can only present a brief outline. That the account is brief does not mean that is not important. North Africa, to give an example, had (and has) a complex multiplicity of histories. Not all of them can be rendered with equal detail.

With the fall of the Umayyad Caliphate in 756, and its replacement by the Abbasids (750–ca. 1100), the political unity of the Muslim world was shattered. Egypt, one of the pearls of the vast Islamic Empire, changed hands from the Tulunids (868–905) to the Ikhshidids (935–969) before the Fatimid dynasty stabilized Egypt's fortunes (968–1171) and extended its power as far west as the region of modern Tunisia (the Maghreb). This allowed the Fatimids to create a vast commercial network that connected the eastern and western Mediterranean. Fatimid rule in Egypt eventually led to the rule of the fabled Saladin. His successful stewardship of Egypt freed it from Syrian influences, ended the crusading kingdom in Jerusalem, and extended Egypt's power south into Nubia and eastward into Syria and the ancient region of Mesopotamia. Although Egypt was in the eastern Mediterranean, its geographical location, access to the Mediterranean through its great port at Alexandria, and growing hegemony in this period made it an indispensable interlocutor between western Mediterranean Islamic political entities and other Muslim polities east of Egypt. As the Geniza documents (mostly records of religious, administrative, and commercial transactions [Jewish merchants played a role in the latter]), made available to scholars by the great Shelomo Goitein, show, Egypt was central to a lively trade joining both the Muslim and the Christian western Mediterranean with the Middle and Far East in complex commercial exchanges. The Fatimids played an important role in the commercial, political, cultural, and religious life of the western sea, and these few comments do not do justice to their enduring importance.[7]

Beyond the Fatimids, the world of western North Africa, what is today Morocco, Algeria, and Tunisia, was a world torn between those claiming to represent the Caliphate and descent from Muhammad's line and Berbers, originating from the Atlas Mountains and the Riff region. The early rulers of Morocco, the Idrisids, traced their lineage to Caliph Ali. For close to 200 years, the dynasty remained in control of most of present-day Morocco until overthrown by the Meknes Berbers from the High Atlas Mountains. Eastward in Tunis (present day Tunisia) or medieval Ifriqiya, the Aghlabid dynasty (801–909) played a significant role in the history of the western sea. Founded by one of the Abbasid high officers and governors of Africa who chose to exert his own rule, the Ifriqiyan Aghlabids launched expeditions into the western Mediterranean that led to the brief conquest of Sardinia, and, far more successful, that of Malta. Sicily and parts of southern Italy also became part of the world of Islam, the former for more than a century. In Sicily, Muslim rule lasted until the Norman invasions of the early tenth century.

Later on, we will have an opportunity to examine the impact of Islamic culture on Sicily, one of those true sites of encounter in the western Mediterranean, but, for now, it suffices to indicate that the Aghlabid invasions of Sicily and other insular outposts on the western sea represented only one of many other incursions by, and contacts with, a triumphant Islam on the northern shores of the western Mediterranean. Through corsair activity and lightning raids, Muslim political and economic relations with Christian Europe continued into the early modern period. An active trade connected North Africa with commercial networks in sub-Saharan Africa. Mali and Timbuktu, among others, connected the southern shores of the Mediterranean with goods from Southwest Africa. North African towns were also deeply connected to Egypt and the commercial activity that linked Egypt with markets further east. North Africa and Muslim Spain, Majorca, and Sicily were part of trade networks that prospered for many centuries.

Politically, Muslim polities and Christian ones carried on extensive corsair raids, followed by periods of political accommodation, in turn followed by armed conflict, and, as shall be seen below, even periods in which they hired each other's soldiers to fight against internal enemies. These ties continue today. While corsairs and slavers no longer ply their trade, or not at least as they once did, legal and illegal immigration remain the most significant form of link between the northern and southern shores of the western Mediterranean. In the present world, where conflict between the West and Islam are part and parcel of conservative discourse, it is proper to remember that in the past, the Mediterranean was, once again, as much Muslim as it was Christian.

Before the Ottoman Empire extended its rule or protection into western North Africa in the sixteenth century, a series of Berber-led dynasties rose in North Africa, swiftly expanding their power into the Iberian Peninsula and over vast areas of the western Mediterranean, holding a firm grip on Mediterranean trade and sailing. In the mid-eleventh century, the Almoravids conquered Morocco and most of the rest of North Africa. When the Castilian king, Alfonso VI, conquered Toledo in 1085, a signal victory over his Muslim rivals in the Iberian Peninsula, Almoravid armed contingents crossed the Straits of Gibraltar and handed a crushing defeat to the Christian armies at the Battle of Sagrajas (1086). The Almoravid victory effectively slowed or stopped the rapid advance of the so-called Christian Reconquest until 1212. The Almoravids, as I have noted earlier, also brought with them more exacting religious practices and a harsher understanding of the Prophet's teachings to both North Africa and Spain. They were less tolerant of other religious groups, showing a far more combative attitude than had been the norm. It did not take long, however, before the strength of their fundamentalist beliefs was somewhat diminished, at least in Iberia, by al-Andalus's lax religious and social practices.

Almoravid rule, in both North Africa and Spain, was overthrown in the early to mid-twelfth century by a new Berber group, the Almohads. In less than half a century, the Almohads conquered present-day Morocco, Algeria, and Tunisia, expelling Norman conquerors that had settled in the region of Tunis or what was then called Ifriqiya. Coming across the Straits of Gibraltar, the Almohads defeated their brethren in Muslim Spain, becoming a formidable rival and deterrent to Christian aspirations. It took decades for the Christians to face down the Almohad challenge. In 1212, a large international Christian army defeated the Almohads at the battle of Las Navas de Tolosa. In many respects, the Christian victory at Las Navas de Tolosa represented a turning point in the history of the western Mediterranean. This was so even though Almohad corsairs, operating from North Africa and the Balearic Islands, continued to control most of the western waters. And though their defeat did not mark the end of incursions from North Africa into the Iberian Peninsula, these military campaigns, such as the Marinid invasion of southern Spain in the early fourteenth century, were most often reactions to Christian threats. After 1212, any hope of recovering the lands of al-Andalus was at an end.[8]

The Almohad Empire, extending throughout most of North Africa, most of Mediterranean Iberia, and to important hubs in the western sea, came very close to recreating a truly western Mediterranean society. Their ambitious imperial program, their architectural design (minarets throughout North Africa and Iberia, see Chapter 10), and their trading policies gave them for a brief period great power along the shores of the western Mediterranean. Islamic Majorca connected Maghrebi merchants, and as noted earlier, with the commercial hubs in sub-Saharan Africa, Mali and Timbuktu. Gold came from the South, while Majorcan merchants, some of them Jews, linked the rising commercial power of Barcelona and Islamic cities in Iberia to Dar al-Islam's wide trade networks.

Yet, the defeat of the Almohads in the peninsula in 1212 fragmented the unity of North Africa and led to the loss of the Balearic Islands in the first half of the thirteenth century. In the region of present-day Tunisia (Ifriqiya), the Hafsid dynasty endured from the early thirteenth century until 1534. Tunis's commercial connections with Italy through Sicily, which served as a natural bridge across the Mediterranean, provided continuous contacts and relations that, although not always peaceful and including the enslaving and ransoming of each other, was part of wider Mediterranean systems of exchange. In many respects, Tunis and Sicily are still connected. The port of Trapani, on Sicily's southwestern coast, receives goods from North Africa, although they are not always legal ones.

Up to this point, I have sought to identify modern geographical and national categories and match them with medieval ones as a way to make the turbulent history of pre-modern North Africa familiar to the reader. The reality is, of course, that these modern distinctions do not reflect the political dynamics of the region from the first Islamic conquests to the coming of the Ottomans in the sixteenth century and to the European colonization in the nineteenth. Before continuing with any attempt to describe local developments, it may be useful to provide a broad view of political developments during the pre-modern period and to identify the main players. As was the case throughout the western Mediterranean, the interplay between mountains and coast was a crucial one. One may begin with the coming of Islamic occupation in the seventh century, the rise of mountain Berber dynasties that throughout the period came to power and gained control across the northern shores of the western Mediterranean into European enclaves in Iberia and southern Italy.

Eventually, these Berber groups declined and were replaced by other Berber dynasties. There are so many of them that one goes dizzy trying to trace their individual histories. One must add to this already heavy concoction the enduring influence of the Egyptian Fatimid Caliphate in the politics of western North Africa, and the Normans' (from Sicily) short-lived ventures into the region. In the next chapter, we shall witness the more enduring Portuguese and Spanish settlements in North Africa (some of them, such as Ceuta and Melilla, still remnants of European occupation), the Ottoman period, a European colonial interlude, and, finally, the countries that emerged from decolonization.

An example of this is the region we know today as Algeria. In the area roughly identifiable today as the modern nation of Algeria, a succession of Berber dynasties or Berber tribal groups gained control of the region after the collapse of the Almohads. They ruled the region until the late 1330s. By that period they were eclipsed by the growing power of the Marinids in nearby Morocco. The latter eventually extended their rule to the region that we know today as Algeria. As we have already seen, the Marinids also tried their hand in Iberia. They clearly perceived that Christians, once they had digested the great conquest of Muslim territories in the 1230s and 1240s (see below), would wish to continue their military campaigns across the western Mediterranean. Defeated by Alfonso XI of Castile at the Battle of Salado in 1340, the Marinids retained, nonetheless, a foothold in the Iberian Peninsula and remained in power in Morocco until 1470. By then, other political players came into play. The fierce Barbarossa brothers gained Algiers in the early sixteenth century as proxies for the Sublime Porte and used the area as a base for their corsair activities in the western Mediterranean. Cervantes suffered through years of captivity in the slave prison in Algiers. French colonial ventures in North Africa, part of the great European colonial and imperial expansion, came to stay in the nineteenth century.[9]

SPAIN: BETWEEN ISLAM AND CHRISTIANITY

If this brief description of the rise and fall of diverse polities in North Africa provides us with any lessons, it is the extent to which the parallel histories of North Africa and Iberia, Sicily and North Africa were closely intertwined before the beginning of the early modern period. In the Iberian Peninsula, those exchanges shaped the historical trajectory of the societies that emerged after 1492. But that was still in the future. In 711, the Muslims crossed the Straits of Gibraltar and swiftly defeated the Visigothic armies. A Visigothic Empire that had enjoyed close to 300 years of continuous existence crumbled in unexpected ways. Two things are important to note. First, the invaders represented a diverse group of Arabs, Berbers, Slavs, and other people united by their faith – and to a certain extent by Arabic, the language of the *Qur'an* – and not by their ethnic identity. Second, the coming of Islam into the peninsula led to numerous conversions from Christianity to Islam (though historians do not fully agree as to the extent of these conversions), above all in the regions along the Mediter- ranean, the newcomers' preferred area for settlement (see Chapter 5).

Although the Muslims swept deep into the peninsula, they did not hold on to all the territory they had initially conquered. The northern mountains in the Basque homeland, the Pyrenean ridges, and the rugged area of Asturias held no attraction for them. As the Romans had done before, the Muslims left the mountains and their people to their own fate. A number of Visigoths or Christians fled to these mountain lairs. From there they would emerge to challenge the hegemony of Islam in the peninsula in centuries to come. In addition, a series of famines and reverses in the mid-eighth century led the Muslims to withdraw south of the Central Mountains, abandoning a central plain which, without any substantial demographic resources or great agricultural potential (in terms of Muslim rural technologies and type of cultivation), held little or no attraction for them. Frequent raids (*razzias*) were conducted by the Muslims throughout the peninsula for the next 250 years as salutary lessons to Christians in the North on who truly held power over the land.

The real history of the Iberian Peninsula or Mediterranean Spain during the centuries between 711 and the onset of the new millennium centered around the establishment of an independent Caliphate of Córdoba in 929. On that date a member of the dethroned Umayyad family, Abd ar Rahman III, declared independence from the eastern Caliphate, beginning the slow political (and elsewhere religious) fragmentation of the Muslim world. The establishment of an independent Caliphate in Iberia did not mean, however, the end of the close connections between al-Andalus and North Africa. They continued uninterrupted for as long as Islam retained a foothold in the peninsula, and, in some paradoxical fashion, have remained, in some modified form, between Christian Spain and Muslim North Africa to this very day. Neither did an independent Caliphate mean a break in the continuity of what one may call a pan-Islamic Mediterranean civilization, so obviously present in the architectural forms, literary tastes, culinary practices, and trade (that later so obviously evident in the Geniza documents) that bound Dar al-Islam into a cohesive world.

In the years between Abd ar Rahman's assumption to the Caliphate and the mid-1030s, when the Caliphate fragmented into a series of small and often warring Islamic petty kingdoms (the so-called kingdoms of *taifas*: Seville, Córdoba, Toledo, Zaragoza, Granada, and others), Islam planted its roots deeply in the region south of the Central Sierra and along the shorelines of the western Mediterranean: from Gibraltar (Cádiz was on the Atlantic) to the region north of Valencia. Along that Mediterranean coastal stretch port cities, such as Algeciras, Málaga, Alicante, Valencia, and others, became, as Figures 3.1 and 3.2 show, part of extensive technological, commercial, and cultural networks linking Muslim Spain to the rest of the Mediterranean.[10]

CATALONIA

Not included in this list of seaports linked to the world of Islam were Barcelona and other Catalan seaports north and south of the city. The area around Barcelona (Catalonia), running roughly from the Pyrenees south and eastward had become part of the expansive Carolingian world in the late eighth and early ninth centuries. By 873, with the rule of Wilfred the Hairy (873–898), the region became an independent Christian county (today Catalonia) with its center on the ancient and quintessential Mediterranean city of Barcelona. I will have a great deal to say about Barcelona in later chapters, but for the present, it

Figure 3.1 Tribunal of the Waters building, where all disputes about water and irrigation took place, Plaza de la Virgen, Valencia. Source: Courtesy of Scarlett Freund.

suffices to say that after the collapse of the Caliphate, a series of new and aggressive Christian polities – the kingdoms of León and Castile, the kingdom of Aragón, and the county of Barcelona – emerged to challenge the Islamic states in the peninsula, as well as each other. Under no circumstance, however, should one describe this as a strictly sectarian divide. Although the slow conquest of most of southern Iberia by the Christians from 1085 onward, and their submission and eventual displacement of Muslims, came to be seen in time through ideological lenses and as forms of crusade and reconquest, the reality was quite different. As I will point out many times in this and subsequent chapters, warfare between the two religious groups was not more frequent than internal strife within each religious group.

THE WESTERN MEDITERRANEAN ON THE EVE OF THE MODERN WORLD

If I have spent so much time in detailing political developments in Late Antiquity and early medieval Europe, it is because patterns of settlement, conquest, and either the development of the vernacular or the imposition of a new language, Arabic, have shaped the history of the entire western Mediterranean to this very day. But, we should not put on our seven-league boots in describing later periods – as Hegel suggested doing for the Middle Ages in his *The Philosophy of History* – without a perfunctory look at Sicily and other European areas of the western Mediterranean before the early modern period.

Figure 3.2 Valencia Cathedral's bell tower (El Miguelete), showing the classical minaret of Almohad building projects. Source: Courtesy of Scarlett Freund.

Although we will return to Sicily as one of those sites of encounter or liminal places characteristic of the western Mediterranean (Chapter 10), the political dynamics during the period between the coming of Islam into the region and the Christian counter-offensive are paradigmatic of the fluid political pattern present in the region.

ISLAM IN SICILY

Between the mid-seventh century – coinciding with the spread of Islam throughout the southern shores of the western Mediterranean – and the tenth, the Muslims launched numerous attacks against Sicily until they formally established their rule there for over a century (965–1072). Because of Sicily's strategic position at the gates of the western Mediterranean and its economic importance, Muslims (mostly from North Africa and the Carthage area) had begun their campaigns against the island as early as 652. Although eventually unsuccessful, North African fleets probed the island's defenses repeatedly throughout the early and mid-eighth century but only to meet stiff Byzantine resistance.

We must not think of this period as one of unremitting warfare. Expeditions against the island, as for example the one leading to the brief capture of Syracuse in 740 or the later sacking of the city, were interspersed with periods of fairly peaceful and active commercial relations. The real conflict, one lasting more than 100 years, occurred after 826 when the Muslims' North African and Andalusi forces established a permanent foothold on the island. Over the next 40 years, they slowly challenged Byzantine rule on the island, in spite of the latter's dogged resistance. The main urban centers, Palermo, Taormina, Syracuse, and others, fell into Muslim hands between 831 and 902. By around 965, the island was fully an important link in the commercial and political networks of Dar al-Islam.

It is important to reiterate that, by the late tenth century, most of the western Mediterranean, with the exception of the Mediterranean shorelines of northern Catalonia, southern France, and most parts of Italy, became part of a Muslim lake. Those areas not under the control of Islam were subjected to frequent raids and Muslim corsair activity. The sea, for all practical purposes, was a Muslim Sea. Sicily became an emirate, ruled from North Africa and, afterwards, from Egypt. In spite of Byzantine attempts to regain the island or revolts from some of the local populations, the Muslims took steps to set their rule on a very sure footing. This was not always easy. Disturbances came from several sources. First, frequent raids from Christian rulers in southern Italy and from Sicilian Muslims into Calabria prevented Sicily from developing a stable working relation with new political entities in southern Italy. This was further complicated by the Ottonian German emperors' growing interest in the South. Even after Otto II's armies were defeated in Calabria in 982, German imperial policies were bound with Sicily's history. Second, Byzantine resistance (by which I mean Greek cultural forms and political aspirations), fanned by Byzantine officials in Ravenna and elsewhere, never really ended and remained a continuous source of difficulties for Sicily's Muslim rulers until the coming of the Normans. Third, as was the case in Muslim Spain, factional struggles within the Muslim ruling class, or conflicting claims between the Fatimids (Shi'a) in Egypt and the Aghlabid dynasty in Ifriqiya (Tunisia), between Shi'a and Sunni, undermined the political vitality of Islamic Sicily.

And yet, in spite of their internal troubles and outside threats, Sicily flourished under Islamic rule. It did so agriculturally and by the introduction of such staples as sugar cane, lemons, and oranges, the latter two fixtures in parts of Sicily to this very day. Islamic husbandry and irrigation technology led to substantial population increase, great building projects, and the full insertion of Sicily into Dar al-Islam trading networks. Its heterogeneous population of

Byzantine Greeks, Roman Catholics, and Jews lived in relative peace as long as Islam was recognized as the dominant religion, and as long as taxes were paid to the Muslim rulers. Sicily as part of the broad Muslim world was also a repository of classical learning, brought into the West by Islamic invaders. But, as had been the case earlier in Muslim Spain in the 1030s, internal conflicts led to decline and eventual defeat. Fractures in the political unity of Islamic Sicily paved the way for the demise of Muslim rule and for yet another change in Sicily's complex political trajectory.[11]

NORMAN AND HOHENSTAUFEN SICILY, CIRCA 1068–1253

The Normans, the descendants of Vikings settled in the mouth of Seine in France in a region that would be named after them, played a signal role in the history of the Mediterranean. For a long while, Norman or Viking expeditions sought to play a role in the Middle Sea. Either raiding the western Mediterranean in seaborne expeditions through the Straits of Gibraltar, sailing south from the Baltic down the Russian fluvial network, aiming for the Black Sea and Byzantium, or as the main protagonists of the First Crusade, the history of the Normans was deeply imbedded in the long history of the Middle Sea. And nowhere was their role in the region as dramatic as it was in southern Italy and Sicily.

Unlike the swift and successful conquest of England in 1066, Norman conquests in Italy were complicated affairs, the difficulties lasting as long as their rule in the region. Appearing first as mercenaries in the endless local conflicts that plagued southern Italy in the early eleventh century (first Norman presence has been dated to 999), by around 1050 the Normans began to claim areas in southern Italy. Defeating papal, imperial, and Byzantine forces, the Normans established firm footholds in Benevento, the Amalfi Coast, and throughout the Calabrian region. Robert Guiscard, invested as a duke by the Pope, provided efficient military leadership that allowed the Normans to create a power base in the south of the Italian Peninsula.

By 1061 Robert and his brother Roger began the conquest of Sicily in earnest. Yet, it would take 30 more years for the major Sicilian cities to be subdued and to firmly establish Norman rule over the entire island. Roger II began his rule as count of Sicily in 1105 before becoming a duke in 1127. With his accession as king (1131–1154) Sicily became truly Norman. Yet, Sicily was not at peace. Noble revolts, attacks from German imperial rivals, papal interference, and the like did not, however, prevent Roger II from presiding over brilliant court-inspired cultural achievements. It would be at Roger II's courts that al-Idrīsī would produce his fabled map of the Mediterranean world (to be discussed in detail in Chapter 7). Ruling over a multi-ethnic, multi-religious, and multilingual island, Roger II carried out important economic reforms and efficiently presided over the overlapping of Byzantine-Muslim-Norman cultures, making Sicily, together with Spain, a true site of encounter between people of different religions (see chapters 7 and 10). Roger II was succeeded by his son William I (1154–1166) and a grandson (d. 1189) by the same name. This second William presided over the building of the splendid cathedral at Monreale, a testimony to the hybrid culture of Sicily.

Dying without heirs, William II's rule over Sicily passed to his aunt Constance, already married to Henry VI, the German emperor. Of that fateful union was born posthumously (his father Henry VI having died before the birth), Frederick II, the great Sicilian and Hohenstaufen ruler. To attempt to summarize Frederick II's (1194–1250) life and activities is a hopeless enterprise. One of the most intriguing rulers of the late medieval Mediterranean, Frederick's court, whether in Sicily or in southern Italy, paralleled that of his predecessor Roger II. Some heretics (although Frederick II's laws were particularly harsh on some types of heresy), dissenters, Muslims, papal enemies, and others found a home at the king's court. His political works or edicts, the Constitution of Melfi most of all, pointed to the Roman past and to renewed ways of looking at questions of power and rulership. His book on falconry borrowed from Muslim knowledge. Sicily retained its place in the western Mediterranean as a site of encounter and cultural production (see Chapter 10).

After Frederick II's death, the short French interlude, and the establishment of an Arago-Catalan dynasty in 1283 after the fabled Sicilian Vespers (when Sicilians rose up in arms against the French and put them to the sword), the island became part of the far-flung Catalan commercial and military ventures in the western and eastern Mediterranean. Some of the dynamics of cultural hybridity waned, and much more so after the Crown of Aragon, under Alfonso V, conquered Naples in 1442. Alfonso V's lifelong fascination with Naples relegated Sicily to a neglected role. Although never isolated and always strategically important, the rise of the Atlantic trade and the shift to Northern Europe as the center of European civilization aggravated the long neglect of Sicily and the underdevelopment and backwardness of the *mezzogiorno*. Yet, Sicily, as was the case with Majorca and the Iberian Peninsula, long remained a place of encounter.[12]

In the next chapter – one single chapter to outline the history of the entire western Mediterranean is not sufficient – I begin by tracing the history of Italian city states that, from medieval to early modern times, or the so-called Renaissance, played such a significant role in the cultural and political emergence of the modern world. We cannot leave this chapter, however, before considering the histories of two Italian city states that, though showing parallels in their genesis as commercial powers in the late eleventh and twelfth century, ended up in very different places. I refer here to Genoa and Pisa.

GENOA

Similar to most cities on the shores of the western sea, Genoa traces its origins to Greek commercial activity along the shores of the Mediterranean. An ally of Rome, the city was destroyed by the Carthaginians during the Second Punic War (209 BCE), became part of the sprawling Roman Empire after being rebuilt, and suffered under Ostrogothic control after the demise of the Roman Empire in the West in the late fifth century. The city experienced, like most of the peninsula, its Byzantine interlude, before the coming of the Lombards into Italy and their final capture of the city and the region (Liguria) in the first half of the seventh century. By the second half of the eighth century, Genoa and its hinterland came under Frankish rule, as the Frankish kings, Pippin III first, and Charlemagne later, defeated the Lombards, Charlemagne taking the Iron Crown of the Lombard's kingdom for himself. The decline of the Carolingian dynasty, internal fragmentation, and raids by the Saracens from North Africa and al-Andalus almost extinguished Genoa's existence, but the period served as one of gestation for its impressive growth and far-flung enterprises in the late eleventh and twelfth century.

Nothing in its previous history foreshadowed Genoa's rise to prominence. Like many other Italian polities, Genoa was, in theory, under imperial jurisdiction, but the German Holy Roman emperors had little real power in the peninsula. For all practical purposes, the city functioned as an independent polity, a mercantile republic. Moreover, one must consider the strategic position of Genoa as an outlet to the rich inland areas of Liguria, Lombardy, and the Piedmont (the area around Turin). Its magnificent bay offered a secure refuge for maritime traffic and for a long time was the only great port between Marseille and Livorno. Genoa had also a long history of transhumance, connecting the city to its rich hinterland or *contado*. Merchant and war ships extended the influence and, eventually, jurisdictional control of Genoa over Corsica, Sardinia, and other Mediterranean islands. Genoa would retain control of these islands until the closing of the Middle Ages, when it was replaced in the western Mediterranean by Arago-Catalan naval power.

Genoa reached its heyday in the twelfth century. Its activities in the eastern Mediterranean – without neglecting its western connections – brought great wealth to the city. Genovese ships carried crusaders to the Holy Land. One may wish to think of the business side of the Crusades and the linking of both sides of the Mediterranean into active trade as mostly a Genoese enterprise. Their success in the East did not occur without opposition from Venice and other maritime powers engaged in the eastern trade. In the western Mediterranean, Genoa expanded its reach beyond the large western Mediterranean islands of Sardinia and Corsica to the coast of North Africa (see below) and, most importantly, to Seville and the Atlantic trade. As bankers and mercantile interlocutors, the Genoese were well poised to take advantage of Spanish (Castilian) expansion into the Atlantic and to be an important part of the re-orientation of Iberian trade from its Dar al-Islam traditional connections to a north-south axis. Although battered by the Black Death and by internal factional struggles among its aristocratic families, Genoa emerged into the early modern world as a faithful ally of Spain.

By the first half of the fifteenth century, Genoa had come under the power of the Visconti in Milan, the Genoese fleet doing most of the heavy lifting in keeping the western Mediterranean away from Arago-Catalan hands. Strangely, Alfonso V (king of the Crown of Aragon, d. 1458) following his capture in a naval battle, and having been sent to Milan, was able to convince his

Milanese and Genoese captors that they should side with him. This they did. Alfonso V captured Naples in 1442, became an Italian Renaissance prince, and showered the Genoese with business and political concessions. Genoese bankers and merchants, as shown recently by Céline Dauverd, had a large presence in Naples' mercantile and banking activities into the early modern period. They strengthened their position – which they had enjoyed since the thirteenth century – in Seville and the Atlantic trade, and under the Doria family became faithful allies of the rising Spanish monarchy. Having tied its fortunes to those of Spain, Genoa enjoyed great prosperity until a plague in the seventeenth century and the demise of Spain as a world power brought the city to its knees. Yet, anyone who travels along the Ligurian coast can see the sprawling size of Genoa today, its teeming harbor and shipyards, and its natural outlet to the rich rural interior and to the industrial areas of Lombardy and the Piedmont.[13]

PISA

With a promising start, Pisa did not achieve the same success as Genoa and had a very different historical outcome from that of its neighbor to the north with which it competed for hegemony in the western Mediterranean. Similar to other ports on the Tyrrhenian Sea, Pisa, situated on the banks of the Arno River as it empties into the sea, experienced successive histories as a Greek, Etruscan, and Roman city. Already a maritime power, it participated in the struggle between the papacy and Byzantium on the side of the former. It suffered a Viking raid and brief occupation in 860 and fought Saracen corsairs at sea and on the North African coast. The eleventh and twelfth centuries witnessed Pisa's heyday as a maritime republic and as a key player in the affairs of the western Mediterranean. As an

Figure 3.3 Pisa's Campo Santo. Source: Courtesy of Scarlett Freund.

enemy of the Saracens, Pisa raided the North Africa coast, expelled the Saracens from their outpost in Sardinia, participated actively in the Crusades, and provided critical support to Roger, the soon-to-be ruler of Sicily, in the conquest of Palermo. It was the rich hoard of gold and precious objects seized after the capture of Palermo that allowed Pisa's city fathers to sponsor the great architectural program of the Piazza del Duomo. Anyone who has braved the throngs of tourists flocking to the Duomo, the Baptistery, the Leaning Tower, and the cemetery cannot but reflect on the wealth of Pisa in the eleventh and twelfth centuries. The future, however, was not promising.

Pisa also had powerful enemies. Because of its Ghibelline sympathies (supporters of the empire against the papacy) and its long and punitive rivalries with Genoa, Venice, Lucca, the papacy, and, eventually, Florence, Pisa would not come to hold the same place assigned to some of its rivals in Italy's political landscape. By the late thirteenth century, Genoa's navy defeated a superior Pisan force at the Battle of Meloria. Pisa's main port was destroyed by the Genoese and, to add insult to injury, the silting of the River Arno's delta left Pisa inaccessible to galleys. Malaria, becoming endemic in the region, also dealt a fatal blow to Pisan aspirations. This was followed by Pisa's falling into Florence's power permanently, with most of the Florentine trade going to Livorno as the most important port for Tuscan goods. Today, besides very prestigious learning centers, above all the Scuola Normale Superiore di Pisa, Pisa is just a few hours stop for tours. Many come to see the legacies of Pisan greatness. Few come to stay.[14]

CONCLUSION

From the waning years of Roman power in the West, the western Mediterranean witnessed the fragmentation of Roman political, cultural, and economic unity under the pressure of Germanic invasions and the rise of local centers of power. Briefly, between the seventh and eleventh centuries, the Muslims sought to reconstruct the Roman Mediterranean world. In spite of their initial success, they also failed. Entropy prevailed. Sicily was lost. Most of Islamic Iberia came slowly to be in Christian hands. New polities rose along the shores of the Mediterranean throughout the Middle Ages. Local languages and cultures, the Berbers most notable among them, came to the fore. Slowly, kingdoms came into being which, with time, became the foundations for modern nations. As the western Mediterranean transitioned into the early modern period, new ideas about sovereignty (mostly in Italy) and rulership came to dominate political discourse. Even while the shadow of Rome remained very powerful indeed, a new and complex world was dawning.

NOTES

1   See Peter L. Brown, *The World of Late Antiquity, AD 150–750* (New York: Harcourt Brace Jovanovich, 1971); as well as the new edition of his monumental *Augustine of*

Hippo: A Biography, new edition with an epilogue (London: Faber and Faber, 2000).

2   See Patrick J. Geary, *The Myth of Nations: The Medieval Origins of Europe* (Princeton: Princeton University Press, 2002).

3   Although much has been written on the Visigoths, the best history of their rule in southern France and Spain is by Roger Collins, *Visigothic Spain, 409–711* (Oxford: Blackwell, 2004). See also the appropriate sections in Joseph F. O'Callaghan, *A History of Medieval Spain* (Ithaca, NY: Cornell University Press, 1975).

4   For the social and political history of the early medieval Mediterranean, see Chris Wickham's impressive, *Framing the Early Middle Ages: Europe and the Mediterranean 400–800* (Oxford & New York: Oxford University Press, 2005).

5   For the early medieval history of what today we know as Italy, see Chris Wickham, *Early Medieval Italy: Central Power and Local Society, 400–1000* (London: Macmillan, 1981).

6   Gottfried Liedl, *Mediterraner Islam* (Wien: Turia & Kant, 2007). See also David Abulafia, *The Great Sea. A Human History of the Mediterranean* (Oxford: Oxford University Press, 2011), 241–285; Thomas F. Glick, *Islamic and Christian Spain in the Early Middle Ages. Comparative Perspectives on Social and Cultural Formation* (Princeton: Princeton University Press, 1979), 217–299.

7   Shelomo. D. Goitein, *A Mediterranean Society: The Jewish Communities of the Arab World as Portrayed in the Documents of the Cairo Geniza*, 6 vols (Berkeley: University of California Press, 1967–1993); see also Jessica Goldberg, *Trade and Institutions in the Medieval Mediterranean: The Geniza Merchants and their Business World* (Cambridge & New York: Cambridge University Press, 2012).

8   Joseph F. O'Callaghan, *A History of Medieval Spain* (Ithaca, NY: Cornell University Press, 1975), 151–519.

9   See Michael Brett's collection of essays on North Africa, *Ibn Khaldun and the Medieval Maghribed* (Aldershot, UK: Ashgate Variorum, 1999), as well as the great work by Ibn Khaldûn, *The Miqaddimah. An Introduction to History*, where almost every chapter relates to the history of medieval western Mediterranean society and to the role of Bedouins or Berbers in the historical development of societies. Translated by Franz Rosenthal, edited and abridged by N.J. Dawood (Princeton: Princeton University Press, 1967).

10 O'Callaghan, *A History of Medieval Spain*, 89–19.

11 On Muslims in Sicily and other parts of Italy in this period, see Alex Metcalfe, *The Muslims of Medieval Italy* (Edinburgh: Edinburgh University Press, 2002).

12 On Norman and Aragonese Sicily, as well as on Frederick II, see Denis Mack Smith, *A History of Sicily: Medieval Sicily, 800–1713* (London: Chatto & Windus, 1980); David Abulafia, *Frederick II: A Medieval Emperor* (London: Penguin, 1988), and his *Italy, Sicily, and the Mediterranean, 1100–1400* (London: Variorum Reprints, 1987); and Ernst Kantorowicz's monumental, *Frederick the Second, 1194–1250* (London: Constable & Co., 1931).

13 The best book on Genoa is Steven Epstein, *Genoa and the Genoese, 958–1528* (Chapel Hill: University of North Carolina Press, 1996).

14 See the still authoritative book by David Herlihy, *Pisa in the Early Renaissance: A Study of Urban Growth* (New Haven, CO: Yale University Press, 1958).

[4] *History in the Mediterranean: The Making of the Modern World*

In this chapter, I continue the historical narrative begun in the previous one. For the sake of avoiding an extremely lengthy political description, I have divided the history of the western Mediterranean into two distinct periods. In Chapter 3, I briefly summarized historical developments in the region from the waning of Roman power in the West to the end of the Middle Ages and the beginning of the early modern period. In truth, of course, in terms of social, cultural, economic, and even, political history, there is an undeniable continuity of the patterns of daily life and in the structures of western Mediterranean societies. Nonetheless, significant transformations took place, above all, in the nature of state power and the rise of empires, the Spanish and the Ottoman in particular. The most remarkable development was the rise of fairly centralized kingdoms, and their ability, to paraphrase Max Weber, to monopolize legitimate violence. In the succeeding pages, we witness the process by which western Mediterranean polities go from fairly decentralized states to the emergence of the modern nation, intense colonial ventures, and, eventually, decolonization. Not everyone, however, developed equally. Italy and Germany, the latter not really part of the Mediterranean world, did not become nation-states until the nineteenth century. Moreover, the processes that led to the eventual construction of nation-states were different from location to location, depending on many factors that were exclusive to particular regions.

There is no need to wait until this chapter's concluding pages to summarize what were the significant developments for the period between the end of the Middle Ages and the contemporary world. Several key developments serve as a broad introduction to the transformations of the western Mediterranean at the onset of modernity. The overarching patterns we find for the period, some of them already foreshadowed in the previous chapter, follow in this sequence more or less: 1) the flow between a remaining sense of political unity, under a waning Roman Empire in the West in the fifth century, and the fragmentation of Roman political authority in the western Mediterranean under the pressure of internal collapse and outside invasions; 2) attempts to re-establish or construct a united western Mediterranean (or, in some cases, to restore unity to the whole sea) by the Byzantine empire in the sixth century, the Muslims in the eighth and ninth centuries, and by Spain and the Sublime Porte in the late fifteenth and sixteenth centuries; 3) as a counterpart to these movements to combat political fragmentation, we see the rise of local powers and the emergence of regional and local identities. France, Castile, and Sicily under the Normans are examples of the first. The Berbers in North Africa, the history of Occitania, and the example of the Italian communes are reminders of the enduring strength of the second.

By the end of the Middle Ages, the signal historical development was the slow emergence of borders and territorial entities in and around the western Mediterranean. Although these processes occurred at different times in the region, it is clear that by the late fifteenth century, many began to think of themselves as living in areas clearly identified by geography and political rule. This complex process of "imagining communities," to use Benedict Anderson's formulation for a later period, was closely related to new territorial boundaries, developments of fiscal borders, and identification of the ruler with a particular territory. Often, religion served (and still serves) as the dominant category in the establishment of communities and regional identities. One development, that is that of nation-states, was characterized by the emergence of territorial entities and what we may call an embryonic patriotism. This often went hand in hand with affiliation, as already noted, in specific religious communities. Similarly, the development of nation-states, colonial rule, and modern polities necessarily interacted with local and regional politics. The recent rebirth of regional resistance to centralizing governments only indicates the reluctance of these regions to be included in these national projects. Religion remains an important element in these recent discourses of unity and fragmentation. And it is to religion that we will turn in the next chapter as an important context for an understanding of history *in* the western Mediterranean.

INTRODUCTION

Having just written the previous paragraph, I must confess that I have always been suspicious of the idea that the rise of the state in Western Europe from the Late Middle Ages onwards was unavoidable. Neither have I been comfortable with the idea that kingdoms were naturally prone to emerge as proto-nation-states, or that the highest achievements of mankind could only take place in the context of large centralized nation-states. Italy in the Renaissance is a counter-example to that view. High cultural achievements were produced, often in a context of war of all against all and without, with the exception of Naples and, perhaps, the papacy, a clearly identifiable territorial and centralized state. Nonetheless, in the transition from the Late Middle Ages to the early modern period, the western Mediterranean witnessed the emergence of highly organized and formal monarchies (not nation-states yet, a far later development). In most of North Africa, the Ottomans gained hegemony in the sixteenth century – though Morocco was able to remain fairly independent – and retained that

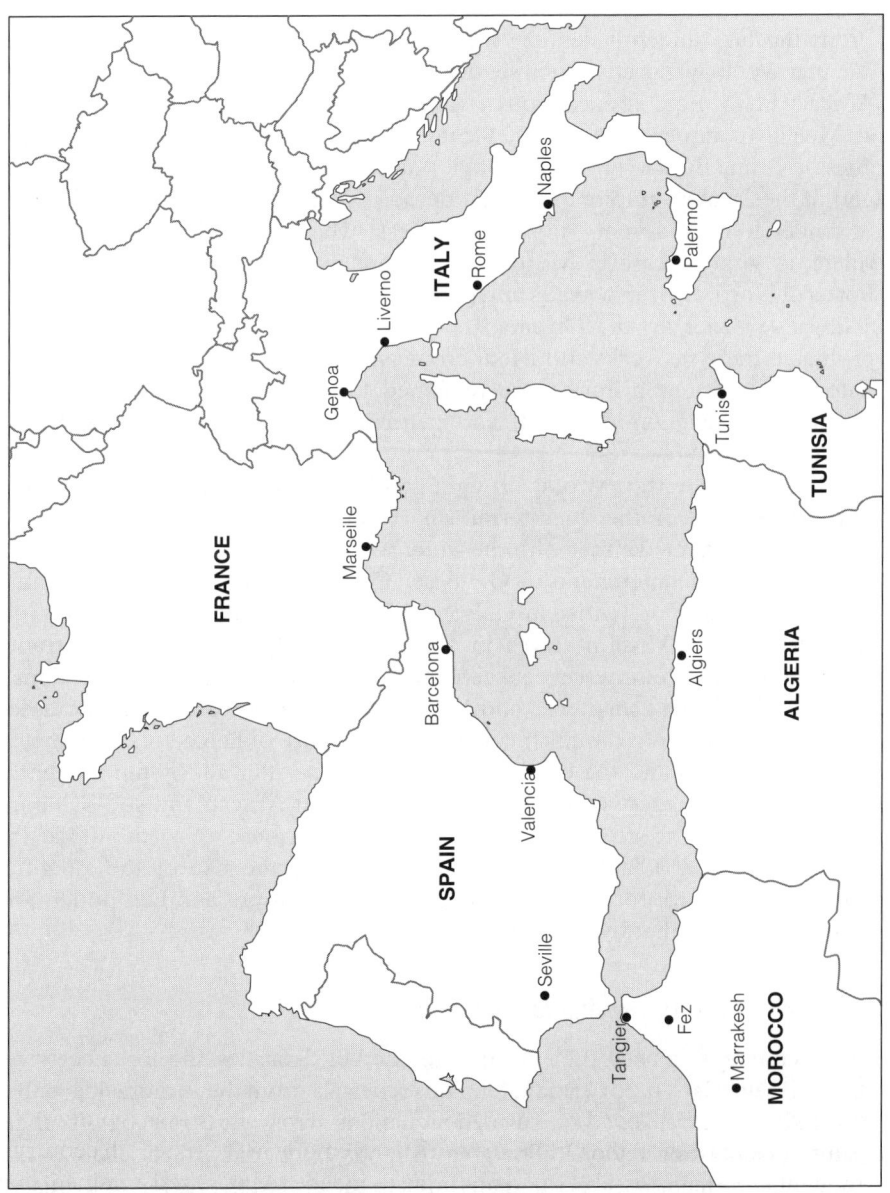

Map 4.1 A map illustrating all countries and cities within the western Mediterranean region during the twentieth century.

control until the eve of the contemporary world and European colonial ventures in the region. A move towards highly developed bureaucracies and closer governmental control (though a great deal less than we have supposed) also took place in the realms of France and Spain. And these two "states" intervened forcefully in Italian affairs. What were the processes that led from the medieval to the early modern period and from the latter into the present age?

NORTH AFRICA

From the late fifteenth century onwards, the political map of the western Mediterranean was pretty much set until the nineteenth century. Most of North Africa, with the notable exception of Morocco and a collection of small outposts at Melilla (conquered in 1497), Ceuta (conquered originally by the Portuguese), Oran, Béjaïa (formerly Bougie), and Tripoli occupied and settled as part of the Spanish empire in the first decade of the sixteenth century, came to be under loose Ottoman rule. Nonetheless, whether ruled by independent rulers, as was the case in Morocco, or under the suzerainty of the Sublime Porte, or North African corsairs and privateers – the fabled Barbarossa brothers, acting as proxies for the Ottomans – the region remained the terminus for profitable trade networks and Mediterranean trade. Economic structures that dated to almost prehistoric time remained firmly in place, pointing to the continuity of economic, social, and cultural patterns across chronological periods.

These commercial networks brought goods from sub-Saharan Africa to the southern shores of the Mediterranean. From these North African ports, merchants connected either with the wider trade networks of the Islamic world or with Christian merchants – Genoese, Catalans, and others. Merchants, whether Muslims or Christians, also doubled their duties as redeemers of Christian and/or Muslim slaves in sixteenth-century prisons and as trade interlocutors for commerce between the two shores and the two religions. Yet, as I will argue in chapters 8 and 12, though trade connections never ceased to exist, they began to diminish considerably because of fierce corsair activity, sectarian warfare, and the opening of the Atlantic. After all, by the sixteenth century the Portuguese could tap directly into West African and sub-Saharan markets without need of intermediaries on the northern coast of Africa. In addition, in what Claire Gilbert has described as the rise of the Atlantic Mediterranean, Morocco's Atlantic ports provided yet another outlet for African products that bypassed the Mediterranean.[1]

Morocco in the Early Modern Period

Morocco had long been the epicenter for Berber dynasties and for successive religious revivals. These periodic religious renewals, from the Almoravids to the Marinids, often translated into armed incursions across the Straits of Gibraltar or into neighboring regions. The great Almohad imperial project came to an end by the thirteenth century and attempts to revive it in the region of Tunis in the early fourteenth century, as shown brilliantly by Hussein Fancy in a recent book, also came to naught.[2] The Marinids also sought to follow on the path chartered by the Almohads, but they met eventually with the same fate. By the late fifteenth century and early sixteenth, new political players came to the forefront. The Berber Wattasid dynasty ruled from the Middle Ages until the mid-sixteenth century. During this period, three significant events impacted Morocco's social, cultural, and political life.

The Spanish conquest of Granada and the Edict of Expulsion of Jews from the Spanish realms sent waves of refugees, Muslims and Jews alike, to Morocco and other parts of North Africa. The first Alpujarra rebellion (see below), in 1499, and the subsequent forced conversion or exile of Muslims shortly afterwards, sent a second wave of Mudejares into Morocco. These exiles brought new and distinct cultural patterns, linguistic influences on the developing Arabic of the region, and new religious sensibilities and awareness, often antagonistic, of the relations between Islam and Christianity in the western Mediterranean. The triumphant discourse of the Iberian realms when it came to their relations with religious minorities in their midst was also paralleled by expansionist moves. The Portuguese had been moving down the coast of Africa since much earlier, and had settled outposts on Morocco's Atlantic coast or, in the case of Ceuta, right at the opening of the Mediterranean. These outposts were not necessarily unprofitable, as they remained essentially coastal outposts, and, as indicated briefly above, connected Morocco to wider trade networks. The Spaniards, on the other hand, sought to continue the advance of the reconquest and to establish beachheads along the coast of Africa. Many of them, including Ceuta (gained from the Portuguese) and Melilla, remain to this very day in Spanish hands. A third major event affecting life in Morocco and weakening the country's economy and Wattasid rule was a major famine in the early 1520s that dramatically impacted Morocco's demographic growth for centuries.

By the mid-sixteenth century, new claimants to the throne of Morocco came onto the scene. Basing their claims to power on their descent from the Prophet Muhammad, the Saadi rulers of Morocco held power for more than a century, from 1549 until 1659. They faced two enduring threats to their efforts to maintain the stability of the Moroccan kingdom. First, Ottoman forces or their proxy rulers, based in what is today Algeria and Tunisia, sought to expand their influence westward and to gain control over at least one shore of the Straits of Gibraltar. The Saadi rulers were successful in blocking Ottoman expansion. Second, Morocco faced continuous threat from the Portuguese and their wishes, under the guise of crusading ideals, to carve a North African colony. In 1578, at the Battle of Ksar el Kebir, known in Iberian history as the battle of Alcazarquivir, the Portuguese forces suffered a crushing defeat. Their young king, Sebastian, died during this battle, and his body was never recovered. The consequences of the battle reaffirmed Saadi dynasty rule in the region, but it also led to the election of Philip II, king of Spain, as the Portuguese ruler. In addition, Sebastian's disappearance led to endless millennial expectations of the return of the king to lead Christianity to Jerusalem and to usher in the end of time. Echoes of beliefs in the imminent return of Sebastian still reverberated in the Canudos rebellion in late nineteenth-century Brazil.

To return to Morocco, under the rule of Ahmad al-Mansur (1578–1603), the victor at Ksar el Kebir, the kingdom reached new relative heights in terms of wealth and stability, after the famine a generation before. For Morocco, the victory over the Portuguese also opened the door for their own expansion south into the Sahara and southern Africa. These gains, however, were ephemeral since Morocco did not have the demographic or economic resources to sustain these expansionist policies. Yet, when Ahmad al-Mansur died, in 1603, Morocco was partitioned among his sons, beginning a period when the kingdom lost a great deal of the influence it had gained at the end of the sixteenth century.

In the late 1660s, a new dynasty, the Alaouite, rose to power and they have successfully remained the rulers of the country until today. Although they traced their presence in Morocco to the thirteenth century, claimed descent from the Prophet, and, thus, held a special *barakah* (blessing), the kind of charismatic power studied in detail by Clifford Geertz, the Alaouite rulers did not command the loyalty of the Berbers, perhaps the most influential group in the kingdom. While unable to restore Morocco to its extensive seventeenth-century borders, Mulay al-Rashid (1664–1672) and Ismael Ibn Sharif (1672–1727) thwarted threats from Spanish and Ottoman forces on the eastern regions of the realm, unified the country, and created a large slave army (the so-called Riffian or Black Slave Army) loyal to the authority of the ruler and able to defend the country's integrity. The taking of Tangier, a strategic port at the Atlantic opening of the Straits of Gibraltar, from England in 1684, and of Larache from Spain in 1689 are clear indications of the new dynasty's military success.

Nonetheless, with Ismael Ibn Sharif's death in 1727, Morocco once again fragmented into different tribal groups, vying for power. For the next 30 years, the country experienced political chaos as Berber and Bedouin groups reasserted their role in Moroccan politics. By 1757, Muhammad III had sought to re-establish some sense of political order and unity, but only by allowing tribal autonomy within the larger Moroccan state. By Abderrahmane's reign (1822–1859), Morocco faced the growing pressure of European powers' colonial ambitions in the entire region. European colonial ventures in the region will be sketched later on, but for now, it is important to note certain things about Morocco's history from the Late Middle Ages to the eve of the European expansion into the region.

Unlike Algeria or what is present-day Tunisia to the east, Morocco had enjoyed more than a millennium of well-developed political identity. Political power oscillated between centralizing rulers, often claiming either descent from the Prophet, special *barakah*, or religious sanction because of their strict interpretation of Islam (as the Almoravids and Almohads did), and tribal allegiances, mostly from the indomitable Berber mountain people and Bedouin desert people. In spite of these contradictory forces pushing and pulling between centralization and fragmentation, Morocco escaped Ottoman rule or extensive European interference (except in some coastal enclaves). Morocco was, after all, fairly wealthy. An active trade with England, funneled through the English enclave in Gibraltar, a productive farming and pastoral economy, access to trade routes in the Sahara, and, for a brief period of time, an actual presence in sub-Saharan Africa made Morocco relatively prosperous during this period. In later chapters, I deal with the region's religion, language, and culture, but, as we move forward to the histories of what would later on become the independent nations of Algeria and Tunisia, it is important to emphasize, once again, that North Africa was not a monolithic society, but a region with diverse political histories and identities.[3]

Algeria and Tunisia from the Sixteenth Century to European Colonization

Algeria. The countries now named Algeria and Tunisia had a very different history from that of Morocco, even though their individual histories were closely intertwined. From the Middle Ages onwards, the regions known as the Maghreb (though only parts of it) and Ifriqiya took very different roads towards nationhood in the modern era. Early modern Algeria and Tunisia, centered around the Mediterranean ports of Algiers and Tunis, respectively, became parts of the expanding Ottoman Empire in the early modern period and coveted possessions for European powers as early as the late fifteenth century and certainly afterwards. After the fall of Granada, Ferdinand and Isabella, fresh from their victories in eastern al-Andalus, plotted a great strategy to reconquer North Africa, which they saw as legitimately, though with no real historical basis, reclaiming the lands of the former Visigothic Empire. Although Italian conflicts thwarted the great western Mediterranean design (see below), Spain established some coastal enclaves on what is today Algeria, the most notable of them in Oran, a city that will be studied in some detail in a later chapter.

The most salient fact in the early modern history of what we know today as Algeria was the Ottoman presence. For close to three centuries, the Sublime Porte ruled most of the southern shores of the western Mediterranean. How they chose to do so, however, was different from Ottoman policies in the eastern Mediterranean, the Balkans, and Anatolia. As shall be seen later, and as already hinted at in Cervantes's description (in a fictional fashion) of his captivity in Algiers, the Ottomans in Algeria and Tunisia ruled through proxies in what has been described as "corsair states." While pirates and corsairs (the second acting under the sponsorship of, or patent from, a ruler) had been a common feature of the Mediterranean throughout its long history, the sixteenth and seventeenth centuries (and even beyond) witnessed feverish activity in Muslim corsair raids on Christian shores and maritime trade and these were reciprocated by the Christians. This was a highly profitable enterprise, bringing not only goods captured but also a robust trade in slaves and significant income from ransoms. These are topics that I will explore in greater detail later on, but, at present, one should remember three important things: 1) Algeria (or what is today Algeria) in this period was under Ottoman rule, though not under the full heavy weight of Ottoman administration as was the case in the eastern Mediterranean; 2) in spite of the economic and military success of privateering, Spain maintained its outposts at Oran (captured in 1509) and Mers el-Kébir, the port of Oran (captured in 1505). Short occupations of Algiers and Bougie in the sixteenth century were quickly repelled by Maghreb and Ottoman armies; 3) finally, through a great part of the sixteenth century, corsair success was the work of the fabled Barbarossa brothers (both of them holding important administrative posts in the Ottoman bureaucracy), whose lives as corsairs and renegades are told in another chapter.

Although Spain made a bid for recapturing some of their North African presidios lost in the early eighteenth century (Oran and Mers el-Kébir were lost in 1708) in 1732 only to sell them back to the Bey of Algiers, it was clear that these outposts proved to be unsustainable. As Ottoman administration waned in the region, Algeria and Tunisia gained a great deal of administrative autonomy from Istanbul. Nonetheless, their continuous corsair activity drew increased military action from European powers that saw their trade with the western Mediterranean and access in and out of the Middle Sea through the Straits of Gibraltar (a favorite spot for corsair activity) compromised by North African state-sponsored privateering. After the Napoleonic Wars ended, restoring some semblance of order to the northern shores of the Middle Sea became an important policy for European powers. North Africa beckoned, and new forms of colonialism came to alter the political life of the Maghreb.

Tunisia. Closer to Sicily than any of the ports on the Algerian and Moroccan Mediterranean coast, Tunis, the ancient Carthage and capital of present-day Tunisia (see Chapter 10), while also an Ottoman province for almost three centuries, played an important role in the corsair wars that were fought in the early modern Mediterranean. Close to the opening to the sea routes to Malta and to the eastern Mediterranean, and with an important Italian enclave at La Goulette (the port of Tunis), Tunisia had closer ties to the Sublime Porte than those lands to the west.

As had been the case in Morocco and Algeria, Spain sought to establish enclaves along the North African coast. These efforts were partly prompted by long-standing ties between the Hafsid dynasty ruling Tunis and the Crown of Aragon. They had intense rivalries, ransoming captives, but also hired each other's troops and had mercantile contacts and representatives. If Sicily was nearby, so was Spain through the Majorcan connection that dated back to a period when the Balearic Islands were part of Dar al-Islam. The most famous of the Barbarossa brothers, Khayr al-Din, Pasha and Admiral of the Ottoman navy, captured Tunis from the Hafsids in 1534, bringing to an end their rule of almost three centuries. Yet, the victory was short lived and over the next 50 years, Tunis changed hands several times. Most of the sixteenth century saw invasions by Ottoman forces from Algiers, corsair attacks, Janissaries' revolts, and Spanish landings and the capture of Tunis, followed by the brief restoration of their Hafsid allies. By the end of the sixteenth century, coinciding with Spain's involvement in the religious wars fought in Central Europe and with the Spanish monarchy's economic and political decline, the Sublime Porte or its corsair proxies established their rule in the region for good.

Although the Sublime Porte also began its own slow loss of power and influence in the wider Mediterranean, as the Mediterranean itself began to lose its centrality in European and North African affairs, nonetheless, Turkish rule made great contributions to the administrative and political practices, legal systems, culture, languages (Turkish and Persian), and patterns of life in the region. Turkish society, although deeply influenced and shaped by Islam, nonetheless had its own peculiar legal sources and cultural traditions that were not the same as Tunisia's existing Arab culture. In that sense, more than Algeria or Morocco (which never came under Ottoman rule), Tunisia, without large groups of Berbers or Bedouins, presented a more receptive culture for Turkish influence. That the region also benefitted from trade networks that connected North Africa to the eastern Mediterranean represented an important aspect of the degree to which Tunisia became firmly a part of the Ottoman Empire. This is not to say, however, that corsair activities, centered most of all on Tunis, did not also play a substantial role in Ottoman Tunisia's economy. Both private businessmen investing in corsair ventures and the Ottoman administrators profited equally from corsair raids and the ransoming of slaves. By the eighteenth century and before the European colonial presence, Algerian and Tunisian corsairs and Ottoman officials also benefitted from the European powers' payments (a form of blackmail) to both Ottoman authorities and corsairs to guarantee safe passage for their vessels.

Throughout the seventeenth and eighteenth centuries, Algeria and, most of all, Tunisia saw the rise of powerful families who as Beys ruled their lands with either support from, or the tacit approval of, the Sublime Porte in Istanbul. In Tunisia, the Bey came to control administrative power over political and financial structures and, most significantly, over tax collection. The Muradid family controlled the office of Bey until 1702, when an Algerian intervention led to a brief interlude in the autonomy of Tunisia. From 1705 to 1881 and the beginning of colonization, members of the Husaynid dynasty ruled over Tunisia, fairly independent from the Sultan in Istanbul. In fact, the French colonial powers preserved the Husaynids' ceremonial role during their rule over Tunisia, the dynasty's role in Tunisian life coming to an end only with decolonization and the establishment of the Tunisian Republic in 1957.[4]

This short introduction to the diverse political pathways followed by North African societies from the Late Middle Ages to the eve of the contemporary world does not do full justice to the important economic transformations that took place in the region during this period: the rise and slow waning of a corsair economy, the role of North Africa, above all Tunisia, as exporters of agricultural products, or the unique role of Sephardim Jews (coming to North Africa in 1492) and two successive waves of Muslim immigrants in 1492 and 1609–1619 (after the fall of Granada and the expulsion of the Moriscos from Spain) in the culture and economy of the region. I will return to some of these points tangentially in later chapters, but it may be well to provide also a short description of the course of North African history from the end of Ottoman rule to the present, before proceeding to the European countries on the northern shores of the Mediterranean. I am conscious that I discuss European colonialism briefly here before discussing Western European Mediterranean developments, but clearly the impact of colonial rule had a greater impact on the histories of Morocco, Algeria, and Tunisia than it did in the respective histories of Spain and France.

NORTH AFRICA IN THE MODERN WORLD: COLONIALISM AND DECOLONIZATION

In spite of waning commerce and exchanges and in spite of the Christian victory against the Ottoman navy at Lepanto in 1571, Muslim polities and Ottoman agents in North Africa also continued to wage successful campaigns in the western Mediterranean against Christian realms and those sailing in the Middle Sea. In fact, as has been seen, Muslim corsairs remained active into the nineteenth century when Barbary pirates even prowled Atlantic waters off the coast of Africa in search of prey. Nonetheless, by the eighteenth century, the Sublime Porte had entered a period of decline, and its influence outside Anatolia had waned considerably. Although it would not be put out of its misery until World War I – and then given new life by the Kamal Ataturk's Young Turks reforms in the twentieth century – the reality is that by the early nineteenth century the Ottomans ceased to play any meaningful role in the western Mediterranean. As early as the late eighteenth century, but surely by the nineteenth century, French and, to a lesser extent, Spanish colonial ventures transformed the North African political landscape. France established a firm rule throughout most of North and Central Africa, with the exception of Morocco, which became partially a protectorate. French architecture spread to new colonial cities or colonial quarters in places such as Casablanca, Tunis, Algiers, and other great cities in North Africa (see Chapter 10). French became one of the official languages in most of western Mediterranean North Africa, and certainly the language of the learned elite. Most of the region became solidly French.

Yet, because there was always resistance to both political and cultural colonialism, the French did not fully succeed. Berber remained the language of most people in the region of Morocco. South of the Atlas and Riff mountains, the desert (as a region) and desert people retained their identity. Nowhere is this more evident, as Sarah Stein has vividly shown, than in the distinction made by French colonial authorities between Jews living in urban coastal areas and granted access to French citizenship, and Jews from the Sahara region who were not eligible for citizenship. Furthermore, even though Algerian troops fought alongside the French in the two twentieth-century World Wars, Algerians also fought a bloody war of insurrection against colonial rule in the 1950s. Paradoxically, when in 2014 the military parade down the Champs Élysées included Algerians soldiers to mark Algeria's contributions to World War I France's efforts, right-wing politicians protested because of the still festering wounds of the Algerian war of Independence. It is, as I have written several times, complicated.

This is so because, after World War II, waves of decolonization and wars of liberation, most notably the Algerian war, led to the eventual demise of French power in the region. The Algerian war was particularly bitter, with atrocities committed by both sides, and right-wing French-Algerians refusing to give up the land they considered their home. One should emphasize the manner in which the French became deeply intertwined with North Africa, above all, with Algeria. France was a great deal more than an absentee landlord or a distant colonial master, as was the case in sub-Saharan Africa. The French migrated to Algeria in large numbers, settled there after military service, and built cities, cathedrals, and opulent avenues. They built them in imitation of their own cities in France. They recreated a France across the western Mediterranean. Through the great French port at Marseille, through Aix-en-Provence, where colonial archives are kept to this day, the French developed a symbiotic relationship with its North African colonies; yet, less so with those in Central Africa. In many respects, parts of the North African coast somewhat resemble southern France. North Africa, above all Algeria, was home for many French men and women. They planted vineyards and olive groves, familiar features of the Mediterranean landscape. Think of the complicated attitude of someone such as Albert Camus, born in Oran, liberal in his opinions about most things, yet deeply attached to a French Algeria and against independence.

It suffices to say that most of the independent realms of North Africa – most of them under the rule of the numerous Berber dynasties that came and went throughout the Middle Ages – fell under Ottoman rule by the sixteenth century. Notwithstanding some European enclaves, the Sublime Porte retained control of the region for the centuries between the end of the Middle Ages and the dawn of the contemporary world. By then, western powers (mostly France and to a lesser extent Spain) captured most of North Africa, either as outright colonies or as protectorates until the decolonization of the region in the 1950s and 1960s. Three countries, each of them with distinct identities – Morocco, Algeria, and Tunisia – emerged into the modern world. Unlike sub-Saharan Africa or the Middle East, where colonial powers created artificial countries for which we are still paying the price in untold violence, the North African polities, though not without civil strife, are recognizable political entities, with long histories and their own unique identities.

Nonetheless, even if it no longer held control over the region, France and its former North African colonies are bound up with each other by immigration, economic exchanges, language, and other factors. When one reads that around 11% of the French population practices Islam and that there are close to 4 million Algerians or people of Algerian descent living in France, one is also saying that North Africans now represent a substantial portion of the French nation. The colonial inheritance in North Africa, however, has also been problematic at times. Morocco, Algeria, and Tunisia have followed very different paths since the 1950s and 1960s, and these paths have been often times rocky and uncertain.

Morocco

Morocco emerged from the Spanish and French protectorate with a constitutional monarchy, though the monarch held extensive administrative rights.

With coasts on both the Atlantic and the western Mediterranean and with its large and assertive Berber population, Morocco holds a strategic position in the region, but Moroccan attempts to expand south into the Sahara and to gain control of the former Spanish colony in the region ran into opposition from local groups, mostly from the Polisario movement. The latter has waged war on Moroccan attempts to gain control of the region for decades. There have been conflicts with Algeria on its eastern border and in the Sahara. Similar to all North African Muslim countries, Morocco also had its "Arab Spring" movement for reform. Unlike Libya and Egypt, where popular demands for greater freedom ended up in bitter civil strife, Morocco seems to have weathered the storm without too much damage.

Algeria

Much larger than any other country in North Africa and rich in natural resources, Algeria has had a troubled transition into the modern world. Its war for independence was one of the harshest of all the wars of liberation from colonial rule. The French resisted Algerian independence and deployed punitive measures against the insurrection. Since independence, Algeria has been plagued by civil war, internal strife, and war with Morocco for control of the western portions of the Sahara. Algerian politics have been dominated by the intervention of the armed forces into national politics and frequent strife between Islamic fundamentalist parties and socialist modernizers. Order was somewhat restored under President Abdelaziz Bouteflika, elected to the presidency in three successive elections, but that did not prevent a round of civil unrest when the "Arab Spring" swept throughout the Arab world. More reforms have been promised and national reconciliation between different political factions continues apace under the watchful eyes of the army.

Tunisia

Tunisia, with its long commercial contacts with Europe, its large Italian migration (mostly to La Goulette and the area of Tunis) in the nineteenth century, and its protected position (protected by a deep desert on its eastern and southern borders), suffered after independence from France from a harsh dictatorship and corrupt governments, but during the "Arab Spring" huge and fairly peaceful street demonstrations prompted a series of political reforms that, at last reading, yielded a re-emphasis on Tunisian secular rule. Although only time will tell whether secular and democratic institutions can survive the opposition of fundamentalist groups, Tunisia's relative prosperity, absence of widespread poverty, and general social harmony (Tunis, the capital of the nation, is one of the most pleasant and civil places to visit or live on the southern shores of the western Mediterranean) perhaps bode well for the future. Caution, as noted earlier, may be after all the most realistic option. Rewriting and revising these pages towards the end of 2017 – in the midst of a wave of terrorist attacks, social upheaval, and large migratory patterns – hope seems, I fear, often illusory.[5]

ACROSS THE STRAITS AND THE MAKING OF MODERN SPAIN

Turning to what we know today as Spain, the end of the Middle Ages marked the closing of a formal Islamic presence in the peninsula. By then, the kingdom of Castile had long enjoyed hegemony in the peninsula. After the Union of the Crowns in 1479, Castile neglected, rather than integrated, the eastern Iberian kingdoms of Valencia, Aragon, and Barcelona (most of Mediterranean Spain). Yet, the eventual control of the eastern kingdoms gave Castile, that is, Spain, a Mediterranean base and a Mediterranean interest. In addition, because of the long struggle against North African corsairs and Ottoman power, and because of Spain's control of Sicily, Naples, and Milan, or its extensive (and oppressive) influence on the remaining Italian state during the early modern period, Spain always kept both a presence and an active interest in western Mediterranean affairs. Yet, Spain was a global power; its involvement in the New World, the Pacific, and Northern and Central Europe limited its Mediterranean role. There are many who have argued that Spain's future was in North Africa or in the New World. We know that Ferdinand and Isabella, and later their grandson Charles I, had planned campaigns in North Africa to conquer the entire Mediterranean coast. Except for a few small enclaves on the Mediterranean African coast, these plans did not come to a successful outcome. Instead, Spain was caught in the fierce religious wars fought in Central Europe and in the northern parts of the Low Countries.

For complex religious, dynastic, and political reasons – most prominent among them the Protestant Reformation beginning in 1521 and Charles V's inheritance of the imperial throne, of Flanders, and of the Spanish realms and their possessions across the Ocean Sea (the Atlantic) and in the Mediterranean – Spain was drawn into a series of exhausting armed conflicts over the next century and a half. These wars had many faces, but they were part of the same struggle for hegemony in Europe and for the rulers' rights to determine the religion of their subjects. Spain fought against France in Italy after 1494 and everywhere else throughout the next century and a half. Although at the battle of Pavia (1525), Charles V's (of Germany, I of Spain) armies defeated the French and captured the French king, guaranteeing Spanish control of Italy, France would prove to be a redoubtable foe, especially under Henry IV of Navarre, king of France 1589–1610, later under Richelieu (Louis XIII's minister), and under their Bourbon successors. England also became a rival from the reign of Elizabeth I onwards and did damage to Spain's trade with its American and Pacific possessions. The Dutch rose in rebellion on matters of religion, seeking independence. Flanders became a quagmire.

Most debilitating of all for the Spanish monarchy were the ferocious religious wars fought from 1525 onwards in Central Europe, Germany, and elsewhere. When they concluded with the Peace of Westphalia in 1648, bringing to an end the savage Thirty Years' War, nothing had been gained – rulers still determining the religion of their subjects. Germany was deeply impacted economically and would not recover for almost a century, Spain was on its way to becoming a third-rate power, and France, Holland, and England emerged as the dominant powers in European politics (see Chapter 12). Clearly, none of them, with the exception of France, was a Mediterranean country. And France's real political interests were in Flanders and, to a lesser extent, in the New World. In Spain itself, the disasters of the wars of religion and against England, the Dutch, and France led to the temporary secession of Catalonia and the permanent break with Portugal in 1640. Although Spain retained its colonial empire, its power had waned in Europe and in the western Mediterranean as well.

By the eighteenth century, the Bourbons had come to Spain (after the War of the Spanish Succession, 1701–1714), bringing to an end the plurality of kingdoms, parliaments, and languages that had been part of the composite Spanish monarchy (even if the eastern kingdoms were neglected). Centralization, following French models, became the fashion. But by then Spain had ceased to be the policeman of Europe. The centers of power, as I noted above, had moved elsewhere: to England, France, and the Dutch Republic. Spanish vessels still patrolled the western Mediterranean from their bases on the Catalan and Valencian coast, from Palma de Majorca, and from Naples, but the economic dynamics of the western sea had declined dramatically (see chapters 8 and 12). A second- or third-rate power in European affairs, Spain went through a series of upheavals in the nineteenth century: a French Napoleonic invasion and the brief imposition of a French dynasty (Joseph Bonaparte) on the peninsula, a successful war of resistance against the French, the almost complete loss of its colonial empire in the early nineteenth century, and endless political upheavals and military coups throughout the rest of that century. The century concluded with a humiliating defeat at the hands of the United States in the Cuban-Spanish-American War in 1898 and the loss of its last New World and Pacific colonies in Cuba, Puerto Rico, and the Philippines.

But the nineteenth century also witnessed the revival of Barcelona as a commercial and industrial hub in the western Mediterranean. That also meant the rise of Catalan and Valencian culture and languages, propelled by a buoyant economy and by the brief interludes of a quasi-federal republic. Significantly, the late nineteenth and early twentieth century also witnessed Spanish colonial activity on the North African Mediterranean coast with the formal incorporation of the Spanish enclaves in Ceuta and Melilla. Spanish protectorates were carved in the ancient Maghreb and along the Atlantic coast of North Africa and in present day Morocco. These short-lived colonial ventures can be briefly listed here: the Spanish protectorate of Morocco (1913–1956); Spanish West Africa (1946–1958); the so-called Spanish Sahara (1884–1975). All these areas are part today of the modern country of Morocco. Spain also had colonial ventures down the Atlantic coast of Africa in Spanish Guinea (1926–1968). Thus Spain became, once again, involved in western Mediterranean and North African politics and in securing strategic outposts on both sides of the Straits of Gibraltar, though Gibraltar itself remained a British enclave from the eighteenth century until today.

The twentieth and twenty-first centuries have reconnected the Iberian Peninsula to North Africa further. North African troops played a significant role in the Spanish Civil War. The military and conservative uprising against the legally constituted Republican government in 1936 had, after all, its epicenter in

North Africa. Paradoxically, while the Franco regime supported a historiography that glorified the reconquest and the Christian victory over Islam – Franco choosing for himself the medieval title of *caudillo* to reiterate his connection to the Spanish medieval past – a Moorish guard with appropriate garments, horses, and weapons protected his residence at El Pardo. And there is now, as mentioned before, an Islamophile movement in southern Spain, as the inhabitants of the region claim a historical connection (of very dubious historical reality) with Muslim rule in southern Spain until the mid-thirteenth century. As I discuss below, Islamophobia, prompted in recent years by migration from North and sub-Saharan Africa, more than counters Islamophile sentiments.

During the long and difficult years of Franco's regime, Spain was fairly isolated from Mediterranean affairs. The allies' victory over Germany and Italy left Spain – a country that had remained neutral during World War II but which had well-known sympathies for, and had received support from, the fascist regimes, and even sent "volunteers" to the eastern front – on the margins of European society. Nonetheless, Spain's recognition by the United States in return for air and naval bases to patrol the Mediterranean and the Straits of Gibraltar, and the economic revival that began during Franco's last years and accelerated after Spain's entry into the European Union, made the peninsula an attractive destination for North African immigrants. Since Spain has also played on its multicultural past and long associations with Islam as one of its attractions for foreign tourists, the country has become, even in spite of the recent brutal fiscal crisis that began in 2007, a magnet for North Africans. Mosques have reappeared in parts of southern Spain after half a millennium of suppression of Islam. Arabic and Berber are now taught in Spain's centers of higher learning. Signs along the roads to Algeciras and Tarifa, ports from which immigrants travel to North Africa by ferry, have Arabic inscriptions to funnel the massive transit of North Africans driving from France to Mediterranean ports as they make their way home during summer vacations (see Chapter 8). This wavering between acceptance and rejection of an Islamic presence and an Islamic past has also taken a toll. There are now frequent and angrily voiced pejorative representations of immigrants, "*los moros*," and even physical attacks against them. The economic difficulties now facing most European Mediterranean countries have only exacerbated these conflicts. Yet, in spite of the present difficulties, and in ways that are often peculiar to the complexity of historical process, Mediterranean Spain today resembles somewhat, in its ethnic, linguistic, and religious composition, what it was 400 years ago, before the expulsion of the Moriscos in 1609–1619. Not unlike Latin American migration to the areas of the United States that were once Spanish and then Mexican, North Africans have returned to a world that was once theirs.[6]

FRANCE

Throughout the Middle Ages and until the end of the thirteenth century, most of what is today part of Mediterranean France was not under the direct rule of French kings and of their administrative capital, Paris. Most of the area located between the Pyrenees and the Rhône Valley was ruled either by the kings (or by members of the royal house) of Catalonia and Aragon (the Crown of Aragon). Such was the case with the kingdom of Majorca, with its capital at Perpignan in what is today France. In the twelfth century, the region of Toulouse also suffered under fragmented lordship. Contentious lords ruled their castles and small domains, perched high on the many fortifications that dotted the hills of the area. Occitania, as historians sometimes call the region when writing of the Middle Ages (see chapters 2, 5, 7, 10, and 11), constituted a distinct cultural and linguistic world, though, as noted, politically fragmented. The crusade launched in 1208 by Innocent III against the so-called Albigensian heresy, allegedly prominent in the region since the middle of the twelfth century, brought to a head the rivalry for political dominance among the different political players in the region. The interest of the Crown of Aragon in Occitania came to a partial end with the defeat and death of Pedro the Catholic at Muret in 1213, and with the ending of the Angevin kings of England's ambitions – also dukes of Aquitaine – with the great victory of Philip II of France at Bouvines the following year.

At Muret, crusaders from the North, mostly French, crushed an army of heretics and Catholics – Peter II, the Catholic, king of the Crown of Aragon, died, as noted above, in the battle while fighting on the side of the heretics. The Albigensian Crusade, as that event has come to be known in history, provided a golden opportunity for the French kings to intervene in southern Mediterranean affairs after the death of the crusade military leader Simon de Montfort in 1218, and to slowly integrate many of these Mediterranean lands into the French Crown. Although the takeover – the French Crown faced stiff regional resistance – was not formally accomplished until the 1270s, already by the middle of the century, Louis IX (1226–1270), later Saint Louis, sought to create a Mediterranean naval outpost at Aigues-Mortes and not only gain a base from which to launch a crusade into North Africa, but also secure an entry point for French interests in the Middle Sea. That attempt, as we already know, failed (see chapters 2 and 11) as the silting of the lands around Aigues-Mortes and changes in the coastline left the town quite inland from the sea.

While the conquest and integration of the Languedoc and great sections of the South were immensely profitable to the French kings, they still did not have a suitable access to the western Mediterranean. Sète or Agde could only permit for the sailing of small vessels. Aigues-Mortes failed, and the great ports close to (or east of) the Rhône delta, Marseille or Toulon, lay beyond French jurisdiction until the early modern period. In a sense, France did not become a real active player in western Mediterranean affairs until Marseille came under French royal authority in the fifteenth century (1482). Under the rule of the Counts of Provence, Marseille – with its ancient maritime pedigree going back to its Phoenician roots – became the most important port in what is today France, but its significance in French political life began only at the onset of the early modern period.

To complicate matters even further, the papacy, relocated from Rome to the banks of the Rhône in 1305, retained its control of Avignon and the area around the city until the French Revolution at the end of the eighteenth century.

Avignon had been the papal see, the locus for the so-called Babylonian captivity, throughout most of the fourteenth century. Although Avignon was not yet part of France, the popes were known for their partiality towards French political interests. When the popes returned to Rome, they did not relinquish either Avignon or its profitable control over towns such as Carpentras (with a substantial Jewish population), or over the equally profitable trade routes that followed the natural highway north along the Rhône River valley. It was not until the period immediately after the French Revolution that Avignon, with its strategic position on the Rhône River and the links to Mediterranean trade coming through Marseille, became part of the French nation.

Toulon, the site of Napoleon's first victory, and other coastal towns east of Toulon, such as Cannes and Nice, did not become part of modern France until much later. Yet, although the French state came late to Mediterranean affairs, the importance of Marseille, one of the quintessential western Mediterranean ports, gave France a major role in the economic and political life of the western sea. I will have a lot more to say about Marseille in a later chapter, but it suffices to say here that the city was, and remains, the focal point of French Mediterranean life. From Marseille and other, smaller French ports on the western Mediterranean, French corsairs plied the western sea in the early modern period as French navy vessels do today. Similarly, it was from its Mediterranean ports that the French would launch their colonial ventures into North Africa in the nineteenth century and it was there – Aix-en-Provence, as mentioned before, being the best example – that its colonial archives would be kept. In the opposite direction, North Africans flocked to Mediterranean ports in search of employment shortly after decolonization, as they continue to do today.

In the transition from the Late Middle Ages to Revolutionary and Napoleonic France, the French Mediterranean faced numerous challenges and difficulties. Its full integration into the French nation – probably, as Eugene Weber argued many years ago, a nineteenth-century phenomenon – followed from revolutionary and Napoleonic administrative centralization. There are many, however, including numerous inhabitants of the region, who will still argue for their own distinctiveness. Toulouse, for example, had developed an important textile industry in the sixteenth century, supplying markets very different from those of textiles centers in northern France and Flanders. Toulouse was also a center for Protestant beliefs, and many influential people died at the hands of Catholics during the massacre of Saint Bartholomew on August 23–24, 1572. Jean de Coras, one of the judges who questioned the false Martin Guerre in that celebrated trial and who left a record of the peculiar circumstances of the case (when a returning soldier pretended to be Martin Guerre, and, after being recognized by his family and fellow villagers as the long departed relative, benefitted from Martin's lands, wife, and child, before being found out as an impostor and hanged for his crime), was killed during the wave of violence that swept France during these sectarian wars.

That Toulouse had a large number of Protestants (called Huguenots in France) is not surprising. West of the Languedoc and Provence was Béarn or Gascony, the homeland of Henry IV of Navarre, one of the leaders of the Protestants in the late sixteenth century. In the early modern period,

Mediterranean France had areas that were in constant flow, neither fully French nor Catholic. Their identities were still to be forged in a distant future after the French Revolution and Napoleonic reforms. Along those lines, Natalie Z. Davis, in her remarkable book on the strange case of Martin Guerre (see above), argues that the false Martin and his wife may have been Protestants, but she also shows how local allegiances and loyalties to the community intertwined deeply within village life. Political borders, as was the case for linguistic and cultural ones, were not yet fully defined.[7] The Guerres were Basque, bringing into their new abodes forms of family organization and inheritance peculiar to their ancestral home. The Roussillon and Cerdagne areas, on the border between France and Catalonia, switched sides depending on the vagaries of war and dynastic alliances. The Val d'Aran, Andorra, and other Pyrenean sites also were liminal places along the emerging frontier between Mediterranean France and Mediterranean Catalonia or Spain. Catalan is still a widely spoken language in the area around Perpignan and as far north as Montpellier. The Catalan flag is displayed everywhere throughout the region, and there are, most certainly for the tourists' benefit, the frequent signs that proclaim the South as the "Land of the Cathars."

The point that I am trying to make through these asides and references is that Mediterranean France, an evolving geographical and political project throughout most of the early modern period and into the nineteenth century, was never an easy territory to digest. The South, as is the case everywhere throughout the western Mediterranean, was different. The cadences of the language were different. The vast number of Roman ruins and even older Greek and Phoenician settlements were constant reminders that the South had origins that were quite different altogether from those of northern France. Those origins and histories were deeply bound with Rome, with olive oil, with fish, with the vine, and with the Mediterranean. Even today, in spite of widespread centralization and cultural homogeneity, there is a culinary – not to mention linguistic and cultural – divide between the northern world of butter and sauces and the southern cuisine of olive oil.

The end of the Ancien Régime, a regime that had fostered – notwithstanding Richelieu's campaigns against local privileges and the revocation of the Edict of Nantes (that under Henry IV had provided Protestants with rights and liberties) by Louis XIV in 1685 – feudal practices, leading in turn to the French Revolution and, far more important, to Napoleonic reform, slowly brought Mediterranean France into an emerging national project. Symbolically, it is important to remember that it was the marching song of Marseille's militias – coming to Paris to face the aristocratic and kingly coalitions gathered on France's northern borders to destroy revolutionary reforms – that eventually became the French national anthem. Hearing it sung with stirring passion at the Champs de Mars on July 14 by French people and recent immigrants was a reminder of how far France has come in the process of building a nation, even with its recent terror attacks and its multi-ethnic, religious, and linguistic diversity.

Today the French Mediterranean coast is the destination for summer travelers. West of the Rhône delta, there are towns that attract the French lower middle class, such as the modern town of La Grande Motte, or even picturesque Sète (see Chapter 11). East of the Rhône, the great and expensive sea resorts at Cannes, Nice, Saint-Tropez, and elsewhere attract a well-heeled international crowd. These are towns that became French only fairly recent. Abrupt topography and the ensuing difficulties in land travel had a great deal to do with the lateness of French control of the region, occurring as it did only in the modern age. Nice and the region of the fabled Côte d'Azur, for example, became part of France only in 1860 as the result of a treaty between the government of France under Napoleon III and the ruler of the kingdom of Savoy-Piedmont (Sardinia), who was then embarking on the process of unifying Italy. It is remarkable the extent to which an area that had its own dialect and its own conflicted identity, between local Italian (Genoese) and French sides, has become so closely bound with the image of France. Nor should we leave this section without commenting that the region became part of the collaborationist Vichy government. Nice became a refuge for fleeing Jews, but also a place from where Jews were deported to the death camps. The city was occupied by Italy briefly and then by Germans, but Nice and other French towns were also places of resistance to the Nazi horror. Today the region still draws well-heeled tourists and cruise ships, but southern France is one of the main entry points for legal and illegal migration and, as shall be seen for Marseille in Chapter 10, a true site of encounters.[8]

ITALY

Milan and Lombardy

Italy as a country had no history between the demise of the Roman Empire in the West in the late fifth century and the Risorgimento in the nineteenth century. Thus, Italy's western Mediterranean political history is complicated. And here it is perhaps appropriate to remind the reader of my preliminary comments at the beginning of this chapter. Unlike all of its other Mediterranean neighbors that developed into large territorial polities or proto-nations, such as France and Spain did by the early modern period, or North African did as well under the rule or protection of the Sublime Porte, Italy did not become a politically integrated region or a nation until past the middle of the nineteenth century. There were, and still are, consequences to that late development of Italy as a nation-state in the midst of other strongly centralized European countries, and there are many who would contend that Italy is not fully a nation yet. Indeed, one of the most salient facts of modern Mediterranean political life is the manner in which medieval regions and localities continue to assert their unique identities and desires for autonomy and/or independence: thus, Catalonia, Corsica, Sardinia, Sicily, and other places in or around the western sea. Emerging from the Middle Ages, and just before the French invasion of Italy in 1494 and the Spanish response to French incursions turned the peninsula into a battlefield for these two kingdoms, Italy was fragmented into myriad republics, despotic states, one theocratic state (Rome), and one kingdom (Naples).

From the thirteenth century onwards, the continuous strife between cities and regional powers had brought forward a series of "states" (if the term could be used for the period in its full significance, though borrowing from Burckhardt's classic formulation) that exercised fairly extensive hegemony throughout their respective hinterlands or in those areas around each specific city that in Italy is called the *contado*. The Treaty of Lodi (1454) had stabilized this situation, as Italian polities sought to preserve the status quo and achieve some balance of power that prevented continuous warfare or the possibility of one large political entity swallowing the others. By that date, at least, five "states," six if one includes Genoa, exercised fairly unchallenged political authority over their respective areas of power. In the North, Milan ruled the rich Lombard plain. Ruled tyrannically by the Visconti from the late thirteenth century until 1447 and then in the mid-fifteenth century by the Sforza, one of the most prominent examples in a line of *condottieri*, or military leaders, who rose to power in Renaissance Italy, Milan experienced a short French interlude when conquered by the king of France in 1492, but, by 1525, the city and most of the Lombard plain had become one of the viceroyalties in the sprawling Habsburg Spanish monarchy. It remained firmly in the hands of Spain – not easy masters by any account – until the end of the Habsburg dynasty in Spain in 1700 and the War of the Spanish Succession. By then, Austria, the remaining Habsburg branch in Eastern Europe, had established firm claims to the region, until the brief Napoleonic interlude in the early nineteenth century. Reverting to Austrian control after Napoleon's defeat, Milan and Lombardy did not become "Italian" until their integration into the emerging kingdom of Sardinia and Savoy, becoming, because of their economic strength (both the city and the region), important components of the new unified Italy by 1861.

Milan and Lombardy never played a major role in Mediterranean affairs. Commercial links connected the city and the region to the West and North, to France and Germany. Through the Rhône River valley and what is today the country of Luxembourg – part of the fabled Spanish road to Flanders – and through the northern lakes of Como and Maggiore, Milan and Lombardy were further linked to Northern European markets. Milan's access to the sea, that is, to the upper Tyrrhenian Sea, or to the western Mediterranean, was not helped by the absence of great ports in the region or by Genoa's control of the Ligurian coast. In an earlier age, Pisa and Genoa had effectively blocked Milanese efforts to expand to the sea. By the Late Middle Ages and the onset of the modern period, Genoa, firmly allied to Spain, held sway over Ligurian and Lombard trade. Yet, Milan, the industrial and fashion locomotive of modern Italy, underwent a rapid industrialization in the late nineteenth century. This recovery was only fitting since Milan had been a prosperous city and region during the Middle Ages, and rapidly made up for the its decline under Spanish and Austrian rule between the early sixteenth century and the onset of the contemporary world.

A hub for air and rail transport, Milan became a magnet for immigrants from the *mezzogiorno* (the South). Overpopulation and the adverse economic conditions that swept most of southern (Mediterranean) Europe in the late nineteenth and early twentieth century sent millions of Spaniards, Italians, Greeks, and Ottoman Jews to the New World. But these migrations, as shall be seen in chapters 8 and 12, also occurred internally. Immigrants from Sicily, Calabria, and Sardinia flocked (and still flock) to Milan and other industrial centers in the northern regions of Italy (Turin, Bologna, and other northern Italian cities). In that sense, although Milan was not a direct player in Mediterranean affairs in an earlier period, it was so in the twentieth century (as it is today), serving as a destination for immigrants, and as one of the poles for the circulation of Mediterranean people from South to North. They bring to Milan their culture and speech patterns, pointing to the enduring connection between the Middle Sea and the inland region, and to other parts of the western Mediterranean, such as Tunisia. Moreover, Milan, because of its thriving textile manufacturing, fashion, and banking, played (and continues to play) a significant role in the modern western Mediterranean economy.

Florence

Florence, because of its thriving medieval textile manufacturing and banking, also played (and continues to play to a large extent) a significant role in the Mediterranean economy. The city is, of course, as is the case for Milan, not on the shores of the Mediterranean. In fact, it is also quite far from the sea, almost in the center of the peninsula, though many in Florence, overwhelmed by the throngs of excursions from cruise ships stopping for the day at Livorno, would argue that it is not far enough. Moreover, Florence had no direct access to the sea through great ports. Only Livorno (Leghorn) offered a good bay for large-scale commercial enterprises. Pisa, which Florence came to dominate towards the end of the Middle Ages and which had been a successful entry point into Mediterranean trade, suffered the same fate as Aigues-Mortes. Thus, we should not be surprised that most of Florence's medieval exports (textiles and luxury items) and imports (wool) were handled by intermediaries (merchants and sailors from Piacenza, Genoa, Castile, and elsewhere).

In the Middle Ages, Florence was a republic, ruled by its proud guilds (the *artes*) until the late fourteenth century. After the unsuccessful revolt of the *Ciompi* (the unskilled laborers seeking to organize themselves into a guild or arte and share in the government of the city) one of the founders of Medici power, Salvestro de Medici (d. 1388) rose to knightly rank, political influence, and wealth on the defeated Ciompi's backs in 1378. By then, the Medici family had already begun its rise to power. By the middle of the next century, they had gained control of the government of the city and of its extensive contado or hinterland. They did so, at least until the early sixteenth century, ruling from behind the scenes and preserving the myth of Florence as a "republic." Because of their significant ability to marry their daughters into royal families (Catherine of Medici and Maria of Medici married into the French royal house in the fifteenth and sixteenth century, respectively) and prominent noble families, and their success in having four members of the Medici family elected to the papacy between the late fifteenth and the early sixteenth century, Florence held on to its international role in spite of the general decline that beset Italy under the Spanish and, later on, under the Austrian Habsburgs. In the case of Florence,

Spanish influence crushed the fabled Florentine liberties that had resisted Milanese attempts to conquer them and/or the enduring papal animosity that had led to armed conflicts in the Late Middle Ages.

But the Florence that had been the effective cultural locomotive of the Italian Renaissance, of international banking – one of the leading groups in the establishment of banking in Florence as one of the most significant economic activities of the city was the house of the Bardi (bankrupted in 1348 by England's default on its debts) – and of fine textile production became over time a memory. With its great painters, sculptors, historians, political philosophers (such as Machiavelli, who was both a historian and a political philosopher), and others, Florence became the trendsetter at the vanguard of cultural production in Western Europe. The Italian Renaissance was certainly not only Florentine in nature, but, clearly, the great names and works of the period were remarkably concentrated on the city on the banks of the Arno River.

And yet, as noted earlier, Florentine merchants often plied the sea in other people's vessels, and the city's manufacturing and exporting economy was not sustainable under Spanish rule. After what Eric Cochrane described as the "lost centuries," the period between the High Renaissance of the early sixteenth century and Spanish dominance on the one hand, and Italian unification on the other – a period when the city languished under foreign rule – Florence has regained some of its prominence and role as cultural and high-end fashion leader. Today the city is one of the most visited destinations in the western world and a center for culture (universities and research centers), fashion, leather goods, and art. Its extraordinary art collections and public and religious buildings make the city a magnet for visitors and a living reminder that cultural innovation in this very Mediterranean city was not ushered in by a centralization of regional or kingdom-wide power, but the result of the special local politics of Renaissance and Mediterranean Italy.

And these unique cultural trophies attracted (and attract) visitors. All of the travel to Italy by members of the upper classes (mostly from England early on and from American by the well-to-do in the second half of the nineteenth century) began in the late eighteenth and continued throughout the succeeding centuries. Florence and Rome became obligatory stops in the Grand Tour and favorite locations for the endless search for antiquities and curiosities (or in the case of young rich American women, poor but noble husbands). Florence and other Italian destinations became the subject of idyllic portraits and/or gripping fictional works (George Eliot's *Romola* and *Daniel Deronda* are good examples, as is Stendhal's *The Charterhouse of Parma*) that sought to recapture the glamor of Renaissance cities – or, in the case of *Romola*, their dangers and political strife. Today, young people, scholars, and tourists crowd Florence's streets (and those of other Italian towns). Cruise ships, as noted earlier, disgorge their teeming and well-heeled masses of passengers upon the city after mooring at (and ignoring altogether) Livorno. In that sense, one from which the proud citizens of Florence profit but which they do not fully enjoy, Florence is fully now part of the Mediterranean world, but at the cost, as is the case with many Italian and European cities, of slowly turning into museum cities.

Rome and Venice

Two other Italian Renaissance powers may be dealt with in a fairly brief fashion. This is not because they were unimportant. It is rather the contrary. If I deal with them here perfunctorily it is because they did not have a significant presence in the western Mediterranean in the early modern period or, at least, not to the extent of other Mediterranean cities.

Rome. The Pope, a theocratic ruler, ruled Rome. Members of the great Roman aristocratic families were often elected popes throughout the Middle Ages. Those families – Orsini, Borghese, Colonna, Barberini, and others – often had members of their own kin groups, besides being elected to the Holy Office, hold extensive control of the College of Cardinals, and the lands around Rome and elsewhere throughout Italy, as Pius II did in Pienza. Rome and the extensive Roman Papal States – reaching from the Tyrrhenian Sea to the Adriatic in a wide band running through central Italy – functioned as yet another political power. It engaged in warfare and diplomacy with (and against) other Italian polities in ways that often did not reflect well on the Church's spiritual mission. Renaissance popes were great princes. They were often very learned Renaissance scholars, as was the case with the noted humanist Aeneas Sylvius Piccolomini (Pius II). They could be warrior-like, as was the case with Julius II, or corrupt beyond words as was, for example, Alexander VI, the Borgia Pope.

As was the case for most of Italy, Spanish rule lay heavily on Roman shoulders. Although the Papal States remained independent and often sought to thwart Spanish policies, the memory of 1527, when the emperor Charles V let his German and Spanish troops loose on the city, was always a grim reminder of the limits of independence. Although papal ships had sailed as part of the great naval battle – and Christian victory – at Lepanto (1571), Rome's role in the life of the sea was minimal. Yet, through its western Mediterranean outlets at Ostia and, more recently, Civitavecchia, Rome also benefits (and suffers) from the hordes of cruise ship excursions that descend upon the city as regularly as clockwork. One should note that in the nineteenth century, the popes resisted and opposed Italian unification, though by the early twentieth century, Mussolini's Concordat with the papacy, in 1929, put an end to the Holy See's hopes of having a territorial political role in the affairs of the peninsula. Of those hopes of territorial sovereignty, only the minuscule Vatican State remains, a rather small consolation for the real political power that the bishop of Rome once held in central Italy.

Other things about Rome, however, call for reflection. First, if Florence was the locomotive of the Renaissance cultural blossoming, Rome was the most important or one of the most important repositories of Classical (and then Renaissance and Baroque) art and culture. Artists came to Rome, attracted by papal and ecclesiastic patronage, and by the Church's ambitious architectural projects. Saint Peter and the art that adorns the great church and its architectural complex are just one example. Another is what the popes and their ambitious urban programs did to the city. Renaissance and Baroque Rome, with its obelisks, bold piazzas (Piazza Navona being one of the most dramatic examples), bridges across the Tiber River, and lavish sculptures, signaled papal interest in making the city the true center of Christendom and of western civilization. It is that Rome, always in competition with its ancient past and monuments, that is an indelible part of the modern world and of Mediterranean society.

Second, for all the struggles between Church and empire, for all its ancient history, for all the transformation of the urban landscape undertaken by Renaissance popes, there are other things that go deeper than a brief summary of Roman political developments allows for. To understand Rome's enduring relation with its past, with its Mediterranean destiny and its Italian present, one needs to walk the city. While most of the old settlements along the shores of the Mediterranean have a layering of past histories and the bricolage of diverse civilizations, Rome has this to the umpteenth degree, matched only perhaps by Istanbul. While the Roman past and Roman ruins dominate the urban landscapes, early Christian churches, eastern Christian shrines, Renaissance buildings, Egyptian obelisks, and Baroque piazzas and monuments mentioned before create a cacophony of architectural forms and cultural messages. Above all, there are the colors of houses and buildings, often with a touch of decrepitude to add to their charm. Northern towns do not always have these Mediterranean colors or, far more important, the shimmering sunlight of the Mediterranean or the tropics – the reds, yellows, almost orange tones – that provide such liveliness to the urban setting. We see them in Sicily, Vernazza, North African cities, the alleyways of Barcelona, and other towns along the shores of the Mediterranean. For Rome, though a bit inland from the sea and depending on its nearby ports to gain access to the Tyrrhenian Sea (the Tiber is barely navigable to even small ships), is a profoundly Mediterranean city, and walking the city – as Michel de Certeau once explained in a luminous essay – is the only way to see the Mediterranean in all of its fullness.[9] Though its commercial and political life did not achieve the extent of that of places like Genoa, Marseille, and others, Rome remains the ultimate destination for what one may consider a true Mediterranean experience. It does so as a living reminder of the unity of the Mediterranean under Roman rule; it does so in the fictional pages of our so often mentioned *Count of Monte Cristo*, when we see the whole world of carnival, bandits, ancient palaces, and cardinals; and it does so to everyone who visits the city. You cannot see the sea from even its highest building, but the Mediterranean is there in the sensibilities and in the tenor of the city's everyday experiences.

Venice. Unlike Rome, Venice was a true Mediterranean mercantile player. Although its main focus of business was the eastern Mediterranean, the Queen of the Adriatic served throughout the Middle Ages and some parts of the early modern period – until the rise of the Ottoman power – as one of the most important interlocutors and middlemen between the eastern and western parts of the Mediterranean Sea. From the late thirteenth century, when its political structure and governmental practices were officially formalized, Venice was a closed oligarchic republic. It was able, because of its strategic position and its

Figure 4.1 Street view of the Trastevere in Rome. Source: Courtesy of Scarlett Freund.

naval power, to retain its independence, until Napoleon conquered the city in 1797 only to grant it to Austria in the same year. As was the case for most Italian polities, it became part of the new kingdom of Italy in 1866. The reality was that by the early modern period the rise of the Sublime Porte had slowly but inexorably pushed Venice out of its eastern Mediterranean outposts (Nicosia, Famagusta, etc.). The Portuguese voyages to India, circumventing the Venetians and Ottomans as the middlemen in the profitable spice trade with Western and Northern Europe, marked the death knell for Venice's unique role in Mediterranean affairs. (See Chapter 12.)

There was, of course, far more to Venice than I describe here. Its galleys played a significant role at Lepanto. Its relations with the Spanish power that almost surrounded it in the North and West were always ambivalent. The city also served as a cultural repository, but one markedly different from Rome, Florence, Naples, and other cities on the western part of the Mediterranean. Its location and romantic allure remain important magnets for modern tourism; yet, the feel of the city is quite different from that of cities on the western shores of the sea.

Naples and Genoa

Naples and Genoa are the two large Italian cities facing the western Mediterranean that have the advantage of great and well-protected ports, although modern harbors, such as La Spezia, also qualify as important ports on Italy's western shore. In the North, Genoa – its early history has already been detailed in the previous chapter and above, but I think one may benefit from retelling it here – connected with the wider commercial networks of the entire Mediterranean. It was a "republic" with a long history of trade, as well as of conflict with the Crown of Aragon and other western Mediterranean maritime powers in the fourteenth and fifteenth centuries. They fought for control of the great islands of the western Mediterranean, Sardinia and Corsica, as well as the profitable trade relations with North Africa. Naples had long been a kingdom, the only kingdom in Italy, from the Central Middle Ages onward. It came under the rule of the Hohenstaufen and imperial rule in Sicily and southern Italy and then saw a French interlude before a successive number of rulers with empty titles as kings of Jerusalem. By 1442, the kingdom had come under the power of the rulers of the Crown of Aragon (Alfonso V). Its political history, as well as its economic structures, could not have been more different from those of Genoa, in spite of its great bay.

Genoa. Dominating its hinterland on the Ligurian coast, Genoa was already one of the most significant political players in Mediterranean affairs by the early twelfth century. With ties to the areas around Nice – in fact, the language spoken in medieval Genoa was connected to the dialect spoken in and around Nice and not to the Tuscan dialect that would become Italian – Genoa played a significant role in the Crusades. The Genoese also established a commercial empire that extended from the Piedmont to Corsica, North Africa, Iberia, and the Levant. In the East, Genoa, a true Mediterranean power, competed successfully with Venice, and defeated, and then lost to, the Catalans in the Tyrrhenian Sea. By the fifteenth century, Genoa suffered through a brief French occupation, and fell under the control of the Visconti rulers of Milan. Losing most of its maritime empire, Genoa was, nonetheless, able to preserve some of its independence and to prosper under the capable rule of the Doria family. Working as a profitable partner to Spain's new imperial ventures in the sixteenth century, the Genoese acquired an important share of the Atlantic trade through its agents in Seville. In fact, one of the main commercial streets of Seville, a city where Genoese commercial interests and bankers had been present since Almohad rule in the twelfth century, is still called Calle Génova (Genoa Street). Genoa's vessels under the leadership of Andrea Doria played a significant role in the western Mediterranean, in patrolling the waters of the North African coast, and in Lepanto. It was a "republic," but one dominated, as was the case in Florence, by a family.

Genoa's dazzling cultural achievements in the sixteenth and early parts of the seventeenth century did not last. The inexorable decline of Spain, Genoa's main ally and most important business partner, made the city and its region vulnerable to attacks. The French and the Austrians took turns in controlling it. It became the Ligurian Republic after Napoleon's invasion of Italy in the 1790s, but France swiftly annexed it in 1805, and the region became part of the kingdom of Piedmont (Savoy) after the Congress of Vienna in 1814. In spite of revolts against Savoy's rule, the city became part of the united Italy by the 1860s and one of Italy's most important commercial and economic hubs in the twentieth and twenty-first centuries. Modern Genoa's expansive shorefront extends for many miles, teeming with manufacturing businesses, docks, and many container ships.

Naples. Naples' history, on the other hand, shared the problems that plagued, and still plague to this very day, the *mezzogiorno*. They are the well-researched problems of most of Southern Europe and the northern shores of the Mediterranean. Always a large city, even in Classical times, Naples' historical roots date to the Bronze Age. Going through many different phases, first as a Greek city, then as part of Rome (the Roman cities of Pompeii and Herculaneum, preserved beneath Vesuvius's volcanic wrath that extinguished their existence in 79 CE, lie close to Naples), Naples came under Ostrogothic rule after the demise of Roman power in the West towards the end of the fifth century. After a brief Byzantine interlude, Naples gained its independence as the Duchy of Naples until the Norman conquest of most of southern Italy and Sicily – an island with which the history of Naples is closely bound – by 1137. The Normans and their Hohenstaufen successors (German emperors), ruled most of Southern Italy until the French Angevin interlude from 1283, the year of the Sicilian Vesper (see Chapter 3), until 1442 when Alfonso V (Alfonso the Magnanimous), king of the Crown of Aragon, conquered Naples, marking his victory with a triumphal royal entrance through a breach in the walls of the defeated city.

From that date onwards, Naples and its countryside came to be fully in the Arago-Catalan sphere. Naples became a Renaissance court, with significant artistic accomplishments, including the philosophical and philological work of Lorenzo Valla, a secretary in Alfonso V's court. As an aside, but an important cultural fact, Naples was also the epicenter for the transmission of Renaissance thought to the Crown of Aragon and Castile in the fifteenth century. These endless connections along the shores of the western Mediterranean explain why to tell the history of one location in relative isolation from the general history of the region is a difficult task. It is difficult to think of Naples without placing it within the wider context of the Spanish monarchy after 1442. In fact, in 1516, when Charles V inherited the Crown of Aragon from his grandfather Ferdinand II (Ferdinand the Catholic), Naples became a part of the far-flung Spanish Empire. As such, Naples played a significant role as a Spanish proxy in the western Mediterranean into the late eighteenth century. Yet, Naples' commerce and mercantile activities were, to a large extent, in the hands of the very successful Genoese diaspora in the city and in the wider kingdom.

When the Habsburg rule came to an end in Spain in 1700, and as a consequence of the War of the Spanish Succession, Naples came to be ruled by the Austrian Habsburgs. After a brief interlude under Napoleon, who installed his relatives or generals as kings, Naples saw another period of Austrian rule until Garibaldi's invasion of the South in 1861. By then Naples and Sicily had been incorporated into the new kingdom of Italy. This very brief outline of Naples' history should not obscure the importance and uniqueness of Naples in Mediterranean history. It was the sole kingdom (besides the papacy) in Italy, never having gone through republican or tyrannical experiences. It was a feudal kingdom, its wealth to be found in its extensive hinterland and in the profit generated by transhumant flocks of livestock. Its commerce and banking were (and have been since), to a large extent, in the hands of the Genoese and the Florentines, respectively. Its magnificent bay became an important base for Mediterranean naval forces, whether the English fleet under Nelson in the late eighteenth century or NATO's forces today. The city has always had a large population, showing that urban growth and urban dynamics were not always dependent on mercantile activities. Naples, together with Valencia, Barcelona, Tunis (with which Naples kept frequent contacts through the immigration of large numbers of Italians to North Africa), Algiers, Marseille, and Genoa, was one of the hubs around which the western Mediterranean revolved.[10]

Naples today is an unruly city, with a Sicilian style criminal organization, the Camorra. The city sent many of its people to the New World, and today it sends them to the manufacturing centers in Northern Italy and Northern Europe. It is a city that, in spite of its civic disrepair, perilous urban life, pressing population growth, and decaying buildings, still has a remarkable and unique beauty that rewards the traveler who dares to disregard the city's perhaps exaggeratedly bad reputation.

For now, having looked very briefly at the individual histories of Italian republics, tyrannies, and kingdoms, we see how these peculiar histories came together to form a united Italy a little more than a century and a half ago. Not unlike Spain, the problem of national identity is still a work in progress, but what is not in doubt about any of the polities we have examined here is their Mediterranean identity. It preceded the birth of nations, and will probably outlive them as well.

CONCLUSION

With that last thought in mind, it is pertinent to remember, once again, the introductory lines to this chapter – as to the nature or validity of the concept of nation-state formation or absence of it – and my further elaboration of these ideas in the pages above. The introduction serves as a conclusion as well. Missing from this description is Sicily, the quintessential Mediterranean society in the Middle Ages and even today. Sicily's history was examined in detail in the previous chapter; it will be central to coming chapters as well when its history will be placed there in the context of encounters and the circulation of people and ideas in religious, ethnic, and linguistic diversity.

By placing the history of soon-to-be nation-states such as France and Spain together with the individual histories of the Italian and North African polities, one is reminded once again of the conundrum we face in describing how the western Mediterranean was organized politically. But there were other factors beyond politics that bound people and polities. Older in many ways than the emergence of centralized kingdoms or Italian "states as works of art," religion, language, and cultural production linked and separated the societies that grew around the shores of the western Mediterranean. As promised in the opening lines of this chapter, it is to a different way of organizing polities along religious allegiances that we turn now.

Notes

1   See Claire Gilbert, "The Politics of Language in the Western Mediterranean c. 1492–1669. Multilingual Institutions and the Status of Arabic in Early Modern Spain." PhD diss., UCLA, 2014.

2   Hussein Fancy, *The Mercenary Mediterranean: Sovereignty, Religion, and Violence in the Medieval Crown of Aragon* (Chicago: University of Chicago Press, 2016).

3   On Morocco, see Mercedes García Arenal, *Ahmad al-Mansur: The Beginnings of Modern Morocco* (Oxford: OneWorld, 2009) and her *La diáspora de los andalusíes* (Barcelona: CIDOB Edicions [Icaria Editorial], 2003). See also Jacques Berque, *Ulémas, fondateurs, insurgés du Maghreb: XVIIe siècle* (Paris: Sindbad, 1982), which explores the role of religion in early modern Moroccan politics, and *Ibn 'Askar, Muhammad ibn 'Ali, The Sheikhs of Morocco in the XVIth Century*, trans. by T.H. Weir (Edinburgh: G.A. Morton et al., 1904), which provides a vivid account of Morocco's rulers in the sixteenth century. The book is available in full through Google Books. See also the work of Julia Ann Clancy-Smith cited in note 4. On the battle of Ksar El Kebir (or the Battle of the Three Kings) where King Sebastian lost of his life, and the subsequent development of a millenarian cult, see Lucette Valensi, *Fables de la mémoire: la glorieuse bataille des trois rois* (Paris: Seuil, 1992).

4   See, among others, Lucette Valensi, *Le Maghreb avant la prise d'Alger, 1790–1830* (Paris: Flammarion, 1969), of which there is an English translation. See also her *Tunisian Peasants in the Eighteenth and Nineteenth Centuries*, trans. Beth Archer (Cambridge & New York: Cambridge University Press, 1985); for the nineteenth century and the rule of the Beys, see the detailed and comprehensive work of Carl L. Brown, *The Tunisia of Ahmad Bey, 1837–1855* (Princeton: Princeton University Press, 1974); for the eighteenth century see Mohamed-Hédi Cherif, *Pouvoir et société dans la Tunisie de H'usayn bin 'Ali: 1705–1740* (Tunis: Université de Tunis, 1986), and the excellent work by Julia Ann Clancy-Smith, *Rebel and Saint: Muslim Notables, Populist Protest, Colonial Encounters (Algeria and Tunisia, 1800–1904)* (Berkeley: University of California Press, 1994). See also note 5. Recently, Jacques Chemla, Monique Goffard, and Lucette Valensi have published a beautiful account (with large number of photographs) of their father's ceramic and tile work in Tunis. Many of these tiles, found today in very upscale Montecito, California, homes, are an aesthetically pleasing reminder of the circulation of art forms, the influence of the Morisco immigrants, and the cultural unity of the western Mediterranean. See *Un siècle de céramique d'art en Tunisie. Les fils de J. Chemla, Tunis* (Tunis: Éditions Déméter, 2015).

5   See the comprehensive work of Julia Ann Clancy-Smith, *North Africa, Islam, and the Mediterranean World: From the Almoravids to the Algerian War* (London & Portland: Frank Cass, 2001).

6   See John H. Elliott, *Imperial Spain, 1469–1716* (New York: St Martin's Press, 1964), and his magisterial *The Count-Duke of Olivares. The Statesman in an Age of Decline* (New Haven & London: Yale University Press, 1986). See also Teofilo F. Ruiz, *Spanish Society, 1400–1600* (Harlow, UK: Longman, 2001); Raymond Carr, *Spain: 1808–1939* (Oxford: Clarendon Press, 1966); Hugh Thomas, *The Spanish Civil War* (New York: Harper & Brothers, 1961); Gerald Brenan, *The Spanish Labyrinth: An Account of the Social and Political Background of the Civil War* (Cambridge: Cambridge University Press, 1950).

7   Natalie Zenon Davis, *The Return of Martin Guerre* (Cambridge: Harvard University Press, 1984).

8   For a history of maritime activities on the French Mediterranean coast over la longue durée, see Jean Jacques Antier, *Marins de Provence et du Languedoc: vingt-cinq siècles d'histoire du littoral français méditerranéen* (Avignon: Aubanel, 1977). For articles on towns and cities in southern medieval France, see *Urban and Rural Communities in Medieval France: Provence and Languedoc, 1000–1500*, eds. Kathryn Reyerson and John Drendel (Leiden & Boston: Brill, 1998); also, for Marseille, see Junko Thérèse Takeda, *Between Crown and Commerce: Marseille and the Early Modern Mediterranean* (Baltimore: Johns Hopkins University Press, 2011). Of course, for this section and all others in this chapter, Braudel's *The Mediterranean* is a must, as is Abulafia, *The Great Sea.*

9   Michel de Certeau, "Walking in the City," in *The Practice of Everyday Life* (Berkeley: University of California Press, 1984), 91–110.

10 For a general history of Italy, see Claudia Baldoli, *A History of Italy* (New York: Palgrave Macmillan, 2009). For Milan under Spain, see Stefano D'Amico, *Spanish Milan: A City within the Empire, 1535–1706* (New York: Palgrave Macmillan, 2012). For Florence in the period of decline, see Eric Cochrane, *Florence in the Forgotten Centuries, 1527–1800: A History of Florence and the Florentines in the Age of the Grand Dukes* (Chicago: University of Chicago Press, 1973). Also Steven Epstein, *Genoa and the Genoese, 958–1528* (Chapel Hill: University of North Carolina Press, 1996); Alan Rodgers, *The Industrial Geography of the Port of Genova* (Chicago: University of Chicago Press, 1960); *Early Modern Italy, 1550–1796*, ed. John A. Marino (Oxford: Oxford University Press, 2002); and Marino's *Pastoral Economics in the Kingdom of Naples* (Baltimore: Johns Hopkins University Press, 1988).

[5] Religions of the Western Mediterranean: Unity and Fragmentation in the Religious History of the Sea

In Braudel's ambitious and expansive work on the Mediterranean in the sixteenth century, one of the most important omissions, besides culture (though one may argue that religion is a category of culture), was his disregard for religion and spirituality, and their role in the history of the Mediterranean.[1] I do not refer here to religion only in its theological and doctrinal sense, but to religion as an important cultural and sociological aspect of the ebb and flow of Mediterranean people. Religion also had a powerful *influence* on architecture, patterns of daily life, and other social and cultural factors. The politics of the Mediterranean in the pre-modern era (and even today) were also shaped by religious beliefs. In subsequent chapters, we will glimpse at the journeys of Muslims in Christian Europe or the different trajectories that brought travelers from one shore of the Mediterranean to the other or on sojourns along the western Mediterranean coast. I am interested, in this chapter, in a different kind of motion. Although individuals' and communities' experiences of religion share many aspects, conversion from one religion to another – whether voluntary or coerced – will, for the sake of convenience, be explored in this chapter as two distinct categories, treating it first as a collective undertaking, then as an individual experience.

The Braudelian Mediterranean was an expansive one, reaching into Northern Europe through trade, waterways, and roads. In terms of religion, however, there came to be a sharp distinction between northern and Mediterranean Europe, as there was already between the southern shores of the Middle Sea (Muslim) and the northern shores (Christian). And this was not restricted to the difference between Protestants and Catholics after 1521, or Waldensians, Albigensians, and orthodox Christians in the late twelfth and early thirteenth centuries.

The Western Mediterranean and the World: 400 CE to the Present, First Edition. Teofilo F. Ruiz.
© 2018 John Wiley & Sons, Ltd. Published 2018 by John Wiley & Sons, Ltd.

Although this chapter aims principally to provide a narrative of the diversity of religious groups and of mass conversion in the western Mediterranean, there are some points – upon which I will elaborate later in this chapter – that should be made at the outset. I would argue that towards the later part of the eleventh century, coinciding with a series of liturgical and ecclesiastical reforms (the imposition of a uniform ritual for the mass, reforms resulting from the Investiture Controversy, and so forth), the western Mediterranean developed a kind of religiosity and spiritual sensibility distinct from that of Northern Europe. In many respects, this was not confined to Catholicism – the religiosity of the eastern Mediterranean was also quite different from that of the European western Mediterranean – but affected Judaism and Islam as well. Furthermore, these diverse vectors along which new forms of religiosity and spiritually developed were not necessarily the legacies of Late Antiquity and the early medieval period. They emerged partially from the contacts and interaction of the three Abrahamic religions along the shores of the western Mediterranean.

MASS CONVERSION

The troublesome issue of mass conversion of peoples along the Mediterranean shores from one religion to another is difficult to access. Whatever is meant by mass conversion – and there are many historians who dispute the extent of these conversions, the numbers involved, or the actual stages of conversion – the reality is that with the triumph of Christianity in the fourth and fifth centuries, and that of Islam (in North Africa, Sicily, and Iberia) in the seventh to tenth centuries, large numbers of people converted. What percentage of the population did so is impossible to say since we even have difficulties in estimating the actual population of North Africa and Iberia in this early period. However, it is safe to surmise that urban populations were both more easily reached than rural and isolated ones, either by conquerors or by missionaries, and more readily swayed by the obvious advantages (philosophical, political, social and/or economic) of conversion, or by the pressures created by conquest, and by rulers' and/or elites' violent interventions on behalf of their own religious views. These different trigger mechanisms – and there were others – often overlapped so that, as shall be seen, large-scale conversions were always complicated, driven by many different factors. Nowadays, it is difficult for many to accept that religiosity is malleable. That was certainly the case historically and, though not limited to the western Mediterranean, the West has known many such changes, ranging from the mass conversions detailed below to the Jewish conversions in late fourteenth-century Spain, to the Protestant Reformation, to the sweeping tide of secularism in Northern Europe.

Individual Conversions and Re-conversions in the Western Mediterranean

Some of these individuals who embraced more than one religion during their lifetime, or who returned to their ancestral belief during some period of their existence, are often lumped under the collective term of either conversos or renegades, depending, as shall be seen, on who is writing their histories. Obviously, there were many different elements at work in these individual conversions – not all renegades or converts were alike. Geographic location, chronology, and political context influenced the nature of conversion, or contemporary understanding of it. These issues will be examined in greater detail in the next chapter.

LARGE-SCALE CONVERSIONS IN THE WESTERN MEDITERRANEAN

The shifting religious identities of the people around the sea offer one way to look at the history of the western Mediterranean over the more than a millennium and half from the fall of Rome to the present. From Roman elite's belief systems (the so-called pagan or pre-Christian religions), to widespread local cults throughout the western Mediterranean world, to Judaism, Christianity, Islam (all three with their orthodox and heterodox variants), and modern secular attitudes, the populations along the shores of the Mediterranean have long understood the importance of preserving their religious identity, or, in some dramatic cases, of changing it when needed. As Jarbel Rodríguez, David Nirenberg, and others have pointed out for medieval Iberia, to give just one example here, the boundaries between religious communities were porous, and it was not always clear whether religious identity was fully fixed. The instability of group beliefs made people, caught in peculiar or changing social, economic, cultural, and political contexts, quite vulnerable to conversion. This chapter therefore explores the nature of these collective journeys from one set of beliefs to another in the western Mediterranean. It aims to introduce the reader to religion as a social, cultural, and political category that parallels the uncertain trajectory of western Mediterranean polities. This inquiry leaves aside the deeper history of personal or communal spirituality and religiosity to consider religion as yet another context for Mediterranean social life.

THE TRIUMPH OF CHRISTIANITY IN THE MEDITERRANEAN

In his impressive and enduring eighteenth-century classic work, *The History of the Decline and Fall of the Roman Empire* (1776–1788), the great Edward Gibbon famously blamed (or partly blamed) Christianity for the fall of Rome. Although Gibbon was not entirely right, his argument resonates with some elements of truth. Roman civilization around the western Mediterranean allowed for local practices and cults as long as taxes were paid and the official rites were conducted and followed. These practices included the cult of imperial authority represented in Dea Roma (the goddess Rome), and the deification of emperors (but only after their death). But Roman religious pluralism and outright insistence on the value of all systems of belief – as long as they did not challenge or threaten Roman hegemony – ran counter to the search for redemptive religions which shaped the life of people along the shores of the Mediterranean after the second century.

The establishment of an enlightened military dictatorship in the second century (for Gibbon, the happiest and most peaceful age ever experienced by mankind) was also marked by a turn away from civic engagement (the true religion of the Classical World) and philosophy to redemptive religions and mystical beliefs. Plotinus (ca. 204/205–270 CE), a Greek Neo-Platonist, was symptomatic of the shift, even among the literate elites, from philosophy to religion and to new yearnings for salvation and redemption. The deep social, economic, and political crisis that almost destroyed the empire in the third century opened the door for a bevy of religions that emphasized mysteries, redemption, and the afterlife. From a variegated menu of religions and beliefs, including the cult of Isis, Orphic mysteries, astrology, magic, Gnostic beliefs, the religion of Mithras, Manichaeism, and many others, a single religion was able to defeat the others and to gain imperial support. It was, of course, Christianity.[2] And Christianity was, most of all, a Mediterranean religion.

The history of the rise of Christianity is well known. Nonetheless, it is worth emphasizing that in the third and fourth centuries, the Mediterranean was a cauldron where many different religious forms competed for new members and often engaged in active conflict with the ancient religions of Rome and local cults around the Mediterranean. The triumph of Christianity was a social and political one. Constantine's Edict of Milan in 313, granting Christians the right to worship freely, and Theodosius's formal adoption of Christianity as the official religion of the empire (395 CE), marked the beginning of Christianity's campaign to ferret out older forms of religion or to combat its competitors.[3]

By the fifth century and the beginning of our story, Christianity was, at least momentarily, the religion of most of the people living on the lands once held by Rome along the shores of the western Mediterranean. This did not mean at all that Christianity was faithfully observed throughout the land. Indeed, the survival of ancient practices in the countryside – areas that had, in fact, resisted Roman civilization over the centuries – remained a reality. The western Mediterranean was Christian, but that Christianity was, at best, a slight varnish, covering old beliefs. It barely registered in such areas where the power of bishops did not reach, or where it did so only faintly. Attempts to Christianize mountain areas of the Mediterranean did not begin in earnest until the end of the Middle Ages and the early modern period, and, in some areas, such as that of Friuli (studied by Carlo Ginzburg), remnants of pre-Christian agricultural cults remained quite vigorous until they were extinguished by inquisitorial activity in the sixteenth century.[4]

This incomplete or partial Christianization of the western Mediterranean – a Christianization that was often limited to urban areas – helps explain, to a large extent, the religious fluidity of the region. Moreover, the triumph of Christianity in Rome and the emergence of the Church, first as a parallel center of power and then as the heir to Roman administrative practices in the West (with the long temporal shift of power within the empire from Rome and Milan to

Constantinople and Alexandria, plus the Germanic settlements in the western parts of the empire), were continuously challenged by the rise of heterodox beliefs and dissent from within.

As the Church declared some of the central tenets of the faith to be dogmas (that is, compulsory for believers) – the dual nature of Jesus as God and man, the Trinity, the Petrine commission (claiming that the bishop of Rome was the direct descendant of Saint Peter, and other doctrinal statements) – numerous groups claimed views that would be declared heterodox. They were branded as heretics and expelled from the church. The list of these heresies is long indeed and to explicate what each of them meant or how they challenged the church would take us far away from the focus of this chapter. A list of them, including Arianism, Pelagianism, Donatism, and others, provides a sense of how Christianity was not static or truly widespread, but a religion very much under construction. Who was orthodox and who was heterodox or heretical came in the end to depend on questions of power, as when Constantine sided with Athanasius against Arius during the early fourth-century controversy over the nature of the Trinity.

To complicate matters further, as the Germans broke into the western regions of the empire – Vandals in Africa, Visigoths in Spain, Ostrogoths and Lombards in Italy – they brought with them Arian beliefs that delayed or prevented their integration into orthodox Christian society. The example of Visigothic Spain illustrates the difficulties faced by a small group of invaders holding Arian beliefs (beliefs considered heretical by the western Church, such as that the different members of the Trinity were not co-equal) against a well-organized Church with an almost unassailable monopoly of culture and the written word. Conversion to the orthodox position, though it took more than a century, became a desirable alternative for the Visigothic kings of Spain in the late sixth century. Conversion allowed the Visigothic rulers to gain the powerful support of the Iberian Church in buttressing their claims to rulership. Similar developments would also be the case with most Germanic invaders throughout most of the western Mediterranean.

Following the pattern established in other chapters in this book, that is, to see the history of the western Mediterranean as a transition from unity to fragmentation and back to some fashion of unity, here we may wish to consider the Ancient Roman Mediterranean between the third and sixth centuries as a world in which regional cults and forms of worship survived under Rome's pluralistic and encompassing religious policies. Imperial Rome seldom took harsh measures against religious diversity – unless religions, such as Judaism and Christianity, made claims, preposterous in Roman eyes, to be the only acceptable form of belief or refused to participate in Roman cults that reaffirmed imperial authority and the unity of the empire. And even then, the Romans were willing to make accommodation, as they did with the Jews, as long as they paid the appropriate taxes. This policy lasted until in the first century CE, when Roman armies led by Titus destroyed the Jew's religious and ritual center, Jerusalem, and dispersed the Jewish population throughout the empire. Resistance to Roman rule, both on religious and political grounds, had become intolerable to the imperial authorities. The destruction of Jerusalem also coincided with persecution of the new Christian sect, a persecution that had begun as early as Nero's imperial rule.

Nonetheless, by the sixth century, even if only in theory, Christianity had become the sole religion of the western Mediterranean basin. The very essence of Christianity rested, as the great von Harnack noted more than a century ago, in its spirited struggle against other religions that the Church thought prone to idolatry, against polytheism, or against heterodox forms within Christianity itself. There were some exceptions to the rule. Jews, because of the deep connection between Judaism and Christianity and because of beliefs that Jews must be witnesses to the second coming of Jesus, were not forcefully converted or eliminated. This did not, of course, preclude violence against, or marginalization of, Jews within Christian society. The polemical literature shows the extent to which Jews were barely tolerated. The western Mediterranean had become a Christian lake, but there were exceptions: pockets of Jews and Jewish religious practices endured and some pre-Christian religious rituals, or even, in some cases, pre-historical cults, survived. Because of their long experience of living in a diaspora, Jews in the fifth, sixth, and seventh centuries remained important players in economic exchanges. As mostly (but not solely) urban dwellers, they represented an element of plurality in a solid Christian world. Yet, as indicated earlier, their position was always vulnerable to attack by the dominant Christian majority.

By the late seventh century, the Visigoths had already been orthodox Christians (what today we may call Catholics) for almost 100 years. Having abandoned their Arian beliefs, the Visigothic Church councils enacted harsh anti-Jewish edicts. These laws sought to restrict Jewish mobility and contacts with Christians. On the eve of the Muslim conquest in 711, the edicts asked for either conversion or expulsion. While in Byzantine North Africa, in Frankish southern France, or in Lombard or Byzantine Italy anti-Jewish measures were not as punitive as those of the Visigoths, Jews lived, nonetheless, under restrictions. In Spain, North Africa, and later on in Sicily, however, the conditions under which they toiled were dramatically transformed by the Muslim conquests of the seventh, eighth, and ninth centuries. Although they were not persecuted elsewhere to the same extent as in Visigothic Spain, the position of Jews, a truly Mediterranean population if there ever was one, remained precarious in this period and afterwards.

THE WESTERN MEDITERRANEAN: A MUSLIM LAKE

We often take for granted the ease with which Islam swept most of the known world; yet, it is still difficult to grasp the reasons for Islam's extensive geographical reach and enduring success. The foundations laid in North Africa and elsewhere beyond the western Mediterranean in the seventh century still endure. That such a change took place, and that the process of acculturation and adaptation to Islam was essentially so swift (or appears so swift in hindsight), is still an elusive idea to grasp. From its humble tribal beginnings in Arabia in the early seventh century, Islam exploded outward after the death of the Prophet Muhammad (632) and conquered most of the known world. Always a minority among the conquered people, the Arabs fostered a culture in which a religion, Islam, and a language, Arabic (a language necessary to read or chant the *Qur'an*), served as the glue that shaped diverse peoples, cultures, and languages into a single cultural unit. Wherever they went in the land(s) of Islam, Dar al-Islam, Muslims found themselves in a fully recognizable world. This is why, as we shall see in a subsequent chapter, al-Idrīsī or Ibn Battūta could travel as far and wide as they did and still feel at home.

By the middle of the seventh century, after the successful conquests of Palestine, Syria, and Egypt, the Muslims – whose armies combined Arabs with many other different ethnic groups – advanced into North Africa, swiftly ending the Byzantines' brief rule in the region. By 711, they had crushed the Visigothic Empire and established Muslim rule over most of what we know today as Spain – which then they held, at least partially, until 1492. The Balearic islands, Sicily, and a series of outposts in southern France and on the western shore of Italy also fell to Muslim armies, either in the sweep of conquests in the seventh century or from raiding parties from North Africa in the eighth and ninth centuries – groups known in western history as the Saracens (see Chapter 3).

CONVERSION AND FURTHER ISLAMIC INCURSIONS INTO WESTERN EUROPE

Two important points are worth reiterating. Although we do not know all the details of this process, the local populations in North Africa and most of Iberia swiftly converted to Islam. The conquering Arabs and other Muslim groups were but a very small minority among the overwhelming numbers of the conquered. How can we explain such effective conversion efforts? Although each region experienced its own rate of conversion, and the context determined the success of, or resistance to, conversion, one could propose some explanations of why this occurred. Most of these explanations are well known or have been discussed by previous historians, but they still do not fully explain Islam's remarkable success.

First and foremost, as noted earlier, the level of Christianization in North Africa and Iberia was still incomplete. In these two areas of the Western Mediterranean, Christianity had not had the early successes that it had experienced in the lands of the Eastern Mediterranean.

If the life of Saint Augustine of Hippo, as brilliantly depicted by Peter Brown in his biography of the Christian bishop or in Augustine's own *Confessions*, is any indication, Christianity faced a mighty struggle for hegemony among the many competing religions, cults, and philosophies vying for late Romans' minds and souls. Spain was not much different.[5] Moreover, both North Africa and Iberia experienced Germanic invaders – Vandals and Visigoths, respectively – who, although nominally Christians, were essentially hostile to the established Church. In the case of the Visigoths, they did not relinquish their Arian beliefs until the end of the sixth century. In the case of the Vandals, they were defeated by the Byzantine Reconquest in the 530s before they had embraced orthodoxy, and, in terms of religious policies, the Byzantines held at best a tenuous hold on the region.

With those who did not share a religious tradition with Islam, the Muslims were fairly uncompromising. Conversion or reprisals were the only options for those not belonging to the Abrahamic faith(s). But why, one may ask, did Christians and also Jews, who as the People of the Book – the *dhimmis* – were given special privileges and allowed to retain their religion from the very early history of Islam, convert to Islam in substantial numbers? In spite of the difficulties in calculating rates of conversion, that seems to have been the case in seventh- and eighth-century North Africa and al-Andalus. Obviously, the combination of an underdeveloped Christianity with the clear material advantages of conversion to Islam triggered seismic waves throughout the western Mediterranean. These conversions, though perhaps lukewarm at the beginning, endured through the centuries and proved to be extremely resilient to Christian pressures in the later Middle Ages to force Muslims and Jews (by then Islam was historic too) to convert to Christianity. The example of the Berbers in North Africa is a telling one: whether non-Christians or barely Christians in the seventh century, they became some of the most fundamentalist and committed Muslims in the West. A commonplace, one that has some solid foundation in fact, is that conversions to Islam have occurred frequently, whereas conversions from Islam to other religions were rare. The historical reality of religious affiliations and the flow between religions in the western Mediterranean attest to that.

Once converted, North Africa remained, in spite of over a century of colonial occupation by Christian European nations, solidly Muslim to the present day. And North African Muslim polities served as the launching pads for the conversion of Central and sub-Saharan Africa in the Early Middle Ages. In Iberia, the story is not too different. Once converted, the inhabitants of al-Andalus remained faithful to Islam until their expulsion from Iberia in the early decades of the seventeenth century. They did so at the cost of their freedom and even their lives during the so-called Christian Reconquest and in a period of Christian hegemony after 1212. In fact, as I have already noted in an earlier chapter, in an even hopelessly romantic gesture, a few Christians or former Christians in western Andalusia today argue that they descend from the Muslims who lived in the area before the mid-thirteenth-century Christian conquest. This has led to some conversions to Islam, which, together with the migration of North Africans to the region, signals a tentative re-igniting of Islam in southern Spain. This claim to a historical descent from previous Muslim inhabitants in al-Andalus is historically improbable, since all the Muslims were expelled from the region after the 1264 Mudejar rebellion. It is nonetheless symptomatic of the manner in which religious identity follows political ideas and autonomous sentiments. Similarly, the many displays that one can see as one travels through the area of the Languedoc in France, proclaiming the region as the "Land of the Cathars," have more to do with modern regional sentiment and with attracting tourists than with the history of the medieval heretics now known by that name (see below).

Under no circumstances should we see the substantial conversions to Islam as marking a uniform shift in religious sensibility. Although Islam, unlike Christianity, had no mechanism for centralized definition of doctrine after the manner of Rome, variation in belief and practice was a frequent source of division. This was certainly the case in North Africa. Beyond the classical split between Sunni and Shi'a, which did not have as much of an enduring impact in the Muslim regions of the western Mediterranean as it does to this day in the Middle East, internal differences on questions of succession to the Prophet, often articulated in political struggle and rivalry, were as constant in Islam as heterodox–orthdox conflicts were in Christianity. The litany of complaints about internal divisions among Muslims and the factionalism that existed in Palestine – complaints voiced by Muslim chronicles around the time of the First Crusade and beyond – had clear parallels in the western Mediterranean. The very idea of jihad required an inner jihad or a process of re-conversion to a purer form of Islam before embarking on campaigns against the infidel.

These internal conflicts and regional differences, resulting from peculiar social and political contexts, created numerous varieties of Islam in the West, even though there was agreement on the basic tenets of the religion. The Almoravids in eleventh-century North Africa, for example – among the most fundamentalist groups found among the Berber and other peoples of the Atlas Mountains – were probably far more observant than Andalusi Muslims. So were the Almohads in the late twelfth and early thirteenth century. Painting this section with broad brush strokes, one could argue that North African Muslims, on the whole, practiced their faith more strictly than their Iberian counterparts. And then there was, and is still, the enduring presence of Sufi saints and mystics among the mountain and desert people. Sufism, a mystical form of Islamic belief, prospered in North Africa, as it did to a lesser extent in other regions of Dar al-Islam, and deeply influenced, as Cynthia Robinson has argued in a recent book, the textual and iconographic representations of Jesus's passion and of the Virgin in late medieval Castile.[6]

Christians and Jews were not exempted from such internal struggles, as they also sought to define their faith. Western Mediterranean Christians underwent significant torment as they sought to establish what orthodoxy was in the face of proliferating heterodox practices and beliefs. As noted above, the formal acceptance of Christianity in the Late Antique world served to bolster it as the religion of a vanishing Roman Empire. This, in turn, led to numberless challenges to orthodoxy and the slow formulation of Church dogma. The nature of early medieval Christian society (widely dispersed over a great geographical distance, with difficult communications, and experiencing a decline in learning), however, precluded the development of large-scale heretical movements. In the twelfth and early thirteenth century, however, dissent from Catholic teaching, increasingly identified as heresy, became widespread among Christians living on the shores of the western Mediterranean, fostered by the shift in cultural sensibilities and the emergence of urban civilization, including mercantile activities, trade, the rise of the bourgeoisies, and other factors. From the middle of the twelfth century, churchmen attributed it to the propagation of heretical teachings by organized sects, especially the Albigensians, anathematized by the Third Lateran Council in 1179. Historians disagree as to whether, or how far, they were right.

THE SOUNDS OF RELIGION IN THE WESTERN MEDITERRANEAN

Before proceeding to a brief exploration of heterodox beliefs on the northern shores of the western Mediterranean, it may be useful to glance briefly at the ways in which religious sensibilities and allegiances to one faith were, and are, conveyed. Although less so in most European Mediterranean cities today than in their North African counterparts, sounds and images remain powerful symbols of religion and religiosity in the everyday life of most people. Having spent a few days in Istanbul in September of 2014, a paradigmatic Mediterranean city (even if not in the western Mediterranean), I was struck, while staying across the street from Hagia Sofia, by the calls to prayer which, five times a day, echoing from minaret to minaret throughout the city, provided a vivid testimony to the enduring and, in some cases, alluring power of religion. Ringing bells would be the equivalent in Christian cities.

By ringing bells, I do not mean those tolling bells that mark the passing of hours, but bells, as was the case in the Christian western Mediterranean, that reminded the faithful of the canonical hours or, as was the case throughout the Catholic world before the Vatican Council (1960s) changes, of the moment when the host underwent its transformation into the Body of Christ. In some of those medieval and modern towns that serve as sites of encounter for different religions – Palermo, Marseille, Seville, Tunis, and others – the call of the muezzin and the ringing of church bells formed a musical point and counterpoint to the shared spaces inhabited by Christians and Muslims. The call to prayer in Istanbul, albeit ignored by most of the inhabitants of that great city, was for me both moving and aesthetically pleasing, even though I follow no religion. So are the tolling bells that commemorate important moments in the liturgical cycle of the day and the year.

Equally, visual clues displayed in garments or in the types of clothing worn signified one's adherence to a faith. They represented a cultural and religious display of one's religiosity. In the late medieval West, Jews and Muslims were forced to dress or wear their hair in prescribed ways as an expeditious manner of establishing their identities in the streets and market places of Christian-dominated areas. That was the case in Castile from the 1250s onwards. That was the case elsewhere as well. Today, no legislation is needed for those observing any of the three Mediterranean religions. They naturally gravitate to sartorial codes deeply imbedded in their religious traditions: the veil, the burka, the wig, the black frocks of Orthodox Jewish men, and proper attire for Sunday mass. Walking in Marseille, French colonial Tunis, or any other large western Mediterranean port, one may discern quite easily the level of religiosity by the clothing, the covering of the hair, and other manifestations of religiosity inscribed in the body of the believer by restrictive enactments, tradition, and piety. But it is time now to return to those who challenged orthodoxy in the eleventh and twelfth centuries.

WALDENSIANS AND ALBIGENSIANS

As noted earlier, Christianity in the West developed by a system of trial and error. Dissenting ideas sometimes triumphed; other times they were branded heterodox, condemned by the official Church, and followers of these doctrinal departures from what had been branded orthodox persecuted. Waldensians was the name given to the followers of Peter Waldo (Valdez or Valdes). Followers of Waldensian beliefs (who sometimes may have joined Protestant Churches in the early modern period) still survive in areas of northern Italy and Switzerland. Peter was a layman with a connection to the cathedral chapter of Lyon in the 1170s. Moved by a desire for ecclesiastical reform and by the new spiritual needs emerging in the twelfth century from the renewal of urban life and the transformation of the medieval economy, he gave up his possessions and engaged in preaching absolute poverty to the laity. Motivated by their rejection of material goods and wealth and by their general enmity against Church authority and ecclesiastical claims that priests were the sole intermediaries between the faithful and Christ, the Waldensians had a signal impact on the religious culture of the Christian shores of the western Mediterranean. Another example of these shifts in spirituality may be Saint Francis of Assisi, who emerged from the same spiritual and social context as the Waldensians. But although Francis preached doctrines not too different from the Waldensian message, the insistence of the latter on translating the scriptures into the vernacular and on lay preaching, and their disregard of ecclesiastical authority, led them into serious difficulties with the Church and lay rulers. It was because Peter refused to make his preaching mission subject to episcopal permission, not through any doctrinal deviation, that he and his followers were excluded from the Church. The Church responded in kind to Waldensian attacks on its wealth, mobilizing its considerable resources in condemning Waldensian practices and beliefs as well as other heterodox practices in 1215 and afterwards, while seeking to eradicate what was considered to be a heresy. Francis, who never challenged the authority of the Church, became a saint. The Waldensians, who did, ended up as heretics and condemned to death by fire.[7]

Heresy, deeply grounded in a series of overlapping contexts, including the ecclesiastical reforms of the eleventh century and their peculiar social and political circumstances, may or may not have been exceptionally pervasive in the territory between the Rhône and Garonne rivers now known as the Languedoc. Certainly, rumors of it were exploited by those, led successively by the kings of England, of Aragon, and of France, who hoped to take advantage of the political fragmentation of the region. By the beginning of the thirteenth century their propagandists and clerical observers from outside the region had convinced themselves that these heretics believed in two gods and belonged to a

Europe-wide heretical movement amounting to an alternative church. Until recently, most historians believed it too, and made of it the "Cathars" who feature so prominently in modern images of the Languedoc, or Occitania, and its tourist industry. In fact, the word was never used there in the Middle Ages. Its most prominent heretics were known in the region as "good men" or simply as "heretics" and by outsiders as Albigensians. How far the account of their beliefs and organization put together by inquisitors after the Albigensian Crusade and the effective subordination of the region to the French monarchy from 1229 can be projected back into the twelfth century remains contentious.

Nonetheless, when Innocent III preached a crusade against the Count of Toulouse as a protector of the Albigensians in 1209, he unleashed a wave of violence against these so-called heretics that was unprecedented in the history of the Church and its dealings with heterodoxy. Northern French warriors invaded the South (what is today southern or Mediterranean France) with the intention of ferreting out religious dissent. Philip Augustus, in fact, did not initially approve the crusade, precisely because he saw it as outside interference with his man, Raymond of Toulouse. He permitted his son, Louis (later Louis VIII), to take on the leadership only in 1219 after the death of Simon de Montfort, the earlier leader of the Albigensian Crusade. Southerners, some Catholics and Albigensians alike, resisted what they correctly saw as an infringement of their regional rights and autonomy. At the battle of Muret in 2013, the northern armies defeated a coalition made up of Catholics from the Languedoc and the Crown of Aragon, as well as Albigensians. In just another sign that politics, and not religion, had a great deal to do with this affair, Peter the Catholic, king of the Crown of Aragon – so named by the Pope after his contribution to the defeat of the Almohads at Las Navas de Tolosa (1212) – died at Muret, in principle defending the Albigensians but also the Crown of Aragon's geopolitical interests in the region. Orthodoxy and heterodoxy were thus imbedded in the wider political life of the entire western Mediterranean.

Neither the savagery of the warfare which continued until 1229, nor the mass slaughter and burnings which accompanied it from the sack of Beziers in 1209 onwards extinguished the heresy: on the contrary, it seems that it was resistance, not emissaries from other lands, that turned heresy into an organized movement. Something more was needed to destroy dissent. From 1233, inquisitorial tribunals, acting directly on papal authority, were set in place throughout most of Occitania, as they already had been in Lombardy. Neither heresy nor persecution were original to the Languedoc. Christianity in general, and the Christian Church in particular, had a long history of often dealing with heterodox movements in harsh fashion. The Inquisition itself also derived from ancient Roman practices of questioning. Nonetheless, unlike previous ways of dealing with dissent – through preaching and conversion – the Inquisition made harsher practices of inquiry (thus the name taken from the Latin, *inquisitio*) and punishment (burning at the stake, torture) the norm.

The use of the *inquisitio* as a legal procedure, both by secular and by ecclesiastical authorities, influenced, according to R.I. Moore and others, the emergence of new patterns of persecution in the Christian West, though one must tread carefully through discussions of heresy, heretical movements, or persecution since they have a long ancestry in western history. As Moore argues in a recent book, and as others have noted, heresy is a malleable category, difficult to pin down, and as much a production of power than of real religious definitions of orthodoxy and heterodoxy. Thus, throughout this and other discussions of religious conflict, one must never neglect the role of political power in these affairs. Religious unorthodoxy was never either a necessary or a sufficient condition for a heresy accusation. Moore has pointed out that the use of *inquisitio* – "a Roman law technique which probably never disappeared entirely – was extended enthusiastically by secular government, notably that of Henry II from the 1160s; bishops are told to use it annually to root out heresy by *ad abolendam* (1184); the innovation in 1233 (but previously, e.g. with Conrad of Marburg in the Rhineland) was over-riding the bishops; what really made it bite, and attract support from lay nobles, etc. was not so much the burnings (actually rather rare once the crusade was over, apart from a spasm in the early 1230s) or other punishments less barbarous than those routinely used by secular rulers, as the confiscation and dis-inheritance of condemned heretics, which Innocent III went in for in a big way to counter communal opposition in the papal states." Moore's argument, that the *inquisitio* was congenial to the persecution of real or imagined minorities because it enabled authorities to go looking for what they thought might be there instead of waiting for someone to complain, perfectly describes the tumoltous events that swept through the Languedoc in the late eleventh and twelfth century.[8]

Regardless of the methodological complications that the term *heresy* carries with it, the Christian western Mediterranean would not witness large-scale heretical movements again. Unless one considers the conversos (Jews converted to Christianity) and Moriscos (Muslims normally converted to Christianity) persecuted wholesale by the Spanish Inquisition (a very different kind of inquisition from the one founded in Southern France in the 1230s) from roughly 1478 to the early seventeenth century as heretical movements (which I do not), there were no widespread heresies along the northern shores of the sea. Throughout the Middle Ages, there was, especially in Calabria and southern Italy, religious and social unrest. This was often the result of Fraticelli (followers of Saint Francis's radical views on poverty) preaching. One also finds remnants of Albigensian and Waldensians beliefs in southern France, northern Italy, and Catalonia. Protestantism made few inroads into western Mediterranean lands in the early modern period, though Protestants (Huguenots in France) were active in the Languedoc, the same area where Waldensian and Albigensian beliefs had prospered three centuries earlier. The Inquisition (whether in its Spanish or papal version) dealt harshly with all these forms of dissent. By the end of the Middle Ages and the early modern period, the most dangerous form of heterodoxy was witchcraft. Although the witch craze that swept most of Europe was not as evident in Mediterranean lands, the rise of the persecution of witches changed the discourse, to a certain extent, from questions of doctrines to questions of practice.

ORTHODOXY AND HETERODOXY IN MEDIEVAL ISLAM AND JUDAISM

In Christine Caldwell Ames's recent book, *Medieval Heresies: Christianity, Judaism, and Islam*, the author places the three great religions of the Book into a comparative framework that explores the links (and differences) in the manner in which the western Mediterranean's diverse religious groups dealt (and still deal) with heterodox beliefs, practices, and dissent.[9] As David Nirenberg has pointed out recently, very often religions (certainly in Iberia) were projects in construction, borrowing liberally from each other as each religion sought to define orthodoxy and heterodoxy. By way of introduction, this is to say that both Islam and Judaism also dealt with dissenting voices and sought to extinguish what was perceived or defined as heterodox. In Islam, departure from orthodoxy (or holding of beliefs that were considered unorthodox) could be dealt with harshly. In Judaism, a religion which throughout most of the period under discussion lacked a "state," Jewish community leaders often sought recourse to Christian or Islamic rulers to punish or exile heretics and dissenters in their midst.

Islam

In Islam, innovation was the locomotive of heretical fears. Whether among the Sunni or the Shi'a, the idea of departure from the teachings of the *Qur'an* or the hadith (collected sayings of Muhammad or accounts of the Prophet's life, and, after the *Qur'an*, the most important source of authority in Islam) meant a break away from the Prophet's message. In a religion without the central authority of something like the papacy in western Christianity, and extending over vast portions of the known world, Islam was often subtly transformed by local practices and devotions, without radically departing from the faith's main tenets, that is, the Muslims' five obligations of prayer, fasting, articles of faith, charity, and pilgrimage. Scholars and philosophers, of course, also argued in favor of some innovations (medicine, for example, or the celebrations in honor of Muhammad's birthday). In that sense, taking into account the breach between Sunni and Shi'a, Islam never faced anything like the Protestant Reformation that challenged the very doctrinal basis of what became Catholic Christianity. A different school of law provided guidance on the observance of Sharia law (religious law that regulated the life of Muslims).

The existence of diverse interpretations of Sharia law and schools of thought as to the correct form of worship within Islam (even if their differences in interpretation and the latitude for innovation was often limited) alerts us to the variety of opinions on doctrinal matters in medieval and later Islam. The Sunni, certainly the dominant group in the areas of the western Mediterranean covered by this book, had several carefully delineated legal approaches to Islam. There were four main schools of legal interpretation, Maliki, Hanafi, Shafi'i, and Hanbali, and a less influential school, Zāhirī. The Shi'a had three legal schools for the interpretation of Islamic law: Ja'fari, Zaydi, and Ismaili. For our purposes, the Maliki School dominated the legal interpretations of Islam in North Africa, sub-Saharan Africa, Islamic Spain, and Sicily, providing guidelines for right conduct and lines of authority. This is not to say that there were not breaches and dissent from established orthodoxy. There were. The Almoravids and Almohads, with their fundamental beliefs and martial prowess, sometime came close to what in western terms may be branded as heresy.

The Maliki School. Dating back to the work of the Maliki School founder, Malik ibn Anas, in the eighth century, the Maliki School emphasized a clear line of authority in the settlement of doctrinal and Sharia law interpretation, beginning with the *Qur'an* and followed by accepted hadiths and other sources of authority in descending order. Maliki's jurisprudence was concerned with questions of apostasy (this applied to converts, unbelief, and living under Christian rule – several North African Maliki fatwas condemned Muslims in Christian Spain), blasphemy, adultery, homosexuality (the latter two both punished by stoning), and other transgressions. All these refer to individual acts by impious Muslims. What about communal forms of dissent?

As noted earlier, the mechanisms for branding a set of beliefs as heretical were not as centralized as they were in Christian society. The fracture lines were not caused by the tension between acceptance and rejection of dogma. Rather, they arose in response to questions of leadership, both political and religious, within the community of Islam. If we are to mention any widespread departure from established Islamic beliefs beyond the great divide on questions of the Prophet's succession (Sunni and Shi'a), the Kharijites are an early example. The Kharijites, in extreme form, argued for the validity of violent means against those practicing less strict or lax forms of Islam. Violence against the relatives of those departing from a high form of orthodoxy was also condoned. As is obvious from recent events, forms of the Kharijite "heresy" are still present in modern-day Islam. Two other doctrinal points (the closest thing to dogma in Islam) identified beliefs universally condemned as "heretical." The first was the denial of the unity of God or absolute monotheism. The second was the belief in further prophetic revelations after Muhammad. Both of these points led to endless conflicts with Christians and, to a lesser extent, with Jews. The Trinity was often seen as a form of polytheism, while the divinity of Jesus (who was seen as a prophet in Islam) was also a stumbling block to both Jews and Muslims. In Islam, the figure of the Mahdi, with the millennial and messianic expectations associated with the term, has been (and remains) closely associated with heterodoxy.[10]

Heresy and Dissent in Judaism

Also without a real center or doctrinal unit (levels of orthodoxy and praxis varied depending on the chronological period and on the location), heresy in Judaism depended on who condemned and who was condemned. To a large extent, this depended on numerous factors, but charges of heresy, to be really effective, had to count on the support or tacit agreement of the ruler or political entity under which jurisdiction Jews lived. Like Muslims and Christians, their faith was not monolithic. And as already noted, unlike Christians, Jews lacked the central authority to impose one system of belief over all Jews. While sharing rituals and a broad understanding of their religiosity, local variations in practice made the Jewish religion a somewhat heterogeneous one, with a certain latitude in practices tolerated without the possibility of necessarily falling into what Christians or Muslims may have considered heresy or dissent. Esoteric medieval Kabbalah mysticism – emerging, according to Gershom Scholem, in late thirteenth-century Castile – was practiced only by a handful of dedicated religious figures, though Kabbalistic mystical philosophy had a Christian counterpart and influenced Renaissance humanists such as Pico della Mirandola. But Kabbalah was open only to the very erudite and pious few, and found, as for example in the polemical works of Leo de Modena in early modern Venice, a good number of opponents. What about the general Jewish population? Massive conversion of Spanish Jews to Christianity supports the contention that group conversion, as a regular pattern of religious practice, was part and parcel of western Mediterranean religious culture from Late Antiquity onwards. In Iberia, massive conversions of Jews occurred in 1391 and after the 1413–1414 Disputation of Tortosa. While it is impossible to determine the numerical extent of those who converted in the late fourteenth and early fifteenth century, historians have argued that perhaps as many as 60% of the Jewish population of Spain (Castile and the Crown of Aragon) converted to Christianity. Whatever the precise number of conversos was in reality, it was substantial and indeed unprecedented in the long history of the persecution of Jews in the West. A large number of conversions also took place in 1492, when, according to Henry Kamen, almost half of the Jews left in the peninsula converted to Christianity rather than choose exile from Spain.

These conversions, some forced, some voluntary, have been described by Benzion Netanyahu as a turning away from Judaism under the influence of secular learning, mostly that of Aristotle and Averroes. Recent historians, most notably Gretchen Starr-LeBeau, have shown the substantial social intercourse and commercial dealings between recent conversos and Jews. The reality is that it is very difficult to determine the "true" religious affiliation of many of the conversos. Sometimes they themselves lived in a liminal world between two religious sets of beliefs and practices. A period of time in which the formerly held religion and the newly adopted one lived in an uneasy relationship may, I think, have been a pattern widespread throughout the western Mediterranean and wherever large group conversions took place.

Of course, there were many, whether in late fourteenth-century Spain or, in an earlier case, in eighth-century Iberia, who converted even without pressure and fervently embraced their new religion. This was the case of the very learned and pious rabbi of Burgos, Solomon (Selomah) ha-Levi, who converted in 1390 (before the violent attacks on Jewish communities through Spain), went to Paris, where he received a degree in theology, had a short sojourn at the papal court in Avignon, was appointed bishop of Cartagena, eventually returned to Burgos, and was elected bishop of the city, one of the most desirable ecclesiastical appointments in the peninsula (see Chapter 6). These narratives of conversion were not exceptional, but easily found in the historiography on the subject. Recently, Paola Tartakoff and Ryan Szpiech have shown, in two superb monographs, the movement from one religion to another (and not just to from Judaism and Islam to Christianity but in the other direction as well) as a reality of religious life in Iberia and elsewhere. And these conversions were not always associated with the critical periods around 1390 or 1412.[11]

When 1492 and the Edict of Expulsion came, some refused to convert, such as Isaac Abravanel, one of the Catholic Monarchs' high officials, who chose exile instead. His patron and old friend Abraham Seneor (or Senior) accepted baptism rather than exile. It was not always clear how resilient religious convictions were or how individuals and families, especially those of very high status in the Jewish community, negotiated the transition from one religion to another. By the sixteenth and seventeenth centuries, Jewish converts were fairly assimilated into Spanish society. This became a reality, in spite of decrees of purity of blood and continuous inquisitorial monitoring (though much lessened after 1525) of converso activity.

Muslims were also given the choice of conversion or exile in the early sixteenth century, and although, as Ana Echevarria has shown, a few Muslims (above all a few high-born Muslims remaining in the Granada area) embraced Christianity, the immense majority at the lower levels of Spanish society converted only nominally while remaining faithful to their ancestral language (Arabic), diet, dress, and Islamic practices. They rose up in arms in bloody insurrections in the Alpujarra Mountains (1499, 1568), were often armed to the teeth, and resisted assimilation by all possible means until their general expulsion from Spain in the early seventeenth century. While Moriscos were often considered heretics and drew increased attention from the Inquisition by the mid-sixteenth century, they were certainly not always seen as such, even if nominally converted to Christianity, by their Muslim brethren across the Mediterranean.

MEDITERRANEAN RELIGIOUS PRACTICES REVISITED

Here I wish to return briefly to some of the issues raised earlier in the chapter about the Mediterranean character of religious change and why the Middle Sea as a whole developed religious practices and sensibilities that differed greatly from those of Northern Europe. Up to 1080, Christians in what is today Spain followed liturgical forms – the so-called Mozarabic rite – that were sharply different from the Cluniac or Roman ritual prevalent throughout most of Northern Europe. Most of Christian Spain celebrated the liturgy of the mass in a fashion that borrowed from the earlier Visigothic Church, Byzantine influences, and adaptations from Islamic practices. Toledo was the epicenter for the use of the Mozarabic rite and favored by the Mozarabs (Christians who had adopted Muslim patronymics, a language – Mozarab – that was written in Arabic script, and Muslim culture) throughout al-Andalus (or southern Spain). It was only at the Council of Burgos in 1080 (five years before the taking of Toledo by Christian forces) that the Roman ritual was imposed in Castile and throughout Iberia, but not without some stiff resistance from those who followed the Mozarabic tradition, including the Cid, who fought as a champion in defense of the Mozarabic ritual in an ordeal by combat between the two liturgies. The Spanish calendar itself was a marker of difference and of distinct religious sensibilities between Iberia and the rest of Western Europe. Until the fourteenth century, Castilians, Aragonese, and others in the peninsula followed a calendrical pattern that was 38 years ahead of the calendar in the rest of Europe. That meant that when it was 1338 in Spain, it was only 1300 in the rest of Europe, with all the consequences for liturgical celebrations and the like.[12]

It is good to remember that the revival or renaissance of the twelfth century – a revival as much religious as it was cultural – like the monastic reforming movements of the tenth and eleventh centuries stemming from Cluny in Burgundy, Gorze in the Rhineland, Camaldoli in Tuscany, or the reform of the papacy itself, had northern origins before the renewed papacy imposed these new practices on Mediterranean lands. Thus, military invasions – such as the Albigensian Crusade – had their earlier religious and cultural counterparts. The religious experiences of the Mediterranean, certainly those related to Christianity in the Middle Ages and during the Reformation period, were often forged in opposition to, or as an adaptation of, Northern European-imposed religious ideals. It may also be proper to emphasize that while the Sunni/Shi'a divide within Islam led also to a great deal of violence and bloodshed, the nature and intensity of religious violence was much less than that generated by the Christian drive for religious unity in Mediterranean Europe (and in the North as well). Shi'a and Sunni may suspect each other, may, at certain times, persecute and kill each other, but there were no theatrical burnings at the stake such as the drive for orthodoxy produced in late medieval and early modern Europe.

Also, as noted earlier, burned at the stake in great numbers in the early modern period were those accused of witchcraft. From the late fifteenth century to the second half of the sixteenth century, perhaps as many as 80,000–100,000 people, mostly elderly women, were burned at the stake or hanged by the neck, accused of worshiping the devil and engaging in a vast conspiracy against Christianity and the state. Here again, the sharp divide between northern and Mediterranean Europe is evident. The geography of early modern witchcraft or witch persecution shows us that there was little systematic persecution of witches in Iberia, southern Italy, or even Mediterranean France, while in the North, especially in Germany, England, and Scandinavia, the persecution and execution of witches rose to extraordinary levels.[13] Similar to the disputes in Iberia over the implementation of the Roman or Cluniac ritual throughout the peninsula, the question of the persecution of witches and, later on, the religious wars triggered by the Protestant Reformation and the Catholic Counter-Reformation, point to larger issues of the divide between northern religious sensibilities, ideas about power, and the obvious social and economic contexts. As to the latter, in Mediterranean Europe, landholding and family structures differed substantially from those of the North in terms of inheritance rights, types of agriculture, and the absence of serfdom (except for Old Catalonia). The extent to which these social and economic factors, most evident in Iberia and Sicily, helped shape the religiosity of the Mediterranean, as opposed to that of the world north of the Pyrenees and the Alps, is worth remembering.[14]

RELIGION IN THE EARLY MODERN AND MODERN MEDITERRANEAN

By the early modern period, the northern shores of the western Mediterranean and Western Europe in general could be clearly seen as sharply divided – with the usual pockets of exceptions – between a Protestant Christian North and a Catholic South. Only in the modern period has there been a change. That change, of course, has been the secularization of institutions, individuals, and daily life. If Northern Europe (certainly its literate elites), under the impetus of new scientific knowledge (the Copernican revolution, Newtonian physics, and the like), was transformed into a more secular society by the time of the Enlightenment and the French Revolution, Mediterranean Europe, with the exception of a few intellectuals who embraced Enlightenment philosophy and liberal political attitudes (and who paid dearly for their ideological position), remained staunchly religious and politically conservative. This was clearly the case in Spain in 1808, when the Spanish people rose against the French throughout the peninsula in opposition to the liberal ideals of the French Revolution (as articulated in a transformed fashion by Napoleon), while embracing the Church-inspired absolutism of Ferdinand VII. Religion had a lot to do with the particular savagery of the Spanish Civil War, and the Catholic Church received many privileges after the defeat of the Republic in 1939. Franco's regime in the twentieth century was openly conservative and religiously traditional. The same could be said, to a lesser degree, of Italy, and, to an even lesser extent, of France, which had a significant Catholic movement in the nineteenth century. Lourdes, one must remember, was part of Mediterranean France.

Yet, the striking thing is that secularism, once again a northern cultural project, has now found a fertile home in formerly devotedly Christian Mediterranean lands. The shift – from traditional Catholicism to modern secular irreligious or agnostic public attitudes – has taken place in a short span of time and almost seamlessly. The most vivid cases are those of Spain after Franco's death and Italy after the 1960s. Although devoted religious communities still play an important role in the nation's life, after Franco's death Spain embraced secular positions that would have been unthinkable a few years before. On the southern shores of the western Mediterranean, however, a contrary development has occurred. Against rising secular trends and education, Muslim societies, or at least, some segments of Muslim society in North Africa, have turned to more fundamentalist forms of Islam. And, far more interesting, they have brought those fundamentalist beliefs into the Mediterranean and Northern Europe as one aspect of migratory patterns in the late twentieth and early twenty-first century. A similar development has taken place among Jewish immigrants from North Africa to metropolitan France. Their revived religiosity is often strikingly dissimilar to that of their mostly assimilated and secularized French counterparts. As I have said many times: it is complicated.

NOTES

1 See Gabriel Piterberg, Teofilo F. Ruiz, and Geoffrey Symcox, *Braudel Revisited: The Mediterranean World 1600–1800* (Toronto: University of Toronto Press, 2010).

2 On the religions of the Roman world and the crisis of the second century, see Robin W. Winks and Teofilo F. Ruiz, *Medieval Europe and the World* (Oxford & New York: Oxford University Press, 2005), 2–29.

3 On this, see Peter Brown's magisterial study, *The Rise of Western Christendom: Triumph and Diversity, A.D. 200–1000*, rev. ed. (Oxford: Wiley-Blackwell, 2013).

4 Carlo Ginzburg, *Night Battles: Witchcraft and Agrarian Cults in the Sixteenth & Seventeenth Centuries*, translated by John and Anne Tedeschi (Baltimore: Johns Hopkins University Press, 1992).

5 See Peter Brown, *Augustine of Hippo: A Biography* (London: Faber, 1967), and his *The World of Late Antiquity, AD 150–750* (New York: Harcourt Brace Jovanovich, 1971).

6 Cynthia Robinson, *Imagining the Passion in a Multiconfessional Castile. The Virgin, Christ, Devotions, and Images in the Fourteenth and Fifteenth Centuries* (University Park, PA: Pennsylvania State University Press, 2013).

7 On the Waldensians or Waldenses, see Christine Thouzellier, *Catharisme et valdéisme en Languedoc à la fin du XIIe et au début du XIIIe siècle: politique pontificale, controverses* (Marseille: Laffitte reprints, 1982); R.I. Moore, *The War on Heresy: Faith and Power in Medieval Europe* (London: Profile, 2012). Throughout this section (and chapter), I have been guided by Robert I. Moore's perceptive comments. I am most grateful.

8 See Moore, *The War on Heresy*, Part Two.

9 Christine Caldwell Ames, *Medieval Heresies: Christianity, Judaism, and Islam* (New York: Cambridge University Press, 2015).

10 The literature on Islamic heresies or dissenting movements is extensive indeed. Some older works provide general guidelines or summaries. See the translation of al-Baghdādī's *al-Farq* . . . translated by Kate C. Seelye, *Moslem Schisms and Sects*, 2 vols (New York: AMS Press, 1966, originally published in 1920). See also Christine C. Ames, *Medieval Heresies: Christianity, Judaism, and Islam* (New York: Cambridge University Press, 2015). On the Kharijites' beliefs, see Jeffrey T. Kenney, *Muslim Rebels: Kharijites and the Politics of Extremism in Egypt* (Oxford & New York: Oxford University Press, 2006).

11 Paola Tartakoff, *Between Christian and Jew. Conversion and Inquisition in the Crown of Aragon, 1250–1391* (Philadelphia: University of Pennsylvania Press, 2012); Ryan Szpiech, *Conversion and Narrative. Reading and Religious Authority in Medieval Polemic* (Philadelphia: University of Pennsylvania Press, 2013).

12 See Teofilo F. Ruiz, *Spain's Centuries of Crisis: 1300–1474* (Oxford: Blackwell, 2007), 1–2.

13 On witchcraft, see the wonderful coverage of the subject in Brian P. Levack, *The Witch-Hunt in Early Modern Europe*, 3rd ed. (Harlow, UK: Pearson-Longman, 2006). The witch craze was clearly not entirely a Mediterranean phenomenon.

14 On the differences in land tenure, patterns of agricultural work, and family structure, see "The Peasantries of Iberia, 1400–1800," in *The Peasantries of Europe. From the Fourteenth to the Eighteenth Centuries*, ed. Tom Scott (London: Longman, 1998), 49–73.

[6] RELIGIONS OF THE WESTERN MEDITERRANEAN: CONVERSOS AND RENEGADES

I N the previous chapter, I have sought to provide a very general and brief account of religious practices along the shores of the western Mediterranean. My emphasis in the pages above has been on group conversions or the religious practices of new religious movements. But what about those individuals who traveled between religions? In this chapter, we go back in time to explore the impact of conversion (and of religious sensibilities tied to processes of conversion) on the cultural and social life of the western Mediterranean.

CONVERSOS AND RENEGADES: CHANGING RELIGIONS

In the opening of Chapter 2, I glossed Cervantes's story of a Spanish captive in Algiers, his daring escape from North Africa, the conversion of the beautiful Muslim woman, Zoraida, and their return to Spain. One of the main protagonists of the story is a renegade: a Christian who had renounced his faith and embraced – whether under pressure, by conviction, or motivated by material gains – Islam. He serves as interpreter or go-between for the captive and the beautiful Zoraida. He moves between the two cultures, eventually returning to Christianity and to the Christian Church.

Words are always laden with ideological meaning, and the term renegade (*renegado*, in Spanish) – the term was most often used for Christians who converted to Islam – carried with it all sorts of negative implications and scorn, above all, in the early modern period when Christianity (Spain) and Islam (North Africa and the Ottoman Empire) fought bitterly for hegemony in the western Mediterranean. But renegades or converts – whose spectacular change in religion marked an age – were important protagonists in the fluid plural religious world of the western Mediterranean. In the lands and islands around the Middle Sea, conversions mattered. From the end of the Roman world to a

The Western Mediterranean and the World: 400 CE to the Present, First Edition. Teofilo F. Ruiz.
© 2018 John Wiley & Sons, Ltd. Published 2018 by John Wiley & Sons, Ltd.

period just before our own contemporary world, one's identity was deeply bound to one's religious beliefs. Even today in many places in the world (including, to a depressing degree, the United States), identity is often defined by religious affiliation. While today conversion to another religion in the European western Mediterranean is an individual choice that comes with no serious penalties – though it may not be so even today in North African western Mediterranean lands – throughout most of the period under discussion, conversion or reneging of one's faith from the dominant religion to a subaltern one often meant death, and being branded with this pejorative term, renegade. It matters, of course, who is narrating the story, who is writing the past. If Leo Africanus, who we will meet in the next chapter, could travel between the worlds of Islam and Christianity and back again without ever being branded a renegade, galley slaves and others who, not unlike Leo Africanus himself, were captured at sea and who embraced Islam would, by contrast, be named renegades if they dared to return to Christian Europe.

CHANGING FAITH IN THE WESTERN MEDITERRANEAN

Here, I re-examine some of the material discussed in an earlier section of the previous chapter, seeking to go from general observations and generalizations to a series of specific case studies or vignettes that, I hope, capture the flavor of Mediterranean religious lives as examined along the fracture lines of conversion. As noted earlier, in the Roman world, just before the chronological setting of this book, no great difficulties existed in adopting a new religious identity as long as you paid your taxes, accepted imperial authority, and were willing to accept the social consequences of joining a new religion that may not be in accord with normal practices. The problem with Jews and Christians was not just their peculiar beliefs. The problem they posed was the political and cultural challenges that their religious beliefs presented to Rome's authority. It is only when a religion, as noted earlier, makes such claims as being the sole repository of truth and charismatic power – ideas fiercely articulated by bishop Ambrose (ca. 340–397) in his controversy with the Roman senator Symmachus (where Ambrose argued for a divine hierarchy of power that was above an imperial one on the issue of the removal of the Altar of Victory from the Roman Senate) – that conversion or reneging one's faith becomes a serious and dangerous matter.

Augustine of Hippo (354–430) was born in Thagaste, a small town in what was then Roman Numidia (North Africa) on November 13, 345. Augustine was paradigmatic of the fluid religious culture found in the Late Antique western Mediterranean world and what happened to that world after the triumph of Christianity. A student in Carthage, and a member of religious and scholarly circles in Rome and Milan before his return to North Africa, Augustine was one of the best examples of a western Mediterranean man, traveling between the two shores of the Middle Sea in search of knowledge, opportunities, and religious commitment. Because of his spectacular and moving autobiography, *The Confessions,* one of the signal literary monuments of Late Antiquity, we are allowed a glimpse into the variety of religious and philosophical options available to a curious mind and to a searching soul on the eve of Rome's demise in the West. In the fluid cultural atmosphere of late fourth-century Roman Africa, Augustine weighed the many options available to him. His *Confessions* is the account of his journey from an early misunderstood knowledge of North African Christianity to a life of the senses, to astrology, Manichaeism, and Neo-Platonism, and finally, with his baptism in Milan in 387, a return to his devoted mother's Christianity. His life's account is also one of physical movement: movement back and forth across the western Mediterranean from northern Africa to Italy and back, and movement across the complex religious and cultural landscapes of the region during the last years of Roman rule in the West. He died in 430 as the Vandals, one of the Germanic bands wreaking havoc throughout the West, besieged his diocesan see, Hippo. He died as all of Roman Africa, and with it most of the West, collapsed under internal pressures and Germanic invasions.[1]

More to the point, Augustine's conversion to Christianity and his militant defense of the Church reveal those new trends in the religious history of the western Mediterranean. As psychologically painful as Augustine's search for truth may have been, according to his own words, there was little risk in trying out different philosophies or alternate religions. By the time he returned to North Africa, Augustine had become an implacable enemy of the different variants of Christianity sprouting throughout the West. As Ryan Szpiech has noted in a book cited below, religious conversion narratives are intimately linked to polemical literature. The harsh polemical tones used by Augustine against those he thought had deviated from orthodoxy had the same fervor as one finds in the autobiographical account of his conversion. His campaigns against Arians, Donatists, Manichaeans, and Pelagians, articulated in several polemical works, were symptomatic of the new hardening attitudes toward religious dissent. On the eve of the chronological starting point for our voyage through the history of religion in the western Mediterranean, that world had radically changed.

Between Augustine's dramatic conversion and the Central Middle Ages, historical accounts of individuals either converting or reneging on their faith were uncommon. As already noted, between the mid-seventh and the early eighth century, mass conversion to Islam took place in North Africa, Spain, and, to a lesser extent, Sicily. The sectarian divide between Christianity and Islam grew harsher. Though conversions unprompted by violent conquests took place along religious frontiers, the penalties for converting had grown exponentially. Both before the coming of Islam and during its heyday, away from the Mediterranean, Anglo-Irish monks, sponsored by the nascent Carolingian power, engaged in the active conversion of northern people. In Iberia, Italy, and southern France (or even much earlier in northern France), German invaders turned from Arian beliefs (a doctrine dating back to Arius, the bishop of Alexandria in the late third and early fourth century and having to do with the nature of the Trinity) to Christian orthodox practices or from non-Christian practices (as was the case of Clovis and the Franks in France) to so-called orthodox beliefs.

The case of Visigothic Spain is representative of the political dimensions of conversion. Under Liuvigild (568–586), the Visigoths affirmed their control of the peninsula, centering their power in Toledo. Yet, the divide between Germanic Arians and Ibero-Roman (or Catholic) orthodoxy remained. When Reccared I (586–601) succeeded his father, he took no time in converting to Catholicism or orthodox Christianity (589). With him, the Visigothic people converted as well. Although Reccared had religious reasons for his conversion, it is also clear that political exigencies led to his decision. There was much to be gained in terms of ecclesiastical support and of the considerable resources of the Church in legitimating his rule and anchoring undisputed Visigothic power throughout the peninsula.

Two points are worth noting in terms of this type of kingly conversion in general and that of Reccared in particular. The first thing to notice is the extent to which many conversions followed political fractures. Not unlike that of Clovis in the late fifth century, a kingly conversion meant also the conversion, whether willing or not, of the king's subjects. Conversion therefore marked a fundamental shift in the Visigoths' allegiance, in this case, to the Christian Church of the Ibero-Roman population who were living in Hispania when it was taken over by the Arian Visigoths. It marked also a dramatic reshaping of one's individual and collective identity. In the case of the conversions that took place in North Africa and Iberia in the aftermath of the Muslim invasions, similar mechanisms were at work. The view of large-scale or kingly conversions has often been that they required great effort and a dramatic shift in one's spirituality. The reality, often times, is that it was rather quick and painless. That in itself raises questions as to the depth of religious commitment. Another significant aspect of the Visigothic conversion to orthodox Christianity was the virulent attacks against the Jews. By the eve of the Muslim conquest in 711, the Visigothic court and Church were moving towards the expulsion or forced conversion of the Jews. The edicts against the practice of Judaism in the seventh century eerily foreshadowed those of the Late Middle Ages.

THE WORLD OF SOLOMON HA-LEVI (PABLO DE SANTA MARÍA) AND OTHER NOTABLE CONVERSOS OR RENEGADES

The history of the Jews saw dramatic changes over the almost millennium and a half of their continuous presence in the Iberian Peninsula. From a period of relative tolerance under the Caliphate of Córdoba until 1035, the Jews faced growing antagonism and limitations of their religious and commercial lives under Almoravid and Almohad rule. As a result, the Jews migrated to the Christian North, finding new opportunities and even sometimes a welcoming attitude from the northern Christian kings and the Church (both profited greatly from Jewish taxes and work). The conditions under which the Jews lived in Christian Spain varied from locality to locality and were often predicated on the economic structure of the urban ruling elites. Nonetheless, these conditions began to deteriorate by the thirteenth century, when Christians became clearly the hegemonic group in the peninsula. They worsened by the mid-fourteenth century and reached a critical point in 1391. That year, a wave of violence against Jews, fanned by the preaching of friars and secular clergy, led to the conversion to Christianity of a large segment of the Jewish population. Jewish communities were erased in some of the large cities throughout Iberia: Valencia, Burgos, Seville, and others. Many conversos (Jews who had converted to Christianity) gained important positions in municipal governments, in the Church, and even among the highest ranks of the nobility. These massive conversions raised other difficulties, but the issue at hand was, essentially, the movement from one religion to another. In Spain, above all in the kingdom of Castile, some of these conversions were truly spectacular.[2]

In the western Mediterranean some conversions had greater impact than others. Not discounting the benefits and actual gains of converting from a subaltern religion (Judaism) to Christianity in late medieval Spain, there were conversions or the reneging of one's faith that signaled important sea changes in the relationship between religions in the western Mediterranean. The Iberian realms, with their long history of co-existence (but not *convivencia*, a term which I have difficulties accepting), though often fraught with violence, between Christianity, Islam, and Judaism, provide us with numerous examples of these movements across confessional lines. One early and influential case was that of Petrus Alfonsi. Born as Moses Sephardi in the eleventh century under Muslim rule, he received Christian baptism in 1106, taking the name of Petrus Alfonsi. A prominent figure in Spain's Muslim courts, Petrus Alfonsi served as an interlocutor between the different intellectual and religious traditions of the three religions. His knowledge of Arabic science played an important role in the reception of new scientific knowledge in twelfth-century northern Europe (especially in England). His polemical works against his former co-religionists also proved to be highly influential in the development of anti-Jewish sentiments, including his arguments for the Jews' responsibility in Jesus's death.

Petrus Alfonsi's case, dealt with here briefly, provides an entry into the more significant issues of individual conversion and spirituality in the western Mediterranean. While one may not discount the religious aspects of these conversions, that is, that they were motivated first and foremost by deep spiritual renewal of one's religious beliefs, one should not neglect the social and economic factors that served as contexts for such conversions. Moreover, changing one's religion from a persecuted one (Judaism or Islam) to a dominant one (Christianity) often led to a combative position vis-à-vis one's former co-religionists. Some notable conversos wrote virulent polemical treatises against those very beliefs they had upheld not too long before. Petrus Alfonsi is a case in point. Another was the case of Abner of Burgos who, under his Christian name of Alfonso de Valladolid, wrote bitter polemical works against his co-religionists, seeking to convince them that the Hebrew Scriptures did support the Christian claims for Jesus's messianic identity.[3] Unlike other conversos from Judaism or Islam to Christianity, who tended to write in the languages of their new co-religionists, Abner/Alfonso wrote in Hebrew, seeking to engage, as he did, other Jewish scholars in his polemics. He based most of his arguments on Jewish sacred texts. Thus religion or changing religions in the western

Mediterranean also functioned as a focus of cultural production, often vitriolic and polemical, but collective cultural production nonetheless.

In the Late Middle Ages, the Iberian realms were torn by civil war and plagued by enduring social, economic, and political crises. There is a long established connection between periods of economic decline and persecution of religious minorities. This setting did not foster peaceful relations between the dominant religion, Christianity, and the minority religions, Islam and Judaism. This was particularly the case in medieval and early modern Spain – the western Mediterranean region with the greatest religious diversity and plurality of culture. Dramatic individual conversions, as opposed to large collective ones (described in the previous chapter), often coincided with those moments when crises, whether individual or collective, reached a tipping point. But conversions did not flow only in one direction, that is, from marginalized groups to hegemonic religious beliefs. Conversion flowed both ways. This was so even though conversion from Christianity to Judaism or to Islam in Christian realms was, as noted above, punishable by death. There is enough evidence to assert that those conversions did take place, even though what have been often documented are those conversions that buttressed Christianity's claims to superiority. In the case of Christians converting to Islam, the possibility of fleeing to Dar al-Islam and finding protection there made the transition from one religion to the other far easier.[4]

Perhaps the best way to enter into the always difficult psychological issue of what goes on at the moment of conversion is to examine a few vignettes that chronologically illustrate the mechanism by which, and the Mediterranean context in which, this reneging of one's ancestral faith and the embracing of another faith took place. One should begin by pointing out that the three religions shared so much in common that transit from one to another was always an intellectual and spiritual possibility. Jesus's messianic role was a stumbling block to both Jews and Muslims, but Jesus and Mary played an important role in Islamic beliefs. Moreover, in the late medieval western Mediterranean, erudite believers in each of the three religions (the group from where our examples come) were deeply connected by their embracing (and sometimes rejection) of Aristotelian philosophy and, much more so, by the learned commentaries on Aristotle's corpus of Jewish (Maimonides), Muslim (Avicenna, Averroes, and others), and Christian scholars (Thomas Aquinas et al.). Whether Christians, Jews, or Muslims, these scholars shared a common set of philosophical beliefs that over the previous centuries had been deeply bound with scholarly attempts at fitting religious beliefs into Aristotle's comprehensive philosophical system.

As David Nirenberg has shown, the three religions, engaged as they were in continuous polemics, were in fact a "co-production," the result of adaptation of one set of beliefs to competing religious practices. Finally, there is always the matter of expediency and choice between faithfully following one's religious beliefs and punishment or death. As we shall see in the next chapter, Leo Africanus was willing to convert to Christianity, avoid slavery, and enter into the intellectual circle around the papacy. Maimonides, living under the strict rule of the Almohads in either Spain or Fez, may have been converted to Islam as a child or adolescent. His famous letter on apostasy (from Judaism) provides evidence on his liberal understanding of forced conversion. What other examples do we have for the Late Middle Ages?

Abner of Burgos (Alfonso de Valladolid)

Allow me to return to this important figure in the history of medieval conversion narratives. Born probably around 1270 and dying sometimes in the late 1340s, Abner of Burgos (known as a Christian also as Alfonso de Valladolid) came of age in the late thirteenth century. His life and conversion coincided chronologically with the composition of the *Zohar,* the most important Kabbalistic text in late medieval Europe. The *Zohar,* and even Abner's life and works, reflected, in part, the failed messianic expectations of Jewish communities in Iberia and the pressures emerging from Castilian social, political, and economic contexts. The realm, Castile, was also torn by civil war, triggered by the successive long minorities of Ferdinand IV (1295–1312) and Alfonso XI (1312–1350). A horrific economic crisis, demographic downturn, inflation, and constant warfare foregrounded religious agitation, attacks against Jews and Muslims, and vitriolic legislation against, and negative literary representations of, religious minorities. Christians sought to segregate Jews and Muslims from Christian society and to tap their wealth for the Crown's benefit.

A doctor by training, but with an impressive knowledge of Biblical and Talmudic texts and Greek philosophy (and seemingly also astrology), Abner converted to Christianity probably quite late in life (in the 1320s), joining, now as Alfonso de Valladolid, the Church as sacristan (a rather modest post) in Valladolid. What marks Abner/Alfonso as a significant player in the flow between Judaism and Christianity is that he engaged in bitter polemics with his former co-religionists and that his anti-Jewish works, as pointed out earlier, were composed in Hebrew. Thus, they were aimed at a learned Hebrew community and were unlike most Christian polemical works in that they were not written either in Latin or in the vernacular. Abner clearly intended his works for the Jewish community. This is a point worth remembering for it allows us a glimpse into the connections between different language communities (a topic to be explored later) in the western Mediterranean.

Abner/Alfonso's works also provide us with a window into the diversity of Jewish religious experiences in Spain. This is shown by his references to Kabbalistic beliefs and to the Sephirots (the 10 emanations of the Godhead), and by his own emphasis on astrology, echoing the interest in the subject found in the respective courts of Alfonso X (1252–1284) and Sancho IV (1284–1295). Kabbalah mysticism, if I may digress here briefly, was always a touchstone for Jewish orthodoxy or heterodoxy. Leo of Modena wrote polemical works against Kabbalistic beliefs and practices in early modern Italy, and his writings, as Yaacob Dweck has shown in his recent and impressive book, *The Scandal of Kabbalah: Leon Modena, Jewish Mysticism, Early Modern Venice,* influenced modern ways in Kabbalist writings, above all, those of Gershom Scholem. Returning to Abner/Alfonso, it is important to note that he went as far as to make accusations to Alfonso XI of Jews performing anti-Christian acts and to take a leading role in debating Jews, ensuring a royal edict banning the use of certain Hebrew formulas in Jewish rituals (for which there seems not to have been any convincing evidence that they were derogatory of Christianity), all of which is part and parcel of the fervor of new converts. They were always ready to point to the errors and mistakes of their former religion and eager to persecute their former brethren.[5]

Abner's conversion was not an isolated phenomenon. The psychological and moral penalties for abandoning one's increasingly persecuted beliefs were more than compensated by the gains (spiritual for some and material for others) to be obtained by embracing a triumphant faith. In medieval Spain and elsewhere, the role philosophy also played is significant in the transition from one faith to another. The context was always important, as was the polemical stance that followed conversion. It was not enough for one individual to forsake his faith, it was also important, certainly for Abner and others, to show to his former co-religionists that his actions were right and to be imitated. Similarly, a polemical attitude was a sure guarantee of the sincerity of one's conversion. Conversion or rejection of one's former faith placed significant stress on demonstrating one's enthusiasm for one's new religion and a corresponding hatred of, or disdain for, one's original beliefs.

Anselm of Turmeda

Anselm of Turmeda was a far more puzzling figure than Abner/Alfonso. His life shows that conversions flowed in many different directions, some of them away from a dominant religion, in this case Christianity in Iberia, to a persecuted one, in this case Islam (though not persecuted in North Africa). I recently saw a YouTube version of his biography told by a former Christian who has embraced Islam, lives in North Africa, and whose Muslim name recalls that of Anselm of Turmeda. The subject of increasing scholarly attention from historians and literary experts – one of my colleagues, John Dagenais, is presently engaged in a book-length study of his life and writings – he is yet another example of the fluidity of western Mediterranean culture. Less known than Leo Africanus – whose life and travels from Islam to Christianity and back to Islam we will have the opportunity to follow in another chapter – Turmeda was born in Palma de Mallorca around the mid-fourteenth century and died in Tunis in 1430. Early in life, he joined the Franciscan Order and learned Arabic and Latin, in addition to his native Catalan. As a multilingual Franciscan he followed a well-established pattern. Ramon Llull (1232– ca. 1315), a towering scholarly, literary, and religious figure, had founded a school of translation in Miramar (Majorca) to teach Arabic as a tool for the preaching of Christianity in Muslim lands.

Majorca was also one of those unique transition points – a site of encounter as was Sicily – with well-established commercial links with North Africa. Jews before 1391, and conversos after that date, carried on a very active and profitable trade with North African ports. Colonies of Majorcan merchants, often Jews and/or conversos, were found along the North African coast. Missionaries and those involved in redeeming captives often made their way to North Africa. Later in the eighteenth century, a Majorcan Franciscan,

Junípero Serra, made his way to Mexico and, eventually, to California, founding missions in this last outpost of Spanish power, and bringing the Mediterranean, once again, in contact with the world at large. In many respects, the Balearic Islands, and most definitely Majorca and its main city, Palma, were liminal spaces, sites of commercial and cultural exchanges between Islam and Christianity, between North Africa and Europe, and between the Mediterranean and the world. So was Turmeda!

In the 1370s, Turmeda, who had studied theology and scientific matters in Lérida (Lleida), went to the University of Bologna, a hub of legal studies but also of Aristotelian thought. In his alleged autobiography, *Tuhfat al-arib fi al-radd ʿala ahl al-salib*, Turmeda refers to Nicolas Martel, one of his masters at Bologna. According to Turmeda, Martel viewed Muhammad as the Holy Spirit or Paraclete. This rather bold interpretation connects Martel, and through him Turmeda, somewhat with Joachim of Fiore's millennial views on the Third Age. Were Islam and the words of the Messenger of God (Muhammad) truly those of the Holy Spirit?

Whether because in truth he was inspired by this philosophical argument or for other reasons, sometime in the second half of the 1380s Turmeda, already a friar, traveled to Tunis where he solemnly renounced Christianity, converted to Islam, married a rich Muslim woman, and entered the service of Tunis's rulers. He took the Arabic name of Abd Allăh al-Turjumăn, and this is a clue to his role as translator (*trujumán* or *trujamán* in Spanish, an equivalent to a dragoman or interpreter in the eastern Mediterranean). As such, he was part of that indispensable cadre of interlocutors and translators (see Chapter 7) who, linked by their knowledge of Arabic and Romance languages, joined the northern and southern shores of the Mediterranean. He died sometime after 1423, having risen to a very high rank in the Sultan's court. His tomb in Tunis (North Africa) remains a site of veneration, paradoxically, for both Christians and Muslims, reflective of the popularity of his works and of his high profile in Tunis.[6]

Not unlike Abner of Burgos, Turmeda's work in Arabic, *Tuhfat . . .*, combines the autobiographical story of conversion with standard Muslim polemics against Christianity. Also not unlike Abner, Turmeda dabbled in astrology. His *Cobles de la divisió del regne de Mallorques*, written in Catalan on the eve of a new century, described the conflicts present in his native island (most notably the violence against Jews in 1391 and its aftermath), providing astrological and magical explanations for the Jews' departure. He was one of the few late medieval scholars as easily at home in Arabic as he was in Catalan.

Living in Tunis, working as a high official of the royal custom service, Turmeda was keenly aware of the shifts in the pattern of trade between North Africa and Majorca. These economic changes, described brilliantly in a recent PhD thesis by Natalie Oeltjen, affected relations between Majorca (and thus the Crown of Aragon) and Tunis.[7] Yet, very differently from Abner or from his better known contemporary, Pablo de Santa María, Turmeda continued to write in Catalan and, most extraordinary, on Christian themes. His *Llibre des bons amonestaments* (probably around 1398 and penned in Tunis), written 13 years after his conversion to Islam, translated into Catalan rhythmic verse Italian catechisms from the previous century. The book was so popular and had such enduring impact that it was still used in Catalan primary schools into the nineteenth century. It led Alfonso V the Magnanimous, king of the Crown of Aragon, and Pope Benedict XIII to request Turmeda's return to Christianity, all things forgiven and great rewards promised. He chose to stay in Tunis.

You will agree that this is a remarkable story, even in the truncated form in which I have offered it here. His life opens a window into the easy transit between religion and language. Turmeda reminds us of those Mediterranean men and women who served as cultural go-betweens, as interlocutors for broader religious and cultural patterns. Anselm of Turmeda or Abd Allāh al-Turjumăn, the author of the very popular Arabic autobiography mentioned above, the *Tuhfat* (translated into Turkish and Persian into the twentieth century), and polemical work against Christianity, and of an equally popular Christian vernacular catechism, a student at Bologna, a friar, married to a rich Muslim woman, a man in the service of Tunis's ruler, he richly represents the different identities available on the shores of the Mediterranean. Conversion from Christianity to Islam was always possible since North Africa was just a short trip across the sea. And in North Africa, there were fewer of the suspicions and limitations that were imposed on recent converts to Christianity in European realms.

Pablo de Santa María

The Middle Ages and the early modern period crawled with these types of conversions from one faith to another. Few, however, reached the level of those learned Jews who, like Abner of Burgos, abandoned their faith, embraced Christianity, and became ardent spokesmen and polemicists for their new religion. Pablo Christiani (who died in the late thirteenth century), a converso, later a member of the Dominican Order, and the main Christian protagonist of the celebrated Disputation of Barcelona (1263), was one of them. His polemics with the learned rabbi of Girona, Moses ben Nahman (Naḥmanides or Ramban), marked an important moment in the Mendicant Orders' efforts to convert the Jews. Joshua Ben Joseph ibn Vives al-Lorqui, who took the name of Jerónimo de Santa Fe, converted shortly after 1390. He also championed the Christian position at the influential disputations of Tortosa (1412–1413), leading to numerous Jewish conversions. Not unlike some of those mentioned before who converted, from Augustine to Turmeda, Jerónimo de Santa Fe also wrote polemical work against his former brethren.[8]

None of these conversions, however, had such an impact as that (already mentioned above) of the learned rabbi of Burgos, Solomon (Selomah) ha-Levi. Historians do not fully agree on whether his conversion preceded or followed the 1391 attacks against Jews throughout most of the Spanish medieval kingdoms. Anti-Jewish violence was particularly serious in Burgos. The city, located in central Castile, served as the most important commercial regional center. Burgos also had the second-largest Jewish community in Castile, second only to Toledo. As to Solomon ha-Levi, we know a great deal about his motives for conversion. When Joshua al-Lorqui questioned him about his abandoning of the Jewish faith, he answered him (as well as other Jewish scholars) describing the motifs for his embracing of Christianity. Clearly, Solomon, now known as Pablo de Santa María, objected to the strong Averroist tendencies of many of his Jewish learned contemporaries. The question of Jesus's messianic nature also came into play. Whatever his real reasons for conversion were, however, sometime between 1390 and 1391 he became a Christian, together with his brothers, sisters, and children. All of them rose to remarkable prominence in Christian society. His brother, Alvar García de Santa María (born in 1370), became the royal chronicler of Castile and author of the *Chronicle of John II of Castile*. Pablo studied theology in Paris. By 1396, he may have been at the papal court at Avignon. Rising rapidly through the ranks, he became the bishop of Cartagena (1403–1415), and then returned to his native city as archbishop, remaining there until his death 20 years later.

A scholar as well as an important ecclesiastical figure and influential member of the royal court, Pablo de Santa María wrote chronicles, glosses or additions to Nicholas de Lyra's work, and some mildly polemical works. His son, Alonso de Cartagena (conceived before Pablo's conversion, of course), was the defender of a fabled *pas d'armes* for John II's royal entry into Burgos in 1421. He was awarded a prize for his chivalrous behavior and martial prowess. Later he succeeded his father to the see of Burgos. Gonzalo García de Santa María, also Pablo's son became bishop of Astorga and Placencia. Other members of the family held other bishoprics throughout Castile. One served as Queen Isabella the Catholic's confessor. For more than two centuries, the family of the Santa María held pride of place in the Castilian and Spanish courts. Members of the family played a signal role in the deliberations of the Council of Trent, and in 1604, Philip III exempted Pablo de Santa María's direct descendants (all of them descendants of Jews at one of the most critical and hostile periods in Castilian history) from the statutes of cleanliness of blood. Their blood, as were their religion and politics, was, and had always been, pure.

If Turmeda's story was a remarkable one, the life stories and successes of the Santa María family and their ascent into the highest ranks of ecclesiastical and political power were exceptional. Although conversion took place throughout the Mediterranean and elsewhere, and although somewhat similar cases of rapid promotion took place in Islamic lands, as I will shortly discuss, Solomon ha-Levi, his brothers, sons, grandchildren, and nephews gained such positions and prestige at a time and in a place where most conversos were looked upon with great suspicion and where they would become the target of the Inquisition in the 1480s. Their dramatic success belies the image of a western Mediterranean society always deeply divided by sectarian antagonism. Religion mattered in the medieval and early modern period a great deal more than it does today (at least in Western Europe), but religious boundaries were porous; beliefs were often interchangeable. To believe or not that Jesus was the Messiah? To believe or not that Muhammad was the Paraclete? These are significant doctrinal questions that separate one religion from another, but, as noted before, these were questions debated within a common frame of reference. Moving from one religion to another, and sometimes back to one's original religion, as many renegades did once back on their own soil, was quite common in the western

Mediterranean. The active commerce of slaves and the business of ransoming captives also fostered conversions and re-conversions.[9]

WOMEN AND CONVERSION

We should not depart this section without some references as to the role of women in late medieval and early modern western Mediterranean religion. While figures such as Catherine of Sienna rose to play significant roles in the spirituality of the late medieval western Mediterranean world (she was the first woman to receive the stigmata, wrote on social issues and widowhood, and was the catalyst for the return of the popes to Rome from Avignon), in this section I am particularly interested in women who were either recent converts, or who had converso connections. As Nathan Wachtel has shown in his wonderful book *The Faith of Remembrance* (see below), women played an important role in converso religious rituals in the Iberian Peninsula and the New World. That their faith was a complex mixture of Judaism and Christianity, linking the Mediterranean to the world at large, only reinforces the point I have been making all along: that the boundaries of belief were porous indeed.

Moreover, as Cynthia Robinson has shown, and as I have previously noted, the cult of Mary had a unique place in the conflation of Islam and Christianity. In Cervantes's tale of the captive (a story that I had referred to frequently), it is the influence of the Virgin Mary and the devotion to her that led Zoraida to seek conversion to Christianity and escape from North Africa. Throughout Christendom, women's spirituality occupied a central role in devotion. Writers such as Christine de Pizan, or the widespread diffusion (and translation) of Francesc Eiximenis's book *The Chariot of Ladies*, had, as Núria Silleras Fernández has shown, a great impact on queens and high-born ladies in late medieval and early modern Spain and Portugal. Regardless, whether humble beguines, Muslim women attracted by the figure of Mary, or the leading women of their age, they were protagonists in the negotiations between, and within, religions.

Here we return to one of the female members of the prestigious converso family of the Santa María. Teresa de Cartagena, a direct descendant of the great Jewish rabbi Solomon ha-Levi, later bishop of Burgos, was someone who, because of her ancestry and her deafness, articulated a special kind of Christian spirituality that was centered on her multiple identities as a woman (who sought equality between the sexes), as a disabled person (who came to see her deafness as a way to withdraw from the world and be closer to God), and as a conversa in a world where New Christians were coming under increasing suspicion. Born in Burgos (the headquarters of her influential family) around 1425, that is, born a generation after her grandfather, Pablo de Santa María, had converted to Christianity, she probably lost her hearing by the middle of the century. Her influential works (though doubts were raised during her lifetime about her authorship) embraced her disability and her gender (and one could also say her ancestry) as important components of her identity as a Christian, a Spaniard, and a disabled person.

In her *Arboleda de los enfermos*, written in the mid-1470s, Teresa de Cartagena deploys her deafness as a way to connect with a "community of sufferers." While the silence in which she lives is for Teresa a way to come closer to God, her deafness transcends the limitations imposed by physical disabilities, connecting her to a larger community and serving as well as the means to connect her and Christianity to others living on the margin. There is no doubt that Teresa was a pious Christian, but in this and other of her works she displays a sensitivity that has often being associated with female piety and with conversas. This is also the case for her namesake, Saint Teresa of Avila (1515–1582), also a saintly woman, also beset by illnesses, and also with converso connections (though nothing in her autobiography indicates she knew about her ancestry). In both cases, illness or social affiliation played an important role in the manner in which they defined their relation to their bodies, to belief, and to society.[10]

The flip side of the relationship between conversion and religious spirituality is found in the work of Francisco Delicado (1480–1535). Probably a converso, a member of the Church living in Rome after the sack of the city in 1527, Delicado's most well-known work, *La lozana andaluza* (*Portrait of Lozana. The Lusty Andalusian Woman*) (1528), portrays the world of lower-class Spanish converso exiles in Rome. Bridging the worlds of Christians, Jews, and conversos, Delicado's picaresque romp shows as, as David Nirenberg and, more recently, Simon Barton have illustrated, that sex (though amorous contact across religious boundaries was severely punished) was one of the other links between believers of the three religions of the Book.

Belief, Unbelief, Syncretism, and Religious Relativism

In later chapters, we will have the opportunity to explore the lives of other notable conversos or "renegades." They will be deployed as examples of the encounter between different religious beliefs because of these individuals' physical travels or movement, not just from one religion to another, but also between the worlds of Islam and Christianity. Nonetheless, there are other themes that should be explored here, even if only briefly. While they do not fall into the category of the large-scale or massive conversions described in the previous chapter, I refer here to two specific themes: 1) the transition from belief to unbelief that occurred among some of the recent conversos along the late medieval shores of the Mediterranean at the end of the Middle Ages; 2) the growing sense that "each individual could be saved in his/her own religion," or what one may describe as religious relativism. In a sense, the faith of conversos and others, in the transition between the medieval world and the early modern period, borrowed from several religions, creating a mélange of religious beliefs which were neither one nor the other.

From Belief to Unbelief

As John Edwards pointed out long ago in a splendid *Past & Present* article, inquisitorial trails of conversos in late medieval and early modern Spain (and for that matter throughout the West) often yielded results that point to unbelief. In spite of Lucien Febvre's famous book on the religion of Rabelais and the question of unbelief in early modern Europe (that is, was it possible to be an unbeliever in the cultural context of the early modern world?), it is clear from Edwards's article and from the Spanish Inquisition records that many of the accused, branded as Judaizers by inquisitorial authorities, were really people who, caught between former and new beliefs, ended up not believing in either. This was the case of a certain Alabert de Almazán, condemned by the Inquisition as a Judaizer for having said that "Paradise was to have money" (*el Parayso era tener dinero*) in 1486. That is, for holding a materialist view of the world and for not believing in an afterlife. Celestina, the eponymous character of the great play/proto-novel by Fernando de Rojas (a converso) and published in 1500, does not think of her poverty as the gift of God. It was precisely from this context of religious confusion, loss of faith, and material yearnings that, as many have argued, Spinoza's ideas emerged in Amsterdam much later.[11]

But it was not simply that some conversos ended up with what may be described as a proto-atheism, resulting from the triumph of science and leading to the spread of secularism (see previous chapter and below). What took place was not so much loss of a belief in God as it was loss of allegiance to one or another religion and the raising of doubts about some of their central doctrines. In the same fashion, as shown by Stuart Schwartz's *All Can Be Saved: Religious Tolerance and Salvation in the Iberian Atlantic World* (2008), inquisitorial trials in the Iberian world showed individuals, more as we progress into later periods, who confessed to each religion's validity as a road to salvation. That is, that a pious Jew, a pious Christian, or a pious Muslim could all be saved if they remained faithful to their particular religions. The belief in a state of religious diversity, and the claim that all faiths were essentially valid (or at least the Abrahamic faiths), was not widespread; yet, there is enough information to point to a shifting religious landscape where individuals along the coast of the western Mediterranean began to make their own personal decisions as to how to be saved or not.

Similarly, some religious beliefs became a mélange of different forms of devotion. As pointed out above, Nathan Wachtel's dramatic accounts of converso life in the Iberian transatlantic world show some of these tendencies. Some conversos kept some semblance of adherence to the faith of their fathers; yet, they could worship such hybrid figures as Saint Sarah, mixing elements of the Jewish faith with Christian worship of the saints. And then there was popular religion, prevalent throughout the shores of the Mediterranean and which – until the Counter-Reformation in the late sixteenth century sought to undo religious syncretism – held pride of place in the ritual life of most western Mediterranean people.[12]

TOWARDS MODERNITY

I fear that in examining the lives and religious conversions of such individuals as Anselm of Turmeda, Solomon ha-Levy, and others, or the questions of converso belief or unbelief, I have made the Iberian experience stand for the whole of the western Mediterranean. It is true that medieval Iberia had a larger population of Jews and Muslims living under Christian rule than any other place in the western Mediterranean. It is also true that there was in Iberia the kind of religious fluidity and the possibility of shifting religious identities that was ideal for conversion. However, examples abound from other regions, often deeply bound with the issues noted in Chapter 4 and subsequent chapters: war, corsair activity, and slavery. In addition, numerous Jews and Muslims migrated from Iberia to North Africa during the high points of expulsion and persecution. Jews from Sefarad transformed the liturgical life of North African Jews. The consequences of these new religious forms can still be seen in present-day Paris and other French cities where Moroccan, Algerian, and Tunisian Jews migrated after decolonization (see below). Similarly, Moriscos brought different ritual practices, culinary preferences, and cultural baggage when they migrated to the Maghreb after the fall of Seville, the fall of Granada, and the final expulsion from Spain in the decade after 1609.

Royal service – Christians and Jews in the service of Muslim rulers, Jews and Muslims in the service of Christian rulers – also provided points of contact, conversion, and antagonism. We know, thanks to the work of Hussein Fancy, of those Muslim soldiers or mercenaries who served the kings of the Crown of Aragon in their struggles against their Christian rivals. Similarly, Christian soldiers, a point I have made elsewhere, served on the campaigns against other Muslims under the leadership of the rulers of Tunis. Miguel Angel Ladero Quesada's recent monumental study of the Guzmán (Medina Sidonia) family traces the beginning of the family's rise to prominence partly to the mercenary employment of the house founder, Alonso Pérez de Guzmán *el bueno* (the good), and his activities as leader of a Christian armed contingent fighting on behalf of Morocco's ruler against his Muslim adversaries. Such examples abound into the modern period.

In an excellent recent article, Brian Catlos traces three episodes, in Granada, Sicily, and Egypt, in which members of one confession served royal masters that held different religious beliefs. Although all three ended up paying with their lives for their alleged political failings (not necessarily religious ones), Catlos argues convincingly that their fates were not related to their religion (while dispelling erroneous notions of why it was the practice of Muslim rulers or of Christian rulers such as Roger II of Sicily to employ members of other religions as royal officials). While pointing to the parallels that existed between these three characters – Yehôsçf (Joseph) ha-Levi, the Jewish wazir, or the equivalent of the most important minister in Muslim Granada, in the second half of the eleventh century; Philip of Mahdia, a converted Muslim accused of practicing Islam in secret, and admiral of Roger II of Sicily (mid-twelfth century); and Ibn Dukhân, a Coptic Christian working in twelfth-century Fatimid Egypt – Catlos argues for the unity of Mediterranean experiences and the importance of "convenience," that is the exigencies of everyday life and political necessity, over doctrinal matters.[13]

If we move to the early modern period, remarkably some of the most notable scourges of Christians in the early modern Mediterranean were renegades, that is, former Christians now turned into Muslims. The same occurred from the other side, that is, renegades from Islam who took arms against their former families and friends. Most of the conflicts that agitated the western Mediterranean from the end of the Middle Ages to the eve of modernity involved the actions of these so-called renegades. Their corsair activities, raids on each other's coastlines, kidnapping, imprisonment, and enslaving of those whose faith differed from their own were part and parcel of Mediterranean experiences. However, we must postpone dealing with this topic until a later chapter. The conflation of conversion, piracy, and taking arms against one's former co-religionists is part of a wider history of encounters and conflicts in the western Mediterranean. One should not leave this chapter, however, without a glimpse at religion in the modern Mediterranean and the recent history of Jews in North Africa. Even today, when religion, and changing one's religion, does not carry the penalties that such actions did in an earlier period, conversion, exile, immigration, the movement of religious conversions across confessional lines, and the circulation of beliefs remain important aspects of the contemporary Mediterranean world.

To a large extent, recent revivals of religiosity or conversions have to be placed in the context of social, political, and economic developments, most of all, in the context of North and Central African migration into Europe. The colonization of North Africa by European powers followed by the waves of decolonization, above all affecting the French colonial empire, had a dramatic impact on the place and role of Jews, as well as Muslims, in the southern reaches of western Mediterranean society. As to Jews, growing animosity towards them – mostly the result of the creation of the state of Israel and the unresolved Palestinian question – and the rise of Islamic religious fundamentalism led to their massive migration – once France had withdrawn from Algeria, Morocco, and Tunis – to France in the latter half of the twentieth century. This phenomenon is, of course, far more complicated than my brief summation a few pages above or here may indicate. Jews in North Africa had a long history. Many Jews lived there in sometimes fairly peaceful relations (and sometimes not) with their Muslim neighbors. Jewish merchants operating from the Maghreb had connected both shores of the Mediterranean from the medieval period onwards, as explored recently by Jessica Goldberg in a sensational article and book.[14]

The expulsion of the Jews from the Spanish kingdom in 1492 and from Portugal a few years after sent another important wave of Iberian Jews to North Africa. The Ottoman presence in the area assured the Jews some modicum of protection and access to the far-flung commercial networks of Dar al-Islam and the Ottoman world. Many works, autobiographical and historical in nature, have examined the role of Jews in the colonial economy of North Africa. The reality is that the end of French rule in the region in the 1950s and afterwards, part of the larger decolonization process throughout the world, together with growing animosity between Muslims and Jews centered on (as noted earlier) the conflict in the Middle East, led to their relocation to France, mostly to Paris, Marseille, and other large French cities. These Jews were far more religious than traditional French Jews who had, in great numbers, adopted a secular lifestyle and assimilated fully into French society. The new immigrants also were not very distinct from their former Muslim neighbors in terms of culinary culture and traditional values. Often they clustered in neighborhoods also inhabited by Muslims, such as areas of the 20th arrondissement in the proximity of the Canal de l'Ourcq. These communities marry endogamously, and have even become part of ultra-religious groups such as the Lubavitch Orthodox Jewish sect with their millenarian expectations. Here is an example of migration reshaping, to a certain extent, the religious identity of Jews in ever so secular France. Because they tend to have large families and attend religious schools, they have become an important component – although enemies of secularism – of a more heterogeneous and religiously diverse French population.

Something similar and far more widespread and significant has happened with Muslim culture in France, Spain, and to a lesser extent, Italy. The wave of Muslim immigration from North Africa to the European Mediterranean had led to new awareness of religious differences. Since Muslims, or at least most of them in their early years of habitation in other countries, tend to live in fairly segregated neighborhoods, retain culinary practices and diets, dress differently, and also, as orthodox Jews do, marry endogamously, their presence has become quite evident throughout Western Europe. This is certainly the case, once again, in the northern districts of Paris, but also in traditional Catalan towns such as Vic, where the mayor of the town in the early 2010s engaged in vitriolic comments against Muslim immigrants, or in the Barcelona neighborhood of the Born, where Muslim immigrants face the threat of ferocious gentrification. The paradox of this is that, of course, in terms of relations between religious groups, nothing is ever black and white. Modern secular democracies on the northern shores of the western Mediterranean do not strictly police the boundaries of religious orthodoxy. When policing is done, it is often internal and done either away from the vigilant surveillance of the state or illegally.

The theoretical end of religious intolerance in twenty-first-century Europe – but, strangely enough, not in America – yields complicated and uneven developments. Muslims can migrate to Europe and choose whether or not to retain their religion, and whether or not to intermarry with those holding different beliefs. Religion, then and now, serves to provide a cohesive community. Religion, then and now, is deeply imbedded in culture – it is a cultural artifact – in culinary practices, language, dress, and the like. The French legislation banning the veil, kippahs, or ostentatious crosses in public schools and state institutions is nothing but a symptom of the conflicting forces of secularism and religiosity still very much at work in the western Mediterranean. As we shall see in the concluding chapter, the issue of immigration and religious affiliation has now become deeply intertwined with the larger history of the Mediterranean and of Western Europe.

Sometimes religious revivals emerge from false historical constructs. Mosques have been multiplying throughout most of southern Spain. Most of them are built to tend to the spiritual needs of recent immigrant; others, especially in western Andalusia, reflect the belief of some people in the region that they are the descendants of the Muslim inhabitants of al-Andalus, overthrown by violent Christian invasions in the mid-thirteenth century and afterwards and forced to convert to Christianity. Even though this contention has, as noted already, a very flimsy historical basis, since all the Mudejares (Muslims living under Christian rule) were expelled from the region in the 1260s, it nonetheless serves as a powerful reminder that religion is often marshaled for historical and cultural purposes. This is not unlike the many announcements throughout southern France, for touristic purposes, as also noted earlier, that the region is the "Land of the Cathars."

When the French National football team won the World Cup in 1998, huge advertisements on the Champs Élysées celebrated the triumph of *Les Bleus*. Led by a North African Muslim, Zinédine Zidane, the photos of the national team and their deeds were equally venerated throughout France, a reminder that in the modern world, sports, especially football (what is called soccer in the United States), is very much another form of religion. It did not matter that most of the players were Muslims and originally from former French colonies in Africa. The same people who cheered for Le Pen or Sarkozy during political campaigns (campaigns that were and still are charged with vitriolic anti-immigrant rhetoric) also cheered for the French team as it progressed to the championship final. The same young people who burned cars in the *banlieu* of Paris a few months earlier in protest against the government ran through the streets of central Paris with large French flags, shouting "Vive la France" after every football victory. And the most remarkable thing is that Franck Ribéry, one of the few Christians in the French National Team in 1998 and later an excellent player in the team of UEFA and German champions Bayern Munich (though close to retirement), married a Muslim woman and converted to Islam. Not very different, one must add, from that English Christian who converted to Islam a few years ago, took Turmeda's name as his own, and expounds on Turmeda's conversion and contribution on YouTube, as we saw earlier. As was the case in Late Antiquity and the Middle Ages, and is even the case today, the western Mediterranean remains a place in which a commitment to a specific faith is closely paralleled by the fluidity of conversion and by the possibilities of self-fashioning and refashioning one's religious identity.

NOTES

1 On Augustine, see the earlier reference to Peter L. Brown in Chapter 5.
2 See Teofilo F. Ruiz's brief discussion of Jews and Muslims in *Spain's Centuries of Crisis*, chapter 7. The most insightful discussion of 1391 and of Jewish and Muslim life in the peninsula is found in David Nirenberg's *Neighboring Faiths. Christianity, Islam, and Judaism in the Middle Ages and Today* (Chicago: University of Chicago Press, 2014).
3 Ryan Szpiech, *Conversion and Narrative. Reading and Religious Authority in Medieval Polemic* (Philadelphia: University of Pennsylvania Press, 2013), chapter 5 et passim.

4   Szpiech, *Conversion and Narrative. Reading and Religious Authority in Medieval Polemic*, chapters 4 & 6 et passim.

5   On Abner and the *Zohar*, see Szpiech, *Conversion and Narrative. Reading and Religious Authority in Medieval Polemic*, chapter 5, and Gershom Scholem, *Kabbalah* (New York: New American Library, 1974).

6   On Turmeda, see Szpiech, chapter 6.

7   Natalie Oeltjen, "Crisis and Regeneration: The Conversos of Majorca, 1391–1416." PhD diss., University of Toronto, 2012.

8   See Yitzhak Baer, *A History of the Jews in Christian Spain*, 2 vols (Philadelphia: The Jewish Publication Society of America, 1966), I: 155–159; II: 95–299.

9   Francisco Cantera Burgos, *Alvar García de Santa María. Historia de la judería de Burgos y de sus conversos más egregios* (Madrid: Instituto Arias Montano, 1952).

10 See Nathan Wachtel, *The Faith of Remembrance: Marrano Labyrinths*, trans. Nikki Halpern (Philadelphia: University of Pennsylvania Press, 2013); Cynthia Robinson, *Imagining the Passion in a Multi-Confessional Castile: The Virgin, Christ, Devotions, and Images in the Fourteenth and Fifteenth Centuries* (State College, PA: Penn State University Press, 2013); Núria Silleras Fernández, *Chariots of Ladies: Francesc Eiximenis and the Court Culture of Medieval and Early Modern Iberia* (Ithaca: Cornell University Press, 2015); Victoria Rivera-Cordero, "Spatializing Illness: Embodied Deafness in Teresa de Cartagena's *Arboleda de los enfermos,*" *La corónica: A Journal of Medieval Hispanic Languages, Literatures, and Cultures*, 32, 2 (Spring 2009), 61–77.

11 See John Edwards, "Religious Faith and Doubt in Late Medieval Spain: Soria, *circa* 1450–1500," *Past & Present: A Journal of Historical Studies*, 128 (1990), 152–161. For Almazán, see Teofilo F. Ruiz, "The Holy Office in Medieval France and in Late Medieval Castile: Origins and Contrast," in Angel Alcalá, ed. *The Spanish Inquisition and the Inquisitorial Mind* (New York: Columbia University Press, 1987), 33–51.

12 See Stuart B. Schwarts, *All Can Be Saved: Religious Tolerance and Salvation in the Iberian Atlantic World* (New Haven: Yale University Press, 2008), and Nathan Wachtel, *The Faith of Remembrance: Marrano Labyrinths*, trans. Nikki Halpern (Philadelphia: University of Pennsylvania Press, 2013).

13 See Brian Catlos, "Accursed, Superior Men: Ethnoreligious Minorities and Politics in the Medieval Mediterranean," *Comparative Studies in Society and History*, 56, 4 (October 2014) 844–869.

14 Jessica L. Goldberg, "Choosing and Enforcing Business Relationships in the Eleventh-Century Mediterranean," *Past & Present*, 216 (August 2012), 3–40; and her *Trade and Institutions in the Medieval Mediterranean. The Geniza Merchants and Their Business World* (Cambridge: Cambridge University Press, 2012).

[7] Language, Culture, and Community in the Western Mediterranean

Not unlike the transformations in religious affiliations that took place over the long history of the western Mediterranean, the ebb and flow of languages followed closely in the wake of decline and conquest throughout the region. Languages were also imbricated in social, political, and cultural changes. In many respects, religious (see chapters 5 and 6), linguistic, and cultural changes, occurring at the local or regional level, were, and remain, closely linked to each other. Large-scale religious conversions paralleled dramatic linguistic shifts or, at least, the acceptance of a dominant prestige language. The best example of this is, of course, the impact of Islam on North Africa as well as on Iberian and Sicilian linguistic developments. Since identity and, to a very large extent, religion are deeply bound with language to this very day, and although I examine language and religion as discrete categories in this and previous chapters, one should always remember their strong connection to each other and, of course, to politics. Islam and Arabic, Christianity and Latin, emerging vernacular languages and the spread of heretical movements are only preliminary examples of the relationships between language, linguistic communities, religion, and the emergence of fairly centralized monarchies.[1]

But the western Mediterranean was first and foremost a place of connectivity. No language completely dominated the linguistic landscape to the exclusion of older autochthonous forms of speech and language. No language remained completely unchanged. They underwent gradual change – although sometimes, in unusual circumstances, it was rapid – by daily practices. Under the weight of quotidian use, languages were reshaped and transformed over *la longue durée*. New words came into usage, different forms of speech emerged; regional cadences and rhythms became part and parcel of these linguistic shifts. Today

The Western Mediterranean and the World: 400 CE to the Present, First Edition. Teofilo F. Ruiz.
© 2018 John Wiley & Sons, Ltd. Published 2018 by John Wiley & Sons, Ltd.

an Arabic speaker in North Africa speaks a language somewhat different from the Arabic spoken in Egypt; a similar distinction can be made between Italian speakers in northern Italy and those in Sicily or Sardinia. Geographical location, the survival of original languages (in the case of Berber in North Africa), and other factors mattered. Even today, after more than a century of efforts to create national linguistic standards through mandatory school systems, the Italian, French, or Spanish (Castilian) spoken in the northern part of each of these countries differ markedly from that spoken on the shores of the Mediterranean. Living in Los Angeles, a multilingual city, the fluidity of languages, their conflation and transformation, is palpable in everyday usage. Languages in the western Mediterranean also overlapped, grafted grammatical and syntactic forms onto each other, and were shaped by cultural encounters and by the circular flow between high and low culture.

In *The Count of Monte Cristo*, a work I have often invoked in previous chapters (and will continue to do in succeeding ones), the crew of the ship hired by Edmond Dantès after his dramatic escape from the Château d'If and his securing of the fabulous treasure promised to him by Abbot Farias, communicated with each other in the *lingua franca*. Although there are scholarly disputes as to whether such a language truly existed, the *lingua franca* of the western Mediterranean, a combination of several Mediterranean languages (see below), was a powerful linguistic mélange spoken on both shores of the Mediterranean. It was a language soon to mostly disappear in a world of nations, documents, and national languages proudly upheld as the hallmark of new political communities. In another passage, already cited in previous chapters, in Miguel de Cervantes's *Don Quixote*, and, specifically, in "The Captive's Tale," a narrative imbedded in the larger novel, a renegade, that is, a Christian converted to Islam, who is a denizen of the *banhos* or prisons in Algiers, becomes the go-between or interpreter for the Castilian prisoner (Cervantes's alter ego) and the beautiful and rich Muslim maiden, Zoraida. The conversation between captives, masters, and the renegade is sprinkled with Arabic words – something that Cervantes does often in *Don Quixote*, a novel with a certain positive appreciation for Arabic. After all, the original version of *Don Quixote*, according to Cervantes's fictionalized account, was written in Arabic.[2]

Language, whether in the not-so-fictional setting of the prisons in Algiers, in early modern Toledo (where Cervantes tells us in his narrative that he had found the story of *Don Quixote* written in Arabic by Cide Hamete Benengeli, and where Arabic or even Hebrew speakers could be found without too much difficulty), in the smaller islands that dot the western Mediterranean, or in the offices of the Consulate of Commerce in Barcelona in the eighteenth and nineteenth centuries (see chapters 8 and 11), was always fluid. Even if there was no such a thing as the *lingua franca*, words from one language intruded into the speech and writing of another language. Masters learned a few words of the language of their servants and slaves and vice versa. It is a process that goes on to this very day because of immigration, not only in the western Mediterranean, but also most vividly in areas like modern-day California, Paris, Marseille, Barcelona, and elsewhere.[3]

LANGUAGES AND LANGUAGE COMMUNITIES IN THE WESTERN MEDITERRANEAN

Not unlike my approach to religion in an earlier chapter, I would like to present a broad portrait of language communities in the western Mediterranean as they developed over time. But, I would also like to complicate matters by examining these points of convergence where different language communities interacted (and continue to interact) with each other. The most interesting sites for an examination of linguistic change are those places where translators and other interlocutors – we may wish to call them, following the work of Claire Gilbert,[4] language brokers – created new cultural spaces and products. In these historical spaces – an example is Oran under Spanish rule in the sixteenth century, another is Marseille or Paris's *banlieu* today – languages overlapped and created means of communication that were new and different. More importantly, these novel language practices were often imbedded in political discourses of religion and identity. So what were the languages of the western Mediterranean?

THE ENDURING PRESENCE OF LATIN

As noted earlier, and not dissimilar to the case for religion, as Rome waned in the West in the late fourth and early fifth century, the linguistic map of the western Mediterranean appeared, at first sight, quite homogeneous. Latin was the administrative language of both shores of the western Mediterranean in the fourth century and until the collapse of the Roman Empire in the West. It would remain so on the North African coast and in Iberia until the coming of Islam in the seventh century and early eighth century, respectively. Latin was, and remained in the Christian Mediterranean, the medium for learned discourse. The remaining members of the Gallo-Roman aristocracy and senatorial groups in southern Gaul, people such as Sidonius Apollinaris (ca. 430–489), wrote in Latin, so did Augustine of Hippo in North Africa in the early fifth century, Boethius and Cassiodorus in Ostrogothic Italy in the early sixth century, Gregory of Tours (538–594) in Frankland in the same century, and Isidore of Seville (ca. 560–636) in Visigothic Spain. Latin was certainly the hegemonic language in cities and towns around the western Mediterranean, much more so after the demise of Greek from most of the western part of the empire.

Yet, Latin's supremacy in the western Mediterranean and beyond – a presence that remained part of the world of culture in the western world into the early twentieth century – faltered outside the urban enclaves that were the heart of *Romanitas* in the West. As Peter Brown and others have shown, the Roman Empire was a sprawling network of towns and cities. Those ruling the cities, the intermediaries or interlocutors between local and central Roman administration, enjoyed the privileges of power and the ability to speak and write in Latin. Below them, those on the lower rungs of the social ladder did not fully partake of the political, linguistic, and cultural benefits of Roman society.[5] In rural areas, local dialects and languages survived as the preferred mode of communication among people. The resilience of local languages was quite extraordinary. Berber, Basque, and other languages not only survived but also became, over the course of time, written languages. Others, such as Provençal, Catalan, Galician, and other Romance forms of speech, slowly developed from late Roman Latin. Over the centuries that followed the collapse of the western parts of the Roman Empire, these languages became the best vehicle to articulate new forms of thought.

By the time Roman power came to an end in the West in the fifth century, Latin was already under great stress. This came from the continuous vigor of native languages never fully erased by Roman presence. As already mentioned, Berber in North Africa, Basque in northern Spain, and other local languages such as Gaelic in Ireland and other Gaelic homelands (Cornwall, Brittany, and elsewhere) survived. In any case, the Latin of Late Antiquity had already been transformed at an accelerated pace by the decline of education, by the progressive ruralization of the Roman western world, and by the movement of people in the wake of the Germanic invasions. Languages are, after all, not static cultural artifacts. They evolved over time then, as they do now. With the waning of central authority and of imperial administration in the western portions of the empire, new words were added, grammatical forms changed, and orthography and phonetic usage were transformed. The general decline in culture and the partial severing of supply lines from Egypt meant a sharp decline in the availability of papyrus. This in turn meant a significant shift from rolls to codices, from paper to parchments, with all the implications that such a transformation had on learning, the maintenance of records, and the like. By the early sixth century, the remnants of classical civilization had become mostly the monopoly of the Church, which also impacted the vocabulary, choice of words, and the diffusion of Latin throughout the western Mediterranean basin.

To complicate matters further, by the mid-sixth century, a critical period in the move from rolls to codices or books – there was a very interesting article in the *New York Times* in 2012 that argued that electronic readers (the ubiquitous Kindle) are, in some ways, a reversal of the process I have described here for the late fifth and sixth century – Latin had been replaced by Greek in the eastern parts of the empire. After Justinian's reign (527–565), Greek became the language of administration in the eastern empire, dividing most parts of the Mediterranean (East and West) into two distinct linguistic communities. In the West, Latin remained the language of the Bible (the Vulgate), of administration, and of whatever culture had been salvaged from the wreckage created by Germanic invasions and internal decline. Local languages and dialects asserted their importance and filled the gaps left by the decline of Roman central power and educational systems. In the East, in what would become the Byzantine Empire, Greek became dominant as the language of liturgy, administration, and culture. There, as was the case in the West, local language communities survived the pressure of privileged forms of speech, but, far more than with the West's experiences with Latin, Greek became the language of preference for both daily exchanges and elite discourse.

As mentioned above, languages in the western Mediterranean also faced the challenge of Germanic invasions. We know today that the different Germanic groups that settled throughout the western portions of the Roman Empire – Visigoths and Sueves in Iberia, Franks in southern France, Vandals in North Africa, Ostrogothic and Lombard groups in Italy – did not constitute homogeneous ethnic groups, nor did they have a common formal language. Although diverse forms of Germanic dialects remained alive among common people in Northern Europe, Germanic ruling elites sought also to preserve Latin as the language of administration. In that sense, learned clerics played a significant role as linguistic brokers. They provided the knowledge to preserve a semblance of a much-cherished *Romanitas*. What is remarkable, however, is the low impact that German or Germanic forms of speech had on the development of early Medieval Latin or on the slowly emerging Romance vernacular languages throughout the northern shores of the western Mediterranean. It has been argued for Spain and North Africa – the first ruled by the Visigoths for more than two and a half centuries, the second occupied by the Vandals for barely over a century until Justinian's reconquest of portions of the western Mediterranean – that few Germanic words survived and became part of local speech, and few places retained Germanic toponyms. The Visigoths' level of assimilation within the Ibero-Roman population and culture, above all after the Visigoths' conversion from Arianism to orthodox Christianity in the late sixth century, may have precluded the development of German as a viable language in the western Mediterranean. In that sense, the experiences of the Mediterranean were dramatically opposed to those of Northern Europe where German or German-influenced languages predominated. Without a deep Romanization of the North, German-influenced languages made great strides in Anglo-Saxon lands, Northern Europe, and even France.

It is nonetheless a testimony to the enduring vigor of Roman culture and of Latin as almost the sole vehicle for the transmission of Classical Antiquity's cultural legacy that for almost 700 years after the waning of Rome in the West, Latin remained almost the exclusive medium for learned discourse and literature. Vernacular literature, reflecting a long oral tradition and development over time, only comes fully into play in the Mediterranean world around 1100, though earlier examples can be found as well.[6] More about Latin later.

ARABIC

On the southern shores of the western Mediterranean, the Islamic conquest of the seventh century established a rival linguistic community, an Arabic one. Although, as noted earlier, regional speech (for example, Berber), Latin-derived languages and dialects, and Greek in North Africa, Spain, and Sicily, respectively, remained alive (as to Greek, it remained strongest in Sicily – see below – and around Rome and Ravenna), these languages presented no threat or competition to the extraordinary success of Arabic in the western Mediterranean. Considering how few of the invaders were ethnic Arab or native Arabic speakers, one should acknowledge the significance of Arabic, first and foremost, as the language of worship and of the *Qur'an*. In Islamic Western Europe, in the Caliphate of Córdoba or in Muslim Sicily, Arabic became the dominant cultural vehicle for exchange. Christians and Jews, while retaining their languages, nonetheless spoke, wrote, and often thought in Arabic. Later in this chapter, we will have the opportunity to revisit the significance of Arabic in the western Mediterranean, both as a language in its own right and as a foundational linguistic component of hybrid languages such as Judeo-Arabic (the language of the Geniza and Maghreb merchants), Mozarab (the language of Arabic-speaking Christians), or *aljamiado* (the language of Moriscos under Christian rule in early modern Spain).

LINGUISTIC COMMUNITIES IN THE EARLY MEDIEVAL MEDITERRANEAN

By 700, the western Mediterranean basin was a site of encounter of two distinct linguistic communities: Arabic and Latin. In each case, authority rested on a claim to be a sacred language. If Latin claims to that heightened state were somewhat spurious – after all, the original language of the Gospels was the Koine Greek, that is, the Greek spoken throughout the Hellenistic world – that was not the case for Arabic. According to Muslim teachings, God had dictated his revelation to Muhammad, who, in turn, recorded sacred speech in Arabic. The supremacy of Arabic and Latin did not mean that local dialects failed to survive. They did, but on the margins of these two linguistic communities. Intellectuals and religious authorities – from Muslim Spain to Christian Italy, whether Jewish, Christian, or Muslim – wrote in either of the two languages. What people spoke in remote regions of the Atlas Mountains, on the fringes of the Sahara, on the spurs of the Pyrenees, or in mountain villages in the Apennines was another matter altogether. In some cases, as was the case in ninth- and tenth-century Iberia or eleventh-century Sicily, Arabic, Latin, and Greek (the latter in Sicily – see also below) served as means of communication between distinct ethnic and religious communities. The case of Sicily will be examined in greater detail below and in Chapter 10, but it suffices here to point out, once again, that Norman Sicily functioned as a true multilingual society in terms of its administrative structures and daily life. To perhaps a lesser extent, so did the Iberian realms in the period between the Muslim conquest and the end of the Middle Ages. The survival of Arabic as the Moriscos' preferred language in the sixteenth century also attests to the enduring quality of bilingual, multilingual, or even diglossic situations. This may also help explain the survival and renaissance of local languages such as Galician, Basque, and, most of all, Catalan in Iberia in the nineteenth and twentieth centuries. The same applies to the attempts at a revival of Provençal in late nineteenth and early twentieth century Occitania (see below).

In the day-to-day affairs of medieval Castile, medieval Catalonia, Sicily in the Central Middle Ages, and Malta in the Middle Ages, litigations or business transactions between Christians, Jews, and Muslims always (certainly in Castile) included the taking of oaths on each community's sacred book, the *Torah*, the *Qur'an*, or the *Gospels*, pointing to the acknowledgment of other languages, not just as parts of daily speech in the marketplace but as part of venerable written (and religious) traditions.[7] I will return to these periods of diglossia later in the chapter to discuss what they meant in terms of the western Mediterranean as a site of encounter, but at present it may be useful to follow the plurality of languages that emerged out of the wreck of Roman authority and cultural hegemony in the West, their evolution over time, and the cultural products that they contributed and continue to contribute to western Mediterranean civilization to this very day.

PRESTIGE LANGUAGES AND THE RISE OF VERNACULAR SPEECH IN THE WESTERN MEDITERRANEAN

It is easy to assume a fairly monolithic linguistic world dominated by high-prestige languages, Arabic, Latin, and Greek, each of them in their own spheres of influence. These languages derived their prominence from political factors and, in the case of Latin and Arabic, from the centuries of political hegemony of Rome and Islam. It is also easy to posit the slow evolution of vernacular speech and written languages from a mother language, as is the case of the relationship between Latin and Romance languages. Although such an assumption is not necessarily incorrect, a sweeping acceptance of the model ignores the long life of certain language groups that either pre-dated Latin and Arabic in the western Mediterranean or co-existed (and co-exist) in an uneasy relationship with those two dominant languages for a long time. Berber is an example of the resilience of certain local languages to centuries of domination by outsiders.

Berber: From Antiquity to the Modern World

Berber is part of a family of languages described as Afro-Asiatic or Hamito-Semitic languages. Thus, Berber shares linguistic ties with Hebrew, Arabic, Amharic, and even with more ancient languages, such as Akkadian and Egyptian. Some African languages, among them Hausa, a language spoken in northern Nigeria, are also part of this linguistic group. The Berber language predominated in North Africa, but, through the Tuareg's far-ranging trade, it reached into Mali, beyond the southern border of the Sahara. My interest here, however, is mostly in the Berber-speaking populations in what are today Morocco, Algeria, and Tunisia, as well as the large Berber diaspora in Western Europe (mostly France and Spain).

Berber was already a written language by the time the Romans conquered North Africa. Written first in the Tifinagh alphabet, an alphabet that still survives among the Tuareg, it did not change to Arabic script until almost 400 years after the Muslim conquest in the early seventh century. Over the past decade, there has been a well-coordinated movement to return to the original Tifinagh alphabet and to abandon Arabic script as the Berber written form. In many respects, the slow linguistic cultural adaptation of Berber to Arabic parallels the emergence of Romance vernacular languages in the European regions of the western Mediterranean. What is abundantly clear, however, from the enduring presence of Berber speech and writing is that, in spite of more than half a millennium of Roman domination and close to a millennium and a half of Arabic cultural influence, Berber is today more vibrant than ever before. Speaking Berber is, of course, closely linked with identity, and such developments as the return to an ancient alphabet, the publication of the *Qur'an* in Berber, or the teaching of Berber to children, whether in North Africa or in the diaspora, tell us a great deal more about the politics of language than about the language itself.

The important point to make here is about the fluidity of linguistic landscapes in the western Mediterranean, or in the Mediterranean as a whole. Berber language and culture withstood the long period of Roman control in North Africa, most probably because Berber dominated the hinterlands of Roman urban settlement, and because the language was an important way of communicating for the all-important Saharan trade. Berber also endured, though not unscathed, the centuries of Muslim (and Arabic) presence in most of North Africa. Written Berber dates back to a period before the Common Era, when it used, as noted above, the Tifinagh alphabet. It changed slowly to the Arabic script after 1000 CE. This cultural hybridity was not uncommon and did take place, as noted above, with *aljamiado* and Mozarabic languages in Spain or Judeo-Arabic in the wider Mediterranean. Significantly, today, affirming the ties between linguistic and national identities, the Berber language, after many attempts by governments in the region to suppress it, has been recognized as one of the "native languages" in Algeria. Since 2011, Morocco has also declared Tamazight and Amazigh (forms of Berber) as official languages of the country. Some schools in North Africa, Central Africa, and Western Europe teach Berber as part of childhood education. More revealing of the long history of quiet resistance to Arabic, Berber has begun to be written in the Latin script.

As has been the case with Basque, modernity and the politics of identity have fostered the development of a unified language and script for the diversity of Berber-related languages spoken throughout most of North Africa, the Sahara, and parts of western Central Africa: Kabyle, Tashelhit, Tamazight, Tuareg, and others. And Berber, like some other autochthonous languages in the western Mediterranean, also has claims to a well-established literary tradition. Among the most important Berber writers, pride of place has long been given to Mohammed Awzal (1680–1748). Writing in Tashelhit (the Berber language found in southern Morocco) and in Arabic, Mohammed Awzal wrote poetical religious treatises, such as *Al-Hawd* (*The Reservoir*) and his *Baḥr al-dumū'* (*The Ocean of Tears*). Both included apocalyptic descriptions based upon a faithful rendering of Islamic law and religion within the Maliki tradition.[8] Another eighteenth-century Berber poet was Sidi Hamou Taleb. Also writing in Tashelhit, he belonged to a poetical troubadour tradition common to both shores of the Mediterranean.

If I have digressed in giving these two short sketches of Berber writers, it is because my intention has been, once again, to underline the resilience of Berber identity and language for almost 1,500 years after the Muslim conquest of North Africa. While Islam has been fully assimilated into Berber culture and little or nothing has remained of their ancestral religions, the vitality of their language has endured as a link to a different identity, one that is today more vigorous than ever and that transcends the regional confines of modern nations. It has been calculated that more than a million Berber speakers live in France (1,800,000 according to Salem Chaker), with large numbers of Berber speakers also in Spain, above all in Ceuta and Melilla, the two Spanish enclaves in North Africa. Salem Chaker, a professor of Berber language in Paris, provides a short narrative on the present state of Berber language and culture, above all, in France, but also in North Africa. From new positions in universities dedicated to the study of Berber, to a novel, *Asfel*, in Kabyle (Berber) written by R. Aliche and published in 1981, to a first Berber television channel, to radio transmissions in Berber by the official French Radio and Television networks, the strong Berber immigrant presence in Paris, Lyon, Marseille, and elsewhere in France has led to the presence of official court translators who can render Berber into French and vice versa in cases involving Berber speakers.

This state of diglossia (the co-existence of a privileged language next to a less prestigious one), whether in North Africa or Western Europe, is not necessarily peculiar to the western Mediterranean, but it is a central part of the linguistic history of the entire region. Although the co-existence, conflict, and development of diverse western Mediterranean forms of speech and writing were bound, as emphasized several times before, with the politics of identity and with religion, the history of the flow from unity to linguistic pluralism was not the same elsewhere. But just two additional short remarks on Berber and Berbers before we cross the Mediterranean into Europe. First, despite my concentration on Berber above, it should be noted that Arabic has been and remains the dominant language in North Africa since the first half of the seventh century. Arabic's literary achievements – from travel narrative, philosophy and philosophical commentaries, poetry, and history, to fiction – would require several volumes to detail. Some of these works are mentioned in other chapters or are glossed below.[9]

The second point has to do with the rendering of the *Qur'an* into Berber. While the *Qur'an* has been translated into many different languages before, including a famous one into Latin in the twelfth century commissioned by Peter the Venerable, the abbot of Cluny, for the Berbers, most of them devoted Muslims, to read the words God dictated to the Prophet in their own language represents a sea change in the cultural history of North Africa. It does so not only in the manner in which religion and identity are formally articulated in one's own ancestral land, but also in the possibility for the emergence of a bilingual (Arabic and Berber) religious culture, rather than a diglossic situation in which one prestige language, Arabic, dominates all cultural production and towers over a less prestigious language, Berber. Finally, and more of a footnote to the above discussion, Berber and its derivatives have long been the language (s) that connected (and still connect) the Mediterranean shores of North Africa to the mountains circling the sea, and to the Sahara Desert. It was the language (together with Arabic) of millennial old caravans, connecting the Middle Sea to the world south of the Sahara. In that sense, Berber linked the Mediterranean to the world.

LANGUAGE DEVELOPMENT ACROSS THE MEDITERRANEAN

Just as Muslim invaders crossed the western Mediterranean and established their rule throughout most of Iberia (711) and Sicily (during the second half of the tenth century), so Arabic and, to a much lesser extent, Berber, established themselves as the languages of a dominant political group in these two regions. But these two languages, above all Arabic, faced linguistic resistance in both societies because of a long-established tradition of Latinity and because of the emergence of vernacular linguistic developments. Latin and the vernacular co-existed and, eventually, overwhelmed Arabic on the northern shores of the Mediterranean, as political changes also brought to the forefront the language (s) of the victors. In what today we call Spain and/or France, the development of Late Medieval Latin and the assertion of local forms of speech led to the emergence of a series of linguistic traditions. These included Castilian (what we incorrectly call Spanish today), Catalan, Occitan (or the *langue d'oc*; it may be useful to point out that Occitania and Languedoc are terms coined after the French conquest and are of French provenance), Provençal, French (after the thirteenth century), and other linguistic variants, such as the speech of Genoa and the area around Nice. Some of these forms of speech did not fully survive the emergence of national languages.

All of these languages were closely related, all Romance languages having a common Latin ancestry. All of them, with the exception of Castilian, remained less privileged languages in relation to Latin until the early modern period or even beyond. All of them had distinct histories and linguistic trajectories. Their development was closely tied to political developments in the regions where these specific forms of speech predominated. Some of them became regional or "national" languages when propelled to heightened prestige by a great literary work, or by the use of the vernacular as the language of translation of a significant sacred book. That was the case, respectively, of Dante's use of the Tuscan dialect as the language of the *Divine Comedy*, and of Luther's selection of a particular form of German for his translation of the Bible into the vernacular. And although of all of these different languages only some have survived as widespread living speech until the present age, all of them were languages of the western Mediterranean and part, by contributing words to it, of the bricolage of languages that was common in the pre-modern Middle Sea.

Castilian

Castilian was not a Mediterranean language until the Late Middle Ages. The shores of the western Mediterranean were Arabic homelands from 711 to the mid-thirteenth century. Arabic speakers also mostly populated them. Castilian, which has incorporated large numbers of Arabic terms and Arabic-derived forms into the language (most words – euphonic words such as *almohada* and others – beginning with *al* are of Arabic provenance), was first spoken and written in the peninsula's northern mountains and the high plains of central Castile. Influenced by other linguistic forms found in the Iberian Peninsula's northern region – Navarrese, Galician, Basque, Late Antique Latin, and others – the first written work in Castilian has long been thought to have been the *Glosas Emilianenses*, dating to the ninth century.

Castilian became the language of an ascendant kingdom (Castile) that between the tenth and thirteenth centuries assumed the leadership of the so-called reconquest and had great success in wresting territories from Islam (Toledo in 1085, Córdoba and Seville in the first half of the thirteenth century). With territorial gains came also a rich literary production in Latin – mostly chronicles, but also vernacular works such as *The Poem of the Cid* (dated by Colin Smith and others to the early thirteenth century), the poetry of Gonzalo de Berceo (mid-thirteenth century), and the anonymous *Poema de Fernán González* (also mid-thirteenth century). Paralleling these literary efforts (whether in Latin or Castilian), robust legal and historical works began to be written in the vernacular from the twelfth century onwards.

Castilian was a very precocious language. Besides these literary achievements, already in the late twelfth and early thirteenth century, Castilian became almost the exclusive language for material transactions, donations, and wills. As I have argued elsewhere, the widespread use of the vernacular in Castile at the local level led to the shift from Latin to the vernacular in the mid-thirteenth century. This was the first instance in Christian Europe in which Latin was replaced *in toto*, and not just partially, as was the case in the Crown of Aragon. Castilian became the language of administration throughout the land, the language of diplomacy in the peninsula, and the language of royal and municipal law, with Latin restricted to some (but not the majority of) ecclesiastical correspondence and a few erudite treatises. The great legal code, the *Siete Partidas* (also mid- to late thirteenth century), the ordinance of the Cortes (parliament), royal charters, and municipal accounts, all were exclusively redacted in Castilian. It is also important to note that the vigor of Castilian in the thirteenth century also fixed the language in its present form. Anyone who reads Spanish today would have little difficulty in reading a medieval literary work or administrative document in Castilian. Not unlike Italian with Dante, but very different from French, the language was very much fully formed by the thirteenth and fourteenth centuries. It will change in succeeding centuries, but not much.[10]

This was precisely the period in which Castilians came to gain political control over the Mediterranean shores of western Andalusia, Atlantic and Mediterranean maritime access to the Straits of Gibraltar on the European side (and, by the sixteenth century, enclaves on the North African coast), and the Mediterranean coast of Murcia. The success of Castilian was, of course, directly related to the kingdom's growing political power. When, in 1492, Antonio de Nebrija published his *Gramática de la lengua castellana*, the first vernacular grammar published in Europe, his dedication to Queen Isabelle mentioned the link between language and empire. It is easy to see the connecting threads between language and politics in the Castilian realm. By 1492, Granada had fallen to Castile and the reconquest had come to an end in the peninsula. Members of the Castilian royal house, the Trastámaras, had ruled the Crown of Aragon from 1412. After 1441, at the Neapolitan court of Alfonso V, the Magnanimous, Castilian was one of the many languages spoken (others were Catalan, Italian, and Latin) and one of the linguistic ranges for literary production there (the *Cancionero de Stúñiga*). The political fortunes of Castile, or Spain after 1492, would allow for one of the most recent vernaculars to establish a foothold in the Mediterranean and to become a truly global language, second only to Arabic in its geographical expansiveness. In the sixteenth century, Castilian was spoken on the Mediterranean shores of Iberia from Gibraltar to Murcia. It was the language of power in most parts of Italy in the early modern period, and in Castilian or Spanish enclaves on the North African Mediterranean coast (Oran, Melilla, etc.). It reached beyond the Mediterranean to the Canary Islands, the New World, and the Philippines. It was the language spoken by Jesuit missionaries in China and Japan. After the dazzling literary achievements of Castile's (Spain's) Golden Age (mid-1580s to 1660s), it displaced Catalan as a language of culture in Valencia and Barcelona, as it would do as the language of administration under Bourbon centralization in the eighteenth century. Castilian became Spanish, standing for the whole even though, in reality, its hegemony was, as we see today in linguistically and politically fragmented Spain, only ephemeral.

If the purpose of this book is, in part, to show the connection between the western Mediterranean and the world, what better example than the spread throughout the world of Mediterranean languages, religious beliefs (Christianity), and political structures that were the locomotives for the emergence of the first global societies in the early modern period. Castilian in most of Latin America (except in Brazil), French in Africa and Indochina, these linguistic connections are legacies (though not always healthy legacies), just as Christianity is, of the global reach of the Mediterranean and of European colonial ventures. But languages were always in conflict with other languages. Bilingual situations were, and are, not uncommon. Castilian fought a battle with Arabic. In its past, there were linguistic moments when hybrid linguistic products such as Mozarab (ca. 800 to the late fourteenth century) or even *aljamiado* (mostly in the sixteenth century) combined the script of one language with the vocabulary and syntax of the other. Translators often had to negotiate the diverse Mediterranean languages' shifting boundaries. Below we will examine some of these language brokers, to use Claire Gilbert's term once again, and their role in these diglossic interludes. But I should not fail to note the ironic reality that, after centuries of struggle against Islam and Arabic by European Mediterranean powers, today numerous Arabic and Berber speakers, in the case of the Spanish Mediterranean, inhabit the shores of the western Mediterranean. Furthermore, on the eastern coasts of Spain, after centuries of suppression, Catalan and its derivative, Valencian, have had a vigorous revival. It is to Catalan, one of the truly quintessential Mediterranean languages, that we now turn.

Catalan

Not unlike Serrat's song with which this book begins, the Catalan language was born in the Mediterranean or, more accurately, in regions that constitute the northern shores and islands of the western sea. A Romance language that emerged from late Latinate forms, Catalan was closely related to a group of Occitan languages spoken on a wide arc from Valencia to Nice. Early Catalan texts appear in the twelfth century with vernacular translations of the Visigothic legal code (the *Forum iudicium* or *Fuero juzgo*), and the so-called *Homilies d'Organyà*. In the thirteenth century, James (Jaume) I (1213–1276), king of the Crown of Aragon and conqueror of the Balearic Islands (1220s) and of Valencia (1238), issued a series of documents in Catalan, including the *Llibre del Consolat de Mar* that regulated trade and maritime activities. Far more significant, he dictated or ordered the composition of a famous autobiography, the *Llibre dels feyts* (*Book of Deeds*) that detailed his accomplishments as king. This is one of the first royal accounts written in the first person in Christian medieval Europe. It was translated into Latin, and, in the original, Catalan is described as "our Latin." But perhaps the most significant Catalan text is the *Usatges de Barcelona* or customary law of the city and region of Barcelona. Versions of the Latin Visigothic codex that included Catalan had already appeared in the twelfth century; versions solely in Catalan had been produced by the thirteenth.[11]

Yet, for all this legal and autobiographical activity, Catalan literature, whether chronicles, lyrical poetry, or religious works, did not fully developed until the late thirteenth and fourteenth century. Unlike in Castile, in the Crown of Aragon (Aragon, Catalonia, and Valencia) Latin remained the language of administration and notarial records until the Late Middle Ages. As Antonio Zaldivar shows convincingly in a forthcoming work, Catalonia's (and Valencia's) language use shows a diglossic situation with Latin remaining the privileged language until the end of the Middle Ages. Nonetheless, as Zaldivar notes, code switching between one language and the other was readily used by the royal chancery for political purposes. The royal chancery also deployed the vernacular in its edicts and correspondence whenever it wished to reach a wider audience in case of emergency or in addressing religious minorities.[12]

The Late Middle Ages were a golden age for the Catalan language. From chronicles by Ramon Muntaner (ca. 1265–1336) to Ramon Llull's (ca. 1230s–ca. 1315) romances (*Blanquerna*), mystical works (*Llibre d'amic et amat*), and theological works, to Bernat Metge's (ca. 1346–1413) *Lo somni* (*The Dream*, 1399), Catalan became free of its debt to Occitan and Provençal, extending its influence from Valencia to Sardinia and becoming the vehicle for a vibrant culture. By the fifteenth century, romances, such as Johanot Martorell's (ca. 1413–1468) incomparable *Tirant lo Blanch,* became best sellers in their printed editions and traveled with Castilian conquistadores into the New World or were read enthusiastically by fictional figures such as Don Quixote in the eponymous novel.

Catalan's heyday, however, was short lived. A Castilian dynasty in 1412, the Union of the Crowns in 1479 after the marriage of Isabella and Ferdinand in 1469, and the linguistic and political hegemony of Castile and Castilian led to the slow suffocating of Catalan as a language of culture. Catalan speakers wrote now in Castilian. In fact, Juan Boscán (ca. 1490–1542), a Catalan by birth, has long been acknowledged as one of the forerunners of the Golden Age through his publication of Garcilaso de la Vega's *Eclogues* in Castilian and his translations of Baldassare Castiglione's *The Book of the Courtier* into Castilian.

Castilian attempts to create a homogeneous linguistic community under the Bourbon monarchy in the eighteenth century (see chapters 4 and 5) and under the rule of right-wing or Fascist regimes during the twentieth century failed to extinguish Catalan. The language became an important aspect for the survival of a Catalan identity, and, during Republican interludes in the nineteenth and twentieth centuries and Republican experiments with federalism, Catalan culture came to the fore with renewed vigor. The Catalan literary renaissance restored the vitality of the Catalan language and literature. The works of Eugenio D'Ors (who my father and I read long ago), Bonaventura C. Aribau, Jacint Verdaguer, Narcís Oller, and many others sought to restore the greatness of Catalan medieval culture. In architecture, painting, music, and other cultural forms, distinct Catalan elements came to the fore after more than a century of repression. In many respects, notwithstanding periods in which the teaching of Catalan in schools was forbidden or when it was banned as a "national" language, the spirit of the Catalan renaissance remained alive and the language itself became a form of resistance to the central government in Madrid. Today, Catalan and its variant Valencian are the official languages in Valencia, Catalonia, Andorra, and, while not the official languages, they also have a strong presence in Cerdagne and Rousillon in France. Sardinia, a polyglot society with different "official" languages, is also a place where forms of Catalan survive into the present. Pockets of Catalan speakers can be found along the shores of the western Mediterranean. The extent to which language, in this case Catalan but the same applies to Arabic and other languages, is so deeply bound with national identity can be palpably felt and seen in twenty-first century Barcelona or Valencia which, in the few decades since Franco's death in 1975, have shifted completely from Castilian as the language of business, administration, and culture to their own autochthonous speech.

The Language(s) of Occitania

The region that encompasses most of southern France today – from the Alps to the Atlantic and north of the Pyrenees – was one of the most thoroughly acculturated regions of the Roman Empire. Great Roman cities – Arles, Nîmes, Narbonne, Toulouse, and others – thrived during the heyday of Roman rule. They were centers of culture, and Latin was the *lingua franca* of the region and of cultural exchanges. Germanic invasions (Visigoths in the fourth and early fifth century, and the Franks afterwards) had minimal impact on the linguistic map of the region. By the Central Middle Ages, however, a series of vernacular dialects or languages began to emerge in the region we call Occitania. Although we may write and speak of an Occitan language or the *langue d'oc* (for the manner in which the word yes was pronounced, as distinct from the *oil* usage in northern French), the reality was otherwise. By the eleventh and most definitely the twelfth century, local linguistic developments had led to the emergence of a series of languages that, although phonetically related, were quite distinct from each other. At the western end of Occitania, the area later known as Aquitaine, Gascon or Basque predominated. Gascon and/or Basque harkened back to Basque pre-Roman linguistic traditions. Although not a Mediterranean language in the real sense of the word, Gascon also had minor connections to the early medieval transformations of Latin. As we move eastward and come into contact with the shores of the Mediterranean, things change dramatically.

By the twelfth century, Provençal, the most important of the Occitan languages, became not only an administrative language (together with Latin), but a formidable literary language as well. Troubadour songs and courtly culture originated in the region. There are, of course, many conflicting arguments as to the origins of troubadour lyrical poetry with its emphasis on love and courtly behavior. Some scholars have traced its origins to Judeo-Arabic lyrical traditions, to the literary articulation of Celtic fantasy, to Ovid's *Ars amatoria* (*The Art of Love*), and to numerous other influences. Regardless of what the origins may have been – most probably a combination of different traditions – Provençal poetry reached high levels of aesthetic sensibility and originality. The language was perfectly suited for the emotions described in troubadour poetry, and Provençal lyrical influence extended far beyond the geographical borders of Occitania, shaping the writing of romances in the English court of Eleanor of Aquitaine, of the *Cantigas de amigo* and *de escarnio* traditions in Galicia and along the road to Compostela, and of Catalan literature. It has been said that Provençal was the language of the papal curia at Avignon (after 1305), or that there are numerous speakers of Provençal in southern France today. Alas! The Albigensian Crusades and the crushing of heretical resistance by the northern French (see Chapter 5) dealt an almost fatal blow to the language's autonomy and vigor. The annexation of most of Occitania into the French royal domain in the 1270s, the legal enforcement of Parisian or Île-de-France forms of speech and grammar in the early sixteenth century (above all among the learned and administrative elites), and the centralization of French education in the nineteenth century, left little room for Provençal to become, like Catalan for example, the real language of a region.

In the thirteenth century, an unknown author (though often identified as Bernardet) composed a long book, *The Romance of Flamenca*. Written in Provençal, the work shows the language's literary possibilities and range. And, once again, it shows the particular qualities of Provençal as a vehicle for lyrical (or in this case humorous irony) writing and long romances. In the nineteenth century, Frédéric Mistral wrote in Provençal. He won the Nobel Prize in Literature in 1904, a testimony to his lyricism and the possibilities of Provençal as a literary language. Mistral worked mightily to revive the language and to teach it to new generations of Provence's citizens. His most important work, *Mireille* or *Mirèio*, was written in Provençal – a work I read as an adolescent when I was far more prone to sentimentality than at present. *Mireille* is a thoroughly romantic story of unconsummated love worthy of the twelfth-century troubadour poems. Yet, in spite of all his efforts and similar efforts by other writers to preserve the language, Provençal is presently a cultural curiosity with no resemblance to the vitality of other regional languages such as Berber or Catalan, which have successfully resisted the linguistic hegemony of Arabic and Castilian, respectively. In many ways, the experience of the Occitan language could have been replicated elsewhere in the western Mediterranean, by a variety of dialects of which some, like Provençal, produced noteworthy literary works, sufficient perhaps to make it into an established regional language. Political events, however, such as the Albigensian Crusade, determined different linguistic developments. In some respects, this could also have been the fate of Italian. It consisted in the Middle Ages and afterwards of different dialects. It had to deal with the political claims of German emperors and with Spanish occupation in the Late Middle Ages and the early modern period. Italian could have suffered the same fate as Provençal, but it did not.[13]

The Italian Language and Tuscan Speech

Of all the Romance languages, Italian is, as should be expected, the closest to Latin. In the Early Middle Ages, after the collapse of the Roman Empire in the West, Italy became politically and linguistically fragmented: the topography of the peninsula also fostered linguistic diversity. Each region developed its own speech pattern. On the Ligurian coast, with Genoa as its center, the language was as close to Provençal and Occitan dialects as it may have been to what we may call Italian. In Calabria and Sicily, at the other end of the Italian Peninsula, a long period of linguistic pluralism (see Chapter 10 and below) witnessed the use of Arabic, Latin, Greek, and, to a lesser extent, Hebrew as administrative languages and daily forms of speech. It is in the South, in late tenth-century Benevento – a region with deep Byzantine or Greek influences and linguistic presence (and soon to fall into the hands of the Normans) – that the first example of written Italian can be found. Other samples of early forms of Italian, an emerging language deeply influenced by Provençal troubadour tradition, appear in lyrical poems and songs of the twelfth century. Yet, there was no serious movement for one of the peninsula's dialects to emerge as a dominant literary language.

Such a development did not take place, in fact, until the very end of the thirteenth and early fourteenth century. Dante Alighieri (1265–1321) can be said to have turned the Italian Tuscan dialect into the normative form of the language. Writing in both Latin and the Tuscan dialect, Dante wrote works of such poetic power – *La vita nuova*, the *Convivio*, and, most of all, *La divina comedia* – in a vernacular version that set the standard for writing in Italian from then on and propelled the Tuscan version of Italian to undisputed prominence. Dante also wrote a defense of the use of the vernacular in Latin, *De vulgari eloquentia*, in which he argued for the vernacular as being as much an important vehicle for literary expression as Latin. Working in the two languages, Dante deployed the Italian vernacular for lyrical and/or autobiographical works, while Latin served as the vehicle for political (*De monarchia*) or philosophical works.

Dante's influence and his use of the vernacular were taken several steps further by Giovanni Boccaccio (1313–1375) and Francesco Petrarca (Petrarch, 1304–1374). Both also wrote effectively in both languages and/or linguistic registers. At the same time, their works were the foundations of a literary and linguistic Renaissance. Their lyrical works, Petrarch's *Canzoniere* and Boccaccio's wonderful collection of tales, *The Decameron,* continued the high standards set by Dante in his deployment of the vernacular Tuscan dialect for literary works. Yet, their Latin works, above all, Petrarch's essay, *On His Own Ignorance and that of Many Others* (1367), emphasized Cicero's rhetoric and set the Italian Renaissance on a very different course. The humanists at the center of attempts to recover the greatness of the classical past preferred Latin over the vernacular. And the Latin in which they articulated their ideas was a Latin that they sought to make as faithful to classical canons as possible. Coluccio Salutati, Poggio Bracciolini, Pico della Mirandola, Marsilio Ficino, and others wrote mostly in Latin. This is not to say that influential works in the vernacular were not produced. Ludovico Ariosto's (1474–1533) *Orlando Furioso* (1516) and Baldassare Castiglione's (1478–1528) *Il cortegiano* (*The Book of the Courtier*) are only two notable examples of the enduring vitality of the vernacular in the face of the onslaught of a Latin-inflicted literary Renaissance, but Latin ruled the learned production of the period.

One can explain the success of the Tuscan dialect not just by the brilliance of Dante, Boccaccio, and Petrarch but also by Florence's unique role as an economic and cultural center in late medieval or early Renaissance Italy. By the sixteenth century, Florence had declined. Most of Italy was in foreign hands or under Spain's heavy-handed protectorate. The Italian language languished and local speech came back to the fore. It has been said that Genoan-born Christopher Columbus did not know or could not write in Italian. This is easily explained by knowing where he was born. Italian was not spoken or taught in Genoa. Through the long centuries between the mid-sixteenth century and Italian unification in 1861, Italian remained alive through music – for vocal expression in opera and song, Italian was the most acceptable language – and a few outstanding literary works. Alessandro Manzoni's brilliant *I promessi sposi* (*The Betrothed*), published between 1825 and 1827, became a harbinger of new literary tastes and a significant marker of a new Italian literary renaissance.

It is important to note that when unification came in the 1860s, barely a small percentage of these new Italians spoke the Tuscan dialect. Each region had its own peculiar speech form. Even after more than a century and a half, differences in speech intonation remain, most notably, the differences between North and South. These diverse pronunciations, choices of words, and accents reflect different economics and political structures, as well as distinct cultural traditions. One last point should be made here. To this day there is an Italian presence in southern Switzerland (around the province of Ticino, in the city Lugano, and in the entire region of Lake Maggiore, for example), areas of the Balkans, eastern Mediterranean France, North Africa, Buenos Aires, Venezuela, and the United States. The presence of these Italian linguistic diasporas has made the Italian language an important cultural player beyond the actual geographical border of the Italian Peninsula. Today, TV, films, and newspapers continue the process of erasing regional differences and completing the development of the Italian vernacular as a national language, a process that Dante began in his *Divine Comedy*.[14]

In the Middle Ages, Sicily, as we continue to move clockwise from North Africa around the shores of the western Mediterranean, was exemplary of the manner in which languages competed for prominence and of the existence of multilingual and multi-religious communities. In Chapter 10 we will have the opportunity to examine Sicily in greater detail, but we should not neglect to indicate, when discussing languages, the unique heritage of Sicily. With its multi-layered linguistic past (Phoenician, Greek, Latin, Byzantine Greek, Arabic, Hebrew, Latin and Norman French, Catalan, Castilian, and finally Sicilian Italian), the entire island functioned, as noted earlier, as an example of polyglotism, or, at least, of the ability to function in diverse linguistic ranges. Of course, not every Sicilian in the Middle Ages or the early modern period was able to function in all these linguistic ranges. But records and administrative edicts under the Norman kings of Sicily, as I pointed out earlier, were issued in Arabic, Latin, and Greek. Hebrew speakers held important administrative roles under Islam. Judeo-Arabic merchants from the area of Tunis traded with Sicily.

The other place that has preserved its similarities to medieval Sicily until today is Malta. Although situated a little eastward of the geographical boundaries of this book, Malta, like Sicily, came successively under Phoenician, Greek, Roman, Muslim, Norman, Spanish, French, and English control and was host to diverse linguistic regimes. Playing, as it did, a central role in the history of the Crusades and in the struggle for the Mediterranean between Spain and the Sublime Porte, the Maltese language today (English is the other official language) traces its origins to Sicilian-Arabic linguistic forms, with Italian and French, and other linguistic influences, thrown in. In many respects, Maltese speakers are very much at home in the western Mediterranean, their language having points of contact and overlaps with most of the languages spoken along the shores of the western sea.

LATIN, HEBREW, AND THE LINGUA FRANCA: LANGUAGES AND COMMUNITY

In the long historical development of languages in the regions around the western Mediterranean and in the nexus between vernacular languages and emerging national identities, a few languages transcended the traditional national divisions that came into being in the early modern period and beyond. While a few vernacular languages triumphed over a large number of local and regional dialects – northern French, or *langue d'oil*, in what is today France, the Tuscan dialect in what is today Italy – elsewhere local languages, such Berber in North Africa, and Catalan in northeastern Spain, to give two examples, were capable of resisting hegemonic speech forms, such as Arabic and Castilian, respectively. One does not need to emphasize the close relationship between evolving vernacular language and national identity. It is a reality. In the nineteenth and twentieth centuries, compulsory public education, radio, TV, and the internet (more recently) have lessened regional linguistic differences, though, as is obvious in places like Spain, Italy, and North Africa, not fully. But what about those enduring speech and literary forms that could be found throughout most parts of the western Mediterranean and which transcended the world of realms and nations?

As Peter Burke has persuasively shown, the "triumph" of the vernacular and the death of earlier narrative languages such as Latin have been greatly exaggerated and need to be problematized. As Berber shows, we can no longer accept such simplistic models. In many respects, watershed markers in the evolution of vernacular languages were always imbedded in the relation between European vernacular and Latin. Antonio de Nebrija, a humanist deeply interested in Latin, famously compiled *Gramática de la lengua castellana*, already mentioned above in my discussion of Castilian. Nebrija, besides his celebrated vernacular grammar (as noted, the first vernacular grammar printed in Europe), composed dictionaries that brought other languages (Latin, Arabic) into play. The *Gramática* itself freely acknowledged Castilian debts to other language, but most of all, to Latin. Other examples abound as well.

Latin was for a long time the preferred register for erudite and scholarly discourse. In the European western Mediterranean and in countries beyond the Mediterranean, for every high school student, whether in 1950s Cuba, as was my case, or early twentieth-century Texas (as was the case with the well-known scholar, Gaines Post), a Latin education – we still use Latin honors as a sign of distinction at UCLA and other colleges and universities throughout the western world, even though few students have studied Latin – was a sign of enlightenment.

Though Latin was in many European locations around the western Mediterranean the administrative language, and the main linguistic vehicle for notarial registers until the early modern period and, in some case, beyond, it was to other literary and religious reasons that Latin owed its resilience. As the official language of the Catholic Church or as the language of Catholic ritual until the Second Vatican Council dictated a return to the vernacular for the Catholic mass in the early 1960s, Latin words – the language of the mass, of prayer, of devout litanies – remained a constant in the lives of most people living on the shores of the western Mediterranean (or elsewhere in the world where Catholicism was practiced) until five or six decades ago. The extent of one's piety did not matter. Ritual formulas were always in Latin, another example of the manner in which the civilizations of the western Mediterranean connected with the wider world.

Giacomo Puccini (1858–1924), whose music, together with that of Verdi, did so much to spread specific forms of Italian throughout the peninsula, wrote his first musical piece, *Agnus Dei*, in Latin and aspired to be a church organist in his native Lucca. His inability to secure that position in Lucca Cathedral, to the great benefit of opera lovers everywhere, also marked his transition from Latin to the Tuscan dialect. The point I am trying to make here, a point inspired by Peter Burke's work, is that Latin resisted emerging national communities, and was as recognizable, above all in its liturgical forms, to a peasant in Sicily as it was to an urban dweller in Marseille, Sète, or Valencia. In that sense, Latin's enduring presence encompassed most of the European shores of the western Mediterranean until the second half of the twentieth century. Today, of course, it still remains the internal language of the Catholic Church. In the recent conclave that selected an Argentinean, Francis I, as Pope, the deliberations from a heterogeneous and polyglot College of Cardinals was conducted in Latin. But Latin also had a vigorous afterlife in academia. Renaissance humanists insisted in restoring Latin to its classical purity. From epistolary traditions in Latin that harkened back to medieval models, to theological, scientific, astrological, and magical treatises, Latin ruled the learned world of Europe's Mediterranean shores (and even Northern Europe). It continued to do so into the modern period. Higher education, for example, was dispensed exclusively in Latin until the nineteenth century, though in Northern Europe the transition into the vernacular occurred earlier. When Krafft-Ebing published his learned treatise on sexual aberrations, his *Psychopathia sexualis*, in 1886, he did so in Latin (an English translation did not occur until the 1960s). Reading of the Latin version was often limited to doctors of medicine and scholars. I would suggest the book was only widely distributed in the 1960s more for prurient reasons than academic ones. This was so in spite of Freud's clear debt to Krafft-Ebing.

Arabic

Although I discussed Arabic earlier, it is important to note, once again, that like Latin, Arabic also transcended the modern world of nations. Although North African western Mediterranean polities experienced the impact of Ottoman Turkish as an administrative language throughout most of the early modern period, Arabic remained the dominant language of all Muslims in the region. During its heyday, in the tenth and eleventh centuries, Arabic was the real *lingua franca* of the western Mediterranean. It was spoken and written throughout North Africa, most of Mediterranean Iberia, the Balearic Islands, and Sicily. As Iberian Christian armies drove Islam out of the peninsula, culminating with the surrender of Granada in 1492, Arabic did not go away. Arabic speakers remained in the peninsula until the early part of the seventeenth century. As I mentioned earlier, Cervantes's *Don Quixote* is fictionally constructed as a translation from the Arabic, the work of Cervantes's alter ego, Cide Hamete Benengeli. The Moriscos, Muslims who had nominally converted to Christianity in the early sixteenth century, never abandoned their linguistic tradition. Even though they often wrote in a hybrid language, *aljamiado*, that is, Castilian words in Arabic script – as Christians had done with Arabic in Mozarabic writings in an earlier period – the Moriscos were committed to the preservation of Arabic, a language deeply bound with their religious, cultural, and ethnic identity. Of course, as we have seen, Arabic is alive and well in Western Europe today, not just on the shores of the western Mediterranean, as evident to anyone visiting Marseille or the Born neighborhood in Barcelona, but also in the very centers of European culture and political power: London, Paris, Berlin, Rome, and elsewhere. Migration and linguistic heterogeneity march hand in hand in our modern world.

Yet, there was more to Arabic than indicated in the above passing remarks. As Claire Gilbert has shown in her forthcoming book, Arabic, while ferociously persecuted in sixteenth-century Spain, was also recognized by enlightened and erudite scholarly elites as one of the languages of culture, sharing the spotlight with Latin, Hebrew, and Greek. Translators, many of them Jews or from local Morisco families, in the Spanish settlements in North Africa, Oran above all, served as interlocutors between Spanish merchants and administration and their Muslim counterparts. In Italy, Pico della Mirandola's *Oration on the Dignity of Man*, the quintessential humanist example of Renaissance thought (1486), makes sure to cite Arabic sources among other ancient works (Egyptian, Hebrew, and the like) that emphasized the centrality of man. But most of all, Arabic, as noted in an earlier part of this chapter, was the language of the *Qur'an*, the language of prayer. I write this while traveling in Italy, where I have seen Muslims kneeling on their prayer rugs facing Mecca and praying in Arabic. I teach at UCLA, where I have also seen young Muslim undergraduates from places as diverse as the United States, Indonesia, Africa, the Indian subcontinent, and the Middle East gathering together for ritual prayers in Arabic. Though its origins were elsewhere in the deserts of Arabia, Arabic, like Latin, was a western Mediterranean language. Arabic was also an important component of that mixture of half-learned languages that, after all, was the true speech of the region.

Hebrew

In a lesser key, since Jews had no nation to protect their interests or to foster their language until the mid-twentieth century, Hebrew was, similar to Arabic and Latin, a language that survived the emergence of nations. Although Jews tended universally to adopt the language of their host countries, Hebrew remained the language of ritual and religious observance. If, under the Caliphate of Córdoba or North African Muslim kings, Jews often spoke and wrote in Arabic, under Christian kings in Iberia they mastered Castilian or Catalan, depending on location. They did so as well with Italian while living in Rome or Venice's early modern sprawling ghettoes. Yet, Hebrew was also a learned language. Religious and erudite works continued to be written in Hebrew. They ranged from the *Zohar* (*The Book of Splendor*), the normative Kabbalistic text written in northern Castile in the thirteenth century, to the elaborate polemical treatises written by Abner of Burgos, a Jewish convert to Christianity in the early fourteenth century (see Chapter 6).

By the Late Middle Ages and the beginnings of the early modern period, printing presses in cities such as Venice and Amsterdam, or in unexpected locations such as Jaca (in Aragon), poured out a stream of religious, philosophical, historical, and polemical books in Hebrew. It was, in many respects, the presence and resilience of Mediterranean Jews on both shores of the sea that allowed them to serve often as translators and language brokers between Christians and Muslims. In Jonathan Israel[15] and Claire Gilbert's works, we can see Jewish families, the Cansinos and the Sasportas, serving as translators for Oran's Spanish officials in their dealings with Muslim rulers in North Africa. In his first ventures across the Ocean Sea, Columbus included Hebrew and Arabic speakers in his crew in the mistaken assumption that such languages were spoken worldwide. It was the profound bilingual or polyglot nature of Mediterranean Jews – in the case of Columbus's first voyage, the converso Luis de Torres was expected to translate the speech of "Indians" because he spoke Arabic, Hebrew, and Aramaic – a trait already present in the Judeo-Arabic writings of the Geniza traders, that allowed them to remain a necessary presence in the commercial networks and diplomatic exchanges between the northern and southern shores of the Mediterranean.

The modern world, of course, has created strange bedfellows. Nationalism and fundamentalism in North Africa in the wake of decolonization sent waves of North African Jews to Israel, France, and other Western European countries. That first generation of exiles and immigrants functioned in a linguistic context that included Arabic, Hebrew, Ladino (or what is correctly named Haketia, the spoken languages of North African Jews whose families traced their origins to Spain), and French. The legacy of French colonial rule has led to the spread of French throughout the region and the borrowing of French terms (*merci* as the best example) in Lebanon, Egypt, Iran, Syria, and elsewhere. Jews, and their ancestral ritual language – although Hebrew as spoken in Israel is a recent language – were also part of the complex and overlapping linguistic and ethnic identities found in the western Mediterranean.

The Lingua Franca

Bearing in mind the already noted disputes as to whether there was a *lingua franca* or not, Arabic Italian or Castilian, for all their widespread use, were never the true language of those who, like Joan Manuel Serrat in the opening lines of this book, were born in the Mediterranean or sailed its waters. But whether or not the *lingua franca* existed linguistically, it certainly did in the imaginary of people who wrote lyrically about the sea. In Dumas's *The Count of Monte Cristo*, a book that I have evoked again and again throughout these pages, the crew manning the mysterious count's swift yacht spoke in a mixed collection of languages that constituted the common form of speech at sea. The heterogeneous crews that served on Edmund Dantès's boat or who were captains on small sailing vessels engaged in coastal trading – as reflected in the "protest against the sea" documentation (see Chapter 9) – spoke a variety of languages all at the same time. A mélange of Arabic, Italian, Catalan, and Castilian deployed in different proportions depending on location and chronological period became the linguistic link that joined people, binding the sea into a linguistic community. That community of different voices and languages transcended and challenged the new identification of people, geography, religion, and culture with a specific language. As we shall see, the so-called *lingua franca* was doomed by new bureaucratic requirements, by official translators and the like, and by the insistence that languages become regulated and precise during the Enlightenment.

Ironically, a new *lingua franca* has emerged in the modern Mediterranean and in the world as a whole. Whether because of the need to tend to tourists, the global and insidious power of the internet, or the hegemony of American material culture, popular music, and sports, English now functions as a *lingua franca*. The crews of those cruise ships that ply the waters of the Mediterranean (or the Baltic, Caribbean, or other seas for that matter) today resemble the ethnic and linguistic diversity of earlier Mediterranean crews. The only unifying characteristic to their diversity – and the crews are diverse in ways far beyond what western Mediterranean crews could have ever dreamed of being in the pre-modern period – is their collective ability to speak English, that is, the language of most of the passengers. The crew members come from Asia, Latin America, Eastern Europe, and myriad other places. They communicate among themselves in English as well. In that, they do not differ from those serving in restaurants, tourist offices, hotels, and the like along the shores of the Middle Sea. English has become a necessity.

CONCLUSION

I do not wish to leave the reader with the impression that the formation of new linguistic communities brought to an end diglossic or multilingual situations. In spite of the emergence of national languages, diverse forms of speech survived. Sometimes these linguistic registers were (and are) persecuted and forbidden. And at other times they are cherished as dynamic contributions to cultural production. What we have seen in broad brush strokes is the linguistic unity – with the usual exceptions – found in the western Mediterranean before the demise of the Roman Empire in the West gave way to a plurality of languages. The western Mediterranean became the site for linguistic transformations as local language emerged into prominence after Rome's demise. A variety of vernacular languages evolved from Late Imperial Latin. A new and dynamic language, Arabic, made its presence felt in the region. Hebrew, Berber, and other less successful languages in terms of their political deployment (Basque or Occitan are also examples) had, nonetheless, a claim to their place at the table of linguistic variety.

Nothing was ever easy. There was no teleological movement from Latin to the vernacular. There was never the rise of one language entirely at the cost of another. As we have seen, diglossia, code switching, and bilingualism were present in late medieval Catalonia, Sicily, and elsewhere. But as new languages emerged – Castilian, Catalan, French, and Italian – they brought with them the heady mixture of emerging national identities and cultural products that were articulated in nascent national languages. Catalan's flirting with independence today or Corsican hopes for a break from France could not be imagined without Catalonia's location at the overlap of Castilian and Catalan, or Corsica's position between two languages, French and Italian. Nor could one imagine the very late Italian unification without Dante. Few spoke "Italian" in 1861, as has been seen, but almost everyone understood that "real" Italian was the one written by Dante in his *Divine Comedy*. The western Mediterranean as part of a global society, as a category of study in world history, has to be seen, first and foremost, as a world of competing linguistic tradition, giving way, reluctantly to the new linguistic reality of a global society. But the echoes and cadences of a distant past still resonate in the ports of Marseille, Trapani, and Barcelona, and in the markets of Tangier and Fez.

NOTES

1 One important guide for the writing of this chapter has been Peter Burke, *Languages and Communities in Early Modern Europe* (Cambridge: Cambridge University Press, 2004).

2 Alexander Dumas, *The Count of Monte Cristo* (London: Penguin, 2003), 201–226. Miguel de Cervantes y Saavedra, *Don Quixote de la Mancha*, ed. Martín de Riquer (Barcelona: Editorial Juventud, 1995), 2 vols. I: 412–429.

3 Cervantes, *Don Quixote de la Mancha*, I: 92–95.

4 Claire Gilbert, "The Politics of Language in the Western Mediterranean c.1492–c.1669: Multilingual Institutions and the Status of Arabic in Early Modern Spain." PhD diss., University of California, Los Angeles, 2014.

5 Peter L. Brown, *Through the Eye of a Needle: Wealth, the Fall of Rome, and the Making of Christianity in the West, 330–550* (Princeton: Princeton University Press, 2012).

6 See the old but still formidable book by Ernst Robert Curtius, *European Literature and the Latin Middle Ages* (Princeton: Princeton University Press, 1953).

7 See Teofilo F. Ruiz, "Trading with the 'Other': Economic Exchanges between Jews, Muslims, and Christians in Late Medieval Castile," in *Medieval Spain: Culture, Conflict, and Coexistence: Studies in Honour of Angus MacKay* (Basingstoke, UK: Palgrave Macmillan, 2002), 63–78.

8 The Sunni Maliki madh'hab, an Islamic jurisprudence school, was the most popular form of education in North Africa during the Middle Ages. Ibn Battūta, who we will meet in the next chapter, was trained in that legal tradition. See also note 9.

9 See the many works by Salem Chaker on the Berber language as, for example, his *Berbères aujourd'hui* (Paris: L'Harmattan, 1989); *Manuel de linguistique berbère* (Alger: Ed. Bouchène, 1991), 2 vols. On Arabic see Jonathan Owens, *A Linguistic History of Arabic* (Oxford & New York: Oxford University Press, 2006) and Sharron Gu, *A Cultural History of the Arabic Language* (Jefferson, NC: McFarland & Co, 2014).

10 Teofilo F. Ruiz, *From Heaven to Earth. The Re-Ordering of Castilian Society, 1150–1350* (Princeton: Princeton University Press, 2004), 12–66.

11 Both texts are available in modern translations and online. For the *Llibre dels feyts* and its historical significance see Jaume Aurell i Cardona, *Authoring the Past: History, Autobiography, and Politics in Medieval Catalonia* (Chicago: University of Chicago Press, 2012).

12 Antonio Zaldivar, "Language and Power in the Medieval Crown of Aragon: The Rise of Vernacular Writing and Codeswitching Strategies in the Thirteenth-Century Royal Chancery." PhD diss., UCLA, 2014, now being revised for publication.

13 Georges Straka, *Les dialectes de France au Moyen Age et aujourd'hui: domaines d'oïl et domaine franco-provençal* (Paris: Klincksieck, 1972). Also, Frédéric Mistral, *Mirèio. A Provençal Poem*, ed. H.W. Preston (Boston: Roberts Bros., 1872); Daniel Vitaglione, *The literature of Provence: An Introduction* (Jefferson, NC, & London: McFarland, 2000).

14 Bruno Migliorini and T. Gwynfor Griffith, *The Italian Language* (London & Boston: Faber and Faber, 1984). See also *Dante, De vulgari eloquentia*, ed. Steven Botterill (Cambridge & New York: Cambridge University Press, 1996).

15 Jonathan I. Israel, *Diasporas within a Diaspora: Jews, Crypto-Jews, and the World of Maritime Empires (1540–1740)* (Boston: Brill, 2002).

PART II *MEDITERRANEAN ENCOUNTERS*

[8] Encounters I: Traveling in the Western Mediterranean

The Mediterranean has long been a place of encounters and travel. Travel, whether for pleasure, faith, or war, was an integral component of the encounters between different peoples on the Mediterranean Sea. While there were spaces or sites of encounter, places such as Sicily, Majorca, Iberia, port towns along the sea shores, and the like (see Chapter 10), individual or group travel introduced a unique dynamic into the history of the Middle Sea. The bibliography of travel accounts fills many pages, extending from the very beginnings of civilization to the present. From the iconic travels of Ulysses or Odysseus to the travel guides for tourists on modern sea cruises and land excursions eager to explore, even if only briefly, the monuments of Mediterranean civilization, these texts provide powerful insights into the mechanisms that propel people to sail the Mediterranean or to voyage along its shores. In this and succeeding chapters, I am mostly concerned with the type of travel that, in Michel de Certeau's formulation, brought one from the familiar to the unfamiliar, from one's own religion or identity to the awareness of "otherness" or alterity.[1]

Traveling in the Western Mediterranean

In the twentieth and twenty-first centuries, Muslims flocked to the northern shores of the Mediterranean from North Africa, the Middle East, and other parts of the world in search of work, learning, or exile. Northern Europeans and Americans (certainly by the nineteenth century) came in large numbers for some of the same reasons, but also for sightseeing and pleasure. Under Rome, people from all corners of the empire came to the capital city or were brought forcefully there. Slaves, merchants, scholars, believers, and others came to serve, to learn, to trade, and to worship from faraway lands in England, Gaul,

The Western Mediterranean and the World: 400 CE to the Present, First Edition. Teofilo F. Ruiz.
© 2018 John Wiley & Sons, Ltd. Published 2018 by John Wiley & Sons, Ltd.

North Africa, and the eastern Mediterranean. In the Carolingian period, kings – Pippin the Short, Charlemagne, Louis the Pious, and many other upholders of imperial power – came to Rome and to other Italian locations to assert their jurisdiction or to receive papal blessings for their rule. By the tenth century, thousands of pilgrims had made their way to Santiago de Compostela, and they still come in large numbers. Although not a "Mediterranean" pilgrimage, the well-transited route to Saint James the Apostle's tomb was also part of the circulation of diverse people in and around the Mediterranean world. This was, after all, part of a pattern of Christian pilgrimages to Rome, the Holy Land, and other significant shrines, or of the obligatory Muslim pilgrimage to Mecca.

Christianity and Islam were, after all, intensely Mediterranean religions. After Rome's emergence as the center of Western Christendom in the eighth and ninth centuries, it became an important destination for religious pilgrimages. In the case of Rome (but an idea that applies equally to many other pilgrimage sites), these circulations of people and relics between northern Western Europe and the Mediterranean brought the two worlds into intense contact. The itineraries of Rome, the careful list of shrines, and other documents compiled in the ninth century by Frankish monks – and insightfully studied by Maya Maskarinec in her published and forthcoming works – provide a stunning view of how the Frankish and Anglo Saxon clergy, among the few literate elites in Northern Europe, perceived Rome and, by extension, the Mediterranean.

As Maskarinec shows, relics from every corner of Europe (but mostly from the eastern Mediterranean) were brought into Rome, a kind of relic exchange that brought foreign saints under the jurisdiction of the ascendant bishop of Rome. Pious travelers, visiting Rome and making the circuit of churches and other holy sites in the city, took some of these relics, regardless of whether they had been initially imported from the East or were original to Rome, back to their homes in the Frankish North. In a real sense, these sacred commercial transactions and the narratives of the travel and purchase of sacred remains were part of the ebb and flow of communication between Northern Europe and the Middle Sea, paralleling in this period the bold voyages of Muslim travelers on the southern shores.[2]

And then, in these exchanges of people so peculiar to the Mediterranean, there was none so dramatic as the movement of Saracens into the Northern European shores of the Mediterranean, above all Sicily, or the migration of the Normans (the descendants of daring Viking explorers and raiders) to southern Italy, to Sicily, and to the Middle East as the core of the first crusading armies in the late eleventh century. Other invaders and travelers eventually followed these Norman warriors: from Goethe, and the American Henry James, to the Grand Tour, and modern cruises today.

In Cervantes's *Don Quixote* (first volume published in 1605, the second in 1615), in one of the many stories within a story that populate his great work, the author offers an almost autobiographical sketch that has been referred to several times before. Borrowing from his experience as a prisoner in the *banhos* (prison in Algiers or Argel in Spanish), Cervantes tells a vivid account of travel and contacts across the western Mediterranean. The "Captive's Tale" describes, in broad brush strokes, the life of a Spanish seafarer and soldier. Beginning his life in Asturias, far away from the shores of the Middle Sea, the main protagonist of the tale joined the Spanish Mediterranean fleet, fought at Lepanto, as Cervantes himself had done, was captured by Ottoman corsairs, just as Cervantes himself had been captured, rowed as a galley slave, and ended in a prison in Algiers as a captive to be held for ransom.

"The Captive's Tale" continues, as we have already seen, with the romantic story of a rich and beautiful young Muslim woman, who, brought up by a Christian captive, had become devoted to the Virgin Mary (the Muslim Mariam). Her desire and hope was to escape to Christian lands and to convert to Christianity. The beautiful Zoraida, for that was her name, chooses the captive as her future husband and as the one to facilitate her journey away from Muslim lands into Christianity. In Cervantes's lively account, we meet renegades, galley slaves, French corsairs, those who spoke the mélange of languages used in the western Mediterranean, as well as catching a host of other glimpses into the Middle Sea's life and sectarians conflicts. The fear of Muslim corsair activity along Spain's southern shores is woven into the romantic tale of the captive and his beautiful Muslim – and soon-to-be Christian – companion. Cervantes's story within the larger story of *Don Quixote*, as well as his other fictional and biographical works about his captivity in Algiers, serves as a window through which to examine the diverse ways in which different people along the western Mediterranean shores encountered, traded with, fought, enslaved, and redeemed each other throughout the long history of the Middle Sea.

THE WESTERN MEDITERRANEAN AS A SITE OF ENCOUNTER

In this and the next chapter, I wish to examine those instances of contact – sometimes peaceful, sometimes antagonistic – that occurred on the waters and shores of the western Mediterranean. If, as I argued earlier, the political history of the Mediterranean could be seen as the flow from unity to fragmentation and plurality, the bonds created by travel, commerce, and even warfare served as the glue that held together what one may describe as a western Mediterranean society. In the pages that follow, I limit myself to a series of vignettes that depict these different types of encounter of individuals with different people and lands. Yet, while focusing on just a few examples, I am, far more important, interested in the transformation of cultures that occurs in those liminal lives that both separated and brought together different western Mediterranean people.

VOYAGES: THE EXPERIENCE OF TRAVEL

One may begin with travelers, those people who, either on their own or as groups, go to see other places to fulfill some pious intent, or in search of knowledge or profit, or both. In doing so, they describe what they see, as for example Ibn Battūta did in the fourteenth century, constructing their awareness of new things based upon what they already know. A few years ago, I completed a two-week-long cruise of Baltic ports – an area of the world unknown to me until summer 2011. I was powerfully struck by the manner in which architectural forms, culinary experiences, and cultural tropes moved from one place to another, following along the fracture lines of travel, military expansion, religious conversion, and trade. The Baltic is much smaller than the Mediterranean, and in sailing it one is powerfully struck by the manner in which the sea links all those maritime locations – I visited Stockholm, Helsinki, Saint Petersburg, Tallinn, Riga, Copenhagen, and other ports. This is a fairly homogeneous world, once linked together by Hansa merchants and trading centers, notwithstanding linguistic, political, and religious differences. The coming and going of ferries, at volumes somewhat matched by similar maritime activity in the western Mediterranean Sea, is testimony to the manner in which a sea serves as a permanent bridge between diverse peoples. The same experience of the connectivity provided by the sea and by travel was evident in 2012, when I sailed the western Mediterranean from Lisbon, through the Straits of Gibraltar, to Civitavecchia, the port of Rome. In 2014, I traveled again, this time from Athens, following Odysseus's fictional journey or the journeys of ancient Greek merchants, to Barcelona by way of Sicily, the Strait of Messina, Italy, and southern France. Even under present conditions and in cruise ships, one can capture the flavor and unity of the Mediterranean, something that can be only known fully through the experience of travel.

TRAVELING IN THE MEDITERRANEAN: MUSLIMS ON THE NORTHERN SHORES

Here I am interested mostly in what travelers saw and felt along their journeys, while acknowledging that travelers often fulfilled other roles as merchants, religious figures, diplomats, and the like. Thus my focus here is not so much on the travelers themselves as on their literary renderings of what they experienced. That is, I am concerned with the travelers' representation of what they saw in worlds that were often quite different from their own, and of the connections they made between their own familiar worlds and the things that were different from their experiences at home. One caveat is in order. In most cases, travel narratives focus on the lands along the Mediterranean shores and on those entry points into the world beyond the sea. The Mediterranean Sea itself plays only a supporting role in these accounts.

Travelers' accounts of their voyages in the Mediterranean are as old as the beginning of literature. The *Odyssey*, though mostly concerned with the eastern Mediterranean, related Odysseus's experiences in the western sea, including his sailing through the treacherous Strait of Messina: the famous episode of the sirens. The *Odyssey*, of course, also reflected the Greeks' early migrations into Sicily and other areas of the western Mediterranean. Herodotus's weaving of his experiences of travel into his histories and Pausanias's Grand Tour of Roman Greece are early examples of the yearning to describe to others a world often new to the traveler, to render that world into words. In an age in which airplanes, trains, and automobiles have replaced sea travel in most parts of the western Mediterranean, sea voyages have become mostly expensive cruises. They are highly managed, and organized with a contradictory and odd mix of didactic and sybaritic elements. The contact with seaports or sights along the shores is often kept to a minimum and mediated by officious guides.

If travelers across the western Mediterranean or along its shores emphasized the land at the expense of the sea, unless a notable storm or a becalmed sea impacted their voyage, these travelers' narratives nonetheless offer an entry into the manner in which travelers experienced the new. Not unlike the experience expressed in Michel de Certeau's luminous and insightful reading of Jean de Lery's voyage to the land of Brazil, in traveling from the southern shore to the northern one, or on the east-west axis along the entire Mediterranean, one replicates a movement, as noted by de Certeau, from "here to there" from "self to other." Yet, unlike Jean de Lery's encounter with the radical "otherness" of the Tupi in Brazil, for Mediterranean travelers it was always a move from the familiar to the slightly less familiar. This is what Lucette Valensi has described so well, in her recent book on Muslims in Northern Europe, as "familiar strangers."[3] Unless you come from outside the Mediterranean world altogether (culturally and geographically), for most people traveling in the region the most evident aspect of the Middle Sea is a sense of familiarity, that is, acquaintance, whether thorough or superficial, with the entire Mediterranean world.

As I have already noted, travelers crossed (and still cross) the Mediterranean or sailed along its shores for many reasons. Religious practices, migration, trade, diplomacy, war, search for knowledge, and myriad other reasons led people to sail the sea. These categories often overlapped. Besides the peripatetic travel of Paul the Apostle through the eastern Mediterranean (Jerusalem, Ephesus, Corinth, and other of the great cities of the eastern Roman Empire) and ending in his martyrdom in Rome, one of our earliest itineraries of Christian pilgrims outlines a long voyage from Bordeaux to Jerusalem in 333 CE. Beyond providing a detailed account of distances, and some short references to the religious highlights seen along the way (especially in the Holy Land), the itinerary of the Bordeaux pilgrim points to the far-ranging possibilities for travel. Significantly, although the trip sometimes followed the Mediterranean coast, the sojourn was entirely on land, veering into Cappadocia and other places, not on a direct line to Jerusalem. Similarly, Maribel Dietz's engaging book, *Wandering Monks, Virgins and Pilgrims*, shows the ceaseless travel of individuals around and across the Mediterranean into the ninth century.[4]

Venetian ambassadors to Spain in the sixteenth century, to provide just another example, often offer us vivid and insightful descriptions of what they saw along the journey. Their reports from their destinations included sensitive political information but also what one may describe today as ethnographic information. Nineteenth- and twentieth-century travelers – often tourists in the modern sense of the word – used pictorial representations, photos, and videos (as tourists do to this day) that recorded the landscape without a more reflective description of the sea and its environs. How then to carry out this inquiry with such an abundance of varied sources? As we have seen, from the very beginnings of writing in the Mediterranean basin, we have had testimonies of travel and of the impact of the Middle Sea on those sailing its waters. Rather than provide a long list of these accounts, I would like to concentrate on a few discrete narratives that convey the writers' experiences of the Mediterranean as a site of encounter.

TRAVELING FROM DAR AL-ISLAM INTO CHRISTIAN LAND

Al-Idrīsī

In their journeys through Christian lands, Muslim travelers often carried with them a vast knowledge of geography and seafaring seldom found in the West in the Middle Ages and even in the early modern period. Their accounts often also showed examples of displacement. These Muslims voyagers did not just journey from one geographical area to another, they also crossed religious boundaries that were, at times, as porous as the territorial ones. Early example of this can be found in the life and works of the twelfth-century cartographer and boundary-crosser Muhammad al-Idrīsī. Born in 1099 or at the turn of the century in Ceuta (North Africa), al-Idrīsī (his full name was Abu Abdallah Muhammad Ibn Muhammad Ibn Abdallah Ibn Idriss al-Qurtubi al-Hassani) traced his ancestry to the Prophet himself. His more immediate ancestors, the Hammunds, had ruled Málaga until their kingdom and city – one of the numerous so-called kingdoms of *taifas* that emerged from the breakdown of the Caliphate of Córdoba in the 1030s – was overthrown by the Muslim rulers of Granada in the 1050s. This led al-Idrīsī's great-grandfather to migrate to North Africa with his entire family. Yet, Muslim Spain, or al-Andalus, remained the cultural and spiritual center for Málaga's exiles. Al-Idrīsī may have studied in Córdoba but also traveled extensively throughout Iberia. He may have also visited Anatolia in his youth, and thus his experience of sailing or traveling along the shores of the Mediterranean was substantial.

Around 1135–1136, al-Idrīsī, for reasons that are unclear, migrated to Sicily and entered the service of Roger II, the island's Norman ruler. Having wrested Sicily from the Muslims (see chapters 3 and 10), the Normans ruled over a multi-ethnic, multi-religious, and multilingual society. Religious fanaticism took a back seat to the production of knowledge, administrative necessity, and the kind of cultural exchanges that were seldom found, with the exception of those at some Iberian sites, in the western Mediterranean. Jews, Christians, Muslims, and Greeks engaged in intellectual debates, traded with each other, and fought with each other, while providing us with a glimpse of the possibilities and travails of plural societies. We will return to Sicily, for its often troubled and variegated history is paradigmatic of the history of the western Mediterranean as a whole, but al-Idrīsī and his travels are now the focus of our attention.

Although the previous representation of Norman Sicily tends to idealize conditions that were not always peaceful or pleasant, the fact is that al-Idrīsī entered the service of Roger II, and the king charged him with producing a map of the known world. This map, however, was not to be just a compendium of scholarly observation and manuscript research, but one that reflected the actual experience of travel. The result, after al-Idrīsī's extensive travels in North Africa and Western Europe, was the composition of an extensive atlas or chart, the so-called *Tabula Rogeriana*. The actual title of the work is closer to the spirit of the project and may be rendered from the original Arabic as "the diversion or solace of he who wishes to travel the world."

This map of the world – one of the most accurate representations of the known world hitherto drawn – was reproduced on a large disc (two meters in diameter) of solid silver. Significantly, in depicting the world – a task accomplished by observation but also by mining the extensive cartographical and geographical knowledge accumulated by ancient and Muslim scholars over the previous centuries – al-Idrīsī placed the northern shores of the Mediterranean at the bottom. Thus, al-Idrīsī located Africa (see Map 8.1) on top, privileging his ancestral home in Ceuta and Dar al-Islam over the Christian West. Geography and map-making have always been (and remain) laden with ideological intent.

Not all of al-Idrīsī's works have survived. A geographical treatise with the title of "Garden of the soul's familiarity and solace" (these titles are approximations to the original Arabic rendering), dedicated to Roger II's son, William I (1154–1166), and referenced in a later work, is no longer extant. What we have, for those who like me are not fortunate enough to read Arabic, is a translation entitled, *Description de l'Afrique et de l'Espagne par Edrisi*, translated and edited by R. Dozy and M.J. de Goeje and published in Leiden in 1866. Al-Idrīsī probably died sometime around 1166.[5]

Al-Idrīsī's account of his voyage took him from Sicily to Africa to the Iberian Peninsula. His sojourns were as much a physical act of moving from one location to another as a kind of cultural crossover. This is something akin to what Sanjay Subrahmanyam describes as "ways of being alien" (and yet a part of the society one inhabits) in a recent book about liminal interior spaces of those who, like al-Idrīsī, lived between two worlds.[6] Al-Idrīsī's *Description de l'Afrique et de l'Espagne* (if we may keep to the title of the late nineteenth-century French translation) begins, in a Braudelian fashion, with a discussion of the climate, dividing the Mediterranean world, and making distinctions between regions, according to climate. For al-Idrīsī, the first of these regions was the sea (the Atlantic) that lies beyond the western sea (the Mediterranean), identified as the "*mer des Ténèbres*" (Sea of Darkness). Following classical authors and earlier geographical manuals, he does not fail to refer to the Fortunate Isles (or Canary Islands). Thus, al-Idrīsī begins by establishing the climatic and geographic link between the Atlantic and the western Mediterranean. The names of a series of towns – not all of them recognizable to us today – introduce us to regions of West Africa close enough to the opening of the Mediterranean as to be part of that expansive Mediterranean world described by Braudel over 50 years ago.

And, then, there was the desert, uninhabitable, Al-Idrīsī says, except for the banks of the Nile. It may have been uninhabitable, but it was crossed

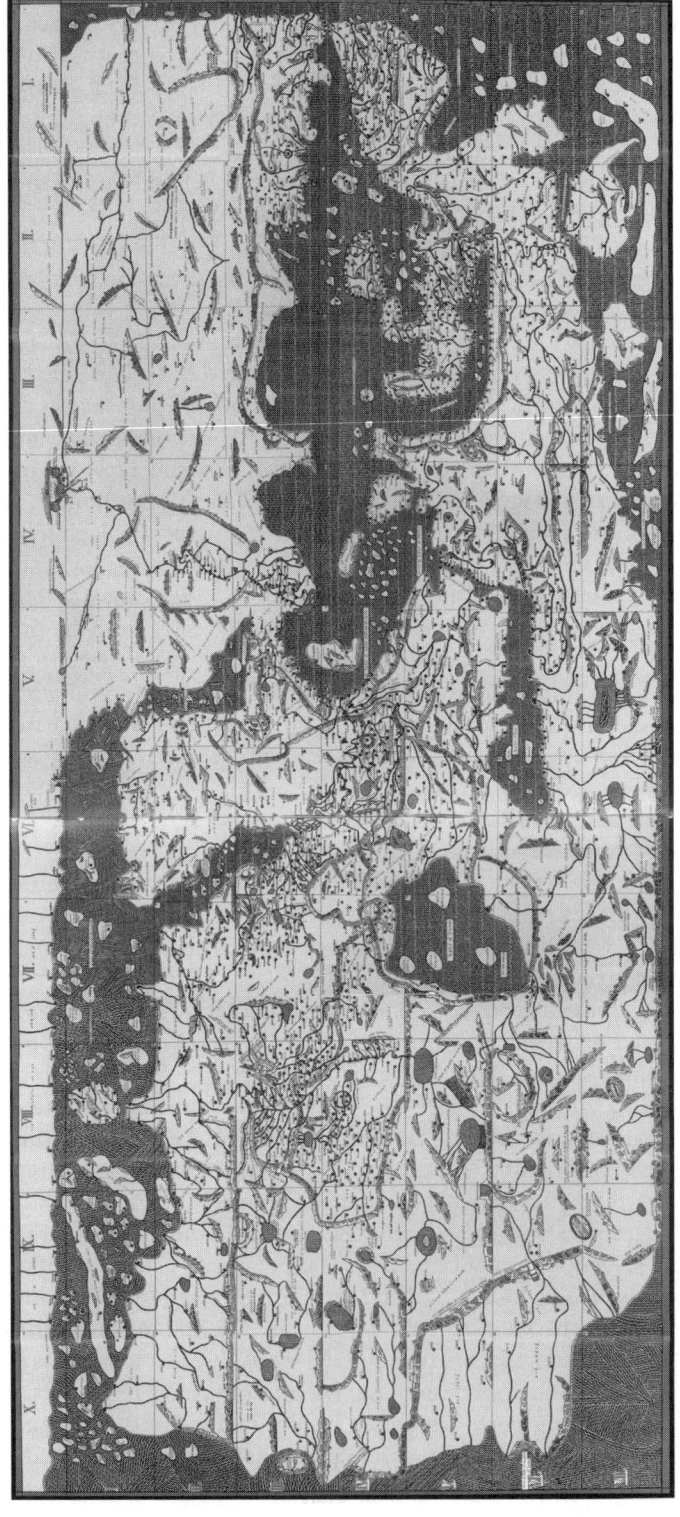

Map 8.1 Al-Idrīsī's map of the world with the Mediterranean at its center and Africa on top. Source: Private Collection/Universal History Archive/UIG/Bridgeman Images.

assiduously by caravans that from the Mediterranean and Atlantic shores of today's Morocco, Algeria, and Tunisia reached south Ghana and proceeded to the heart of the sub-Saharan region. As a good observer – and in line with numberless travel accounts that would follow over the next 10 centuries – al-Idrīsī reports on economic activities: what was grown in each region and, therefore, what was consumed or traded. His list includes millet, wool, slaves, gold, fish, goats, and other items. He includes descriptions of these types of commodities and links them to frequent observations and remarks about social differences, signaled by the wearing of certain fabrics and types of cloth. "The rich people wore robes of cotton and *manteaux* (coats)." Al-Idrīsī was also interested in the number of days or journeys that it took to travel from one location to another, tracing on the page a textual map of the areas visited or studied and providing a guide to distance. This awareness of place and distance is clearly reflected in his meticulous rendering of the number of days it took him – traveling at the regular speed of caravans – to go from one location to another in Africa. Although the Nile river is mentioned too often in relation to Ghana and the western Maghreb for us to feel comfortable as to al-Idrīsī's actual awareness of the geography of northern Africa, Ghana, the land of gold, is described as being linked to northern Africa, and thus to the Mediterranean by the caravans plying the desert.

The *Description* wanders east to the better known world (for al Idrīsī) of Nubia and Egypt, by his lifetime already well established regions of Dar al-Islam. In describing these locations, he could borrow freely from a well-established and ancient knowledge of Egypt. His first climatic region, therefore, extends from the Atlantic shores to the lands irrigated by the Nile, reaching south into sub-Sahara Africa. As the author reminds us in the introduction to his "second climate," he sought to render an account of all that is remarkable in term of "towns, villages, mountains, cultivated and uncultivated soils, as well as animals, minerals, seas, islands, kings and nations, manners, customs, and religions." Although his descriptions, as noted earlier, do not always vouch for al-Idrīsī's ambitious program or actual minutely detailed knowledge, his capacious expectations and geographical reach provide a window into what his patron, Roger II, hoped for in this description. They also allow us to see how the writer himself wished to provide a complete and comprehensive description of the lands stretching south of the Mediterranean (which for him meant north of the Mediterranean).

Along the way, as he continues his description of Africa, al-Idrīsī also collects the same old stories that either: 1) engaged in pejorative representations of Black Africans and of mythical androgynous lands with little difference between the sexes, or 2) depicted humans who dressed themselves with the leaves of trees, speaking an unintelligible language, and engaged in a perennial struggle with sea monsters. Dragons also appear in his narrative, with Alexander the Great making the obligatory appearance and, as befits heroes, defeating the monster to the eternal gratitude of the island's inhabitants.[7] In al-Idrīsī's narrative, the description of monstrous races – appearing at the margins of the civilized world and away from the western Mediterranean – reflected the author's mixture of personal observation, knowledge of his immediate world, and a propensity to fantasy that he shared with earlier geographers and his contemporaries, whether Christians, Jews, or Muslims. However, when describing the Maghreb, Al-Idrīsī is on more solid ground. In twelfth-century North Africa – present day Morocco, Algeria, and Tunisia – al-Idrīsī describes actual distances between one point and another, as opposed to how many journeys were usual to reach a particular destination. He notes the presence of Jews, their wealth, and the restrictions imposed on them by Muslim rulers.[8] One also learns of trade between Muslim Spain and the coast of Africa and the patterns of trade within the western Maghreb. His descriptions of Fez, for example, reflect a first-hand acquaintance with the city, and they are a reminder of Fez's importance and vitality in the twelfth century. The city functioned as the focal point of the western Maghreb, a hub for commerce and the distribution of its rich agricultural production, and a site for political primacy in the region. Yet, al-Idrīsī, while describing Fez and its hinterland positively, does not neglect to tell us about the bloody social and factional conflicts agitating the city.[9] Also coming to life in al-Idrīsī's narrative are the different sites in North Africa that served as Almoravid centers of power: Fez, Tlemcen, Oran – all three already connected by trade and politics to the Iberian Peninsula in the eleventh century – and Algiers, also flourishing in the eleventh and twelfth centuries. One place mentioned prominently was Bougie, the capital of the central Maghreb and a communications hub for the region. Beyond the region lay Tunis and Carthage. Significantly, al-Idrīsī does not fail to connect the Muslim world of North Africa to its Roman past and to note the ruins of a great Roman settlement, silent witness to the enduring presence of Rome along the shores of the Mediterranean. He also condemns the Arabs for destroying some of the riches of the region, while heaping praise on his patron – the great king Roger – and on his conquest of Tripoli in 1145.[10]

I could fill many pages with a summary of al-Idrīsī's description of Africa. But here what matters is not so much how many sites are mentioned or described in some detail (a lot of them) or al-Idrīsī's at times expert, first-hand knowledge of these locations, nor his descent into myth for others, what matters is the combination of personal observations and the deployment of ancient sources and hearsay that are at the heart of travel narratives. Before proceeding to his travels in and descriptions of the Iberian Peninsula, a world in which Christians and Muslims shared a space on terms of some equality in the twelfth century, it may be useful to examine what al-Idrīsī, the traveler, wrote about his ancestral land. Strangely, Ceuta, his hometown, is rarely mentioned as he describes the world of Dar al-Islam in North Africa for his Christian patron. Not unlike Leo Africanus in the sixteenth century (see below), al-Idrīsī emerges as one of those "trickster travelers," to use Natalie Z. Davis's description of Leo Africanus, a man negotiating the mental space and difference between the two worlds that he inhabited. Unlike Leo Africanus, however, al-Idrīsī remained a Muslim, since conversion, a point worth emphasizing, was not a requirement for royal service in twelfth-century Sicily.

In depicting North Africa, there are tropes evident in his work, as was often the case in subsequent traveler accounts of the western Mediterranean. The sea, though not directly described, is ever present. Special attention is given to those localities close to the Mediterranean Sea and distances are often given for these locations as numbers of days of sea journeys (as imprecise a count as that may be). The impression is that, in addition to the extensive caravan trade into the interior and across the Sahara, North Africa in this period also knew a vigorous coastal sea trade.

Al-Idrīsī is also concerned – as most medieval guides, such as the pilgrim from Bordeaux visiting Jerusalem, mentioned above, or as I have noted for al-Idrīsī before – with actual measurable distances. He felt the need to inform the reader of how many journeys were necessary between one point and another. Far more crucial for an understanding of the economy of Mediterranean North Africa is the manner in which al-Idrīsī wrote about movement or travel centered around specific locations or transportation links. It was not sufficient just to mention the number of journeys between one location and another, but to detail how all the locations, whether centering on Fez, Tunis, or elsewhere, connected with many others. What emerge are patterns of trade that permit us to see the crisscrossing of the Maghreb by the movement of people and goods. Al-Idrīsī also pays careful attention to the economic resources of diverse regions, confirming, as would be the case in Europe north of the Mediterranean, the character of agriculture in the Middle Ages and the reliance on those basic staples and livestock grown or tended on the lands around the sea: cereal grains, fruit, olive oil, goats, and the like.

Religion, on the other hand, does not play a central role in al-Idrīsī's description of Africa. Was it because, writing for his Christian master in Sicily, he did not wish to emphasize Islam – though notices of Islam's expansion into Central and sub-Saharan Africa are included? Jews appear in the narrative, as do, notwithstanding the theoretical religious unity of Islam, the factious Muslim politics of the region. The past, as already noted, is ever present. The shores of the Mediterranean embraced a common classical cultural inheritance, one of which al-Idrīsī must have been fully aware in Sicily with its Greco-Roman sites and contacts with the East, but to which he could also attest while traveling in North Africa and Iberia.

AL-IDRĪSĪ AND IBERIA

Although a traveler going from North Africa to al-Andalus in the twelfth century remained in Dar al-Islam, al-Idrīsī makes a clear distinction between these two worlds – the latter a peninsula, between the Atlantic (the *mer des Ténèbres*) and the Mediterranean. For him, the Atlantic, the Ocean Sea, is *terra incognita*. It is filled in his narrative, as was the case in some of his descriptions of Africa, with mysteries appropriate to its immensity and unknown extent. The Mediterranean was once a lake, or so al-Idrīsī tells us, inserting into his narrative a bizarre account of how Alexander the Great, aware of the continuous antagonisms between North and South, dug a canal (the Straits of Gibraltar) separating the two lands. Al-Idrīsī, who tells us that he had navigated the Straits of Gibraltar, notes the difference in height between Atlantic and Mediterranean waters and how Atlantic waters flow into the Mediterranean – an explanation for the swift current that made sailing out of the latter sea so difficult.

Al-Idrīsī's accounts of the European and African shores around the Straits show a first-hand acquaintance with the region. This is as it should be from someone born in Ceuta and who understood the close relationship between towns on both sides of the Straits (Ceuta, Tarifa, and Alcázar Masmuda, a town in North Africa, 12 miles across the sea from Tarifa). His knowledge of Iberia's geography is considerable, encompassing not just Muslim Spain but areas under Christian rule as well. It is a knowledge that also includes a fairly good grasp of history. In describing Algeciras, he retells the story of the Muslim invasion in 711, while tracing Algeciras's geographical links to the lands beyond the shores of the Mediterranean. Our narrator describes in perfect detail two distinct ways to reach Seville from Algeciras: one sailing the Straits into the Atlantic to Cádiz and then up the Guadalquivir to still Muslim Seville, the other a land route that followed river valleys north to the city.

Similar to his account of Africa, al-Idrīsī emphasizes distances, that is, is how many journeys (sometimes identified as short journeys) are necessary between one location and another. Since one may calculate journeys as between 35 and 50 kilometers a day (depending on terrain and mode of transportation), one gets an appropriate sense of distance, even more so when distances are spelled out in miles. For example, he provides accurate distances as follows: from Castella by the Sea to Tarifa is 14 miles, from Tarifa to Santa María del Algarve 12 miles, and so forth. One must not underestimate the strategic importance that map-making, whether the cartographic representation of the *Tabula Rogeriana* or al-Idrīsī's textual mapping, had for commerce and politics. Roger II wished for an empirical depiction of that Mediterranean world in which the Norman rulers of Sicily had to live. Al-Idrīsī provides him with that and more. Also, as is true of his African description, he is sensitive to the economic resources of each of the areas he describes (olive oil from the Aljarafe), to the religious buildings (the mosques at Santa María del Algarve), and to language.

In a wonderful aside on language – one that connects with one of the themes I explore in this book (see Chapter 7) – al-Idrīsī comments on the inhabitants of Silves, a town close to the Atlantic, three journeys from Badajoz. The population of Silves and its hinterland, al-Idrīsī informs us, is composed mostly of Arabs from Yemen who "speak a very rare Arabic dialect . . . have the ability to versify and are eloquent and spiritual whether [they are] humble people or from higher social standing."[11] His ability to distinguish between different forms of Arabic and to establish a linguistic hierarchy show a clear understanding of the linguistic plurality found in the Mediterranean, one to which an educated man, as al-Idrīsī was, would have always been sensitive. On an interesting note, our guide provides an eyewitness account of the management of water in Mérida and elsewhere that shows his understanding of the western Mediterranean ecology and economy, even if, shortly afterwards, he relates a somewhat fantastic story about eight adventurers sailing into the Atlantic – the moral of the story being that it was not a very good idea to venture into that ocean.

What happened when al-Idrīsī crossed from Dar al-Islam to Christian lands? He had already left his Muslim homeland in North Africa and had settled in

Sicily in the privileged court of Roger II. Then, at his patron's prompting, he had embarked on a voyage of observation, entering into his account a host of information – some fairly accurate, some of it fictitious – that would have provided Roger II with a grasp of the lands around the western Mediterranean. Al-Idrīsī thus traveled back to the lands of Islam on both sides of the Straits of Gibraltar, but while in Iberia, either through direct observation or through reliable informants' accounts, he also visited or described Christian lands that were, during the year of his visit, engaged in frequent warfare with the Muslim kingdoms of *taifas*. Two of his descriptions deserve comment. The first is that of Toledo, conquered by the Castilian king Alfonso VI in 1085, that is, decades before al-Idrīsī's description, and the second is that of Santiago de Compostela's, one of the most important Christian pilgrimage sites in Western Europe and never held by Islam.

Al-Idrīsī's account of Toledo is written in the first-person style, as someone who had seen the city with his own eyes. His narrative shows an understanding of the city's history, its topography, waterworks, and monuments. He was clearly aware of Toledo's Visigothic past, and he reminds the reader of Toledo's political importance as capital of the Visigothic Empire and as a hub of road communications for the entire peninsula (something that Toledo had also inherited from its Roman past). Although he mentions the capture of the city by Islam in the early eighth century and the Visigothic treasures found there, there is no mention at all of the Christian Reconquest or of the actual multi-religious character of the city in the middle of the twelfth century. As to Santiago, al-Idrīsī compares the church – still then the smaller ancient church that would not be rebuilt until almost a century later – to that of the Holy Sepulcher in Jerusalem. He mentions the pilgrims that had begun to pour into the city in large numbers around the twelfth century. He describes the 300 gold and silver crosses found within the church and the numerous priests that performed the liturgical services, but little else. The description is superficial, as is his mention of Barcelona, for example, and raises questions as to whether he actually saw these places for himself or described them second hand.

If one accepts that he did, what would it have been like to travel through Muslim and Christian lands with his compromised identity of a Muslim scholar working as an agent for a Christian king (albeit a fairly eclectic one)? What does that tell us about the world of the western Mediterranean? Or about those few scholarly travelers who, as shall be seen in the next chapter, brought to their narratives a substantial knowledge of history and a keen sense of the economic, geographical, and cultural aspects of the lands they visited and described?

Al-Idrīsī is only our first example, but one can already discern the manner in which movement across the Mediterranean from Islam to Christianity and back was possible (perhaps even more so than it is today), and the inquisitiveness of those who traveled and wrote about their experiences. Whether it was because travelers felt the necessity of rendering their experience of that newly acquired knowledge into words, as Ibn Battūta did, or whether, as was the case with al-Idrīsī and much later with Leo Africanus, their positions as aliens in an alien world forced them to so do, their writings reveal a moment of encounter between the two worlds on the two shores of the Middle Sea.

But was a twelfth-century educated man born in the region, or for that matter a twenty-first-century woman or man, ever fully an alien anywhere in the western Mediterranean basin?

Ibn Battūta

Abu-Abdullah Muhammad Ibn Battūta's sense of the topography of the entire Mediterranean is imbedded in his travel narrative, the *Rihal* (translated with notations by H.A.R. Gibb as *The Travels of Ibn Battūta*). Born in 1304 on the Atlantic side of the Straits of Gibraltar in Tangier (Morocco) to a prestigious Berber family with a long tradition of judicial service, Ibn Battūta went wandering through Dar al-Islam and probably beyond in what is perhaps the most remarkable feat of travel in the pre-modern era. Considering that he did his extensive travel, reaching India and perhaps China in the East, sub-Saharan Africa in the South, and Granada across the Mediterranean, mostly by joining traders or pilgrim caravans, his almost 30 years of travel (1325–1354) are truly unprecedented. But if his voyages were unique, his narrative power, keen sense of observation, and voracious curiosity also make him one of our most significant sources for understanding what traveling along the shores of the Mediterranean and across the sea meant in the fourteenth century. Far more significant, his account and the very nature of his travel show us the global reach of Islam during this period. Someone who was born and died (in 1368 or 1369) on the shores of the western Mediterranean did travel to the far reaches of the known world, and the world he described was both familiar and unfamiliar.[12] Such was the power of his observations that, through his narrative, this world, both known and alien, comes alive, fully alive, for his readers. Is that not, after all, what traveling is all about, the recognition of the familiar in the context of the strange and unknown?

As tempting as it may be to follow Ibn Battūta on his far-ranging voyages, and to experience what it was like for a western Mediterranean man, born by the shores of that sea, to travel to India, to Central Asia, to Mecca, to Timbuktu, I focus here on his travels throughout North Africa and into al-Andalus. Knowing that, chronologically, he visited most of the North African coast early in his life – he was only 21 – on the occasion of his first pilgrimage to Mecca (the *hajj*), and then, after his return from Mecca, the Maghreb and al-Andalus in his middle years, one can see the comparisons he often made between home and other places. Although he tells us that he wished "to travel the earth," in the end, he returned home to continue his sojourn, as it were, through writing.

NORTH AFRICA IN 1325

In June of 1325, Ibn Battūta departed from Tangier on a pilgrimage to Mecca and Medina. Traveling along the coast, our narrator and his companions – part of a group of merchants, two qādis (or judicial officials), and others from Tunis – traveled by a coastal road that linked Tangier to Tlemcen, Algiers,

Bougie, and eventually Alexandria. Ibn Battūta tells us little about the geography of the region or of these towns themselves, but two things are clear and telling for us: 1) that the travelers chose land routes over coastal sailing to Alexandria; 2) that the roads between North African cities were thick with bandits, a well-known feature of medieval and early modern Mediterranean life. Upon reaching Tunis, Ibn Battūta's narrative emphasizes the city's local political and, above all, religious practices. His travel narrative is marked by religious utterances or by descriptions of religious festivals and behavior, such as the breaking of the fast at the conclusion of Ramadan or his noting of the tomb of a learned Malik scholar and Imam.[13] Besides details of his own marriage, on rain (which would have been a rarity at certain times of the year in coastal North Africa), and on the continuous threat of roving bandits, we learn little about North Africa, as Ibn Battūta travels beyond the shores of the western Mediterranean on his way to Tripoli, Mecca, and the East.

Nonetheless, a closer reading of the text reveals much. Pilgrims and merchants travel together, some for profit, others for pious reasons. Traveling alone in fourteenth-century North Africa, or in Europe for that matter, was not safe. In North Africa, the journeys took them from one important urban center to another. In Dar al-Islam pilgrims were welcome – as was the case with Christian pilgrims in Christendom – as custom and traditions of hospitality were carefully observed on either shore of the Mediterranean.

While Ibn Battūta's travels in the East have had an enduring hold on the scholarly imagination as a Muslim counterpart to the better-known writings by Marco Polo (though I would suggest that Ibn Battūta's writings are far more informative and expansive than those of the Italian traveler), his later travels into al-Andalus and into the heart of Africa have received far less attention. For us, these voyages are of greater significance as they show the human traffic across the Straits of Gibraltar. These are links that remain very much alive – and in far greater volume than during the peregrinations of a Malik scholar in the fourteenth century. Today, in a parallel between the distant past and the present, North Africans working in the European community, most of them Muslims, return home from Northern Europe during the summer holiday. At the same time, legal and illegal immigrants travel, as we shall see in detail in Chapter 12, in the other direction. But what Ibn Battūta shows us in convincing fashion is the manner in which the western Mediterranean connected the two shores of the sea providing access from the North African coast to the great markets south of the Sahara. Map 8.2 shows the extent of these travels and conveys the extent of Ibn Battūta's peripatetic travels.[14]

His narrative of these travels, when he was approaching by then his fiftieth year of life, begins with a touching mention of his journey to visit his mother's tomb in Ceuta. Having suffered from illnesses for three months, he marked his recovery by joining a jihad. He indicates that this took place after the death at the siege of Gibraltar in 1350 of Alfonso XI, the only Christian king vanquished by the plague. Thus, Ibn Battūta's narrative provides us with a glimpse of conflict between Muslims and Christians in the Iberian region around the Straits of Gibraltar and of the struggle for control of that most strategic Mediterranean outlet. Ibn Battūta's language is combative and bellicose. "Alfonso XI was" a

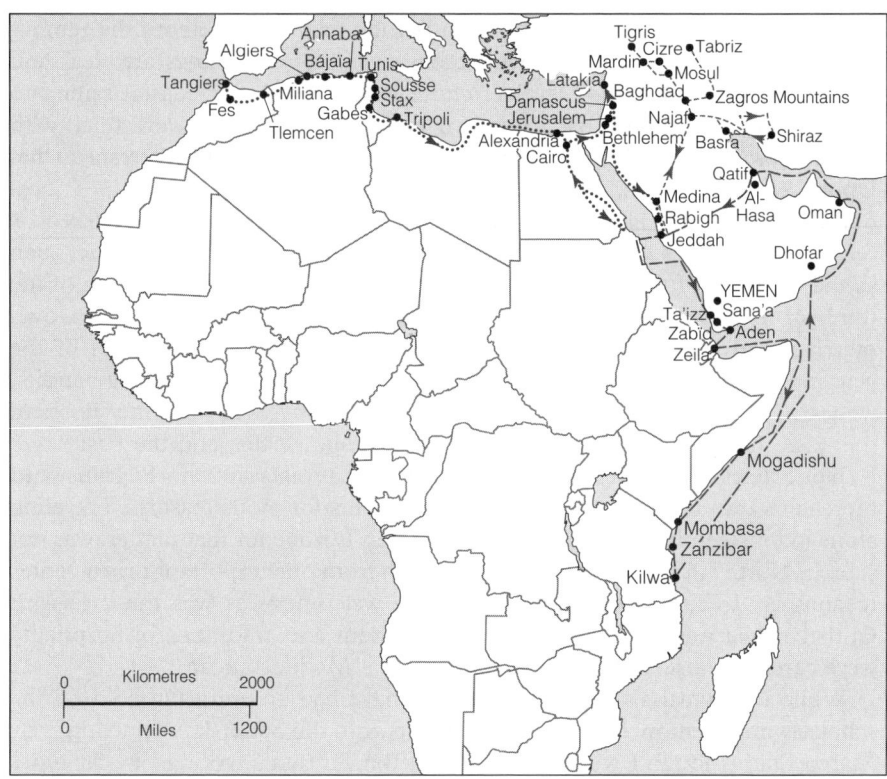

Map 8.2 Ibn Battūta's itinerary in North Africa and Spain from 1349 to 1354.
Source: Sladew, https://en.wikipedia.org/wiki/File:Battuta-path-1325-1326.png.
Used under CC BY-SA 3.0, https://creativecommons.org/licenses/by-sa/3.0/deed.en.

"Christian tyrant . . ." "The Christians are idolaters." Placing his account within the long historical context of the Muslim's conquest of Spain, Ibn Battūta heaps high praise on the fortifications and works in Gibraltar (Jabel) and on the nearby town of Ronda – as beautiful today as he described it in the fourteenth century. He does not fail to mention that some of his own relatives held positions of authority in Islamic Spain, reinforcing his connections to al-Andalus.[15]

Yet, the Marinid rule (the ruling house in North Africa promoting campaigns in southern Andalusia) in western Andalusia was, at best, a tenuous one. Traveling to Málaga by land as they followed roads that bordered the sea, some of his companions, who had gone on ahead of him, were captured by Christian raiders. Ibn Battūta's short but dramatic narrative retells a common western medieval and early modern Mediterranean story. Four Christian galleys landed troops in the area, took his companions by surprise, killed one of the travelers and a fisherman caught by chance in the fray, and imprisoned 10 of them. In a later chapter, we shall see the dynamics of these recurring patterns of raids, ransom, and slavery generated by violent encounters between Christians and

Muslims on both shores of the Mediterranean. Ibn Battūta, to our fortune, for otherwise we would not have his impressive travel narratives, was not captured. He tells us how, upon his arrival in Málaga, the Muslim religious authorities were already at work collecting funds for the ransom of the 10 prisoners – let us not forget that ransoming, though mostly studied from the Christian side, went equally both ways.

The best of Ibn Battūta's narrative power in this section of his account of travels in Spain is dedicated to Granada. "Its environs," he tells us, "have not their equal in any country in the world." Going to Málaga and to Granada was for Ibn Battūta, a return home. His description of the Vega de Granada, the orchards and gardens that encircled the city, serves as a reminder of how, in the mid-fourteenth century, when the fate of Islam in the peninsula was already pretty much decided, the Muslims could still build places of beauty and rule cities that remained centers of learning. The Alhambra was already well under construction when Ibn Battūta visited the city. And Granada was a cosmopolitan city: Persians, including dervishes from cities on the Silk Road, and even Indians inhabited the city. Returning to North Africa by retracing his steps to Málaga (Granada's main port, which maintained an active trade with North Africa until the end of the fifteenth century) and traveling by sea across the western Mediterranean, Ibn Battūta made a detour back to Marrakesh and Fez before embarking on yet another extraordinary voyage across the Sahara to Mali and back to Fez by way of Timbuktu and Buda.[16]

Few voyagers have ever traveled as far or as extensively as Ibn Battūta did. He wished, most of all, to travel the earth, and he did. His sojourns in North Africa, al-Andalus, and the Sahara, though not sharing in the exotic nature of his descriptions of India or Central Asia, nonetheless provide us with a window onto what Dar al-Islam in the West felt like. They show us a world with the Mediterranean as its center. They show us the movement of goods and people, the networks of roads, the seafaring, and the caravans that brought that world together and also kept it apart. For Ibn Battūta, the Christians were idolaters and enemies. His narrative, as ambitious and expansive as it was, did not encompass the world of Christianity. The western Mediterranean was often, and remains, a site of encounter, and in the fourteenth century, not unlike the twenty-first, those encounters were also often violent ones.

Leo Africanus

Al-Hasan Ibn Muhammad Ibn Ahmad al-Wazzan, better known to his Christian contemporaries as Leo Africanus, is perhaps not the best example of those who, traveling in Dar al-Islam, give us a glimpse of the Christian world. He may be better placed among those conversos or renegades I have already mentioned in an earlier chapter. But his life – and any attempt to understand that life and to place it in the context of Islam and Christianity – powerfully rendered by Natalie Z. Davis in a wonderful book, *Trickster Travels: A Sixteenth-Century Muslim Between Worlds*, is a magnificent example – far better than that of al-Idrīsī or Ibn Battūta – of what it meant to cross that liminal space between religions. That space, in this particular case, was the western Mediterranean.[17]

Born in Granada, the last Islamic outpost on the Iberian Peninsula, on the eve of its surrender to Isabella and Ferdinand's armies in 1492 (he was probably born between 1480 and the very early 1490s), his experience of youth, after a few early years in Granada, was one of exile in Wattasid Fez. Not unlike Ibn Battūta, for whom Fez was the hub of his numerous travels, al-Wazzan's scholarly upbringing had Fez and travel as context. Anyone who has been to modern Fez or who has seen photos or movies of its medina and market can easily imagine what it felt like to live in al-Wazzan's Fez: a bustling city, a hub for North African commercial exchanges and trade from beyond. Fez connected, through North African ports, to European Mediterranean destinations across the sea. It connected eastward (whether by road or by sea) to the wider world of Dar al-Islam. But Fez, as Natalie Z. Davis points out, had also become a center of learning in Islamic law and religion (Sunni). In early sixteenth-century Fez, one would have found immigrants from al-Andalus and Maghreb natives working together in the compilation of legal decisions. They also generated a significant body of historical and biographical material. As Davis describes it, and as is echoed in al-Wazzan's (Leo Africanus's) famous *Description of Africa* and in his own life, one fundamental question was being asked: What was to be one's attitude towards dissent within Islam and what should one's attitude be towards Jews, Christians, or renegades? In a world of encounters between the two shores of the western Mediterranean that was, and remains, a central issue.[18]

The question was, of course, not an idle one for al-Wazzan. Early in his life he engaged on diplomatic and administrative missions in North Africa, a period when Portuguese and Castilian forces were putting added pressure on the Maghreb. Not unlike Ibn Battūta a century and a half before, al-Wazzan crossed the desert to Timbuktu and beyond into sub-Saharan Africa. Like al-Idrīsī and Ibn Battūta, he visited Egypt and probably went on the *hajj* to Mecca. It was on his return trip (a sea voyage) to North Africa in 1518 that he fell into the hands of Spanish corsairs, seeking captives in the eastern Mediterranean and away from their own shores. After a brief imprisonment in the Castel Sant'Angelo in Rome, al-Wazzan was presented as a gift to Pope Leo X and baptized in the church of Saint Peter (already then in the construction phase) in 1520. He took as his Christian name Giovanni Leone, in honor of his sponsor, the Pope. Leo X was, of course, a Renaissance Pope, and he recognized al-Wazzan, now the newly named Giovanni Leone or Leo Africanus, as an important cultural addition to his court. I should explain that the sobriquet Africanus appeared first in the Venetian publisher Giovanni Battista Ramusio's edition of al-Wazzan's *Description of Africa* (*Della descrittione dell'Africa et delle cose notabili . . . per Giovanni Lioni Africano in 1550*). Through the patronage of Leo X, he was given access to the Vatican library and worked on Arabic manuscripts there, but Leo Africanus was also an important source of information on North Africa at an important strategic moment in the growing conflict between Christian kingdoms and the rising power of the Ottoman Empire.

Once a Christian, Leo Africanus was able to travel throughout Italy, collecting material for an Arabic-Hebrew-Latin vocabulary or proto-dictionary that gives a sense of his linguistic skills. He also engaged in the composition of an Arabic grammar. Both of these works are extant only in small fragments, but they are revealing of the fluidity of languages among Mediterranean learned elites. Back in Rome, and still enjoying papal patronage, Leo Africanus embarked on the composition of his *Description of Africa*. Persuasively, Natalie Z. Davis has argued that in 1527 or shortly after, al-Wazzan/Yuhammad al-Asad (as Davis identifies him), or Leo Africanus, as I describe him here, left Rome, returning to North Africa and to Islam. Considering the upheavals created by the sack of Rome by Charles V's German and Spanish troops in 1527, one could see that the confusion of those months may have both prompted, and permitted, Leo Africanus's return to Dar al-Islam.

There is little more we know of Leo Africanus's life, except for some fragments of information that Natalie Z. Davis has ferreted out from the scarce extant sources. If I am interested here in Leo Africanus's biography, it is, above all, because of his physical, religious, and intellectual wanderings from Africa to Italy, from Islam to Christianity, from traditional Muslim scholarship to the Vatican library and Renaissance culture. Davis describes him as a "Trickster Traveler," and she is concerned with determining his true allegiances to one faith or another. Although these are important questions, for me Giovanni Leone, or al-Wazzan, represents one of those cultural brokers that plied the Mediterranean as merchants, translators, and diplomats. Not unlike some of the renegades or converts – such as Anselm of Turmeda, a fascinating character we have already examined in some detail in a previous chapter on religion (Chapter 6) – who created new knowledge at the intersection of two overlapping worlds, Leo Africanus did the same. He brought with him knowledge of Africa to which only mostly Muslims had access and made it available to Christians across the waters of the western sea. His *Description of Africa*, written, after all, for his Christian patrons, shows, as Davis argues, the kind of cultural hybridity in which knowledge of Africa, barely understood or known to Christian scholars, was rendered in terms borrowed from the western tradition.[19] As an example of the kind of cultural production generated by the constant contact between North and South, Islam and Christianity, in the western Mediterranean, Leo Africanus's work borrows, as did that of al-Idrīsī and Ibn Battūta, from ancient Greek knowledge of geography, mostly Ptolemy. This was a text well known and available in Arabic throughout Dar al-Islam, providing a common frame of reference for Christian and Muslim alike. Nonetheless, the nomenclature of geographical terms represented a crossover from one cultural and religious world to the other, what Davis describes as "a double vision."[20]

In many respects, while al-Idrīsī and Ibn Battūta's narratives reflected the intellectual superiority of Islam over Christian Europe, certainly in terms of geographical knowledge, by the early sixteenth century, the relationship between the two worlds had begun to reverse in the western Mediterranean. If the Ottomans' power still waxed strongly in the East and was applying increase pressure to the West, on the shores of the western Mediterranean, European powers, Portugal and Spain above all, were slowly carving enclaves in North Africa and venturing into the Ocean Sea (the Atlantic) in a fashion that transformed geographical knowledge in the known world (see Chapter 12). But what should one say about his *Description of Africa*? While it is not certain that his description of North Africa reflects al-Wazzan's (to return to his Muslim name) personal experience of place – his accounts of sub-Saharan Africa may have been borrowed from earlier writers – nonetheless, there are sections of the book that tell us a great deal about the Mediterranean at the onset of the early modern period. In al-Wazzan's division of Africa into different regions, I am mostly concerned with his description of the Maghreb, that is, the area running from Tunis to the Atlantic, or western Mediterranean Africa. Al-Wazzan's *Description of Africa*, sprinkled with autobiographical references, provides a closer look at the Mediterranean world of North Africa and at the possibilities of travel within Dar al-Islam. In these autobiographical asides, Leo Africanus, writing in Italy, evokes not only the geography of Africa (and al-Andalus), but also its culture and history.

Of his four-part division of Africa – Barbary, Numidia, Libya, and the "lands of the Blacks" – my focus is on the first one, Barbary, and, to a lesser extent, Numidia. One must remain, however, keenly aware of the manner in which all these artificial geographical divisions resulted from the experiences of religion, travel, and trade. Similarly, in Leo Africanus's *Description*, the Mediterranean and the Atlantic are linked not just through the Straits of Gibraltar, as Europeans would first think, but through numberless roads and trade routes linking North Africa's Mediterranean urban centers to their Atlantic counterparts. In the first part of his *Description of Africa*, Leo Africanus makes rather pejorative observations about race (distinctions between white and black Africans), as well as providing some engaging reflections on language, religious conflicts within Islam, and the vices and virtues of Africa's inhabitants. One can see with how much interest his Italian readers would have received his work. Some of his observations – one must describe them as almost anthropological in nature – on those nomadic North Africans who lived in tents, echo Ibn Khaldûn's greatest work, *The Muqaddimah*, with its emphasis on Bedouin life.[21] Some of his historical references, such as, for example, the size of armies or the number of people killed in battle (in one case 1 million people) are blatant exaggerations. At the end of Part I, after a delightful little anecdote or allegory about a bird who could live underwater and paid no tribute to either the king of fishes or the king of birds by continuously switching from one realm to another, Leo Africanus reveals his own liminal status between two worlds. If Africans are usually harshly described and represented, in his writing Leo Africanus would emphasize his Granada origins and emphasize not being from Africa. Yet, he would also emphasize that he had been educated in Africa and not in Granada.

His approach to the description of place is comprehensive. In describing Tunis for his Christian readers, he begins with the etymological origins of the word, tracing its Latin and Arabic roots. He provides a history that goes back to the demise of Carthage, presents ethnographical material on such topics as the peculiar spinning techniques employed by the women in Tunis, and includes a careful description of the politics of Tunis during his own lifetime. Although Leo Africanus is not as thorough for every town he mentions, this is a remarkably comprehensive guide to the North African Mediterranean world.[22] Having traveled extensively through the Maghreb, he was also familiar with

Mecca, Istanbul, and other great cities in the eastern parts of Dar al-Islam. He had witnessed, as he lets us know in casual remarks when describing specific regions or cities, the constant armed conflicts between the diverse kingdoms of the Maghreb and the Portuguese and Spanish forces. The latter sought to establish footholds on the North African coast – as they did in Oran – or to attack North African ports that served as bases for Muslim corsair activity. Most notable is the passing reference to Barbarossa, one of the most formidable corsairs in the first half of the sixteenth century and someone who, along with his brother, will be discussed later on in far greater detail.[23]

Thus, in Leo Africanus's *Description of Africa*, a work purposely written as a convenient reference for his European masters and to help assuage the growing enmity between Ottomans (and North African Muslims) and Christians, we also see the historical hybridity of Mediterranean societies and their continuous encounters, often violent, such as those involving invading Portuguese and Spaniards or Muslim corsair raids. Yet, at other times, the encounters were intrinsic to learned exchanges. Proof of that second point are the work on geography undertaken by al-Idrīsī, working at the Sicilian court of Roger II, and Leo Africanus's own intellectual exchanges with his Italian counterparts or with his friend Egidius of Viterbo. In many respects, the *Description of Africa* is a quintessential example of the western Mediterranean as a site of encounter and cultural production. Leo Africanus, a "trickster traveler" for sure in Davis's formulation, was also a scholar and diplomat who served as an interlocutor between two cultures, a bird who could live among the fish (the Christians) as he did among his own kind (the Muslims).

MUSLIMS IN THE WEST RECONSIDERED

If I have spent this inordinate amount of time on the biographies of three Muslims traveling in the western Mediterranean and serving as cultural inter-locutors between the two shores of the Middle Sea, it is because these three figures stand for myriad other travelers and learned men (and women in the modern age) who experienced first-hand different religious, linguistic, and cultural communities, who wrote about them, and who allow us to see visions of otherness at precise moments in the chronological development of the West. In the next chapter, we will find some of these figures as merchants and corsairs, as well as their Christian counterparts. The *funduq*, that hospitable and commer-cial institution so magisterially described by the late and much missed Olivia Remie Constable, was one of those places of meeting and exchange.[24] In the pages that follow, I exchange the kind of monographic detail provided until this point for a broader vision of Muslims in Europe from the end of the Middle Ages to the present.

Lucette Valensi, whose life and work also bridge the Mediterranean, writes in her *Ces étrangers familiers. Musulmans en Europe (XVIe–XVIIIe siècles)* of the relevance of those who traveled, worked, learned, and taught in early modern Europe. Most of all, the experiences of some of these Muslims, experiences that were and are very different from those described above, parallel the lives of the millions of Muslims who live in Western Europe today. In a world where many of our leaders subscribe to such formulations as "the clash of civilizations," and where Islam is seen as a monolithic front facing the West, the Muslims of early modern Europe provide us with salutary lessons on how to face the present.[25] In Valensi's book, we met a whole gallery of Muslims who served Christian princes as valuable advisers and who served Christians as slaves. We see those who came to Europe as diplomats, those who were redeemed from their bondage, and even those who converted to Christianity (as Christians also converted to Islam). What her book does, above all, is to remind us that between the final expulsion of Moriscos from Spain in the early seventeenth century and the massive immigration of the twentieth century, Muslims never ceased to be a familiar presence in Europe. They did not really go away, but remained part of the structure of Christian Europe, as Christians did on the southern shores of the Mediterranean. They were, in Valensi's formulation, both "strangers and familiar."

Although most of the vignettes that Valensi explores for the early modern period are Mediterranean stories that tell of the vicissitudes of Moriscos, corsairs, or renegades (see chapters 5 and 7), one of the most fascinating accounts is that of Mehemed Riza Beg, an ambassador of the Shah of Persia to the court of Louis XIV of France at the end of Louis's reign, in 1714–1715. The subject of engravings, of fictionalized accounts, of hatred and interest, Riza Beg described aspects of his visit and impressions of the French court. Most significantly, among his observations is his description of the presence of women in the court and in the streets: women "who participated actively in dinner receptions, who spoke openly and danced in public."[26] If we learn anything from this description it is that, although "familiar," a great deal of strangeness remained in the perception of one group by the other. Cultures different from one's own could be described, but the sense of difference was always present just below the surface. Ambassadors from the Sublime Porte or from Persia, as well as slaves brought forcibly from their homelands, had experiences that were quite different from those of immigrants today. Rather than give accounts of personal experiences that differ remarkably depending on whether one sojourns to Europe from North Africa in search of employment or to study in a center of higher learning, whether one is a fervent believer or not, or whether one is a woman or a man, here I try very briefly to capture what is to be a Muslim immigrant in the West today (see also a discussion of immigration in chapters 9 and 12).

THE MODERN TRAVELER

In this age of airplanes, fast ships, and bullet trains, the experience of travel is radically different from that of medieval and early modern travelers, or even from that of nineteenth-century ones. Advances in transportation technology, however, are not the sole explanation for the different manner in which travelers experience the process of, in de Certeau's formulation once again, going from "here to there." In many respects, the growing sense of two distinct cultures and the erosion of familiarity between one shore of the western Mediterranean and the other have clear historical precedents. Already by the nineteenth century, the colonial occupation of North Africa by European powers, a topic that I refer to often throughout the book, propelled the creation of a discourse of difference, most notable among the French, that essentialized and romanticized Muslims in the eyes of most Europeans. This is most obvious in the depictions (some of which I explore in the next chapter) of North Africa as "oriental" and exotic. This was, of course, not limited to North Africa but applied to parts of the European Mediterranean, as for example Merimée's vision of southern (Moorish) Spain.

Yet, in an ironic fashion, the globalization of the world makes familiar what was once unfamiliar and alien. Alienation does survive, but its edge is now social (and sometimes religious) rather than to do with differences in material culture. The sharing of modes of dress, music, and the like, even by some of the poorest people on earth, removes some of the thrills of the new. How did al-Wazzan react to the sight of Rome? Surely, he knew great cities in Dar al-Islam. Some of them shared similar monuments with Rome – not surprisingly given the enduring presence of Rome in North Africa's ancient urban centers – but Renaissance Rome must have left an indelible mark on our "trickster traveler."

Today, especially for the international set, but even for humble immigrants, photos, emails, stories told by fellow travelers, guide books, and the like remove most of the mystery. There are still exotic places and fairly inaccessible tourist destinations, but there are no real unknowns or things to be discovered for the first time. In dealing with travel accounts of Muslim travelers in Europe in the contemporary world (as opposed to the issue of immigration in the twenty-first century), the difficulties of traveling from one culture to another reside not so much in the travel itself as in the individual process of acculturation and social adaptation, or, in many cases, the rejection of any form of assimilation. Those who write do not need to tell what they have seen, as the thrill of the new has been watered down by previous knowledge. For many of those for whom the new cultures they encounter across the narrow waters of the western Mediterranean must be jarring, their voices are often muted.

Emily Ruete's autobiographical *Memoirs of an Arabian Princess from Zanzibar* offers a prelude and contrast to contemporary accounts. Born Sayyida Salme, a Muslim princess, she traveled in Europe in the nineteenth century. Like all travelers, especially women travelers – think, for example, of Flora Tristan – she was "always an exile in spirit."[27] She traveled in Africa, Northern Europe, and the Middle East, a new Ibn Battūta, sojourning, however, in a very different world from that of the great fourteenth-century traveler. She was, after all, a convert to Christianity. She married a German merchant and escaped her family connections in Zanzibar for a domestic life in Germany, but, as Roxanne L. Euben astutely points out, "in contrast to a *rihla* (a true travel account a la al-Idrīsī or Ibn Battūta), in the preface, Salme describes her published work first as some 'sketches of my life,' then merely as a 'personal memoir' written after the fact."

By the nineteenth century then, narratives of travel had become essentially a conscious literary form of self-reflection. Today such narratives are mostly about interiority and acculturation, or, far more painfully, about the failure to acculturate. As for the other things, for the descriptions of landscape and buildings, types of food, good restaurants, and so on, we have travel guides such as the Michelin Green Guides that open windows into every world. I mentioned before that I had traveled through the Baltic region by boat. Although I had never been there before, I arrived with a significant amount of knowledge about what I was going to see. Maps or Google allowed me to walk the cities on the Baltic virtually and to follow those walking tours designed by guide books for my greatest enjoyment of monuments and sights. While most voluntary travel is in pursuit of pleasure and knowledge, what of another kind of travel, that undertaken out of need, fleeing either unendurable religious or political conditions – the political or conscience exile – or harsh economic conditions – the legal or illegal immigrant?

In the next chapter and, far more so, in the concluding chapter, I will explore the nature of immigration across and around the Mediterranean in the twentieth and twenty-first centuries – for this is an ongoing process with long-term effects on western Mediterranean culture, religiosity, and politics. But, I do not wish to leave this section without listening to the voices of a few among the many who crossed the Mediterranean in search of safety and work. Their voices, part of an oral history project undertaken by Behzad Yaghmaian, capture not so much the civilization of the western Mediterranean but the difficulties of crossing – because of education, religion, anti-immigrant feelings, and other factors – that these individuals found in places that for them could never be home. Al-Wazzan, a scholar and diplomat, would find far better conditions, but that was, of course, as long as he accepted Christian baptism and a new name.

THE VOICES OF IMMIGRANTS

I wish to begin with a short personal recollection. Almost 40 years ago, I traveled by car with my young family from Venice to Madrid. One of our stops along the road was at the town of Fréjus. It coincided with our need to rest, and it was the place where Napoleon had landed on his return from exile in Elba – another Mediterranean crossing worth remembering. We arrived at night and had the misfortune to choose a hotel by the train station. The next morning, as we prepared to continue our journey, right by the train station there were hundreds of North African young men. It was never clear to me whether they were expecting a train or had gathered there in hopes of daily work. Nonetheless, I have never forgotten the image, a powerful reminder of alienation and displacement. In chapters 9 and 12, I would like to trace the movement of people across national boundaries, whether legally or illegally, but if I tell this small story it is to remind myself that, unlike al-Idrīsī, Ibn Battūta, or al-Wazzan, these travelers, these immigrants I saw at Fréjus in the late 1970s, most probably left no accounts of their journeys, no recollection of their ancestral home, except perhaps as fragments of plaintive conversations, oral transmissions, and memory.

Rather than concentrate on the well-known history of North African migrants from Dar al-Islam to European countries, I follow here briefly some of the oral histories collected by Behzad Yaghmaian of Kurdish and Afghan immigrants to Paris. The stories often revolve around questions of sexual identity, persecution, and marginality. But they have in common the movement from their respective countries of Iran – the Iran of watchful mullahs and morality policing – Afghanistan, and the Kurdish regions north of Iraq. From Turkey and Greece, these illegal immigrants traveled by boat to Italy. Then, through a series of adventurous attempts, often failed attempts, they moved across the border, illegally traveling by train to Paris, Calais, London, and other places where illegal work or charity allowed them to survive. Their interviews reflect either the suffocating restrictions on their sexuality or individuality in their countries of origin, or the harshness of their new surroundings, as they sleep in parks, on benches, or grass patches, hassled by the police, fed by philanthropic or governmental programs. There are no accounts of the crossings, and there is often bitter reflection on their new settings. One untypical case is that of a woman identified as Ferial, probably an Afghan pretending to be an Iranian. Ferial rails against the unnaturalness of borders, as she does against gender distinctions. The stories of these immigrants from Dar al-Islam to Christian Europe, living on the margins, travelers across the eastern and western Mediterranean in the early twenty-first century, are striking by the absence of religion in their accounts, by the utter alienation both from their original homes and from their new place of exile.[28] Their stories, dark and moving, serve as a reminder of what had so dramatically changed, of how, while the physical Mediterranean of medieval and early travelers remained, the conditions of travel and the political and cultural contexts had been transformed. In many respects, these stories remind us of those people, who, reneging their religion or serving as interlocutors between two sides of the Mediterranean, lived often "betwixt and between."

NOTES

1 Michel de Certau, *The Writing of History*, trans. Tom Conley (New York: Columbia University Press, 1988). See especially the chapter entitled "Ethno-Graphy."

2 Maya Maskarinec, *Building Rome Saint by Saint in the Early Middle Ages* (Philadelphia: University of Pennsylvania Press, 2017); *"Foreign Saints at Home in Eighth- and Ninth-Century Rome. The Patrocinia of Diaconiae, Xenodochia and Greek Monasteries,"* in Cuius Patrocinio Tota Gaudet Regio. Saints' Cults and the Dynamics of Regional Cohesion, *eds. Stanislava Kuzmová, Ana Marinković and Trpimir Vedriš, Bibliotheca Hagiotheca, Series Colloquia, 3 (Zagreb: Hagiotheca, 2014), 21–37.*

3 Lucette Valensi, *Ces étrangers familiers. Musulmans en Europe (XVIe–XVIIIe siècles)* (Paris: Éditions Payot & Rivages, 2012).

4 See *Itinerary from Bordeaux to Jerusalem. The Bordeaux Pilgrim (333 A.D.)*, trans. Aubrey Stewart (London: Palestine Pilgrims' Text Society, 1887); Maribel Dietz, *Wandering Monks, Virgins and Pilgrims* (State College: Penn State University Press, 2005).

5 On Al-Idrīsī and other Muslim travelers and geographers of the period see *Géographes et voyageurs au moyen âge*, edited by Henri Bresc and Emmanuelle Tixier du Mesnil (Nanterre: Presses Universitaires de Paris Ouest, 2010).

6 Sanjay Subrahmanyam, *Three Ways to be Alien: Travails and Encounters in the Early Modern World* (Waltham, MA: Brandeis University Press, 2011).

7 Al-Idrīsī, *Description de l'Afrique et de l'Espagne*, trans. R. Dozy and M.J. de Goeje (Leyden: Brill, 1866), 61–62.

8 *Description de l'Afrique et de l'Espagne*, 81.

9 *Description de l'Afrique et de l'Espagne*, 86–90.

10 *Description de l'Afrique et de l'Espagne*, 138–143.

11 *Description de l'Afrique et de l'Espagne*, 217.

12 On Ibn Battūta, see Ross Dunn, *The Adventures of Ibn Battuta: A Muslim Traveler of the 14th Century* (London: Croom Helm, 1986); for his work, see *The Travels of Ibn Battūta, A.D. 1325–1354*, edited and translated by H.A.R. Gibb (Cambridge: Hakluyt Society at Cambridge University Press, 1958–2000) and pages ix–xvii for what little we know about his life and the history of the text. There is a new abridged edition by Tim Mackintosh-Smith (London: Picador, 2003).

13 *The Travels of Ibn Battūta, A.D. 1325–1354*, vol. I: 3–17.

14 *The Travels of Ibn Battūta, A.D. 1325–1354*, vol. I: 130.

15 *The Travels of Ibn Battūta, A.D. 1325–1354*, vol. I: 310–311.

16 *The Travels of Ibn Battūta, A.D. 1325–1354*, vol. IV: 946–49.

17 Natalie Zemon Davis, *Trickster Travels: A Sixteenth-Century Muslim Between Worlds* (New York: Hill and Wang, 2006).

18 Davis, *Trickster Travels: A Sixteenth-Century Muslim Between Worlds*, 3–87.

19 Davis, *Trickster Travels: A Sixteenth-Century Muslim Between Worlds*, 125–152.

20 Davis, *Trickster Travels: A Sixteenth-Century Muslim Between Worlds*, 127.

21 Ibn Khaldûn, *The Muqaddimah*, trans by Franz Rosenthal, ed. N.J. Dawood (Princeton: Princeton University Press, 9th paperback edition, 1989), 35–43.

22 There is an English translation of Leo Africanus's work available online through Google books. There are also partial translations in French, Spanish, and other languages. See *The History and Description of Africa and of the Notable Things Therein . . .* translated into English by John Pory in 1600, edited by Robert Brown (London: Hakluyt Society, 1896), 3 vols, III: 716–725.

23 *The History and Description of Africa and of the Notable Things Therein . . .* , vol III: 701–702.

24 Olivia Remie Constable, *Housing the Stranger in the Mediterranean World: Lodging, Trade, and Travel in Late Antiquity and the Middle Ages* (Cambridge & New York: Cambridge University Press, 2003). See chapter 7 for a description of the *funduq*.

25 Valensi, *Ces étrangers familiers*, 7.

26 Valensi, *Ces étrangers familiers*, 212–222. Susan Mokhbery's fine work deals with the Persian ambassadors to France in luxurious detail, "France and Persia in the Age of Absolutism." PhD diss., UCLA, 2010.

27 Roxanne Leslie Euben, *Journeys to the Other Shore: Muslim and Western Travelers in Search of Knowledge* (Princeton: Princeton University Press, 2006), 157.

28 Behzad Yaghmaian, *Embracing the Infidel: Stories of Muslim Migrants on the Journey West* (New York: Delacorte Press, 2005).

[9] ENCOUNTERS II: THE MEDITERRANEAN AS A SITE OF CONFLICT, MOVEMENT, AND ENCOUNTER

In the previous chapter, I glossed a series of vignettes – most of them chronologically located in the Middle Ages and the early modern period, the period perhaps of most intense awareness of religious difference – that trace the presence of Muslims in Western Christian Europe. Through their works, this handful of individuals served as interlocutors between the Muslim and Christian shores of the western Mediterranean. In spite of the centuries that separated al-Idrīsī, Ibn Battūta, and Leo Africanus, or the great span of time between them and our present, the flow of Muslims to Europe continues. Nowadays, it is far less the erudite scholar – though there are certainly North African scholars working and/or lecturing in Europe – brought to Christian Europe by patronage, as was the case of al-Idrīsī's employment at Roger II's Sicilian court in the early twelfth century, or that of Leo Africanus caught and sold as a slave to Rome in 1518, than it is, as shall be seen in detail in the concluding chapter, immigrants desperately in search of better economic conditions and security.

This chapter attempts the near impossible: to depict the many different ways in which, over two millennia, men and women met, fought, traded, converted (or not), and intermingled in what was, and remains, a site of encounters. In writing it, I also hope to bring the story closer to the present (without forsaking the past) and to convey, by a series of examples, short narratives, and poignant vignettes, the enduring nature of the Mediterranean as a setting for the flow of people from one shore to the other. While crossing the body of water that separates Africa from Europe has been reduced to a few minutes or hours by airplanes and swift ships, for many such a crossing represents a momentous transformation and a challenge to long-held values and one's own particular culture.

In the western Mediterranean – for almost all of its history and until the colonization of most of northern Africa by European powers in the nineteenth

The Western Mediterranean and the World: 400 CE to the Present, First Edition. Teofilo F. Ruiz.
© 2018 John Wiley & Sons, Ltd. Published 2018 by John Wiley & Sons, Ltd.

century – conflict was often intertwined with trade, cooperation, and cultural exchanges. Moreover, throughout the Middle Ages and into the early modern period, conflict between religious groups, as I have noted before, was not more common than conflict within them. Christians fought against other Christians a great deal more than they did against Muslims. The same can be said of Islamic realms. They engaged in battle with other Muslims as they did with Christians. In spite of the discourses of crusade and jihad in the eleventh and twelfth centuries – and in centuries afterwards – religious differences, while providing an important incentive for strife, were far from the sole reason for war. Often, small differences within a specific religion led to greater conflict than that created by the encounter between two different religious systems. Thus, as we have seen in an earlier chapter, or as we read in the press today, the conflicts between Sunni and Shi'a and between Protestants and Catholics, or the brutality unleashed in the persecution of heretics, have generated as many wars and as much violence, if not more, than the clashes between Christian, Muslims, and Jews.

The point, of course, is that different groups met, fought, and cooperated in the western Mediterranean according to a series of vectors that included (and includes) religion, race, linguistic identities, geography, social status, commercial rivalries, and other factors. These diverse contributors to conflict between different religions were deeply grounded in shifting historical contexts. They yielded unique situations which, when taken as a whole, provide a complex portrait of Mediterranean societies. What then prompted these exchanges and encounters? In the previous chapter, we gazed on a discrete number of Muslim travelers and emigrants who wrote about Dar al-Islam while employed or traveling in Christian lands. Here, the category of travel narratives is also examined from the perspectives of Muslim writers, but with the addition of Jewish and Christian as well as non-religious modern writers. Another important category is that of trade with the *funduq* (briefly mentioned before) as a site for the encounter of merchants. Slavery, corsair activity, and redemption provide us with yet another entry into those points of contact between the diverse religions, languages, and polities of the western Mediterranean. Finally, immigration and modern travel provide us with a further window into the past (see also Chapter 12).

CHRISTIAN TRAVELERS IN THE LANDS OF ISLAM

As Adeline Rucquoi has shown in a series of remarkable articles, most signally, "Las rutas del saber: España en el siglo XII" (The Roads of Knowledge: Spain in the Twelfth Century), the Iberian world (mostly Toledo, Córdoba, Barcelona, and other significant sites of encounter for Muslim, Jewish, and Christian scholars) became an important location for the acquisition of new knowledge (mostly Ancient Greek science and philosophy and their Muslim translations as well as Muslim commentaries and original works) for Christian medieval scholars. That new knowledge, in turn, would propel cultural changes throughout the medieval West. Scholars from France,

England, and Germany flocked to the South, to the Mediterranean lands of Dar al-Islam. There, through the mediation of Muslim, Jewish, and local Christian scholars and translators, exchanges of people and ideas took place. The same pattern of intellectual exchanges applied to Sicily, where the Norman royal court served as a site for the conflation of several learned traditions, hence, al-Idrīsī.[1]

There have always been curious Christians who, from the ninth century onwards, sought the knowledge available in the lands of Islam. The Muslims were the great transmitters of Classical culture and knowledge brokers throughout the Mediterranean world. The number of Christian scholars (Herman of Carinthia, Robert Ketton, and many others) traveling to Iberia (mostly to Toledo or Barcelona), to Sicily, and, after the end of the eleventh century, to the Holy Land is considerable indeed. Here, for the sake of brevity, I recount the stories of just a few.

Before the twelfth century and the revival of learning in the West, Christian savants had already visited the Mediterranean region in search of the knowledge that Islam had preserved from the collapse of the Classical age. One of the best-known examples is that of Gerbert of Aurillac (ca. 946–1003). Born in the kingdom of France, a monk at the monastery of Saint Gerard d'Aurillac, Gerbert accompanied the ruler of Catalonia back to Barcelona from his northern monastery in the 960s, lived in Vic and Ripoll (both important centers of learning and repositories of Arabic texts), and was part of the bishop of Vic's entourage on a diplomatic mission to Córdoba. Córdoba in the late tenth century (before its demise in the mid-1030s) was one of the great centers of learning in the Islamic world. There, Gerbert became fascinated with math and astronomy, encountered the abacus, and learned about the so-called Arabic numbers (which were not really used around the Mediterranean by Christian scribes until the thirteenth century). He returned then to Northern Europe, served in the court of the Ottonian emperors, held an important position as a teacher at Reims Cathedral (the ritual center for the French monarchy), and ended up as Pope Sylvester II (999–1003). He is one of many who were instrumental in the circulation of knowledge between the Islamic Mediterranean and the Christian North. He was someone who had seen the glory of a Mediterranean Muslim city (Córdoba). For his effort, he was branded a sorcerer, and his memory and legacy were besmirched. That fact also tells us something: that Muslim science was, for many medieval people before the twelfth century, a form of magic.

Peter the Venerable (ca. 1092–1156), abbot of Cluny, friend of Abelard and Heloise, and one of the most powerful clergymen of his age, also came to Iberia (probably to the area of the Rioja), promoted Cluniac monasteries along the Road to Santiago, and was deeply interested in knowing about Islam, its doctrines, and its culture. Peter commissioned a translation of the *Qur'an* as an indispensable tool for learning about that religion, rejecting the many diverse and bizarre descriptions of Islam circulating in Christian Europe. It seems like the more things change, the more they remain the same, as bizarre stories about Muslims are part and parcel of political discourse in Europe and in the United States today.

THE ITINERARIES OR TRAVELS OF BENJAMIN OF TUDELA AND IBN JUBAYR

Born probably around 1130 in Navarre, a small kingdom in the Pyrenees straddling France and Spain, Benjamin of Tudela, probably a Jewish merchant and/or pious pilgrim, departed the kingdom on his way to Jerusalem probably around 1165. His account compares, though not favorably, with far better-known travel accounts by Ibn Battūta or Marco Polo, written almost two centuries later. Although his main preoccupation throughout his voyage was to report on the number of Jews living in the places he visited and to provide the names of the most influential Jewish inhabitants, he also contributes significant insights into some of the places he visited, the Christians' and Muslims' treatment of Jews, and the peculiar position of a Jew, in this case himself, sojourning widely from one end of the western Mediterranean to the important cities on the eastern part of the Middle Sea. His observations about Middle Eastern shrines and cities offer evidence of the keen awareness that at least a few people had of the broad and diverse nature of the entire Mediterranean world in the twelfth century. Passing references to trade also illuminate Benjamin de Tudela's observations on what we may broadly describe as the Mediterranean economy, duly recorded and paralleling the pious descriptions of Jewish shrines in Palestine. Finally, his itinerary traces the nature of people's movement over land and by sea around and across the Mediterranean.

Although we are not to take too seriously Benjamin's description of the number of Jews in specific locations – it is impossible for 40,000 Jews to have inhabited Baghdad when he visited, and the fact that he usually gives more or less the same figure of 300 or 200 as the number of Jews living in different locations is almost as unlikely – it is true that he traces a veritable semantic map of Jewish inhabitation along the shores of the Middle Sea or inland from the Mediterranean. Reaching as far east as Persia (the ruins of Nineveh outside present-day Mosul) and today's Saudi Arabia, he filled his itinerary with references to other far-away places that he did not visit but that were known to his sources and interlocutors: China, Tibet, and German imperial cities. Here we see the Mediterranean linked to the known world at large.

Traveling by land from Navarre to Zaragoza, the capital of the kingdom of Aragon, and by way of the Ebro River to the city of Tortosa, Benjamin of Tudela reached Barcelona. He carefully lists the names of the leaders of Barcelona's Jewish community, but he does not fail to describe Barcelona as a trade hub for the western Mediterranean and beyond.

> This is a small city and beautiful, lying upon the seacoast. Merchants come thither from all quarters with their wares, from Greece, from Pisa, Genoa, Sicily, Alexandria in Egypt, Palestine, Africa and all its coasts.[2]

We thus know, as verified by other historical sources, that Barcelona kept an important trade connection with Italian maritime and commercial centers such as Genoa and Pisa, but also with Sicily and markets far to the east.

Benjamin of Tudela, beyond the adjective beautiful, has little to say, however, about Barcelona's monuments, while he would not fail to describe monuments elsewhere, especially the Jewish holy places in Palestine. More than a careful description of places along his route, his narrative is a journey into Jewish settlements along the shores of the Mediterranean. In many respects, Ibn Battūta's far more comprehensive and extensive travelogue emphasized in similar fashion the presence of Islam, of Islamic hospitality, shrines, and religious practices that he observed and described in his long journey. As Ibn Battūta would do through Muslim settlements, Benjamin journeyed in the Mediterranean through a network of Jewish settlements. Travel and religion in the Middle Ages were inexorably bound up with each other. In many respects, the pattern still remains. Perfect strangers always invite my Jewish students in Paris for the Sabbath's ritual meals. Muslim hospitality is always practiced in European settings. One often moves, even today, through long-established ties of religion, culture, nationality, and language that determine the nature of hospitality.

If we place Benjamin of Tudela's description of Messina in Sicily, and of the island itself, next to that of Abu 'l-Husayn Muhammad ibn Ahmad ibn Jubayr, both accounts reveal a great deal of what it was to travel in the Mediterranean. Ibn Jubayr was born in Muslim Valencia in 1145, just 15 years after Benjamin's celebrated voyage. He served in the court of Granada's ruler, and in 1183 left the eponymous kingdom on the way to Mecca to fulfill one of his duties as a Muslim. The entire sojourn took him two years before his return to his duties in Granada's court. His itinerary, which I examine below, provides a blueprint of the manner in which travel in the period provided a glimpse of the nature of the interaction between Muslims and Christians between conflict and co-existence.

Ibn Jubayr's "Comments on Sicily" reflected his observations of the island and its people on the return from his pilgrimage to, and long sojourn in, Mecca from August 1183 to March 1184. Let us see first what Benjamin of Tudela, who had also made parts of the same journey earlier, after his extensive travels through the Holy Land, wrote about the island in general, and Messina and Palermo in particular.

Thence it takes twenty days by sea to Messina, which is the commencement of Sicily and is situated on the arm of the sea that is called Lipar, which divides it from Calabria. Here about 200 Jews dwell. It is a land full of everything good, with gardens and plantations. Here most of the pilgrims assemble to cross over to Jerusalem, as this is the best crossing. Thence it is about two days' journey to Palermo, which is a large city. Here is the palace of King William. Palermo contains about 1,500 Jews and a large number of Christians and Mohammedans. It is in a district abounding in springs and brooks of water, a land of wheat and barley, likewise of gardens and plantations, and there is not the like thereof in the whole island of Sicily . . . And a reservoir has been made there which is called Al Buheira, and in it are many sorts of fish. Ships overlaid with silver and gold are there, belonging to the king, who takes pleasure-trips in them with his women. In the park there is also a great palace, the walls of which are painted, and overlaid with gold and silver; the paving of the floors is of marble, picked out in gold and silver in all manner of designs. There is no building like this anywhere. And this

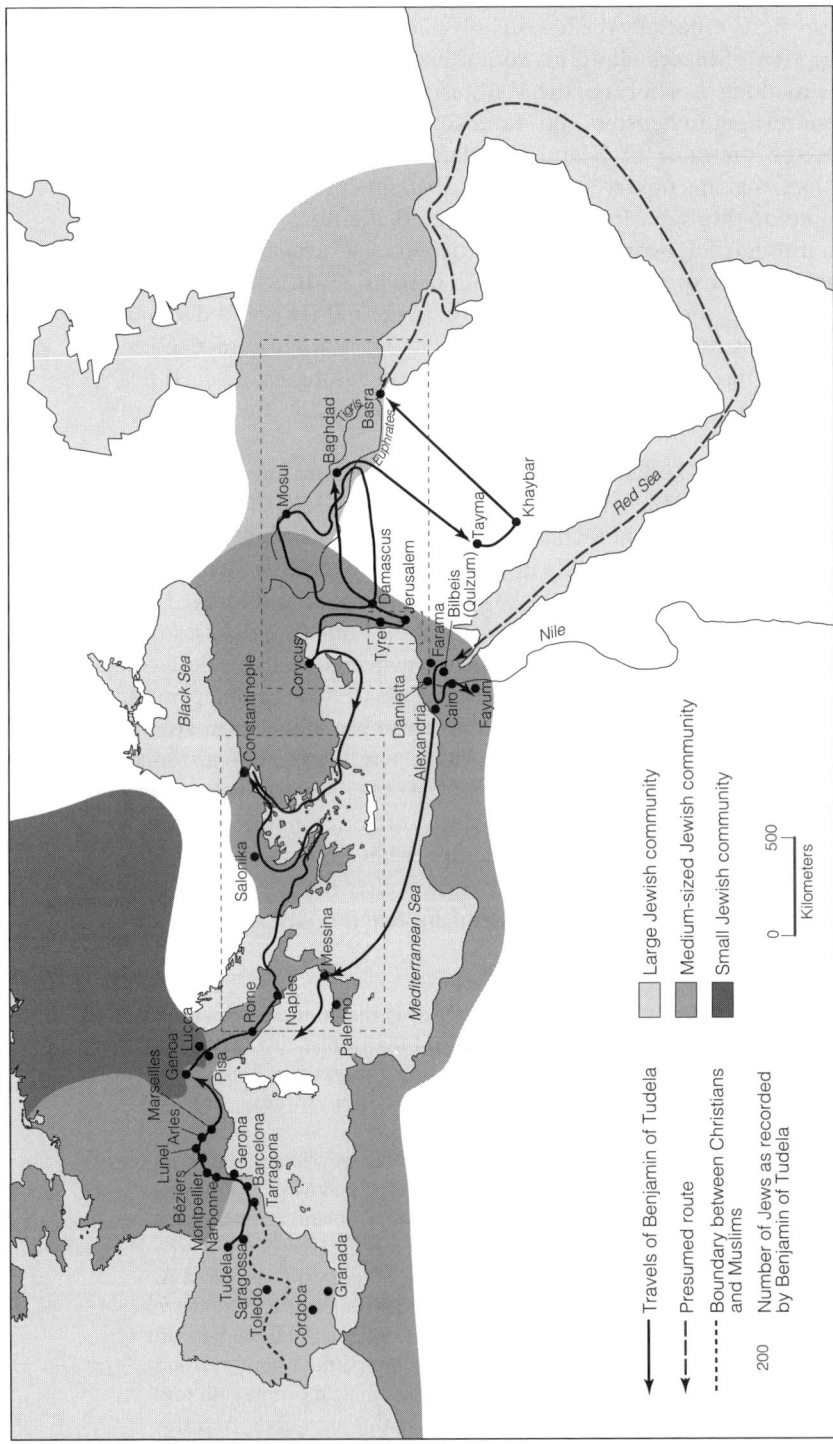

Map 9.1 The Jewish communities visited by Benjamin of Tudela and religions along his route. Source: From https://en.wikipedia.org/wiki/Benjamin_of_Tudela.

island, the commencement of which is Messina, contains all the pleasant things of this world. It embraces Syracuse, Marsala, Catania, Petralia, and Trapani, the circumference of the island being six days' journey. In Trapani coral is found, which is called Al Murgan.

Not unlike that of Benjamin of Tudela, Ibn Jubayr's vision of Messina and Sicily is seen through the lens of his own faith, though nuanced by the recognition of Roger II and his son William's multicultural rule, and influenced by what should have been a greater knowledge of Mediterranean geography than that of his near contemporary, Benjamin of Tudela.

The prosperity of this island surpasses description. It is enough to say that it is a daughter of Spain in the extent of its cultivation, in the luxuriance of its harvests, in its well being . . . But it (Sicily) is filled with the worshipers of crosses . . . The Muslims live beside them with their property and farms. The Christians treat these Muslims well and "have taken them to themselves as friends" (Koran XX, 41), but [the Normans] impose a tax on them [the Muslims] to be paid twice yearly, thus taking from them the amplitude of living they have been wont to earn from the land. May Almighty and Glorious God mend their lot, and in His goodness, make a happy recompense their heritage.

Yet, Ibn Jubayr also attested to the relative freedom and privileges enjoyed by Muslims under King William's rule, devoting some telling passages as to the role of Muslims in the Norman administration, the Muslim faith of the king's concubines and servants, and the fact that the king is "admirable for his just conduct, and the use he makes of the industry of the Muslims . . ."[3]

Ibn Jubayr's description of Messina is far more extensive and detailed than that given by Benjamin of Tudela, combining negative comments and acerbic religious observations with a recognition of Messina's teeming commercial life: "The city is the mart of the merchant infidels, the focus of ships from the world over, and thronging always with companies of travelers by reason of the lowness of prices . . . it is cheerless because of unbelief, no Muslim being settled there. Teeming with worshipers of the Cross, it chokes its inhabitants, and constricts them almost to strangling. It is full of smells and filth; and churlish too, for the stranger will find there no courtesy."[4]

These two brief summaries of some of the salient points in the respective itineraries of Benjamin of Tudela and Ibn Jubayr provide a wealth of information on western Mediterranean life. Compare with the difficulties that exist today in moving across the borders of sovereign nations, especially if one is, like these two travelers, an outsider. Yet, a Jew and a Muslim journeyed through Christian lands in the twelfth century with a great deal of ease. Benjamin traveled across Christian realms in Iberia, France, and Italy and through Muslim territories without any semblance of difficulty. Ibn Jubayr went from al-Andalus to Ceuta in North Africa, and then on to the Balearic Islands (still, in the late twelfth century, in Muslim hands). Having traveled on to Christian Sardinia, he then embarked on the long ship voyage to Palestine before eventually reaching Mecca. On their respective returns, each traveled to

Sicily, crossing the island from east to west before returning to their homes in Christian Navarre and Muslim Spain, respectively.

Both pilgrims moved along well-known networks of co-religionists who were bound, by the laws of hospitality and religious solidarity, to provide shelter for travelers. As already noted, both Benjamin and Ibn Jubayr saw the places through which they traveled through the lens of their own religion: How many Jews lived in the locality? Under what conditions did Muslims live in the lands of idolaters and infidels? Their contact with Christians was certainly not extensive and, in most cases, it was non-existent. Both wrote lyrically about the holy places of their respective religions. They spoke equally enthusiastically about the prosperity of Sicily and of Palermo's attractions under their Norman rulers. Both entered the island through Messina, the exit and entry port for those traveling from the western Mediterranean to the East and back. Both returned to Spain from Trapani (still today a link to North Africa), described, at least by Ibn Jubayr, with the same references to active trade and international flavor that he had used for Messina.

Significantly, although parts of each of their voyages were undertaken over land – mostly so in the case of Benjamin of Tudela – the important segments of their journeys were made by sea. Benjamin reports needing 20 days to come from the East to Messina. Ibn Jubayr took almost a month to negotiate the distance from Acre to Messina. Genoese ships seem to have been the main source of transport, carrying passengers and trade from the shores of Spain and Sardinia to the Holy Land and back to Sicily. These references attest to the unique role of Genoa as a maritime and mercantile power in the twelfth-century Mediterranean and to its ties, through Crusade and trade, with the eastern portions of the Middle Sea. In the accounts of these two travelers, one can also see the diverse personalities of the western Mediterranean: Jewish, Muslim, Christian, Italian, French, and Mediterranean.

LITERARY TRAVELS AND ENCOUNTERS

As we all know, travel narratives that take form in the imagination are often never realized. We (I certainly do) are always planning voyages and walks that we may never carry out. We travel in the mind to obscure corners of cities or to remote locales. In Cervantes's *Don Quixote* or Dumas's *The Count of Monte Cristo*, often mentioned in these pages, a great deal of the action revolves around movement and travel. Whether the peripatetic activities of the Knight of the Sorrowful Figure or Edmund Dantès's travels in the Mediterranean, fiction and reality overlap. Travel is about encounters, and so are some of the most cherished fictional works of the medieval and early modern Mediterranean. A paradigmatic example of the inclusion of travel within a literary work is the romance of *Flores y Blancaflor*. Of a true Mediterranean provenance (probably the story, though redolent with references to the *One Thousand and One Nights*, had a southern French origin in the twelfth century as *Floire et Blancheflor*), *Flores y Blancaflor* became one of the most popular fictional works of the Late Middle Ages. It was translated into (or derivative versions were written in) most

European languages, including a version in Norwegian. The story was incorporated as historical truth in the *Estoria de España*, the influential thirteenth-century vernacular history of Castile.

Flores y Blancaflor had all the essential plot lines of a potboiler. The royal heir to King Fines, the Muslim ruler of Almería, Flores grew up in close company with Blancaflor, the Christian child of a captured French noble-woman, held as a hostage (or slave) in the court of Flores's father. Growing up together, they of course fell in love. Flores's father became greatly alarmed by his son's love for a Christian and the possible consequences of that love for his succession and the politics of the realm. Without Flores's knowledge, the king sold poor Blancaflor into slavery and contrived a story of her death. When, after untold misery, Flores learns the truth, he embarks on a long journey through the Mediterranean in search of his lost love. Of course, as is the usual case in these romances, love triumphs: Flores, now king of Almería, marries Blancaflor and, this being a Christian story, he converts to Christianity with all his subjects.

First and foremost, the story is about encounters and the amorous relationship between a Muslim and a Christian. As we have seen in an earlier chapter, recent works, especially those of Simon Barton, explore the sexual encounters between people of different faiths. As troublesome as they were in the past (and remain today), religious differences could be overcome by love and the lovers' perseverance. Second, the story is about travel, in this case, Flores's extensive search for Blancaflor throughout the Mediterranean. Taking in many adventures along the way, the story reflects on the possibilities of travel and mobility within the boundaries of Dar al-Islam. Third, Flores's conversion (and that of his subjects) may reflect some of the actual armed conflicts between Christians and Muslims over Almería in the twelfth century. That Flores converted for the sake of his love for Blancaflor was fiction. Nonetheless, there is a long tradition of conversion prompted by love (or marriage), whether in the case of Clovis in late fifth-century Frankland or in the Mediterranean. Such conversions triggered by love or desire could also be presented as real in the porous borderlands between the two (often three) faiths in the western Mediterranean.[5]

RECENT TRAVELERS

In most nineteenth- and twentieth-century travel accounts written by Europeans about the Islamic Mediterranean (and in some of these narratives Iberia and southern Italy were often also seen as "orientalized" destinations), the interest resided in either the ruins of the ancient past, whether Roman or medieval, or the exotic. What Benjamin de Tudela and Ibn Jubayr described as new and/or not seen before, have become, with the passing of time, places described in travel books, inundated by tours, and depicted, most often with great exaggeration and inaccuracy, by avid local tourist guides. Ways of seing today differ radically from those of the past. We gaze on these places through what Mary Louise Pratt defined as "Imperial Eyes."[6] It is very clear that the colonization of North Africa by European powers in the nineteenth century, mostly by France, transformed the way in which these areas and their past were experienced.

Ali Bey

Traveling meant, in some cases, adopting the identity of others. Domingo Badia y Leblich was born in Barcelona in 1766, studied Arabic in Spain and England, and, under the assumed name of Ali Bey al-Abbasi (he pretended to be not just a Muslim but a descendant of the Abbasid caliphal family), traveled to Morocco. He lived there for two years (1803–1805), made the pilgrimage to Mecca (the *hajj*) disguised as a Muslim, and then returned to Spain and served Joseph Bonaparte during the liberal French interlude. After the defeat of the French in Spain, Domingo Badia moved on to France, revealing his affinity for, and the extent to which he was influenced by, the Enlightenment. His accounts of his experiences in the Holy Land were published in French in 1814, translated into English two years later, and have appeared in several Catalan editions (I am using an 1888/1889 Catalan edition). Returning to the East, he died in Damascus in 1818. An explorer, most probably a spy, his life and travels are representative of a certain the type of voyager. They blend into their surroundings, and, unlike most travelers today, become other, aiming to observe from within. That many thought he was truly a Muslim and bought into his disguise and pseudonym as Ali Bey al-Abbasi speaks torrents as to his ability to create a different and believable persona and, thus, gain access to different worlds from those he had inhabited before. He is exemplary of the manner in which travel often creates new identities and ways of looking at oneself and the world.

Although his visits to Mecca and other sacred places in the Middle East are of great interest, it is his time in Morocco that is closer to the geographical limits of this book. Although some of his ideas were perhaps a bit far-fetched – that the Atlas Mountains were the remains of the lost world of Atlantis – Domingo/Ali Bey drew fairly accurate maps of Morocco, identifying some sites hitherto unknown to Europeans. Although some scholars have claimed that Ali Bey's accounts contain a great deal of fantasy, nonetheless, the most recent critical assessment defends his originality.[7] Traveling in a small boat from Tarifa to Tangier across the Straits of Gibraltar in four hours, Domingo/Ali Bey describes the feeling of moving from a known world to a completely new and unknown one. He notes the differences in customs, language and behavior that make Moroccans as different from Spaniards as "a Frenchman would be from a Chinese." We are already in a world where boundaries and access are carefully watched. Domingo/Ali Bey is carefully questioned, his passport minutely examined. Almost seven centuries had passed since the travels of Benjamin of Tudela and Ibn Jubayr, and movement was carefully monitored, especially between Muslim North Africa and Christian Europe.

In his journal or travel account, Ali Bey/Domingo writes from a Muslim point of view, and that religious ambivalence is perhaps what is most interesting about his biography. He defines himself as a Muslim, shaves all his hair, goes to the mosque for Friday service to pray, participates in the feast held in honor of the birth of the Prophet, and performs the prescribed ablutions; yet, as has been argued by scholars who have studied his life, he was a child of the Enlightenment and probably a deist. His descriptions – of dress, behavior, and festivals, and of his horror at the circumcision of young and old – reflect a modern traveler's sensibilities to difference and to otherness, a perspective very much inherited from the Enlightenment. At the same time, his careful descriptions of Tangier's defenses, of its inhabitants' equestrian prowess, and of the nature of trade and commercial exchanges speak of his role as an outsider, an observer, and a spy. But his observations are also directed towards culinary practices – with a delightful description of how to cook couscous – weddings, and other ethnographic details that place him in line with modern anthropological practices.

In Ali Bey/Domingo's writings we can see the manner in which Islamic North Africa, so familiar to traders, missionaries, and those redeeming slaves in an earlier period (as well as to corsairs) has become utterly "other." For Ali Bey, this was a curious place entirely different from the traveler's home. His reflections on the manner in which the Jews are treated and the inequality between Jews and Muslims, his pejorative description of Tangier's architecture, and his far-fetched understanding of the geography of Africa's interior provide enough material for a book. One must note, nonetheless, his careful description of Fez and other Moroccan sites, as well as the continuous trope of contrasting Muslim "ignorance" with European enlightenment – taking the *Qur'an* as entirely representative of the former and placing it in opposition to what he considered to be the superiority of European science. His summary of Muhammad's life and the careful description of Muslim prayers (with the Arabic forms and translations) attest to Ali Bey's curiosity beyond strategic considerations. We are far away from the world of Ibn Battūta, Benjamin de Tudela, and other medieval travelers.[8]

Isabelle Eberhardt

Almost exactly 100 years after Ali Bey traveled in North Africa, a bold Swiss woman spent a great deal of time in Algeria. Born in Geneva, Isabelle Eberhardt (1877–1904) lived a great deal of her short life in North Africa. The child of an unconventional couple, descended from German-Russian and Armenian parents, she came to North Africa when she was 20, traveled extensively disguised as a male, converted to Islam, and was, in fact, buried as a Muslim after her tragic death in a desert flood. She was only 27 years old. Like many before and after her, the haunting beauty of the desert, of its dunes and expanse, captured Isabelle. She married an Algerian and wrote books, among them the poetical *Dans l'ombre chaude de l'Islam* (*Under the Warm Shadow of Islam*). Written with a collaborator, it is a travel account as much of the spirit as it is of the physical spaces she described. It is a very sympathetic account, far removed from the pejorative descriptions found in the work of Ali Bey and other writers.

Isabelle's is not an "imperial" gaze nor is her writing part of a colonial discourse; rather, it is the contrary – hers is not a feigned conversion but closer to that of someone like Anselm of Turmeda (see Chapter 6), whose sympathetic encounter with Islam prompted a true conversion. Her writings and life were counterparts to what was actually happening in North Africa, where European powers already held sway. Yet, in spite of her enchantment with the world that is revealed to her in her travels, *Dans l'ombre chaude de l'Islam* also reports on the strong Spanish and Jewish presence, and on Jewish artisanal activities in Kénadsa. She describes lyrically the small towns on the edge of the desert and the nomads that inhabited those spaces. She notes the black slaves, the separate lives of women, what she calls "le petit monde des femmes," and their arguments and bickering, often laced with anti-Jewish insults. She is moved by the public Friday service of a "religion where there are no mysteries, no sacraments, nothing that requires the intercession of a priest." For Isabelle Eberhardt the quality of sunlight and the luminosity of sunrises over the desert bring a sense of belonging that belies a particular moment in western society when North Africans became colonized subjects. Few can write as sympathetically as she does about a Mediterranean world that had once been united in the waning years of Rome, and which now, at the beginning of the twentieth century, was severed into two shores, divided by religion and colonial rule.[9]

TRAVELING THE MODERN MEDITERRANEAN

Paul Theroux

Almost a century later, Paul Theroux, a well know twentieth- and twenty-first-century travel writer, sought to describe his impressions of his journey along most of the shores of the Mediterranean. His *The Pillars of Hercules* traces his voyages, mostly by train, by bus, or by sea, from the Straits of Gibraltar – or the gateway into the Mediterranean from the Atlantic – and back to Tangier in a somewhat incomplete clockwise progress from the European regions of the Mediterranean to the Middle East and African shores. His reflections could often be described as dismissive indictments of some of the regions he visited and of other travelers he encountered in the western Mediterranean. In line with much of the writing in his other travel books, the personal comments and the acerbic descriptions of uninformed or prejudiced travelers are constant tropes, though less pronounced as Theroux ventures into regions less commercialized or open to tourism. American tourists, commenting on crime in Marseille, come in for special indictment. There is not, or very rarely, a sense of enchantment in the book, unless it is about Corsica or Tunisia. One would not find here the reflections found in those earlier narratives I have examined in Chapter 8 or above. Although the Mediterranean described by Theroux in the late 1990s is very different – in terms of political and economic patterns – from the Middle Sea today, we can witness in press, TV, and radio coverage of the 1990s the same reports of anti-immigrant sentiment that are, unfortunately, commonplace everywhere today.

Underneath the author's, at times, unsympathetic vision of the Mediterranean and its people, one gets hints of the geography, climate, and demographic distinctiveness of the areas through which he traveled. Unlike medieval and early modern narratives, Theroux's underlines, in an almost essentializing way, the differences between nations. The Spaniards are sharply different from the French. The Corsicans and Sardinians are something else. The French are described, in the usual stereotypes, as obstreperous and perverse people. The *vendaval* and the tramontane winds are mentioned. The *étangs* (swampy or marshy lagoons) that line the French Mediterranean coast come up in frequent references. Stereotyping, something that is profoundly ahistorical, abounds in his narrative. The distinctions are no longer between Muslims, Christians, and Jews, but between national types, national identities.

The Arabs (by which we must understand, in Theroux's formulation, North African and African Muslims) are described as being ubiquitous on the northern shores of the Mediterranean. Many of these North African immigrants, according to Theroux, often engage in crime. They are to be feared or are feared by some of the local population who warn the traveler against them. One should walk outside one's hotel with as little money and jewelry as possible, he recommends. Marseille has "all the different races" of the Mediterranean, though "different races" is a rather simplistic term to be applied to those who inhabited the shores of the sea. Senegalese can be found even in Sardinia, plying their trade as they do throughout most of Western Europe today. Theroux's description is a grim reminder of the massive and desperate migration from sub-Saharan Africa to Western Europe (see Chapter 12). From Sicily, southern Italy, and Venice, Theroux made his way to the eastern Mediterranean. A great deal of his narrative is given to his voyages there, with sojourns inland.

Theroux returns to the western Mediterranean by way of Trapani in Sicily (not unlike Benjamin of Tudela or Ibn Jubayr), and the short ferry ride to Tunis. Tunisia is for him "an island," surrounded it seems by countries which, due either to the political climate or to civil unrest, do not provide a welcome to a western traveler. But Theroux revels in Tunisia, in the Berbers selling carpets at Tunis's medina, and in Tunisian faces, "more the face(s) of the Mediterranean than anywhere else." Unable to visit Algeria, he goes to Morocco and Tangier by a circuitous route that brings him back to Italy and then to Spain to take the ferry to Tangier from Algeciras. All of Theroux's account in this book is an elaborate literary voyage in which the places described by and former dwelling places of a whole roster of European writers, old and new, are visited, evoked, re-seen through the traveler's eye. Is not all travel an exercise in memory? Is it not a kind of seeing the world first through the eyes of travelers that saw these places before us, places we see through their accounts? Then, and only then, do we see these places each in our own ways. We aim to see these locations in the same way as those who were there first and who, in their writings, convey to us a sensibility and awareness to which we hope to add our own experiences. But there were others who traveled, and travel today, not to see or delight in what they see but to trade and profit from their efforts.[10]

THE SINEWS OF COMMERCE

Whether in ancient times or today, commerce and economic exchanges have brought people from different areas of the Mediterranean and from beyond the

Middle Sea into close contact. Trade, religion, and warfare are different aspects of the encounters that define Mediterranean civilization. None is more revealing of those points of contact than the *funduq* or *fondaco*. Elsewhere in this book, I have already referred to the *funduq* and to its importance. The late and much missed Olivia Remie Constable's admirable book on the *funduq* examines the origins and development of the institution from the Classical period until its high point in the Middle Ages. *Housing the Stranger* is the most authoritative description of this peculiar institution.[11] But what was the *funduq*? Modern travelers to Venice may walk by, and relish in, the Fondaco dei Tedeschi, or even the Fondaco dei Turchi, without realizing the connections to a world now vanished.

Whether in North Africa, in the eastern Mediterranean, or on the European shores of the Middle Sea, the *funduq* was something similar to a hotel or hostel. Merchants, the "stranger" in Constable's formulation, stored their merchandise in the *funduq*. There they also found a place to rest, or to practice their religion without fear of local interference or persecution. It was – and the word is used today in the same sense by the tourist industry in North Africa – an example of the hospitality found throughout the shores of the Mediterranean, fostered by bonds of reciprocity, gift-giving, and trade. The Fondaco dei Tedeschi housed German merchants and their wares for more than 600 years. With storage, clerical, and housing facilities (with room to house over 150 merchants), the Fondaco served as a haven and secure place for outsiders, whether Muslims or Christians of all persuasions, as they traded in each other's lands. The Fondaco dei Turchi was a haven for those Ottoman merchants and envoys keeping safe the ties between the Sublime Porte and the Serenissima. In many respects, hotels located near research and business hubs, or often at airports, fulfill today some of these same purposes. These hotels for business-people provide an abode away from home. There, one may find like-minded people. Transactions, business deals, and exchanges of information take place in such settings, and secure rest is found. In the wider Mediterranean, where the flow of merchants and merchandise across the sea often linked the Muslim and Christian Mediterranean into one single economic unity, the *funduq* was the best example of that world without borders that slowly became a thing of the past in the transition to modernity.

CORSAIRS

Trade and corsair activity were also part of the flow of goods and people from one shore of the western Mediterranean to the other. In that world, renegades, a topic already explored briefly in an earlier chapter (see Chapter 6), played a significant role during the height of sectarian warfare in the western Mediterranean in the Late Middle Ages and the early modern period. While religious conflicts had always been part and parcel of Mediterranean relations since the early years of the Islamic conquest, they rose in intensity in the waning years of the Middle Ages and at the onset of the modern age. It was only with the European colonization of North Africa that strife at sea was relegated to the struggles in the African continent between colonized and colonizers.

But it was in this period, that is, from around 1400 to 1600 and even beyond, that corsair activity, mostly carried out by renegades (Christians who had converted to Islam and vice versa), set the tone for transactions between North and South. Here I am not interested in what these changes in religious affiliation – that is, conversion from Christianity to Islam and vice versa – meant, but rather in what these corsair activities signified in terms of the exchange of goods and people. Corsair activity in the period was most famously epitomized by the Barbarossa brothers. For an entire generation, their naval activities created havoc throughout the western Mediterranean, securing Ottoman hegemony at sea until Lepanto (1571). The four so-called Barbarossa brothers, born in the Aegean sea, probably of Christian ancestry but converted to Islam, played a signal role in securing Ottoman naval superiority in the eastern Mediterranean, while defeating Spain in the western parts of the sea, expelling the Spaniards from Algiers and most of their settlements on the North African coast, raiding Valencia, Minorca, and the Spanish and Italian Mediterranean shores, and capturing merchant vessels that dared to sail too far from the European coasts. The best known of the four Barbarossa brothers was Hayreddin Barbarossa, who was born Khizr or Khidr around 1478 and died in July 1546. He rose to the title of Pasha, acting as the effective ruler of most of the Ottoman possessions in North Africa, and carrying out vigorous campaigns against Christian Mediterranean polities and commercial activities in the West. It would be futile to attempt here a full biography of Barbarossa. He is one of those historical protagonists whose legendary activities are as important, or even more so for the early modern imaginary, as his actual real life. He stood for a new type of confrontation or armed encounter in the western sea. The consequences of his corsair activities and those of his corsair opponents transformed the nature of trade and the relationship between the northern and southern shores of the Middle Sea.[12]

But the Barbarossas were not alone; nor did Muslims have a monopoly on corsair activities. David Coleman's work on corsairs, outlined in a superb presentation at a meeting of the American Historical Association in Chicago, examines the life of Juan Martínez de Briteos, a Morisco corsair (descended, that is, from a Muslim nominally (or truly) converted to Christianity in the early sixteenth century). He became a formidable and most feared corsair in the 1520s and 1530s, the critical period for the recrudescence of corsair activity in the Alboran Sea. He often raided the coast of North Africa, while, at the same time, carrying on normal trading activities from the ports of Málaga, Marbella, Gibraltar, and elsewhere along the Mediterranean coast of Castile. As Coleman shows, Martínez was able to accumulate a substantial fortune; yet, unlike those who converted to Islam, because of his ancestry and the growing suspicions of Moriscos in the early sixteenth century, Juan Martínez remained an outsider not fully trusted by his Christian patrons and commercial partners.

While Spain was a site of malleable religious identity and political allegiances, Mediterranean France, where religious diversity did not exist, had its shares of corsairs and renegades. Bartolomé Bennassar has shown, from a careful mining of inquisitorial records, how numerous men and women from Mediterranean Europe converted to Islam in the sixteenth and seventeenth centuries. These were identified by Bennassar as the "people of the border-lands." They were soldiers, merchants, and sailors caught between two polities, two religions, two different cultures, yet sharing in a broader Mediterranean civilization that transcended the limitations of nationality, language, and religion. Many of these people, like Juan Martínez, became renegades. Whether captured in corsair raids on the Mediterranean coast, taken at sea on the western Mediterranean, the Atlantic Ocean close to the Straits of Gibraltar, or the waters off West Africa, or whether they were truly willing to embrace another religion, these people, caught in liminal spaces, would become impor-tant interlocutors between two worlds. Some, as Claire Gilbert shows with careful details, became translators and go-betweens in Spain's North African possessions and elsewhere. Many, as Bennassar eloquently describes, became renegades. Some, of course, were ransomed, as Cervantes was, through the tireless efforts of such orders as the Mercedarians, committed to the ransoming of Christian slaves in Muslim North Africa. Muslim captives were also ran-somed and returned home, or exchanged for Christian captives. Others, as noted earlier, converted to Islam for practical reasons; yet others underwent a heartfelt conversion. Corsair activity and strife in the western Mediterranean, however, had some other important consequences that went beyond the flow from one religion to another.[13]

The first was the increased importance of slavery in the western Mediterra-nean and Atlantic worlds. Whether as galley, domestic, or other type of slave, their number grew, as did the development of a discourse, certainly among Christians, that justified slavery by appeal to patristic sources and Aristotelian philosophy. Valencia, as Debra Blumenthal has shown, became an active market for slaves and for slaves' conversion to Christianity.[14] Many of the natives defeated by Castilian forces in the Canary Islands ended up being sold as slaves in Valencia and elsewhere. Moriscos defeated in 1570–1571, after their rebellion in the Alpujarras Mountains in Granada's hinterland, were also sold as slaves. Seville had a large number of slaves among its rising population. *Lazarillo de Tormes*, the first European picaresque novel, begins with the story of a freed African slave. Cervantes himself, as we have seen in other sections of this book, became a slave in Algiers before being ransomed. Capture by a corsair in the open sea or on coastal raids meant sure slavery and, in some case, a very hard life rowing in either Christian or Muslim ships. And to become a galley slave was about as hard a fate as one may have. The ubiquitous nature of slavery on both shores of the Mediterranean was, to a large extent, a conse-quence of corsair raids, of religious conflicts, and of continuous warfare at sea.

The other, less noticeable, trend resulting from the increase in corsair activity and warfare at the onset of the early modern period was the decrease in trade between the two shores of the western Mediterranean. This is not to say that trade and opportunities for profit disappeared. They did not. The Genoese maintained their settlements outside Tunis. Other merchants traveled across the sea to ply their trade, but the intense commercial relationship that had flourished in an earlier period, in spite of war and religious differences, slowly vanished. Similar to the eastern Mediterranean, where Ottoman forces pushed out the Venetians and other western traders from their long-held outposts in the

Aegean, in the western sea corsairs and Ottoman naval forces targeted merchant ships as easy prey. So did Christian corsairs and Christian naval forces. "Mediterranean commercial connectivity" suffered from these new conditions. As shall be seen below, by the eighteenth and nineteenth centuries, the evidence for trade across the Mediterranean would, for all practical purposes, be non-existent. By the nineteenth and twentieth centuries, and the rise of colonial enterprises in North Africa, new commercial ties were forged that reiterated European hegemony over the southern shores of the western Mediterranean.

TRADE REVISITED

To chronicle the entire history of commerce in the western Mediterranean, a topic well studied, would require several books. As shall be seen in a later chapter, or as we have seen in small vignettes up to now, the western Mediterranean was connected to great and diverse trade networks (the commercial world of Dar al-Islam, the Genoese commercial emporium beginning in the twelfth century, the Silk Road, the sub-Saharan trade routes, the Atlantic world, and other trade systems) from ancient times. Phoenicians traveled to England to buy tin and to Atlantic Africa for other goods. Braudel has shown the expansive commercial reach of the Mediterranean into the Baltic, the North Sea, Central Africa, and the Atlantic. Rather than tackle this broad topic, in the pages that follow, I focus on a case study. I have used the evidence of the "protests against the sea" in earlier chapter to provide some element of specificity to my discussion of the western Mediterranean climate. Here I turn, once again, to the evidence provided by the Barcelona protests against the sea to paint a limited portrait of trade in the late eighteenth and nineteenth century, just at the point when the Atlantic had fully replaced the Mediterranean as the focus of Western European life and just at the time that marks the beginnings in earnest of European colonial ventures in North Africa.

Throughout its long history, the Mediterranean served as a commercial link for Mediterranean goods, as well as for those from regions beyond its shores. The late eighteenth- and nineteenth-century protests against the sea (a collection of documents from Barcelona already described in Chapter 2) provide a case study and a lens through which to observe a brief history of patterns of trade in the western Mediterranean and beyond. These documents reveal the complex world of trade (and of sea captains) that, through the Straits of Gibraltar and the Red Sea, connected seaports along the northern shores of the Middle Sea to a global economy. The depositions against the sea and bad weather extant in the archives of the Consulado de Comercio and housed at the Archivo de la Corona de Aragón allow us to see what goods were brought into the port of Barcelona for a little bit over a century. They also provide a portrait of the flow of trade in the western Mediterranean and of Barcelona's links to Northern European and Atlantic markets. The changes from the late 1760s to the late 1860s were dramatic indeed, reflecting not just the evolution of commerce and manufacturing as we approach the contemporary world, but also Barcelona's rebirth as a lively industrial and economic center in the second half of the nineteenth century. Moreover, the protests against the sea examined here represent just the tip of the iceberg. Consulates of Commerce or Consulates of the Sea existed in all the major ports of the western Mediterranean. If we were to examine all of them we would most probably have over 100,000 such protests, revealing patterns of trade and weather conditions over a century. But we must return to our Barcelona case study to get a small sample, at least, of what was taking place in the western Mediterranean at the onset of the contemporary world

What goods came into Barcelona during the century covered by the protests again the sea? Where did these goods come from? Before attempting to answer these questions, it is important to reiterate that the more than 25,000 protests against the sea allow us to see only a fraction of the goods coming into the port of Barcelona during this period. Moreover, my sampling of a single decade of the documentation represents only a partial view of what the entire Barcelona trade may have been like in the late eighteenth and early nineteenth century. Nonetheless, the extant documents available among the records of the Consulado de Comercio offer a rough but pretty accurate portrait of Barcelona's trade in the period.

The Movement of Goods in the Western Mediterranean, 1766–1868

One of the most striking features of the documents extant at the Archivo de la Corona de Aragón is the absence or, at best, paucity of references to trade with North Africa. Even though corsair activities and antagonisms with Islam still plagued the western Mediterranean into the late eighteenth century, it is inexplicable that in the broad sampling of the documentation that I undertook there was no obvious mention of trade between Barcelona and northern Africa ports. We know that as late as May 1790 Genoese and Spanish ships sailed from Genoa to pursue Berber corsairs. There are other references to conflict and corsair activity (from both sides), but we also know that there have always been frequent mercantile contacts between the two shores of the Mediterranean before the European conquests in, and colonization of, the Maghreb. So the absence of any reference is puzzling indeed. In many respects, this points to the kind of watershed moment when the almost millennium-long encounter between merchants from the two shores of the western Mediterranean came to an end. As noted above, one may probably date this break to the early modern period when corsair activity and the sea-wide struggles between the Sublime Porte and western powers dealt a fatal blow to the commercial unity of the western Mediterranean. That vaunted unity would not be restored until the colonization of North Africa by western powers. Of course, political unity was restored only to the disadvantage of the colonized. As Theroux points out correctly, even Corsica and Sardinia became "colonies" of the Western European mainland.

The other important absence is that of trade with the eastern Mediterranean. The references to ships sailing from eastern ports found in my sampling are few in number. Does it mean that goods from the eastern Mediterranean and beyond may have been funneled through Italian ports or the merchandise transferred there? Or does it mean that in the late eighteenth century the trade between the two halves of the Middle Sea was negligible? With these two caveats and unresolved questions, let us see what it is that the documents tell us about the movement of goods.

In 1766, the protests against the sea from those sea captains sailing strictly in the western Mediterranean mentioned only a limited range of products. Although the depositions did not always include a complete inventory of the goods carried by the ships – often the testimonies mention only "diverse merchandises" or additional cargo without specifying what it was – there is no evidence from the extant documentation of any complex or diverse exchanges of goods. A total of 122 protests against the sea were submitted that year, in which wheat is mentioned nine times, and a general category of cereals once. Cotton appears four times, while unspecified goods or "*merca-durías*" are mentioned six times. If we extrapolate from this information, one may conclude that commercial exchanges in the western Mediterranean were mostly limited to foodstuffs and raw materials. The extant protests against the sea do not always, however, let us know what goods most of the vessels affected by the weather carried or what Barcelona exported to other countries in the region.

When we turn to trade that came into the Mediterranean from Atlantic ports in Europe and the Americas, the number of insurance claims grew exponentially, reflecting the longer voyages and more perilous conditions, especially at the Straits of Gibraltar. Wheat alone elicited 52 entries, with grains in general or flour in particular adding 23 more entries. Captains protesting about damages to their cargo from sea and weather conditions listed "diverse" (and unspecified) merchandise 16 times, salted fish (probably cod but also including sardines) seven times, and cotton once. Their depositions also mentioned tin (twice), wine (twice), fertilizers (once), rice (once), and beans (once). If the depositions for 1766 were representative of the next two or three decades, then most of the provisioning of Barcelona in the late eighteenth century came from Atlantic locations. Clearly, the Barcelona hinterland could not produce enough grain to satisfy the needs of its urban population. It may not be too far-fetched to argue that such may have been the case for most of the large western Mediterranean seaports. While there was some movement of grain within the western side of the sea, the bulk of foodstuffs and other needed supplies came from beyond the Straits of Gibraltar.[15]

One hundred years later, a great deal had changed. By 1866, Barcelona was clearly fully connected to the global economy. The goods imported reflected Barcelona's manufacturing and building expansion. From the Mediterranean, we have notices of new and different goods: industrial oil (thrice), hides (twice, some from Marseille), sulfur (thrice), soda-ash (once), iron (once), coal from Sardinia (once), cotton (twice, including a shipment from Smyrna), drugs (once), and marble (thrice). Compared to a century earlier, these items offer evidence of a more diversified pattern of trade. Wheat and flour (and some wine), which had represented the bulk of the imports into Barcelona in 1766, are barely part of the overall trade, with only two mentions. Remarkably, mentions of wheat and other grains are fairly absent from the depositions of captains sailing into Barcelona from non-Mediterranean ports. Cod and other types of fish garnered the most mentions, with 25. This was followed by wood, mostly from Scandinavian ports, with 24 entries. Cotton shipped to Barcelona from Pernambuco (Brazil), New Orleans (US), and elsewhere also accounted for 24 entries. Other items mentioned, such as coal, tar, machinery, iron (from Gijón on the northern coast of Spain), sugar, cacao, and other raw materials, showed the broader range of the traded merchandise. A glimpse is also provided of the widespread geographical span of Barcelona's commercial links. Besides diverse European Atlantic and Baltic seaports, we have a growing number references to Buenos Aires, Havana, Matanzas (in Cuba), Pernambuco, New Orleans, New York, Manila, and a host of other far-away locations.[16]

The absence (or very small number) of references to wheat and other cereal grains in the depositions against the sea in 1866 may alert us to a possible shift in the provisioning of Barcelona. Better and safer roads may have provided Catalonia in general, and Barcelona in particular, with access to the cereal producing areas in central Spain (the plains of Old Castile). Yet, as the evidence for 1868 shows, that year a large amount of wheat was imported (mostly from the region of the eastern Mediterranean and the Baltic but also from England and even Oran). The rise in the price of wheat and other cereal grains, which began in earnest in the late eighteenth century throughout most of the rest of Western Europe, may have led to incentives to seek new sources for cereals, above all wheat, and may have made the higher cost of transportation more bearable.[17]

MARITIME ROUTES IN AND OUT OF THE MEDITERRANEAN: SHIPS' PLACES OF ORIGIN

Implicit in the protests against the sea is evidence for the wide range of ports from which goods were shipped to Barcelona. Although the Consulado de Comercio's clerical spelling of some of the names of these ports leave a great deal to be desired, one can see the origin for traffic within and without the Mediterranean on the way to Barcelona. One must assume that a similar pattern existed for other great ports in the western regions of the sea. This information is best rendered in two tables that summarize the archival evidence for the first year in which the Consulado began to keep records of the protests against the sea (Table 9.1 and Table 9.2).

That a ship was registered in a particular port or country, or that the captain was not from Spain or Catalonia, did not always reflect the ships' actual ownership. Such is the case for many ships registered in Liberia or Panama today, regardless of place of ownership. Cruise lines, for example, often fly the flag of the Marshall Islands. But the evidence for 1766, with some exceptions, is that place of registration also identified the owners' nationality. As is clear from Table 9.2, the majority of the ships coming into Barcelona originated in a European port not located in the Mediterranean.

Table 9.1 Registration by Country of Origin, 1766.

Country of Registration	Number of Mentions
England	53
Netherlands	40
France	24
Spain	2
Denmark (including a Danish-registered ship, making the route between Alicante and Barcelona)	2
Malta	1
Sweden	1

Source: From ACA, Consulado de Comercio. *Indice de los registros de protestas de mar (1766).*

Table 9.2 Mercantile Routes into Barcelona, 1766.

Route	Number of Mentions	Route	Number of Mentions
Amsterdam-Barcelona	15	Rotterdam-Barcelona	10
Cádiz-Barcelona	7	London-Barcelona	5
Philadelphia-Barcelona	5	Malta-Barcelona	5
Lisbon-Barcelona	4	Lubeck-Barcelona	3
Maryland-Barcelona	3	Dunkirk-Barcelona	3
Marseille-Barcelona	2	Christiansand-Barcelona	2
Falmouth-Barcelona	2	Alicante-Barcelona	2
Daus?-Barcelona	1	Nantes-Barcelona	1
Dereja (is this Djerba, and thus a North African port?)-Barcelona	1	Castellamar-Barcelona	1
Naples-Barcelona	1	Dorchester[a]-Barcelona	1
Hamburg-Barcelona	1	Civitavecchia-Barcelona	1

(continued)

Table 9.2 (*Continued*)

Route	Number of Mentions	Route	Number of Mentions
Tenerife-Barcelona	1	Swinworth-Barcelona	1
St Malo-Barcelona	1	Middleburgh-Barcelona	1
Aui? Agde?-Barcelona	1	Whitby-Barcelona	1
Vannes-Barcelona	1	Hoidreg?-Barcelona	1
Rouen-Barcelona	1	Cádiz-Barcelona	1
New York-Barcelona	1	Berwick-Barcelona	1
Crezi?-Barcelona	1	Arundel-Barcelona	1
Seine (river)-Barcelona	1	Gonjeuti?-Barcelona	1
Honfleur-Barcelona	1	Trieste-Barcelona	1
Terranova-Barcelona	1	Tepel?-Barcelona	1
Exeter-Barcelona	1	Portsmouth-Barcelona	1
Luim?-Barcelona	1	Quebec-Barcelona	1

Source: From ACA, Consulado de Comercio. *Indice de los registros de protestas de mar (1766)*.
a) Dorchester is inland. The nearest port is Weymouth. There is also Dawlish further west. Could the clerk have misspelled the location or was Dorchester the origin of the goods and mentioned here even if not a seaport? I am thankful to R.I. Moore for this information.

1866

By 1866, the structure of ownership and the ports of destination had changed dramatically. The data is so abundant for that year that rendering all the information in tabular form would require a very long and tedious table. This is a simplified version.

Altogether, 77 cities (instead of countries, as had been the case in 1766) are identified as different places where the ships listed in the protests against the sea were registered. Barcelona barely appears in the documentation noting port or country of registration in 1766, but in 1866 it led the way with 47 different ships (from those making depositions or protests against the sea) registered in the city (Table 9.3). After Barcelona, Bilbao makes the next highest number of

Table 9.3 Trade in 1866 (a sample). Seventy-seven cities are mentioned altogether.

Port of Origins of Trading Vessels	Number of Entries
Barcelona (Spain)	47
Christiansand (a Norwegian port)	13
Havana (Cuba)	11
Pernambuco (Brazil)	10
Bergen (Norway)	8
New Orleans (United States)	8
Bilbao (on the Bay of Biscay, Spain)	8
Villagarcía (Galicia, Spain)	7
Gijón (Asturias, Spain)	4
Palma de Mallorca (Spain, in the Mediterranean)	4
Mataró (near Barcelona, Spain)	4
Liverpool (England)	3

Source: From ACA, Consulado de Comercio. *Indice de los registros de protestas de mar*, 4, 129 (1866).

appearances in the record, with eight; Villagarcía follows with seven. Neither of these towns, however, could match Barcelona's seemly extensive control of the trading vessels coming into the city. Gijón, Palma de Mallorca, and Mataró (a port within Barcelona's jurisdiction), with four mentions each, and Liverpool, with three, are the only ones that receive more than two mentions in this long list. Not shown in the table but worth mentioning are some interesting points of origin, such as Kiev and Reykjavik. While numerically Mediterranean ports had the upper hand (because of the numerical strength of Barcelona registrations) as the locations for ships engaged in trade within and in and out of the Mediterranean, in terms of the geographical breakdown that shows where merchandise came from, most of the ports were on the European or American Atlantic coasts and outside the western Mediterranean.

As to mercantile routes, the documentation of the protests against the sea for 1866 lists 81 different ports with which Barcelona traded in this period (from the limited sample). The port mentioned most often in the protests was Christiansand or Kristiansand (a port in Norway, different from Kristiansund, a major exporter of salted cod to Spain in the nineteenth century) with 13 entries. Havana, Cuba (11), Pernambuco in Brazil (10), Bergen (also in present-day Norway), and New Orleans (8) followed behind. The Americas appear prominently in the documentation. American ports are mentioned 58 times, including two South American Pacific ports, Guayaquil, Ecuador, and Callao, Peru. Northern European ports (in Scandinavia, England, Iceland, and Germany) appear in 64 of the documents. But the Mediterranean and Spain's Atlantic ports are not mentioned even half as many times as the other two geographical regions mentioned above. One reference, to Manila (in the Philippines), points to the wide range of Barcelona's trade.[18]

Some patterns are clearly discernable from these tables and data summaries. In 1766, the range of countries represented in the depositions against the sea was small indeed. Three countries, England, the Netherlands, and France, gathered the lion's share of registrations. The ships' registration – with the caveats already voiced before – clearly reflected these three countries' economic dominance, not only in the world at large but in the Mediterranean as well. Non-European or North American nations are not represented in the records, though some names are almost undecipherable and may correspond to ports or areas outside both Europe and North America, as for example the mention of a port that may have been Djerba, an island off the coast of Tunisia in North Africa (and a city with a long involvement in trade with Europe). Ship registration – the evidence is, of course, fragmentary and limited to ships damaged by bad weather, to specific sample years, and to those ships with Barcelona as a terminus – reflects the economic dominance of these three nations (though a good number of Scandinavian registrations can also be found) not only in the Mediterranean but in the world at large as well.

In 1866, ship registration identified the city in which the merchant vessels had been registered rather than the country, as had been the case in 1766. Barcelona, Bilbao, and Villagarcía – in the Mediterranean, on the Basque coast, and in Galicia, respectively – overwhelmed other ports of registration in terms of mentions in the extant depositions. How may one explain such a radical shift? Does this mean that English, Dutch, and French entrepreneurial concerns now found it easier or more profitable to register some of the vessels in their large commercial fleets in Spanish ports? It is very difficult indeed to come up with a certain answer. The ports of origin, the nature of the trade, the name of the captains, and other evidence seem to indicate the staying power of English, Scandinavian, and American economic interests in the western Mediterranean economy. Nonetheless, Barcelona experienced an unprecedented economic expansion in the second half of the nineteenth century and that may have also influenced the nature of the evidence.

THE GLOBAL MEDITERRANEAN TRADE

Barcelona actively traded with Scandinavian ports (trading mostly wood and cod) and with its traditional non-Mediterranean commercial partners, England, France, and the Netherlands. The city also carried out important commercial exchanges with Spanish Atlantic ports (Gijón, Bilbao, and Villagarcía), as well as with the Americas. As to the trade with Spanish Atlantic ports, it is a reflection of Spain's backward internal road links (certainly from the Northwest of the peninsula) that what today would be carried by truck or rail was then transported from Iberia's Atlantic ports through the always troublesome Straits of Gibraltar and into the western Mediterranean. American ports on the Atlantic – Pernambuco, Havana, Santiago de Cuba, Philadelphia, New York, Buenos Aires, New Orleans, ports in Puerto Rico, and Rio de Janeiro – were the origin of long-distance trade with Barcelona. Even ports on the Pacific coast, Guayaquil and Callao, appear in the documentation, as does distant

Manila. Two things are clear from the limited evidence of the depositions against the sea in the one-year sampling from 1866. By that year, Barcelona's merchants had connected with four distinct global markets. The first secured a constant supply of much needed Scandinavian wood (for construction) and other important raw materials. The second ensured an extensive trade with the Americas, with the remaining Spanish colonies (Cuba, Puerto Rico, and the Philippines) having the lion's share of entries. A third stream of goods came from English ports, most often consisting of manufactured goods and machinery. Finally, Barcelona's traditional trading partners in the western Mediterranean (that form a pattern of commercial exchanges that dated from Roman times) remained an important part of the city's commercial life.

Once again, the absence of mentions of North African ports (or the scant number of them, if one considers some of the names that I have been unable to locate as possible African ports of origin) adds to the puzzle, since we know that by 1866 Spain was already engaged in a colonial project in North Africa. One additional caveat is necessary. The frequency of mentions may be deceptive. One may justly assume that ships sailing from far away – Pernambuco, Cuba, Scandinavia – had far greater chance of facing inclement weather and rough seas than vessels making short voyages and engaged in the coastal sailing typical of the Mediterranean. Even so, and although the evidence for mishap in the western Mediterranean remained quite compelling, one is still left with the sense that while sea trade was a perilous enterprise, economic needs and the promise of high profits trumped the risks of seafaring. For our purposes here, the evidence shows that ships and sailors from almost every corner of the world (with the noted exceptions) poured into the port of Barcelona and other western Mediterranean ports. These encounters included more than just the transfer of goods from one country to another or the linking of Barcelona to global patterns of trade. These encounters brought people from different parts of the world, as they do today, to the heterogeneous and bustling atmosphere of maritime enclaves on the shores of the Middle Sea.

SHIPS

We may not leave this discussion without revisiting, even if briefly, the question of ships, an issue raised by Braudel in his *The Mediterranean*. By 1830, the registers of the protests against the sea began to note the ships' tonnage and to describe in detail the type of ships trading with Barcelona. This was still a world of sails. Few if any of the vessels mentioned were steamships, though heavy iron ships were, in general, less vulnerable to bad weather, though of course they could also sink. The types of ships and the tonnage often contrasted sharply between those plying the western Mediterranean exclusively and those coming from beyond the Straits of Gibraltar, though exceptions could be found. A very large frigate, drawing 600 tons, sailed between Scandinavian ports and Barcelona, with a cargo of wood. The captain complained about damage to his cargo by rough seas and duly entered his formulaic protest against the sea on January 4, 1866. The Santander-registered brigantine *Victoria* left Havana for Barcelona on January 15, 1866, with a cargo of sugar, cotton (probably from an earlier stop since cotton was not a Cuban export), and other merchandise. On January 28 and 29, the *Victoria* met severe weather, taking on as much as six inches of water in its cargo area. Only two months later, on March 18, did the captain enter a protest against the sea at the Atlantic port of Cádiz. Leaving Cádiz on March 25, the *Victoria* reached Barcelona only on April 9, when Captain Gerónimo Casanova entered a second protest against the sea. The *Victoria* drew 228 tons, a considerable tonnage but far below that of the Scandinavian frigate. Beyond noting what seems an exceptionally long time to cross the Atlantic and parts of the western Mediterranean (almost four months), including 15 days between Cádiz and Barcelona, one may also note that even larger ships such as the *Victoria* could meet their share of misfortune in unpredictable seas.[19]

While frigates and brigantines often connected the western Mediterranean to the outside world, within the region a whole assortment of smaller ships with considerably less tonnage was often the norm. The 38-ton *lancha* (boat, lighter[20]) the *Clotilde* carried trade between Alicante and Barcelona in 1866. A 48-ton *goleta* (schooner) carried trade between Marseille and Barcelona the same year. A 60-ton *balandro* (sloop) sailed between Alicante and Barcelona. A 62-ton laud, *San Antonio*, made the crossing between Palma de Mallorca and Barcelona, while a 57-ton laud did the same between Málaga and the capital of Catalonia. Exceptions, of course, can also be found. In the same year for which we find these protests against the sea, a very large brigantine, drawing 368 tons, sailed between Trieste and Barcelona, while two small schooners, drawing 73 and 101 tons, respectively, made the Atlantic crossing from New York and Cuba into the western Mediterranean in 1866. These exceptions aside, the evidence from the protests against the sea reflects that the patterns of coastal sailing, so typical of medieval and early modern Mediterranean seafaring, still remained in place into the nineteenth century. Moreover, it is important to note the predominance of sail over steam in 1866. Whether large ships sailing south from Northern European ports or across the Atlantic, or smaller ones sailing the western Mediterranean, long periods of time may have been needed to complete some of those crossings.[21]

1868

It would, however, be foolish to assume that findings based on the evidence of one single year, 1866, stand for the whole of imports into Barcelona and maritime disasters. While my portrait of the western Mediterranean, provided by the evidence of the 1866 protests against the sea, is faithful to the evidence, in 1868, just two years later, three significantly different conclusions may be derived from the extant evidence. First, for the first time in all the years I have examined, the protests against the sea for 1868 include a good number of references to steamships ("*vapor*"). Most of them did not have large tonnages, but some did. Most of them were registered in Gijón on the northern coast of Spain. A good number of them carried on trade with the eastern Mediterranean or between England and Barcelona. Their cargo was, unlike entries for sail ships, often described as a "variety of goods" (*"diferentes generos"*), but when engaged in trade with the eastern Mediterranean their cargo was almost exclusively wheat and, sometimes, flour. Three of these steamships appeared twice in the protests against the sea during the same year (one, the steam ship *Campeador*, appeared three times), indicating either bad luck, incompetence, criminal intent, or that steam ships were indeed not so secure against the fury of the Mediterranean Sea after all. The second point is a brief one. Unlike in the evidence for 1866, two years later Barcelona did not maintain its dominant position in terms of ship registration. The third point has already been alluded to above. Unlike what seemed a trend of replacing the import of cereal grains (mostly wheat) with other products, by 1868 a veritable river of wheat came, mostly from the eastern Mediterranean, including a mention of trade with North Africa (Oran). Nonetheless, the same patterns of trade are confirmed by a careful reading of the protests: wood and cod (*bacalao*) from Scandinavia; sugar, cotton, and coffee from the Americas; and wheat (though in much larger quantity than in 1866) from the eastern Mediterranean.

CONCLUSION

We have traveled far and covered variegated topics in this chapter. All along, the short descriptions provided throughout this and other chapters have sought to bring to life the experience of travel, of encounters. These encounters varied from the experiences – rendered into travel accounts – of an erudite Muslim and a learned Jew as they journeyed through Christian Europe, to those of Europeans or Americans traveling and living in Islamic lands. Encounters could also be harsh and brutal. Corsairs played an important role in the life of the late medieval and early modern Mediterranean, but they did so too in Roman times and in Atlantic waters. Missing from this account, but briefly noted elsewhere in the book, are the activities of Christian missionaries in North Africa. Their demise – or the absence of Muslim missionaries in Europe in the same period – points dramatically to the changes that occurred as a result of the increase in corsair activity and naval conflict on either side of 1500, and to the beginnings of the European colonization of North Africa. But missionaries or monastic interlocutors in the ransoming of captives also played an important role in connecting different areas of the western Mediterranean.

These sketches, beyond providing glimpses of, and a taste of, Mediterranean life, serve to confirm, and sometimes add to, Braudel's description of the Middle Sea. Finally, here, as I have done in other chapters in this book, I have drawn on archival material to provide a more focused view of specific issues in the history of the western Mediterranean. One of the most interesting aspects of these protests against the sea is the question of language, a topic already examined in an earlier chapter (Chapter 7). That the depositions were written in Castilian and not in Catalan tells us a great deal about the politics of language in the late eighteenth and the first half of the nineteenth century in Spain. While in the Late Middle Ages – and even into the sixteenth century – Catalan had been the language of culture and business, Bourbon centralization (see

Chapter 4) sought to end Spain's linguistic plurality in the eighteenth century. This is quite evident in the protests against the sea. By the eighteenth and nineteenth centuries, merchant captains had the choice of making the deposition themselves or doing so through interpreters. These were formal documents and, thus, did not use the so-called *lingua franca* that for so long had been the language used by merchants, slavers, corsairs, and others to communicate throughout the Mediterranean, and which still was alive in the pages of Dumas's *The Count of Monte Cristo*. That *lingua franca* may still have been the common language of people at sea, but it did not have any validity for the depositions entered at Barcelona's Consulado de Comercio. Instead, translators (usually the consul in Barcelona of the particular country from which the sea captain hailed) served as interlocutors for their compatriots and for others. The depositions against the sea and against bad weather, while confirming most of Braudel's findings for an earlier period and expanding the scope of his inquiry, also provide us with a window onto Barcelona's trade – and that of the western Mediterranean – in the eighteenth and nineteenth centuries and the unpredictability of the sea. The documents offer testimony for the encounters between Mediterranean seafarers and an angry sea, and for the dramatic changes in Barcelona's and the world's economy in their transition to an industrial society.

NOTES

1 Adeline Rucquoi, "Las rutas del saber. España en el siglo XII," *Cuadernos de historia de España*, LXXV (1998–1999), 41–58. See also her "Éducation et société dans la Péninsule ibérique au Moyen Age," *Histoire de l'éducation*, 69 (janvier 1996), 3–36.

2 *The Itinerary of Benjamin of Tudela*, edited and translated by Marcus Nathan Adler (first edition 1907, republished in New York: Philipp Feldheim). Available in The Project Gutenberg EBook of *The Itinerary of Benjamin of Tudela*, 2. http://www.gutenberg.org/files/14981/14981-h/14981-h.htm.

3 *The Travels of Ibn Jubayr*, trans. R.J.C. Broadhurst (London: Jonathan Cape, 1952), 339–340.

4 *The Travels of Ibn Jubayr*, 338–339.

5 *Crónica de Flores y Blancaflor*, ed. David Arbesu (Tempe, AZ: ACMRS, 2011).

6 Mary Louise Pratt, *Imperial Eyes. Travel Writing and Transculturation* (London: Routledge, 1992). Although Pratt's emphasis is on South America and Africa, some of her perceptive descriptions apply to Mediterranean North Africa and to certain areas of the Western European Mediterranean where the Muslim imprint endures in monuments, culinary practices, and behavior.

7 See Patricia Almarcegui, *Ali Bey y los viajeros europeos a Oriente* (Barcelona: Bellaterra, 2007). See prologue by Roger Mimó Lladós. Also M. Carme Montaner and Anna María Casassas, "Between Science and Spying: Maps of Northern Africa and the Near East in the Works of Ali Bey el-Abassi (1766–1818)," *Eastern Mediterranean Cartographies*, 25/26 (2004), 181–196.

8 *Viajes de Ali Bey el Abbassi por Africa y Asia durante los años 1803, 1804, 1805, 1806, 1807*, vol. I, trans. by P.P. (Valencia: Librería de Mallén y Sobrinos, 1836).

9 Isabelle Eberhardt and Victor Barrucant, *Dans l'ombre chaude de l'Islam* (Paris: Librairie Charpentier et Fasquelle, 1906), 41, 62, 65, 67, 84–85, 90 et passim.

10   Paul Theroux, *The Pillars of Hercules: A Grand Tour of the Mediterranean* (New York: G.P. Putnam's Sons, 1995).

11   Olivia Remie Constable, *Housing the Stranger in the Mediterranean World: Lodging, Trade, and Travel in Late Antiquity and the Middle Ages* (Cambridge: Cambridge University Press, 2003).

12   Ernle Dusgate Selby Bradford, *The Sultan's Admiral: The Life of Barbarossa* (London: Hodder & Stoughton, 1969); Paul Achard, *La vie extraordinaire des frères Barberousse, corsaires et rois d'Alger* (Paris: Les Éditions de France, 1939).

13   Bartolomé Bennassar et Lucile Bennassar, *Les chrétiens d'Allah: l'histoire extraordinaire des renégats, XVIe et XVIIe siècles* (Paris: Perrin, 1989). See also his engaging fictional/historical account of a well-known figure, Mustafa des Six-Fours, *Les tribulations de Mustafa des Six-Fours* (Paris: Criterion, 1995).

14   Debra Blumenthal, *Enemies and Familiars: Slavery and Mastery in Fifteenth-Century Valencia* (Ithaca, NY: Cornell University Press, 2009).

15   Archivo de la Corona de Aragón (hereafter ACA), Consulado de Comercio. *Registro de protestas de mar*, 4/1, 129 (1766).

16   ACA, Consulado de Comercio. *Registro de protestas de mar*, 4, 129 (1866).

17   On the economic transformations of modern Catalonia, see Pierre Vilar et al., *La formació de la Catalunya moderna* (Esplugues de Llobregat: Ariel, 1970); Pere Pascual, *Agricultura i industrialització a la Catalunya del segle XIX: formació i desestructuració d'un sistema econòmic* (Barcelona: Crítica, 1990).

18   ACA, Consulado de Comercio. *Registro de protestas de mar*, 4, 129 (1866).

19   ACA. Consulado de Comercio. *Indice de los registros de protestas de mar* (1766–1868). Indices for 1866. ACA, Consulado de Comercio. *Registro de protestas de mar*, 4, 129 (1866), ff. 22r–22v.

20   A lighter is a flat-bottomed barge, used principally for loading and unloading ships offshore and transporting goods in shallow waters.

21   ACA, Consulado de Comercio. *Indice de los registros de protestas de mar* (1766–1868). Indices for 1866.

[10] Between Two Worlds: Iberia, Sicily, Tunis, Algiers, and Marseille[1]

T HE entire Mediterranean region has long been (and remains) a site of encounter, a place where different cultures, religious beliefs, and ethnic groups have commingled (as they do to this very day), fought with each other, cooperated, and co-existed (or not) over time. Often, the dynamics of such encounters have generated new cultural products through the overlapping of different sensitivities and aesthetic impulses. At other times, they have led to destruction and grief. The former outcome is most obvious in some of the monuments and structures that dot the shores of the Mediterranean or that mark the passing of a culture through a specific location. The latter is present in the historical accounts of explosive armed conflicts and in encounters generating, at best, mistrust, pejorative representations, and marginalization. At worst, these antagonisms have led to furious displays of violence, death, and/or exile.

To describe the manner in which the contacts between one civilization and another led to new cultural forms would require an entire book and more. To the impact of Qur'anic chants on medieval music or that of Judeo-Arabic Spanish lyrical poetry on the genesis of courtly culture and troubadour poetry, or the role of Muslims and Jews in the transmission of Greek philosophy to the medieval West at locations such as Toledo, Sicily, and Palestine (see previous chapter), one may also add the influence of Kabbalah and Muslim learning on the culture of the Renaissance. Or, if we wish to consider the modern age, one may note the impact of migration from the Mediterranean on the culture and cuisine of modern Northern Europe and America. These and many other points of contact and cultural production are only a few examples of the flow of culture from one group to another. Jews in the Caliphate of Córdoba wrote in Arabic. Castilian Christians under Islamic rule developed a language, Mozarab, that reflected the influence of Arabic. Spanish Muslims and Moriscos (Muslims nominally converted to Christianity), influenced by the Castilian language, followed the same route in the Late Middle Ages and the sixteenth century with *aljamiado.* Jews fleeing Spain carried a new dialect, Ladino, with them to the ghettoes in Rome and Venice and to the Ottoman lands, including North

The Western Mediterranean and the World: 400 CE to the Present, First Edition. Teofilo F. Ruiz.
© 2018 John Wiley & Sons, Ltd. Published 2018 by John Wiley & Sons, Ltd.

Africa. I could go on piling up these examples, but what I have listed above is sufficient to illustrate the complex network of cultural influences that flowed from one group to another and back.

With the end of the Roman Empire in the West, the subsequent fragmentation of political, civic, and religious unity (see chapters 3, 5, and 6) led to centuries of accommodation, continuing even to the present day, to the new realities of the Mediterranean world. It also led to strife. Those complex processes of cultural formation and the emergence of regional identities – often bound up in questions of religion and language – that resulted from the encounters between different groups are still palpable and ongoing in the immigrant enclaves that are found from Gibraltar to Palermo or in the historically recent exile or repatriation of Jews and colonial settlers (*pied noir*) from North Africa following the demise of the French colonial empire there over five decades ago.

SITES OF ENCOUNTER

Although, as noted above, the entire Mediterranean was, and is, a site of encounters, some locations or regions on or near the shores of the Mediterranean Sea seem to have had a longer history of conflicts and cultural diversity and creativity. The Iberian Peninsula, and specifically cities such as Toledo, Seville, Barcelona, Valencia, and Granada, was certainly one of those points of convergence. The Balearic Islands, Majorca most of all, and Sicily were special places for the commingling of different people. Marseille today is the hub of successive waves of immigrants that have incontrovertibly shaped the present life of the city. This has also been the case in other locations along the shores of the western portions of the Mediterranean. The flip side of this is the flocking of people from different parts of the Mediterranean to other countries or continents around the world, contributing to a vibrant and diverse popular culture in their host countries. Thus, in the pages that follow, I would like to present short sketches – not actual histories of these locations, which would not be possible in the space allotted – that reflect and describe those moments of convergence and divergence when cultural artifacts and cultural production occurred. Emphasis is placed on those locations that reflect the conflation of contributions from a diversity of cultures. Special attention will be given to buildings, urban landscapes, and ceremonial spaces that show the layering of cultures at specific moments in time.

IBERIA

The Iberian Peninsula was, together with Sicily, the quintessential melting pot of the western Mediterranean. We have already seen (Chapter 3) the successive waves of invaders that settled in the Iberian Peninsula and contributed to its historical and cultural development. Greeks, Phoenicians, Carthaginians, Romans, Germanic tribes, Berbers, Arabs, Slavs, and Jews found in Iberia a land to conquer, a place in which to trade, a land of refuge, a productive site, and a vibrant and, often times, dangerous mixture of cultures. In Iberia, as elsewhere, these contacts and this cross-cultural fertilization often had as counterpart eruptions of violence.

Iberian languages, to give a preliminary example, evolved from these contacts. Castilian is the vernacular emerging from Late Imperial Latin, but it also borrowed abundantly from Galician and Arabic, and even includes some contributions from Hebrew. Catalan, also a vernacular deeply shaped by its Latin ancestry, was deeply influenced by the Occitan languages, Castilian, and Arabic. There is no peninsular language, one may emphasize, that is not itself a bricolage of different linguistic traditions. With the adoption of certain terms and linguistic forms there was also the kind of cultural borrowing and influence that transformed the cultural landscape from which literature and quotidian forms of expression emerged. For example, *ojalá*, a term used to emphasize that one wishes something would happen, is used frequently in Castilian and, even more so, in Latin America Spanish. It is an adaptation from the Arabic *Inshallah*. Similar adaptations appear in many other salutations and expressions that move from one linguistic and religious context to another with little effort at all. In many respects, though the fluidity of languages remains a global phenomenon to this very day – most obvious in the significance of English and the borrowing of English words to describe aspects of a material culture deeply influenced by American models – in the Late Middle Ages and the early modern period, the western (and also the eastern) Mediterranean was clearly a cauldron for the overlapping of linguistic and cultural traditions. How did this work at the local level? How did it work in the commingling of different people in specific urban spaces and in its architectural monuments?

Seville

Today, Seville is the capital of the autonomous region of Andalusia and the most important city in southern Spain. A manufacturing, cultural, and artistic center, the city has been among the most populous in the peninsula since its heyday in the Late Middle Ages and its moment of glory as the sole Spanish link to the New World. Although the city was connected to the Atlantic through the Guadalquivir River, the silting of the river in the late early modern period had, by the seventeenth century, prevented the galleons that connected Spain to America from sailing directly into the city. But Seville also played a signal role in connecting the Atlantic with the Mediterranean and with the rest of the world. The Genoese established a long-lasting mercantile outpost there in the Middle Ages, leaving an important imprint on the city's commercial and social life. And they used the city as a base through which to connect the Mediterranean to the Atlantic.

Seville has had a long history, reaching back into the Classical period. That history attests to the presence in the city of different civilizations and disparate ethnic and religious groups. An important urban center during the long centuries of Roman control over Iberia, Hispalis (its Roman name) played a significant role in the Roman connections with the Atlantic through the port at

Gades, or Cádiz. Sevillians in the Middle Ages, the early modern period, and even today are extremely proud of their Roman origins, or even of the preposterous claim that the city predated the Roman conquest of Iberia. The legend that Hercules himself had founded the city during his visit to the Straits of Gibraltar, or Pillars of Hercules, was also one of the most important mainstays of Sevillian self-representation. The reality, of course, is that Hercules was claimed as a favorite founding father by many towns and cities throughout the peninsula, as well as being an important motif in the early modern Spanish Monarchs' iconographical program.

Nonetheless, though many of these claims were spurious, many local histories produced throughout the early modern period emphasized Seville's ancient origins. The extreme to which this self-fashioning of the city was carried out can be easily seen in one detail of Philip II's royal entry into Seville in 1570, when the municipal officials of the city proposed to the king that they receive him while dressed in Roman senatorial robes. Of course, Philip took very little time in deflating such expectations and in reminding the city's municipal council that, at least in Castile (though not in the Crown of Aragon), he was the undisputed master.[2]

The collapse of Roman power in Iberia towards the early fifth century and the successive invasions of Vandals and Visigoths that followed were not beneficial to Seville. The Vandals' presence was ephemeral, and the Visigoths established their capital in Toledo, north of Seville. Nonetheless, the ancient Hispalis still played a role in the mostly rural economy of the Visigothic realm (because of the rich agricultural Sevillian hinterland), as well as in its cultural life. After all, Seville was home to one of Visigothic Spain and early medieval Europe's greatest polymaths, Isidore of Seville. Yet, the great Church councils during the Visigothic period took place in Toledo, Braga, and elsewhere.

Seville's ascent to a prominence in the peninsula began with the Muslim invasion in 711 and with the Muslim presence in al-Andalus in the succeeding centuries. Although Córdoba – easily connected to Seville by the Guadalquivir River – became the capital of the new Caliphate and the central point for Umayyad rule of the peninsula, Seville played an important role in the commercial and agricultural life of Iberia because of its unique strategic location. Through the river, the city had easy access to the Atlantic. Through a series of river valley routes, it also accessed the Mediterranean at what is today Algeciras or Gibraltar. Moreover, there was a way to sail from North Africa to present Cádiz by navigating north from Tangier and avoiding the treacherous waters around the Straits of Gibraltar. This was the manner in which some of the North African armed contingents reached the Iberian Peninsula in the Late Middle Ages.[3] As noted, the Sevillian hinterland, the fabled Aljarafe, was one of the best-cultivated and most productive regions of Muslim Spain, with only Valencia as a serious competitor. It was there that the Muslim green revolution began in the peninsula. It was there that grain, olive oil, and grapes became the main staples of Muslim agriculture. It was there that new husbandry techniques deeply influenced the course of southern Spain's agricultural practices. It was there that irrigation and water technology were deployed to improve agriculture.[4]

With the breakdown of the Caliphate of Córdoba in the 1030s, Seville became an independent kingdom, one of the so-called kingdoms of *taifas.* Economically, it was one of the strongest of the Muslim kingdoms that emerged from the wreckage of the Caliphate. Because of its significance, it soon attracted the attention of Almoravid (late eleventh century) and Almohad (late twelfth and early thirteenth century) invaders from North Africa (see Chapter 3). Under the Almohads and their imperial ambitions, Seville thrived as one of the centers of al-Andalus trade and culture. Its population included Italian merchants, a substantial Jewish contingent, Christians under Muslim rule, and, of course, Muslims, both those whose families had lived in Iberia for centuries and newcomers from North Africa.

This pluralistic society came to an end when the Christians, led by Ferdinand III (1217–1252), conquered the city in 1248. Following the conquest, and after an uprising by Mudejares (Muslims under Christian rule) in the 1260s, the city and the countryside were emptied of their Muslim population as the king of Castile, Alfonso X (1252–1284), sought to repopulate the region with Christians. Seville became Alfonso X's favorite city, and Jews and some Muslims slowly resettled in the city and its environs, restoring some of its former heterogeneous population. By the late fourteenth century, even before the Castilian forays into the Atlantic Sea, the city was the largest in Spain and the economic locomotive for the Andalusi economy. After 1492, it became the sole port of departure and entry for commercial exchanges with the New World. As such, its prosperity was more than guaranteed. Seville, thus, became a bustling entrepôt, attracting settlers from the rest of the peninsula and from other parts of the world, most of all, from Italy. So that's some of the history, but how was Seville a site of encounter and cultural production?

SEVILLE AS A SITE OF ENCOUNTER AND CULTURAL PRODUCTION

In the center of the city of Seville, and within a short walk of each other, we find architectural sites that illustrate not only the historical evolution of Seville but also the conflation of different cultures and architectural vocabularies. The late medieval Gothic cathedral, built on the site of the main mosque of the city after the conquest of 1248, still has a courtyard and a bell tower, the fabled Giralda (the symbol of the city, redolent with its Almohad Muslim past), that were part of that mosque and symbols of Muslim life in the peninsula.[5] Just a few minutes walk from the cathedral one finds the Royal Alcázar. To this very day, the Alcázar, a building of twelfth-century Almohad origins, though rebuilt and added to by Peter I (1350–1369), serves as a residence for the Spanish royal family. Adjacent to the cathedral and the Alcázar is the neighborhood of the Santa Cruz, a former Jewish and, after 1391, converso enclave that still retains, notwithstanding its name, a great deal of the flavor of what Jewish life may have been like there before 1391. Not too far away is the Archivo de Indias (the general Archive of the Indies), dating to the sixteenth century and built in the

Renaissance style as a mercantile lodge (Casa de Contratación) before being converted to a repository for the extensive collection of documents related to the Castilian presence in the New World. In the direction of the Guadalquivir River and also very close is the Torre de Oro, the Muslim Golden Tower that kept watch over the river. From it a chain could be extended across the river to block invading ships. And not too far away is the site of the eighteenth-century Royal Tobacco Factory (La Tabacalera). It was the epicenter for Spain's internal monopoly over the distribution of tobacco and the making of cigars, the site for Prosper Mérimée's "orientalist" novella, and Bizet's great opera, *Carmen,* and Carlos Saura's flamenco-inflected film rendition of the story. All these cultural products were greatly influenced by music and dancing associated with the Roma (gypsies) of Spain. Today, the building partly houses the University of Seville.

As is obvious from these brief descriptions, these buildings tell us of a history of encounters. They tell us about cultural artifacts that incorporated elements of different provenances, conflating them into something else and allowing us to see change over time. Two in particular are poignant in their blending of architectural styles and in their role as markers of political and religious change in the peninsula. The first is the architectural complex that includes the cathedral and the Giralda. Not unlike the cathedral at Córdoba, where the Christian invaders plonked a Gothic cathedral right in the middle of the exquisite forest of arches that are the trademark of the great mosque there, in Seville, the Christian victors, following a well-established practice in Reconquest Spain, turned the main mosque of the city into their temple. This Mediterranean practice, if you would allow me this digression, was carried across the Ocean Sea into the New World, where Marian shrines would be placed in Mayan and Aztec temples in an attempt to sacralize indigenous ritual spaces and cover them with a veneer of Christianity.[6]

SEVILLE CATHEDRAL

When the city of Seville was conquered in 1248, all of its Muslim and Jewish inhabitants were expelled from the city. Ferdinand III, the Castilian king, waited until the city had been emptied out before making a proto-royal entry into the city escorted by Castilian magnates and other royal officials. He walked through the empty city to the site of the main mosque, a building that had already been blessed by ecclesiastics and converted into a church. There a Te Deum, a mass of thanks, was chanted to celebrate Seville's conquest.[7] The mosque had originally been built under Almohad rule. It began to be constructed in 1184 and was completed shortly afterwards in the early 1190s. It was turned into a cathedral dedicated to the Virgin Mary in 1248. For over a century and a half after the conquest, Christians in Seville worshiped in a temple that reminded them continuously of the Muslim past. They were called to prayer by bells in the Giralda, the ancient minaret of the mosque, from where the muezzin had called the faithful to prayer in that haunting cry echoed today in the *cante jondo,* or deep song, of flamenco.

Figure 10.1 Seville Cathedral's bell tower (the Giralda), a minaret of Almohad origin. Source: Courtesy of Tom Flethcer. http://www.nyc-architecture.com/ARCH/ARCH-notes-municipal.htm.

It was not until the early fifteenth century, in 1401, that, after an earthquake had destroyed most of the ancient Almohad building, the citizens, of what was then the most prosperous city in Iberia, decided to build a new cathedral. Built over the next century, it is the largest cathedral in Christendom, but its builders retained the bell tower, the ancient minaret of the mosque, and, as noted earlier, a courtyard, the Patio de los Naranjos, or Orange Tree Courtyard. The double gate leading to this yard or garden, also of Almohad origin, consists of two elaborate horseshoe arches of bluish tint. It is decorated with Arabic inscriptions and typical Muslim decorations in the style that it is also known as

Mudejar, and was built by local artists under Almohad rule. It is a beautiful arch and a beautiful garden. Together with the Giralda, these remains of a Muslim past stand in sharp contrast to the gaudiness of the Gothic cathedral. They serve as reminders, encapsulated in the buildings and syncretistic use of space and architectural design, that cultures co-existed, even after the expulsion of the Mudejares from southern Andalusia.

Virgins and Saintly Tombs

Seville Cathedral is a very good example of what I wish to convey here because of the architectural vocabulary present in its fabric to this very day. But there are other elements to consider beyond the conflation of architectural styles. In a recent and wonderful book, Amy Remensnyder describes how an image of the virgin – or such was the belief of early modern Sevillians, as shown in Alonso Morgado's book of 1576 – had been found in the Almohad mosque. Dated to the Visigothic period before the Christian conquest of the city, the cult of this particular virgin, the Virgin de la Antigua, gained great popularity among the New World explorers and conquerors. But, of course, Muslims, as Remensnyder shows throughout her book, also venerated the Virgin Mary.[8]

Besides housing the Virgen de la Antigua, Seville Cathedral was the burial place of its Christian conqueror, Ferdinand III. Upon his death in 1252, the king, as was often the custom in Castile, was buried in the city that had seen his greatest victory. His tomb, remade and renovated over the centuries, occupies a central place in the cathedral's sacred topography. The original mausoleum incorporated two important iconographic references. The first one was the sword with which Ferdinand III had taken the city. That symbol of Christian victory over Islam would be redeployed at numerous times in the history of the Castilian monarchy and during festive displays of power. The other was the original inscription on the tomb. Written in Latin, Castilian, Arabic, and Hebrew, the three latter renderings praised Ferdinand as a just ruler over the three religions. Only the Latin, which could only be read by the few, included triumphalist statements about the victories of Christianity over Islam. This iconographic reference to Castilian kings as rulers of a heterogeneous religious realm had a long history. Alfonso VI (1065–1109), self-proclaimed emperor of all the "Spains," also claimed to be the emperor of the three religions. Alfonso X, Ferdinand's son, chose Seville as his favorite residence and a great deal of the cultural work of his scriptorium brought together Jewish, Muslim, and Christian scholars in fruitful intellectual cooperation.

The Alcázar

This layering of different cultural tropes and architectural styles is also evident in the magnificent Almohad royal palace or Alcázar. Rebuilt and modified somewhat by Peter I (1350–1369) – though still faithful to its original Mudejar style – the entire palace is a gesture to the great architectural and imperial ambitions of the Almohads. Nowhere is this more evident than in the impressive gate to the palace, the Puerta de la Montería, often referred to as the Puerta del León, or Lion's Gate, because of its sculptural details. Although the gate of the Montería has undergone many different transformations over the centuries, any casual or uninformed tourist can easily see its Muslim provenance. The color, a splendid red, the tile works depicting a lion, other elements in the architectural history of this gate, and the contiguous courtyard, the Patio de los Leones, all attest to its Almohad origins, linking Seville with other Almohad buildings in North Africa.[9]

Peter I, while building his palace in the second half of the fourteenth century, was fairly faithful to the original ornamental program for the building. He injected into it, however, all the intrigues of his court and his tempestuous romantic affair with his beloved mistress, María de Padilla. The city resonated with the stories of their love affair, of Peter I's rejection and imprisonment of his lawful wife, of the conflicts with his half-brothers, the Trastámaras, and of his eventual assassination at the hands of his half-brother. All these dramas played out in and around the Alcázar. But in the overlapping that occurred in these sites of encounter, there were other cultural tropes. It is not a coincidence that Peter, who so openly favored the architectural language of his Muslim enemies, was also quite supportive of his Jewish subjects. In fact, he was accused of being the illegitimate child of a Jew, and the Jews fought on his side during the civil wars that plagued the realm in the 1360s.

Allow me to return to the Alcázar. Long after a new dynasty came to power which preferred Valladolid over Seville, by the Late Middle Ages and the beginnings of the early modern period, late Gothic and Renaissance architectural elements were incorporated into the fabric of the palace. The Alcázar, as is the case with other buildings, is an organic cultural structure that underwent continuous changes, either in its function or in the juxtaposing of contrasting architectural styles. This is also the case with one of the most famous Islamic palaces in Europe, the fabled Alhambra. Built in the Late Middle Ages, when the Islamic presence in Spain was already doomed in the face of Christian advances, the Alhambra reflects the wealth and sophistication of the Nasrid rulers of Granada, even as its realm came to be besieged by Christians. Charles V, grandson of the conquerors of the Alhambra, Ferdinand and Isabella, built a Renaissance palace on the grounds of the palace-fortress. The clash of architectural design articulated messages about Christian power, but also dramatically altered the site's functions. The organization and use of space always matters. How contemporaries read these subtle messages of domination and rupture is hard to say, but the reality remains that out of distinct elements buildings were transformed, appropriated anew, and put to uses for which they were not intended.

By the seventeenth and eighteenth centuries, as Spain and Seville began their precipitous decline, the leading citizens of Seville, most of them originally form Flanders and who had made their fortune in the trade with the Indies, turned, as Amanda Wunder has magisterially shown, to the building of religious monuments.[10] At a time when economic and social crises demanded radical action, it was to religion that the leaders of Seville turned. By then, the city was also the epicenter, as Elizabeth Perry has shown, of scam artists, petty criminals, and the like. In that sense, Seville remained a place for the commingling of people unlike any other in Iberia.[11]

Throughout its long history, Seville has remained a site of encounter. Today, in spite of the awful economic crisis that began in 2007–2008 and remains fairly unabated into the second half of the 2010s, the city is a great commercial and manufacturing center, attracting Muslim immigrants from North Africa. Also, related to the recovery of Islamic aspects of the city, a curious phenomenon has been developing throughout not only Seville but most of southern Spain (Andalusia) as well. In response to the needs of the Muslims who had settled in the region as permanent residents, the wealthy Muslims who keep residences and yachts in the tourist enclaves on the Costa del Sol (Marbella above all), and some Spaniards who, as noted earlier, have converted to Islam because of the romantic notion that they are descendants of the Muslim inhabitants of the region robbed by Christian invaders of their ancestral identity, mosques, some small places of worship and other large ostentatious structures, have sprouted throughout the region. This is also the case in Seville, where there is a substantial Muslim population, both legal and illegal, today. In the district of the Macarena, the home of many of the Roma people and the site for the worship of the Virgin of the Macarena, there are now numerous small mosques. In 2010, despite numerous protests and conflicts, the municipality of Seville allowed for the construction of a large mosque on one of the islands on the Guadalquivir (see also below for conflicts in Marseille over the building of a large mosque). The island of the Cartuja had been the site of the World's Fair in 1992. It is today a business and financial center. Minarets and the calls by the muezzin have now returned to Seville. They have returned not without strife, but then strife was part and parcel of medieval life as well.

PALERMO AND SICILY

Sicily

Few places in Europe have had such a long history of experiencing waves of invaders and settlers as Sicily in general and Palermo in particular. Located off the southernmost tip of the Italian Peninsula and forming, together with the underwater ridge that links the island to North Africa, a clear boundary between the eastern and western Mediterranean, Sicily has long been a true melting pot. Phoenicians, Greek settlers (mostly from Corinth and other polities on Greece's western shores), and Carthaginians (from nearby Africa) came to Sicily and fought for control of the island. Each group left a contribution to the island's history. As evident from extraordinary architectural sites, such as the stunning Greek temple ruins at Agrigento and elsewhere, Sicily was already a place for commercial and cultural exchanges (as well as armed conflict) long before Rome occupied the island and turned it into one of its most important suppliers of grain for the capital city's needs from 241 BCE onwards. The enduring Roman presence (over six centuries) has left enough evidence to mark the island as one of the most Romanized regions of the empire and as a link between Roman Italy and Roman Africa.

With Rome's decline in the fifth century, the island was not spared the turmoil caused by the Germanic invasions. Briefly seized by the Vandals in 439, it was then conquered by the Ostrogoths and added to their peninsular kingdom in the late 480s. Ostrogothic rule, however, was short-lived. Under Justinian (527–565), the eastern Roman Empire (later the Byzantine Empire) launched attempts to recover or reconquer most of the western parts of the former Roman Empire lost to Germanic invaders from the fifth century onwards. Successes in recovering parts of North Africa, outposts in Italy, and most of Sicily did not obscure the relative failure of Constantinople's military campaigns in the West. Sicily, however, came to be fully in the hands of the Byzantines. Since, shortly after Justinian's death, the eastern empire reverted to Greek as the language of administration, religious liturgy, and culture, Sicily underwent its second Greek phase. Unlike the first Greek settlements in the region, the Byzantine presence on the island, above all in its eastern region, would have an enduring impact on Sicilian life and government long after Byzantine imperial administration came to an end. Greek remained one of the administrative languages and a vehicle for material exchanges in Sicily until the twelfth century. Greeks or Byzantines also played a significant role in the island's political conflicts.[12]

Islam in Sicily Between the mid-seventh century – coinciding with the spread of Islam throughout the western Mediterranean – and the tenth, the Muslims launched attacks against Sicily until formally establishing their rule there for over a century (965–1072). Because of Sicily's strategic position at the gates of the western Mediterranean and its economic importance, Muslims (mostly from North Africa) had mounted campaigns against the Byzantine-controlled island as early as 652. Although these early raids were essentially unsuccessful, North African fleets probed the island's defenses repeatedly throughout the eighth century. We must not, however, think of this period as one of unremitting warfare. Expeditions against Sicily, as for example the one leading to the brief capture of Syracuse in 740 or the later sacking of the city, were balanced by periods of truce and commercial relations. The real conflict, one lasting almost a century, began after 826 when North African and Andalusi Muslims established a permanent foothold on the island. Over the next 140 years, the Muslims slowly conquered most of Sicily. The main urban centers, Palermo, Syracuse, and Taormina, fell to the Muslims between 831 and 902. And by around 965, Sicily had become fully part of the "world of Islam."

It is important to note that by the late tenth century, with the exception of the shores of Catalonia, southern France, and parts of Italy, the shores of the western Mediterranean and the sea itself were under Muslim control. Those areas not under the direct control of Islam were subjected to frequent raids and corsair activity. The sea, for all practical purpose, was a Muslim sea, and Sicily, now an emirate, played a central role in Islam's western Mediterranean strategy. In spite of stiff local Byzantine resistance, raids from Christian rulers in southern Italy, and internal disturbances prompted by conflicting claims between the Egyptian Fatimids (Shiʻa) and the Aghlabid dynasty in Tunis

(Sunni), Sicily flourished under Islamic rule. It did so agriculturally and by the introduction to the island of such staples as sugar cane, lemons, and oranges, the latter two still a fixture in parts of Sicily to this very day. Islamic husbandry and irrigation technology led to substantial population increase, great building projects, and the full insertion of Sicily into Dar al-Islam trading networks.[13] Sicily's heterogeneous population – Byzantine Greeks, western Christians, and Jews – lived in relative peace as long as Islam was recognized as the dominant religion and taxes were paid to its Muslim rulers. Membership of the larger Muslim world also allowed for the circulation of Classical learning that Islam brought into the West. Yet, as had been the case in Muslim Spain in the 1030s, internal frictions led to the weakening and eventual defeat of Islamic power in Sicily, and to another dramatic change in Sicily's complex political trajectory.[14]

Norman and Hohenstaufen Sicily, circa 1068–1253

The Normans, descendants from the Vikings who had settled at the mouth of the Seine, played a signal role in the history of the Mediterranean. For a long while, Norman and Viking expeditions sought avidly to play a role in the Middle Sea. Whether raiding the western Mediterranean in seaborne expeditions through the Straits of Gibraltar, sailing south from the Baltic down the Russian fluvial network and aiming for the Black Sea and Byzantium, or as the main protagonists of the First Crusade, the history of the Normans was deeply imbricated in the history of the Middle Sea. Nowhere was their role in the region as significant as in southern Italy and Sicily. Unlike the swift and successful conquest of England in 1066, however, Norman conquests in Italy were complicated affairs, lasting as long as their rule in the region. Appearing first as mercenaries in the endless local conflicts that plagued southern Italy in the early eleventh century, by around 1050 the Normans had begun to claim areas in the southernmost tip of Italy. Defeating papal, imperial, and Byzantine forces, the Normans established footholds in Benevento, on the Amalfi coast, and throughout Calabria. Robert Guiscard, invested as duke by the Pope, provided efficient military leadership. By 1061, Robert and his brother Roger began the conquest of Sicily in earnest. It would take 30 more years for the major Sicilian cities to be subdued and for the Normans to establish a firm control over the island.

First a duchy and then a kingdom under Roger II (1105–1154), Sicily was not yet fully at peace. Noble revolts, attacks from German imperial rivals, papal interference, and the like did not prevent Roger II from presiding over brilliant court-inspired cultural achievements. It would be under Roger II's rule that al-Idrīsī produced his fabled map of the Mediterranean world and a comprehensive geography of Africa. Ruling over a multi-ethnic, multi-religious, and multilingual island, Roger II carried out important economic measures to restore Sicily's prosperity, presiding over the overlapping of Byzantine-Muslim-Norman cultures. This commingling of cultures made Sicily, together with Spain and the Balearic Islands, a true site of encounter between people of different cultures, religions, and languages.

If I have spent so much time in laying out Sicily's political development, it is because every conqueror, every settlement of new people on the island, left

Figure 10.2 The coronation mantle of Roger II of Sicily was made in 1133/1134. In the mantle appears an Arabic inscription of the Hegira date of 528. The artists remain unknown. Source: Courtesy of Michael Greenhalgh.

monuments and an imprint in Sicily's history. It is not sufficient, however, to have a revolving door of new conquerors to be able to lay claim to being a site of encounters and cultural production. What marks Sicily as distinct is the hybridity that emerged from this mixing of populations. In art, in the laws enacted in three different languages, in the Norman administrative system, and in the people themselves, each of these groups left imprints. These cultural products, like the great cathedral at Monreale or the Norman kings' burial place at Palermo (see below), had elements that remind the viewer of the bricolage of different civilizations. These buildings were also new and original cultural artifacts.[15]

Palermo

Palermo shared fully in that history. Over its long past, dating almost three millennia, Palermo experienced the whole range of different presences. The city was founded by the Phoenicians, knew a Greek interlude, served as the launching point for the Carthaginian naval attacks against Rome during the First Punic War, and became part of the Roman Republic and later the Roman Empire. Towards the chronological beginning of this book, with the waning of the Roman Empire in the West, Vandals first, and Ostrogoths later, occupied the island and the city. The Germanic interlude did not last, as Byzantine attempts to reconquer the western parts of the empire brought a long Greek interlude. By the ninth century, Muslim raids from North Africa had led to the eventual capture of the island and city (see Chapter 3 and above). The Muslims prospered in Sicily, and Palermo and the island prospered with them as well. The Islamic interlude of more than a century came to an end with the coming of the Normans. Choosing Palermo as their capital, the Normans and their Hohenstaufen successors (German emperors) ruled the island and southern

Italy from Palermo until the French gained control of the island and the city (1266–1283). After the Sicilian Vespers, when the population of Palermo and of Sicily rose up in arms against the French, the Crown of Aragon gained possession of the island, though keeping it administratively apart from the other realms that constituted the federated realm of Aragon. Eventually, during Spanish rule (1479–1713), Sicily and Palermo came under the rule of the House of Savoy for a brief period, then that of Austria, and then that of Bourbon rulers of Naples. In 1860, the island, with Palermo as its capital and cultural center, became part of the unified kingdom of Italy (see Chapter 3).

This brief account of Palermo and Sicily's history points to the different historical layers that, like sedimentary strata in a deep canyon, accumulated over the centuries. But the idea of layering and sedimentary deposits gives a very wrong impression of what really took place. With the exception of the French, whose rule of the island was brief and who were few in number, one group was not replaced by another; rather, each new group blended with the existing population. In the same manner, cultural tropes, architectural styles, linguistic forms, and culinary practices became a robust mixture of different cultures, of different architectural nomenclatures, of different speech patterns and intonations, and of diverse culinary practices. Walking through the streets of Palermo today, one is struck by the difference between that city and other Italian northern cities, such as Milan, Turin, and Florence. It is not just that one is in the *mezzogiorno*, the South, where the climate and people are different, it is also the sense that Palermo is a true Mediterranean city and, thus, closer to Marseille, Tunis, or Barcelona in spirit and artistic form than to its northern Italian counterparts.

Not unlike those in Seville, Palermo's architectural complexes, which in this case also include the great cathedral at Monreale (a mere 15 kilometers outside Palermo proper), are the enduring example of the commingling of different people and cultural strains, proclaiming Palermo (and Sicily) as a true site of encounter and cultural production. It was, after all, at Palermo where, as mentioned before, al-Idrīsī made the famous map of the Mediterranean for his Norman king, Roger II. It was from Palermo that these same Norman kings ruled a multilingual and multi-religious island with administrative practices borrowed from the former Muslim rulers of Sicily and using Arabic, Latin, and Greek. It was at Palermo that they chose to be buried in tombs made of porphyry that imitated eastern Mediterranean practices. And above all, a series of buildings, most of them dating from that unique period of cross-fertilization, show the mélange of cultures, artistic forms, and aesthetic sensibilities that were representative of the Mediterranean's long history of cultural adaptation, conflict, and creation of the new.

Monreale

We should begin with the extraordinarily beautiful cathedral at Monreale. Dedicated to the Assumption of the Virgin and built under the sponsorship of William II in the 1170s, the last of the Norman kings before the Hohenstaufen (he and his father are buried at Monreale in impressive porphyry tombs), the cathedral at Monreale borrows from French (Norman), Byzantine (Greek), and Arabic architectural tropes to produce a building of unique beauty and one of the most impressive Christian churches in the western Mediterranean. The deployment of different architectural styles (Italian basilica, eastern churches, Gothic features, Arabic themes and colors), the extensive use of marble, the impressive mosaics covering most of the large dome of the cathedral, and the inscriptions in Latin and Greek reflect the hybrid nature of the building and of Sicilian civilization. Some of the exterior colors and carvings speak vividly of Arabic influences.

One would imagine that such a mélange of contrasting architectural styles would clash and yield very poor results. Nothing could be farther from the truth. The result of the mixing of all these decorative elements and architectural designs is not a mismatch of styles; rather, the uniqueness and impressive beauty of sacred space results from this overlapping of different cultural products into something new and very different from Norman (French), Byzantine, or Muslim buildings. It is a reminder of the possibilities provided by the Mediterranean's multicultural environment.

A few more examples from medieval Palermo are in order before we turn our attention to the modern city. The first example is the Palazzo dei Normanni (Palace of the Normans). Built on top of Punic, Carthaginian, and Roman ruins, as well as a ninth-century Muslim castle/fortress, the Palace of the Normans became the seat of government for the Norman kings of Sicily. It served as an administrative center for the Hohenstaufen rulers (though Amalfi and other towns in southern Italy drew them away from Palermo). It was there where Frederick II (1194–1250) gathered his unusual court. It included Jews, heretics, and Muslim scholars who often served as advisors. Capable of speaking several languages, including Arabic and Greek, Frederick II, not unlike other western Mediterranean rulers, kept a Muslim guard as his personal escort. Muslim rulers would do the same with Christian mercenaries in North Africa in the fourteenth century. The architectural themes of the palace, thus, parallel the personal policies of its Norman builders and Hohenstaufen successors. It is not a coincidence that Frederick II's ceremonial cape during his coronation was supposed to be of Muslim origin and to have inscriptions in Arabic. Nor is it a coincidence that his tomb, in spite of his being excommunicated four times by the Church, stands to this very day in Palermo Cathedral, a tomb that imitates the great porphyry tombs of his ancestors, the Norman kings of Sicily. In Frederick, the son of the German Holy Roman emperor Henry VI, Northern European elements of rulership came together with the rich multicultural civilization of Palermo, Sicily, and the western Mediterranean.

The royal palace also served as the seat of government for the rulers of Sicily who succeeded Manfred, Frederick II's illegitimate son. From the French Angevins' short interlude in control of the island, to the rulers of the Crown of Aragon, and to the present, the Palace of the Normans has remained the central focus for Sicilian and *mezzogiorno* politics, housing the Sicilian regional parliament today. But, even today, after renovations and rebuilding carried out in the sixteenth century, the palace retains sections that evoke its Muslim

Figure 10.3 Capella Palatina (Sanctuary), Palermo (Sicily), dating from the Norman period. Source: From www.theapricity.com.

past, while gardens and courtyards, built in the eastern Mediterranean Muslim style, tell us of the close connection between Norman Sicily and Muslim culture. Nowhere, however, is the overlapping of architectural styles more vivid in Palermo than in Roger II's splendid chapel, the Cappella Palatina, or Palatine Chapel.[16]

Words are insufficient to describe the chapel's unique beauty. Built initially under Roger II's patronage, the chapel weds, more so even than Monreale itself, Byzantine, Arabic, and Latin architectural and decorative elements. It is a stunning mix of three styles into a sacred space of inexpressible beauty. From the Byzantine-style mosaics that parallel those of the dome in Monreale, to the Muslim's intricate wooden ceiling with its decorative star design that actually forms a cross, the building is a graceful joining of different cultures. Any description would fall short of grasping the effect achieved by the blending of cultural references to Byzantine, Muslim, and Latin culture. Equally stunning are the inscriptions, mixing the three languages in celebration of Roger II's multilingual administration, and the tombs of Roger II himself and other Norman kings and members of the royal family.

Also in Palermo, and part of an extension of the palace complex, there was a hunting lodge or summer residence known as the Ziza that today serves as a museum for Islamic art. As with most of the other buildings in Palermo described above, a Muslim architect built the Ziza on behalf of the island's Norman kings. Unlike the other great structures in the city, the twelfth-century palace was originally designed strictly as a Muslim edifice. The original style was only altered two centuries afterwards with the addition of northern Christian elements. The architectural plans, the inscriptions in a form of Arabic on the entrance, and other details point to the manner in which, under Norman rule, the kings of Sicily and southern Italy sought to erect palaces and churches that captured the presence of Islam and of other civilizations on the island.

Finally, to complete this short tour of Palermo's buildings, one should note that the borrowing of architectural styles is also present in many of the city's medieval churches, None, however, is more blatant in imitating Arabic or Muslim models than the church of San Giovanni degli Eremiti, or Saint John of the Hermits. Built in the sixth century as a Christian church, it was converted into a mosque, in a process of appropriation of sacred spaces by one religion from another so common in the Mediterranean, during the Muslim interlude on the island. During Norman rule, the mosque was converted, once again, into a church. Conversion to a Christian temple did not mean, however, a complete erasure of Islamic elements. Gardens, wells, and domes in the eastern Muslim fashion (and now painted in red) make the building an archeological site in which different religious and architectural forms and design strata can be seen imprinted in the fabric of the church. Also of note as an example of the mixture of different influences is the Church of Saint Mary the Admiral (Santa Maria dell'Ammiraglio), also known as "La Martorana." The building, dating from the mid-twelfth century, serves the Albanian community in Palermo. The liturgy of the mass at La Martorana follows Byzantine liturgical form, and the church combines a series of different styles, reflecting Sicily's rich historical diversity.

PALERMO AND SICILY TODAY

So far, my emphasis has been on medieval Palermo as a unique period in which, under its successive Muslim, Norman, and Hohenstaufen rulers, the city and the island became sites of encounters. But Palermo also has other claims to diversity and to a global importance in our story beyond its richly textured medieval past. As we have seen (Chapter 3), from the early modern period onwards a combination of economic shifts and neglectful political rule led to the diminishing importance of the island within the history of the western

Mediterranean. Palermo as a city and Sicily as a region fell behind under the pressures created by the transformations that swept northern Italy in the late nineteenth and early twentieth century. Poverty and excess population haunted the city and the island. The slow pace of modernization was reflected in that sure barometer of change, language. The Sicilians, while required to learn Italian if they wished to prosper in the new Italian nation, chose to preserve their own dialect. They carried that Sicilian dialect to many other parts of the world.

In the late nineteenth century and early parts of the twentieth century, a rapid increase in population and oppressive land tenure practices led to substantial emigration from the island to the New World (the United States, Argentina, Brazil, and Venezuela). Italians in general and Sicilians in particular (most of them from rural environments) flocked to New York, Boston, and other urban centers throughout the United States. Although the large majority of these immigrants engaged in manufacturing work in their new countries, a good number of them migrated to California and tended vineyards and olive groves. In Brazil, they tended coffee plantations after the emancipation of slaves there in the late nineteenth century. These immigrants brought with them peculiar forms of speech, culinary practices, and Mediterranean codes of honor and shame. Although many came with the idea of a swift return home, few made that journey. Nonetheless, their links to the island and to Palermo remained strong and have played a significant role in popular culture to this day, as, for example, in the Godfather saga, both in Mario Puzo's novel(s) and in the films of Francis Ford Coppola.

Another wave of migration went to Argentina, a country that was, in the early twentieth century, in the midst of an economic boom. One of the great neighborhoods in Buenos Aires today, Palermo, has been named after the capital city of Sicily. Venezuela also received a substantial number of Italian immigrants. Once again, elements of Mediterranean culture traveled across the sea to new destinations, linking Sicily to the other parts of the world. By the mid-twentieth century, with the economic revival of Northern Europe after World War II, people from the *mezzogiorno* migrated to Switzerland, Germany, and elsewhere. There was also an important internal migration to the manu-facturing centers at Milan, Turin, and Bologna. This second wave of migration and the difficulties found by these immigrants (mostly from Naples and/or Sicily) in adapting to their new circumstances have inspired numerous books and films. By raising the social and economic issues that have affected the South in general, and Sicily in particular, through trenchant social critique or humorous depiction, these books and films – think of Lampedusa's *The Leopard* or Lina Wertmüller's many films set in Sicily – reflect the problems that beset Sicilian society in its slow and still ongoing transition to modernity.

And yet, there is a tragic fashion in which Sicily – and Palermo, its capital and financial center – remains a site of encounter. From the town of Erice in the southwest corner of Sicily one can see, on a clear day, the coast of Africa. In fall 1989, when I spent a week in Erice for a conference on Frederick II, I could sometimes see Africa vaguely in the distance. Trapani, the port just below Erice, is the major entry point for drugs (or was in the 1990s). Today, news reports and TV newsreels remind us that immigrants, mostly from North Africa and

Albania, risk their lives attempting to reach Sicily and thus achieve entry into the European community. The drowning of immigrants who dare face the cruel Mediterranean sea (see Chapter 12) and the atrocious conditions at the little island of Lampedusa or the refugee camp in Mineo, Sicily, where a video was shot of abuses against illegal immigrants that shocked Europe, are vivid reminders that sites of encounter and the commingling of cultures do not always yield beautiful cultural products such as those found at Monreale and the Cappella Palatina.[17]

TUNIS

From Sicily to Tunis is just a short sea voyage or an even shorter plane ride. The route between the two regions, Sicily and Italy on the hand, and Tunis and the Maghreb on the other, is as frequently traveled today as it was in Antiquity and in the Middle Ages. Jewish merchants, the so-called Maghribi traders, operating from the area of Tunis, traded with Christian Sicily in the eleventh and twelfth centuries. Part of a complex pattern of trade that extended from Fatimid Egypt and North Africa to Christian Europe, the abundant Geniza's Judeo-Arabic documentation attests to the extent of these contacts and trade.[18] For our purpose here, the point to be emphasized is that the city of Tunis, not unlike other western Mediterranean entrepôts, had long been a place where many different cultures met, made their own unique contributions, overlapped and fought each other, or influenced each other's developments. The final product is still a work in progress. Not unlike some of the locations I have described above (or will describe below), ancient, medieval, early modern, and contemporary – in the latter time period, the legacies of a colonized past – cultural artifacts co-exist architecturally and culturally in Tunis's pluralistic ethnic and linguistic history(ies).

Located on the western Mediterranean coast of North Africa and blessed with a large gulf and lake facing the city and a fairly good port, Tunis was one of the most important gateways to the Maghreb and the Sahara. Its port city of La Goulette (see below) provided a good launching point for trade, corsair activity, and military forays into the western Mediterranean. Its strategic location on the coast allowed Tunis's sailors easy access to Sicily, as noted earlier, but also to Sardinia and Malta. The latter island, though not discussed in this book, was an important gateway to the eastern Mediterranean. Sailing westward along the coast led to other important Maghreb and North African ports, Algiers above all. Sailing eastward along the African coast, Tripoli and Alexandria were easily accessible. Tunis also had good connections to the interior and to the outskirts of the great desert and the profitable trade with sub-Saharan Africa. It is not surprising that fierce renegade corsairs the Barbarossa brothers used Tunis as their main base in their naval raids and campaigns on behalf of the Sublime Porte in the western Mediterranean (see Chapter 5).

Although most probably an early Berber settlement, Tunis's history is nonetheless deeply bound with that of later settlers, the founders of Carthage. The ruins of the great Punic city are part of the suburbs of Tunis today. It was from that strategic location on the coast of North Africa that the Carthaginians built a great maritime empire, and settled in Sicily and other Mediterranean islands and lands (Spain above all). There is not much that we actually know about the history of Carthage or the early history of Tunis, except from the accounts of their conquerors, the Romans. Literature, however, provides an approximation to Carthaginian life. Gustave Flaubert, the great nineteenth-century French novelist, wrote a richly textured and seductive historical novel, *Salammbô* (based on Polybius's account of the war). It captures, though in an orientalized fashion, aspects of the city's history after the First Punic War (264–241 BCE). Flaubert's remark, as quoted by Walter Benjamin, that "few will be able to guess how sad one had to be in order to resuscitate Carthage," contains immense wisdom. It is very hard for present historians to approximate what that history was. One should point out that there is, of course, a little town named Salambo, 14 kilometers from Tunis, which points to the historical continuity of names and ideas.

Tunis, together with Carthage, was destroyed and then rebuilt by the Romans. The city became an important part of the Roman Mediterranean world and a center for the export of grain and fish sauce to the Roman port of Ostia, which catered to the insatiable needs of Rome's population. Over the centuries of Roman control, Tunis, playing a supporting role to Carthage, became also a Christian city. The ruins of Carthage present in Tunis's urban sprawl contain a large number of impressive Roman monuments, lending to the importance of the city (and thus of Tunis) as a tourist destination today with its many surviving examples of the Romans' presence in North Africa. These Roman ruins are just one layer of the sedimentation of different civilizations over the long history of the city. In Late Antiquity, it was to Carthage that Saint Augustine traveled to further his education. He sailed to Rome from there to find Christianity in Milan under Saint Ambrose's guidance. Nonetheless, it was the Arab invasion in the first half of the seventh century that shaped Tunis's history from then onwards. Although Tunis maintained regular trade relations (as well as being involved in military conflicts) with Christian Europe, the region as a whole became indelibly linked to the expansive world of Islam.

Successive Berber dynasties rose and fell in what we know today as Tunisia or medieval Ifriqiya. Sunni–Shi'a conflicts also swept the land. Under the Almohads and Fatimids, the city of Tunis, no longer in the shadows of Carthage, rose to become one of the most important cities in the western Mediterranean. Its medina, dating to the seventh century, bustled with activities and products from almost every corner of the known world. Throughout the Middle Ages, Almohads, Normans, and Fatimids struggled for control of the city, its rich hinterland, and far-ranging commercial networks. Significantly, each one of these political powers represented those geographical areas (Almohads, the region of Morocco; the Normans, Sicily; and the Fatimids, Egypt) with which Tunis also had important economic ties. Tunis also had other significant connections to the northern shores of the Mediterranean that were not necessarily economic. Saint Louis laid siege to the city in July 1270, while on his hopeless attempt to reach Jerusalem overland from North Africa. He died there in August 1270. However, when the Christians lifted their siege and returned to France, the peace treaty assured Christian merchants access to Tunis's markets and to members of religious orders to care for the souls of Christians and to serve as go-betweens for the ransoming of Christian prisoners and slaves. As we have seen earlier, Anselm of Turmeda came to Tunis in the fourteenth century. There he converted to Islam, married a rich Muslim woman, and rose to an important position in the Tunisian court.

By the sixteenth century, Tunis became, except for a brief Spanish interlude after Lepanto, one of the important Ottoman outposts in the western Mediterranean and the main naval base for maritime campaigns and trade in the western parts of the Middle Sea. By the late nineteenth century, the French had established a protectorate over the city and reshaped Tunis along European architectural lines. Italian workers also flocked to the city and the region, establishing an important presence there. After occupation by German troops during World War II and restoration of the French colonial administration, the city and the country gained their independence in 1956 as part of the great wave of decolonization that swept Africa and Asia in that decade.[19]

This brief history of Tunis describes the city's complex levels of historical development, but, as it was the case with Seville and Palermo, my interest here is either in buildings that incorporate different cultural tropes or in the city's diverse demography and urban landscape. Urban spaces in which different elements co-existed (and co-exist), creating something different and new. Even given the few Carthaginian and Roman ruins, sites mostly for the benefit of archeologists and historians or for avid cruise tourists, Tunis's life and dominant architectural elements begin with the medina. A warren of alleyways, small streets, and densely built urban spaces, Tunis's medina is today a UNESCO World Heritage site. The medina, located a few kilometers inland from the lake of Tunis and the shores of the Mediterranean, dates from the early centuries of Muslim conquest. Under the Almohads and Hafsids, the city became one of the leading urban centers in the Islamic world. Its markets teemed with life and with products from the entire known world. Many historical monuments are preserved between the boundaries of the medina, or souk. These buildings reflect architectural choices that are replicated in Muslim cities from Iberia to India. Many mosques dot the medina, including the main mosque of the city. Most notable are the Kasbah and Zitouna mosques. The minaret of the latter mosque reminds one of the Giralda in Seville, both buildings sponsored by Almohad rulers. In a reminder of the transmission of traditions and architectural vocabulary across the Mediterranean and sectarian divides, these two minarets are replicated by a third and modern one, presently found at the Great Mosque of Paris in the 5th arrondissement, facing the Jardin des Plantes.

The medina today is encircled, bound as it were, by wide boulevards. On the one side is the boulevard du 9 avril 1938. The Place du Gouvernement also divides a corner of the medina from the rest of Tunis and rue du 2 mars 1934 before the new street nears the great Kasbah mosque and melts away into the narrow streets of the medina. A series of wider streets on the other boundary of the medina, the rue Bab Souika, rue des Glacières, and the imposing avenue de France, mark the transition to the new town of colonial

French provenance. Within the boundaries of the medina numerous substantial residences, religious schools, and the like mark the importance of the medina up to the modern era.

Unlike other Mediterranean cities in which significant portions of the ancient foundations were destroyed by natural causes or razed to give way to more modern buildings, Tunis, as was the case with Barcelona, built an entirely new city next to the old one. Traveling east from the medina, the new city, built from the beginnings of the French protectorate onwards, is a perfect example of French colonial architecture. The names of the streets – avenue de France, Charles de Gaulle, and others – still echo the colonial past. Of the wide boulevards, most notable is the boulevard of Habib Bourguiba (named for the well-known former Tunisian leader and built in imitation of the Champs-Élysées in Paris), close to the great Catholic cathedral dedicated to Saint Vincent de Paul, a French saint. The boulevard of Habib Bourguiba leads to the port of La Goulette and the sea. There is not the juxtaposition of conflicting historical styles seen in Seville and Palermo. In Tunis, each historical style keeps to its own well-defined space and architectural tradition: the encounter is not one of juxtaposition but of parallel existences. At one end of the city, Punic and Roman ruins are now overrun by new constructions. At the other, a typical medieval Arabic-Muslim city, harking back to the very early period of the Islamic conquest, co-exists with modernity. But Tunis is also yet another city: the colonial French city, borrowing its architectural vocabulary from the European Middle Ages – the Cathedral of Saint Vincent de Paul built in the Gothic style – and from French modernity.

As a site of encounter, Tunisia had also a long Jewish presence, most of all on the island of Djerba, linked to Tunis by sea lanes. Lavish synagogues, such as the Great Synagogue of Tunis, also appeared in the old city. Jewish merchants operated from Tunis and Djerba as part of the great trade networks that linked Egypt, Africa, and Europe. Jewish merchants from Majorca, though they mostly sailed with their goods to western North African ports, also had a presence there. This Jewish presence, dating from Roman times, remained a fixture of Tunisian life until the second half of the twentieth century. Following the flow between cultures so peculiar to the Mediterranean, Jewish synagogues in the Middle Ages borrowed architectural features from Muslim mosques. The language of trade and quotidian affairs was the Judeo-Arabic found, in written form, in the Geniza documents. After the expulsion of the Jews from Spain in 1492, some fled to North Africa, taking with them their own Judeo-Spanish languages. Moriscos, when expelled from Spain in the early seventeenth century, also flocked to North Africa, taking with them elements of Spanish culture and their own Arabic-Spanish writings and language (*aljamiado*).

Christians also came to Tunis. They did so as merchants to profit from the trade opportunities. They came as mercenary soldiers for the Hafsids rulers of Tunis. In their service contracts, as was the case in the peace agreements with the French crusaders in 1270, these Christian mercenaries in fourteenth-century Maghreb demanded places of worship and religious advisers so they could practice Christianity as they fought rival Muslims while in the service of their Tunis masters. Christian monks flocked to the slave markets of Tunis to ransom Christian captives or to exchange Muslim slaves for Christian ones. Italian immigrants and settlers also came in abundance to Tunis. From the Middle Ages onwards, the Genoese had a significant trading outposts on the island of Tabarka (see Chapter 11), near the Tunisian coast. By the middle of the nineteenth century, Italians had migrated to Tunis in large numbers, establishing a strong Italian enclave in the city, most of all at La Goulette, the main port of Tunis. After 1881, when the French established a protectorate over what is Tunisia today, the Italians came to be seen as a threat to French interests. Nonetheless, the Italians, immigrants from the Ligurian coast and the South, added one more ethnic and linguistic component to the complexities of Tunisian life. The connections between Tunis and Italy are evident even to this very day, as attested by the frequent ferries that link Tunis to Genoa, Palermo, Salerno, and Trapani. The latter port, Trapani, on the southwest corner of Sicily and closest to Africa of any of the Sicilian ports, is, as already noted, a well-known entry point for drug smuggling and illegal migration from Africa into Europe.[20]

DJERBA AND LA GOULETTE

We should not leave Tunis and Tunisia without a brief glossing of two locations already mentioned in our discussion of Tunis, and closely linked to the city. The first one is the island of Djerba, the largest island off the western Mediterranean's North African coast. Although not adjacent to Tunis, the island is very close to the Tunisian continental landmass. Djerba is a microcosm of all the different trends we have been describing in the previous chapters and will address in succeeding pages. As was the case with other Mediterranean sites, Djerba had a complicated and multi-layered history. Inhabited since Early Antiquity, a producer of dyes for textile manufacturing throughout that period, the island was part of the sprawling Mediterranean Roman Empire. With the demise of Roman power in the West, Djerba experienced a Byzantine interlude before being conquered by a Berber Muslim sect, the Kharijites (Ibadite). Berber is, in fact, still spoken on the island.

Because of the island's strategic location, Djerba became a highly contested territory. The Normans from Sicily and their successors, the Crown of Aragon, gained a foothold in Djerba in the twelfth, thirteenth, and fourteenth centuries. By the early sixteenth century, the Ottoman corsairs, including one of the famous Barbarossa brothers, gained control of the island for the Sublime Porte. Genoese (as a proxy for the Spanish monarchy) and Spanish fleets also briefly occupied the island until an Ottoman fleet regained it in 1560. The island remained in Ottoman hands until 1881 when the French established their protectorate over all of Tunisia.

The presence of different groups in strategically important and contested territories is, of course, one of the features of the Mediterranean. What makes Djerba worthy of notice is the co-existing of three religious groups in a small and densely populated island. Many small mosques survive from the early days of

Berber conquest. As previously noted, the Jewish population of Djerba was substantial from the beginning of the Common Era until 1967. The El Ghriba synagogue is one of the oldest in the western Mediterranean, with a history of close to 2,000 years. Jews, mostly engaged in trade but also active in a variety of other economic activities, were an important part of Djerba's society until they migrated to France and Israel, following the Arab–Israeli war of 1967. The synagogue, the target of attacks by Muslim fundamentalists in 1985 and a major bombing by Al-Qaeda in 2002, has undergone many different alterations over its two-millennia history, but the style of the main building and splendid courtyard is Moorish, or what in Spain would have been called the Mudejar style, serving as another example of the manner in which one group borrowed an architectural style from another. Christian churches were also erected in Djerba, to serve the religious needs of numerous Maltese Catholic fishermen who settled in the city.

Djerba's history is somewhat paralleled by that of La Goulette (La Goletta in Italian), the name given to the port of Tunis by the many Italian immigrants to the region. It has, of course, an Arabic name, Halq al-Wadi. La Goulette is today a stop for cruise ships visiting Tunis and North Africa (which they do less and less as tensions rise throughout the world). It combines the modern facilities of a major cruise stop with architectural elements that reflect the port's ancient and conflicted history. Whitewashed buildings (with blue motifs), typical of the Mediterranean, alternate with imposing and ancient brick and stonewall fortresses. Charles V built a large castle, the Kasbah, during Spain's short interlude in control of the island. Similar to Djerba, La Goulette was a contested entry point into North Africa until the Ottoman conquest in the sixteenth century. What is significant in terms of the themes explored in this particular chapter is the juxtaposition of styles, fragments of the past, remembrances of different periods, and architectural styles that to this very day adorn the streets of La Goulette and other towns and cities on the shores of the Mediterranean.

ALGIERS

Writing in the late sixteenth century (but not published until 1612), Diego de Haedo, a Franciscan friar, wrote the *Topografía e historia general de Argel*, one of the most comprehensive descriptions of early modern Algiers. The work is important for several reasons. First, it provides a comprehensive description of the city's topography and history from the perception of a religious man who saw the presence of Islam in the region as a threat far more dangerous than that of the Protestants in central Europe, bemoaning Philip II's attention to central Europe and his disregard for North Africa. Second, it emphasizes the tribulations and, often, martyrdom of Christians in Algiers, revealing to us a whole world of captives, rescues, renegades, and conflicts. Third, the book plays a significant role in telling the story of Cervantes's captivity (though Cervantes had made sure to document his years as a prisoner in the *banhos* of Algiers). As such, the book, written and published before Cervantes's death, is a testimony to the importance of the great writer's captivity in the overall architecture of his work. If I begin with this allusion to de Haedo, it is because it also shows the manner in which, not unlike today, Christian Europe is deeply imbricated with the history of Mediterranean North Africa.[21]

In many respects, what we have described for Tunis also applies, to a large extent, to Algiers, a city known also as Alger la Blanche ("Algiers the White") for its whitewashed buildings so typical of the Mediterranean – from Greece to North Africa to Andalusia. The city's history also harks back to its diverse Phoenician, Roman, and Christian pasts, as embodied by its monuments. After the Islamic conquest of the region, Algiers came to be under the rule of a Berber dynasty and, by the twelfth century, part of the sprawling Almohad Empire. Frequent European (mostly Spanish) attempts to gain a foothold in the city and the region, the most prolonged of which was a Spanish military presence on a little island (El Peñón) by the entrance of Algiers port, lasted until the Ottomans established their rule in the city, one of the strongholds of the Barbarossa corsair proxy state.

The city, similar to Tunis, consists of different layers that reflect historical periods, religious affiliations, and a colonial presence. The Cabash (Kabash), or old city, is located on a hill, slopping to the Mediterranean. A new French colonial city fills the space between the ancient Almohad and Ottoman city and the sea. In many respects, the topographical organization reminds the viewer of Málaga, with its Moorish *alcázar* on the hill, dominating the new city. The Ketchaoua mosque, close to the foot of the Casbah, was originally a mosque, turned into a Catholic church (conforming to a very Mediterranean pattern of appropriating one's rival's sacred spaces), and then turned back into a mosque again as recently as 1962. The building could be transported to Palermo and fit into the architectural complexes there without missing a beat. The Catholic basilica of Notre Dame d'Afrique's bell tower would make for a perfect minaret in a mosque.

Algiers was far more than a contested space, refuge for Moriscos fleeing Spain, center for corsair activities, or city with a large number of renegades and slaves. Algiers was also, as we have already seen, the epicenter for resistance to France during the Algerian War of Independence in the 1960s. The violence and excesses of the contending factions marked one of the crucial turning points in the decolonization of North Africa, captured impressively in Gillo Pontecorvo's dramatic rendition of urban guerrilla warfare, the iconic film *The Battle of Algiers*.

NORTH AFRICA AND IBERIA AS PARTS OF DAR AL-ISLAM

Those buildings, described above, that integrate different architectural styles, reflecting the commingling of different cultures and religions (mostly in the Middle Ages), were not restricted to those locations discussed in the previous pages. On the shores of the western Mediterranean, in North Africa, Iberia, and Sicily, examples of these hybrid architectural styles or of contrasting urban landscapes are the norm to this very day. This is obvious in mosques, synagogues, and churches in Toledo, Valencia, Barcelona, Málaga, and elsewhere in the Iberian Mediterranean, as well as even in interior continental cities. This is also the case in other Sicilian locations beyond Palermo, or in North African coastal and interior cities, where the medinas, as is the case in Fez and Marrakesh for example, stand in sharp contrast to the modern French colonial buildings, the Gothic cathedrals erected by Christian conquerors, and the ritual places built by pockets of Jews and Muslim exiles from Spain. The locations examined above, as representative of sites of encounter and cultural production and, above all, in terms of their built space, all had something in common.

These were locations were, regardless of whether Islam or Christianity were hegemonic, three religious groups shared a common space, borrowed from each other, and imitated each other's architectural styles. Nowhere, to give an example beyond the ones already discussed, is this more obvious than in the synagogue of El Tránsito in Toledo (a city that may not qualify as a Mediterranean location, but bound to the Mediterranean world by the trade networks of Dar al-Islam before 1085 and to Castile's control of most of the western Mediterranean shores after the mid-thirteenth century). The synagogue of El Tránsito was built in the fourteenth century at a time when Islam was being effectively pushed out of the peninsula or neutralized. It was also built at a time when Jewish life in Iberia had come under serious attacks and restrictions. Nonetheless, the building, constructed under the sponsorship of one of the Jews in the royal service, Samuel ha-Levi, closely resembles a Muslim edifice. After the Jews were either forcibly converted or exiled from Castile in 1492, the synagogue became a Christian church with few additions to its original fabric, except for a bell tower with Romanesque windows. The Christian additions contrasted with the horseshoe-shaped windows of the early Moorish architecture of the original building. Here is yet another dramatic example of the blending of cultural tropes in a building of rare beauty.

But what conditions would be found in a western Mediterranean town where no communities of either Muslims or Jews existed in large numbers or at all in an earlier period? Or, far more significant, what about cities on the European western Mediterranean where Muslims never held power, or where Jews did not play the signal economic role they did elsewhere in Sicily, Spain, or Djerba? Were such places also sites of encounter? Below, in Chapter 11, I explore the nature of small towns and islands that did not function necessarily as sites of encounter. They were, of course, important contributors to Mediterranean daily life and its history without buildings and monuments exhibiting the juxtaposition of different artistic elements. Here, however, I wish to examine very briefly one example of a city where modern encounters between Muslims and Christians (and Jews) generated (and generates) a different kind of co-existence, without the concomitant history of political rule by one group over the other. It is important to assess, therefore, what kind of new cultural products these encounters produced and continue to produce.

MARSEILLE

Marseille is one of the quintessential western Mediterranean cities. As a recent writer, Jean-Claude Izzo, argues, it is a city of garlic, mint, and sweet basil where the possibilities for happiness and also for a Mediterranean noir are endless. Marseille's strategic location as a gateway to Provence and its rich agricultural and cultural life, the superb layout of its port for medieval and early modern sailing and of its superb new cruise ship terminal, its bold and attractive topography, with its high promontory where the gaudy basilica of Notre Dame de la Garde sits, all of these things and more make the city special. For those of us who have grown up with unhealthy doses of nineteenth-century Romantic novels, Marseille is also the site for *The Count of Monte Cristo*. For me, going to Marseille meant seeing the Château d'If, sailing around the castle and seeing it from the striking perspective of Notre Dame de la Garde (Figure 10.4). It meant walking on the Plage des Catalans, the residence of those Catalan descendants from an earlier migration to Marseille and the home of the fictional Mercedes. But Marseille was, and is, a great deal more that my own or others' romantic musings. It was a busy slave-trading center in the Middle Ages and at the beginning of the early modern period. Its proximity to Africa, to which it is connected by sea and air, makes the city the main entry point for North African migration into France. Though the city has been aggressively gentrified and has lost most of its famous (and attractive, I should add) edge, Marseille remains one of the most intriguing locales on the western Mediterranean, a place of the mind, of imagination, and of gustatory and olfactory pleasures.

As one of the most important settlements in the western Middle Sea, Marseille harks back to the Paleolithic period. It became an important Greek

Figure 10.4 View of the port of Marseille with the Château d'If. Source: Courtesy of Scarlett Freund.

colony in the seventh century BCE and a significant trading center for Greek connections with the western sea. Through fluvial networks – the same river links described by Braudel in his *The Mediterranean* – Marseille's trade reached into the heart of France, as well as connecting the eastern Mediterranean to the area of the Straits of Gibraltar or Alboran Sea and the Atlantic. By the third century BCE, Marseille entered the orbit of Roman power, profiting as a middleman in Rome's trade with Gaul, but by the eve of the Christian era, Marseille lost its independence and became part of the expansive world of Rome. As such, the city still enjoyed great prosperity, as its Greek and Roman ruins still reflect.

With the waning of Roman power in the West, the city and its hinterland experienced brief periods of Visigothic rule, followed in the sixth century by the presence of early Frankish rulers and eventually the Carolingians' expansive empire. For the northern Frankish realm(s), Marseille and, to a lesser extent Barcelona, represented important outlets to the Mediterranean. During the Middle Ages, the city experienced tumultuous political change, as the Count of Provence, the House of Anjou, and others vied for control of the region. The Black Death that swept Europe in general and most of the western Mediterranean in particular also had a devastating impact on the demographic resources of the city. In 1482, the city became part of the French realm and, although not a peaceful union, it would prove to be one of the most strategically important locations for the French monarchy's ambitious plans for expansion in Italy and North Africa. During the early years of the French Revolution, Marseille's militias marched to Paris to join the revolutionary armies fighting invaders on the northern borders of the nation. Their rousing marching and battle song, *La Marseillaise,* inspired the revolutionary armies to victory at Valmy and elsewhere. The vagaries and connectivity of history never cease to amaze me. On July 14, 2013, I, along with a large group of Californian students, sang *la Marseillaise* at a celebration of the overthrow of the Bastille at a great party at the Champs de Mars in Paris. That the theme of the celebration was the iconic proclamation of the French Revolution, *liberté, egalité, fraternité,* and that Martin Luther King's speech, *I Have a Dream,* was prominently cited, only points to the manner in which Mediterranean ideas and, in this case, cultural products have a global reach.

But the Marseille of the revolutionary anthem in the late eighteenth century is very different from the Marseille that followed in succeeding decades and, particularly so, from the twentieth- and twenty-first-century city. The second-largest city in France, Marseille today is a multi-ethnic, multi-religious, and multilingual city. A great deal of this diversity has led to friction, but also to creativity and blends of cultures that parallel, though as part of the actual life of the city, that juxtaposition of architectural forms we saw in the buildings and urban landscapes of the locations examined above. With a population of around 850,000 inhabitants, more than 20% of the inhabitants of the city come from somewhere outside France. The bulk of these immigrants to the city are now Berbers and Arabs from the Maghreb. A substantial number of other immigrants have come from Corsica, Italy, Spain, and elsewhere, as they have flocked into Marseille in search of work or as a point of entry into the European community. The number of Muslims has been calculated at over 150,000, though some sources give numbers as high as 250,000. Mosques can be found throughout the city, reflecting the growing presence of Islam both in the city and in France generally. In 2010, permission was granted to build one of the largest mosques in Europe, the Great Mosque of Marseille (probably to be completed by the middle of this decade, see below), which encompasses a large religious complex and a very prominent minaret that would compete with some of the high spires of Catholic churches throughout the city.

Marseille is also the home to around 80,000 Jews, making it the third-largest Jewish urban community in Europe. Neither Muslims nor, to a certain extent, Jews, however, played a significant role in the earlier history of Marseille. Muslims were rare until the beginnings of French colonial ventures in North Africa. Jews had always played a role in Marseille's life, even though their community was numerically low. As merchants, Jews in Marseille negotiated their place in society with municipal authorities, maintaining a certain amount of autonomy. The city was a center of Jewish learning in the Middle Ages, and a place of refuge for Jews fleeing Spain, until the French edict of expulsion in the very early sixteenth century. Nonetheless, Jews filtered slowly back into the city, and the pace of Jewish migration accelerated after Algerian independence since most Jews in northern Algeria had been granted French citizenship in the late nineteenth century.

In twenty-first-century Marseille, large communities of Muslims and Jews commingle with their Christian counterparts. Such diversity of population and religious affiliation is often associated with encounters and cultural hybridity, but such qualities are not exclusive to the Mediterranean. London, Paris, Los Angeles, and New York, for example, are places where the boundaries between different groups are often porous and exchanges, commercial, cultural, and otherwise, take place. In Marseille, these encounters are palpable in the creative imaginary, in the markets of the city, and in its buildings.

MARSEILLE'S IMAGINARY

Dumas's *The Count of Monte Cristo* has been a continuous presence throughout the pages of this book. What may be more fitting than to begin this more focused discussion of Marseille with it? In the novel, the opening paragraph already provides us with a vivid account of the city's topography and urban landscape. The three-masted ship, the *Pharaon*, has been sighted from the lookout at Notre Dame de la Garde. In 1815, the fictional beginning of the novel, the church that stood on the present site of the imposing neo-Byzantine basilica (consecrated in 1864) dated back to the thirteenth century, with ample renovations in the fifteenth and sixteenth centuries. Notre Dame de la Garde rose on the highest point in the Marseille area. From this site, there are magnificent views of the Old Port, the city, the Château d'If, and the expansive Mediterranean. Why, one would perhaps ask, was the new church built in a neo-Byzantine style with clashing Romanesque elements? It had to do, I think, with the peculiar taste of late nineteenth-century France. Not unlike the Sacré Coeur in Paris, it was

Figure 10.5 Streets in Marseille's old neighborhood near the port. Source: Courtesy of Scarlett Freund.

erected in a high place with privileged views to compensate, I fear, for its tasteless artistic values.

The *Pharaon*, the name redolent with connections to Egypt, arrived from Smyrna, Trieste, and Naples after, as we know, an unexpected stop on the island of Elba. It was reflective of the city's trade connections with the eastern Mediterranean and the Ottoman lands. We follow the ship, which was guided by a pilot who had met the vessel at the Château d'If and sailed through the narrow entrance into Marseille's well-protected harbor to safe mooring at the city's busy port.

Health authorities and customs officials, as would be the case decades later in Barcelona and other western Mediterranean ports, boarded the ship to carry out the necessary inspections. Dantès, eager to see his aging father and his beloved Mercedes, walked from the port to the broad boulevard of La Canebière, as charming a street today as it may have been in the early nineteenth century. From there, he made his way to rue de Noailles and to his father's house. Noailles is one of the most popular and diverse neighborhoods of present-day Marseille. The site of a daily popular market often described as "the stomach of Marseille (*le ventre de Marseille*)," the neighborhood is home to a large population of North and sub-Saharan African residents. It pulsates with Berber and Arabic, and with the culinary aromas of Maghrebi and African cuisine. Although developed at the same time as La Canebière, in the second half of the seventeenth century, and equally as aristocratic, the street and the neighborhood witnessed a change of fortune by the end of the eighteenth century and had become, by the time Dumas described it in the early nineteenth century, a popular and impoverished neighborhood. It remains so, though with greater ethnic and religious diversity, to this very day.

From Noailles, and after fulfilling his filial duties, Dantès quickly made his way to Les Catalans. The name dates back to the seventeenth century, when a group of Catalan fishermen fled Catalonia (probably escaping the disturbances around the revolt of the Catalans in 1640 and the turbulence of civil war, Catalonia's secession from Spain, and its brief interlude as part of France) for Marseille and established a small colony by the sea and east of the Old Port. Although today few would consider walking from La Canebière or the Old Port to the beach at Les Catalans, for Dantès, propelled by his love for Mercedes, the distance was only a short one. Les Catalans' buildings were described as a combination of Moorish and Spanish styles. And we know that, besides fishing, the inhabitants of Les Catalans were actively involved in smuggling, their coastal location outside the Old Port allowing for the possibility of skipping customs officials. Of all of Marseille's features none, however, plays such a significant role in Dumas's novel as the Château d'If. Located on a very small island, barely a mile from Marseille – which is why Edmund Dantès could think of swimming to shore after his escape – the castle and prison dated from the sixteenth century, serving as a perfectly located protection to the entrance to the Old Port, and now a favorite tourist destination. But it is not only the Romantic imagination that provides us with an entry to Marseille's changes and diversity of population.

A *New York Times* article in 2009 called attention to the French soap opera *Plus Belle la Vie*, commenting that it was watched regularly by one-fifth of the French population. That was eight years ago. Now, after more than a decade of extraordinary success and popularity in France and abroad (it is shown in TV5Monde French international TV broadcasts and followed avidly by Francophone people throughout the world), *Plus Belle la Vie* is an excellent example of Marseille as a site of encounter, cultural experimentation, and diversity. With Le Mistral neighborhood in Marseille as the location for the recurring daily events (a fictional neighborhood but somewhat identified with the 2nd and 3rd arrondissement of Marseille, an area west of the Old Port adjacent to the Mediterranean Sea), the soap opera's endless twists and dramas bring, as the *New York Times* describes it, a multicultural, multi-ethnic, multi-religious, and political set of characters to reflect Marseille's own population.

> There is the Marci family, which owns the Bar du Mistral; the Nassri family from Algeria; the Torres family from Spain; the Lesermans, whose matriarch survived the Holocaust and is a Communist; the wealthy Frémonts with their shady business dealings and lesbian daughter; the Chaumette family, transplanted from Paris; the Estèves, with their son, who divorced, has a daughter and loves a man; and the Castellis, who, as the show's Web site says, are "living to forget the past."

The interrelationships between these families – their disputes, love affairs, business dealings, and tragedies – both transfix the French and educate them, at

Figure 10.6 The setting for *Plus Belle la Vie*, France's longest-running soap opera, in Marseille's old neighborhood. Source: Courtesy of Scarlett Freund.

least a little, about cultural differences, as well as about social issues such as the presence of Islam in Marseille, racism, drugs, homosexuality, teenage pregnancies, and other problems, present even among the members of the police force.[22]

The cast of the series reflects Marseille's diversity, conflicts, and overlapping cultures, both as they exist today and as they were in the past. Sharing a space, the mythical Mistral neighborhood (the name of both a cold wind from the North that creates havoc for navigation and of the great Provençal writer), all the different ethnic groups present in the city, all the different gender preferences, and the well-known (but now very much reduced) criminal activities are represented as art. One may argue that it is a low form of art, but it is one that informs French people of the possibilities to forge a city and a nation from difference. This is most remarkable when one thinks of the rising attraction of anti-immigration parties in France (and in Europe as a whole), exemplified by Marine Le Pen's electoral success (until she was, fortunately, defeated in the French presidential election runoff on May 7, 2017) and by her strident anti-immigration rhetoric.

MARKETS

Marseille has other sites of encounter besides the fictional *Plus Belle la Vie*. The city abounds with markets: from the fish markets around the port to specialty markets for Christmas and Christmas decorations. None of these markets approaches the already mentioned daily market of Noailles (*Le Marché de*

Noailles). The stores and stalls there owned mostly by people from the Maghreb, the market at Noailles (near where Edmund Dantès's father supposedly lived), transports you, as do markets in Paris in the neighborhood around Barbès Rochechouart, to another place that is and is not France. The market at Noailles is a testimony to the long-term impact of immigration. Tourists today flock to the market at Noailles to experience the colorful display of products from every corner of the world, the mélange of races, the variety of speech sounds, and the quaint stores. They come to vicariously experience some of the dangers of Marseille, for which the city was duly famous or infamous. They often fail to see what the market tells us – very much what the soap opera tells us – about the commingling of cultures, of religious groups, of social distance, and how in Marseille, at least some of the time, this commingling yields something new. In 2005, when race riots erupted throughout most of France, especially in Paris, Marseille and the Noailles neighborhood remained calm.

BUILDINGS

As noted earlier, Marseille was never under Muslim rule, nor did it have a substantial Jewish population in an earlier period. Buildings that borrow from architectural forms belonging to these cultures and that have acquired the patina of time are not to be found in the city. Unlike Paris, which aims for architectural harmony and enjoys architectural continuity, Marseille combines the old and the new, and everything in between, with admirable panache. Greek and Roman ruins, most of them collected in a wonderful museum of antiquities (on the edge of the neighborhood for which the Mistral neighborhood may stand), share space with some magnificent ancient buildings and Romanesque churches. Although often rebuilt and reshaped, the Abbey of Saint Victor dates from the fifth century and provides an architectural continuity to Marseille's buildings. The church of Saint Laurent in the popular 2nd arrondissement neighborhood remains pretty faithful to its original Romanesque plan. Other churches, such as the previously mentioned Notre Dame de la Garde, or the Cathedral of Sainte Marie Majeure, the city's main Catholic church, were entirely rebuilt in the nineteenth century, though remnants of the old Romanesque cathedral still stand. Both adopted a Byzantine-Romanesque style with striped lines that had more connections with Italy than with the northern French Gothic.

The city's prosperity is evident in its many fine baroque buildings and nineteenth-century structures. Above all, Marseille has some impressive Le Corbusier and other modern buildings. Whether apartment complexes or museums, they reflect the eclectic nature of Marseille's built space. More than an example of overlapping of styles, these diverse architectural choices reveal to us Marseille's adaptability to changing tastes and the city's willingness to experiment. In that sense, Marseille is not unlike other cities in the Mediterranean. Barcelona is another example. There, a new modern city, l'Eixample, was built adjacent to the old one (the Barrio Gótico and the Born). It is in Marseille's mosques and synagogues, however, that we see the mixture of

Figure 10.7 View of Notre Dame de la Garde from Marseille's port. Source: Courtesy of Scarlett Freund.

different architectural vocabularies that reflect the flow between cultures. These religious structures had been sites of conflict as well. Not unlike the synagogue at Djerba, Jewish temples have seen terrorist attacks during waves of violence and anti-Semitism that swept France in the late twentieth century. That was the case with the Or Aviv Synagogue, reduced to ashes in a terrorist attack. The building of the Great Mosque met with endless opposition from the National Front and other anti-immigrant and Islamophobic groups.

The main synagogue of Marseille, la grande synagogue, was built in the second half of the nineteenth century in the city's 6th arrondissement. Though heavily protected and walled, except for the absence of a cross on top of the building, it strongly resembles a small pre-Renaissance Italian church. In fact, it reminds me very strongly of Florence's Santo Spirito. The synagogue was built in that Romanesque-Byzantine style that seems to have been Marseille's architectural folly in the nineteenth century. As such, the synagogue, built around the same period as the Cathedral of Sainte Marie Majeure and Notre Dame de la Garde, followed the lead of those two Catholic structures. Unlike places, such as the Jerusalem Synagogue in Prague, that borrowed an exaggerated architectural vocabulary that referred back to Sephardic/Spanish roots, the outside and interior of the nineteenth-century main synagogue in Marseille followed patterns common to other religious buildings in the city.

The plans for the mega-mosque to be built in the city, on the other hand, have suffered from years of fierce opposition (as already noted). A first stone was dedicated in 2010. Then there was a judicial reversal of the permits for the mosque's construction in 2011. This was soon followed by a court of appeals' approval of the building permits. At the publication of this book, the building has not yet even been started. The original plans and model of the new mosque follow an architectural design that joins streamlined Islamic themes, corresponding to a Muslim place of worship and redolent with Arabian references – main entrance, a very tall minaret, and arches – with modern touches that remind one of some of Le Corbusier's buildings in the city. In the absence of a real building, for the issue is still hotly contested, other mosques in the city, six of them at last count, all date from the twentieth century and reflect the growing presence of Muslims in the city. These small mosques follow very traditional plans. They are, however, integrated into the urban fabric of the city. Often, the number of the faithful is so large that on the Friday service they overflow into the streets, blocking the traffic, a resounding statement as to the presence of Islam in twenty-first-century Marseille.[23]

CONCLUSION

In the same manner in which the architectural layout of Tunis and Algiers was replicated in other North African Mediterranean cities – Tangier, Tétouan, inland Fez, and others – the example of Marseille was also replicated in other European Mediterranean towns. The difference for Marseille, as opposed to Djerba, Tunis, Valencia, and so on, is that the Muslim and Jewish population has been a recent import. Marseille, unlike other places, does not have a long history as a site of encounter; yet, the dynamics of the commingling of three religions and their diverse cultures is somewhat similar. Each of the places briefly described here form part of those complex tapestries that marked, and still mark, the western Mediterranean as a site of encounter.

In spite of its decline relative to other regions of the world, the Mediterranean Sea's long history as a place where different civilizations meet has remained a model for a new global society. On its islands and shores different cultures, ethnic groups, religions, and linguistic communities met, cooperated, fought, and influenced each other, producing new forms of political organization and cultural products. One could say that the European patterns of conquest and settlement in Africa, Asia, and the New World had already been tested in the Mediterranean, as for example in Sicily, North Africa, the Balearic Islands, and elsewhere. These lessons were then applied to new colonial models. These cultural artifacts, ways of living, and ways of accommodating diverse people within one polity often resulted from the flow from unity and forced homogeneity to creative heterogeneity and back. Many books have been written about these meeting places: the sites for the encounter of different peoples and cultures. And here in this chapter, we get just a brief taste of the enduring, charming, and at times threatening contradictions and gifts to be found along the shores of the western sea.

NOTES

1 "A site of encounter is a geographical location where people from different cultures construct networks designed to exchange objects, customs, and knowledge according to shared norms." Teofilo F. Ruiz, "Sites of Encounters and Cultural Production: An AHA Initiative for an Action Thématique," *Perspectives on History* (2007), available at http://www.historians.org/perspectives/issues/2007/0712/0712vic1.cfm; Nicole Gilbertson, "Sites of Encounter in World History," *Perspectives on History*, 50, 5 (2012), 32–33.

2 Teofilo F. Ruiz, *A King Travels. Festive Traditions in Late Medieval and Early Modern Spain* (Princeton: Princeton University Press, 2012), 89–99.

3 Hussein Fancy's excellent book, *Mediterranean: Sovereignty, Religion, and Violence in the Medieval Crown of Aragon* (Chicago: University of Chicago Press, 2016), on Muslim mercenaries and other armed contingents traveling across the Straits includes references to sailing from Tangier.

4 See Thomas F. Glick, *Islamic and Christian Spain in the Early Middle Ages. Comparative Perspectives on Social and Cultural Formation* (Princeton: Princeton University Press, 1979), chapters 2, 7, and 8.

5 There is a popular *sevillana* (a song) that tells the story of the Giralda, the "most beautiful tower in Spain," and how the tower was left bereft and abandoned when the "*moros*" (Moors) were expelled from Spain.

6 *El conjunto histórico de Sevilla. Rehabilitación singular*, eds. Ana Reyes Morales Hevia and Marcos Alvarez (Seville: Ayuntamiento de Sevilla, Gerencia Municipal de Urbanismo, 1996).

7 Ruiz, *A King Travels*, 77–78.

8 Amy Remensnyder, *La Conquistadora: The Virgin Mary at War and Peace in the Old and New World* (Oxford & New York: Oxford University Press, 2014), 215. Also see Santiago Montoto, *La Catedral y el Alcázar de Sevilla*, 2nd ed. (Madrid: Editorial Plus Ultra, 1951).

9 Rafael Cómez, *El Alcázar del rey Don Pedro* (Seville: Deputación de Sevilla, 2006).

10 Amanda Wunder, *Baroque Seville: Sacred Art in a Century of Crisis* (College Park, PA: Pennsylvania State University Press, 2017).

11 Mary Elizabeth Perry, *Gender and Disorder in Early Modem Seville* (Princeton: Princeton University Press, 1990) and *Crime and Society in Early Modern Seville* (Hanover, NH: University Press of New England, 1980).

12 See M.I. Finley, Denis M. Smith, and Christopher Duggan, *A History of Sicily* (London: Chatto & Windus, 1986).

13 Jessica Goldberg, *Trade and Institutions in the Medieval Mediterranean* (Cambridge: Cambridge University Press, 2012).

14 Alex Metcalfe, *The Muslims of Medieval Italy* (Edinburgh: Edinburgh University Press, 2009).

15 Donald Matthew, *The Norman Kingdom of Sicily* (Cambridge & New York: Cambridge University Press, 1992).

16 David Abulafia, *Frederick II: A Medieval Emperor* (London: Penguin, 1988).

17 *The Royal Palace of Palermo*, ed. Maria Andaloro (Modena, Italy: Franco Cosimi Panini, 2011); Nora Nouritza Nercessian, "The Cappella Palatina of Roger II: The Relationship of its Imagery to its Political Function." PhD diss., UCLA, 1981.

18 See note 13 and Jessica Goldberg, "Choosing and Enforcing Business Relationships in the Eleventh-Century Mediterranean: Reassessing the Maghribi Traders," *Past & Present*, 216 (August 2012), 3–40.

19 Hédi Slim, Ammar Mahjoubi, Abdelmajid Ennabli, and Khaled Belkhodja, *Histoire gènèrale de la Tunisie*, 3 vols (Tunis: Sud Èditions, 2003–2007).

20 *Tunis: évolution et fonctionnement de l'espace urbain*, ed. Pierre Signoles et al. (Tours: Centre National de la Recherche Scientifique, 1987); Signoles, *L'espace Tunisien: capitale et etat-région* (Tours: Laboratoire URBAMA, Institut de geographie, 1985), 2 vols.

21 Diego de Haedo, *Topofrafia e historia general de Argel* (Madrid: Sociedad de Bibliófilos Españoles, 1927–1929), 3 vols.

22 "Melting Pot of Melodrama Enthralls French Nightly," by Steven Erlanger, *New York Times*, March 2, 2009. Accessed on March 27, 2017. http://www.nytimes.com/2009/03/03/world/europe/03marseille.html?pagewanted=all&_r=0.

23 *Marseille: une métropole entre Europe et Méditerranée*, eds. Philippe Langevin and Jean-Claude Juan (Paris: La Documentation française, 2007); David Crackanthorpe, *Marseille* (Oxford: Signal Books, 2012).

[11] ON THE WATERS OF THE WESTERN MEDITERRANEAN: ISLANDS AND TOWNS

SEVERAL years ago, Richard Kagan, a renowned historian of early modern Spain and a dear friend, emphasized to me, while discussing writing a history of the Mediterranean, that the real story of the Middle Sea was to be found in the collective histories of little towns on its shores. He argued that the histories of the great iconic cities, while important, were not representative of the actual tenor of life in the region. I have never forgotten Kagan's comments and these pages are an effort to address his remarks.

Through September and October 2014, I sailed almost completely across the Mediterranean. Beginning in magical Istanbul, I flew to Athens, where I led a UCLA Alumni group and gave lectures. We sailed from Athens to some of the Aegean islands, to Ephesus, and from there to Taormina, Messina, the Amalfi coast, Civitavecchia (the port of Rome), Livorno (the entry port for tours to Florence, Pisa, Lucca, or Cinque Terre), Monaco, Marseille, and Barcelona. The trip, besides giving a brief taste of almost the entire Mediterranean and some of the highlights of urban settlements along Europe's Mediterranean shores, served as a vivid reminder that, notwithstanding modern forms of transportation, what bound the cities and towns from the Black Sea to the Straits of Gibraltar or, in Joan Manuel Serrat's moving lyrics with which this book opens, "from Algeciras to Istanbul," was always the sea. The experience of place is always dramatically different when one approaches, or leaves, these sites from the sea. Nothing, however, was as memorable as sailing through the Strait of Messina, as Odysseus had done long ago. Alas! The sirens did not sing to me.

In Chapter 10, I examined a few discrete places as examples of the kind of fruitful encounters that forged, and still forge, new cultural artifacts along the shores of the Mediterranean. Here, I take a very different tack. Not every city along the shores of the Mediterranean was a site of encounter. Not all of them witnessed the commingling of people, their adaptation to new ways of living, or their resistance to them. The Mediterranean was far more than that. All the great cities and islands that dot the sea or crowd its shores have already received a great deal of attention in the abundant Mediterranean historiography. Yet, it

The Western Mediterranean and the World: 400 CE to the Present, First Edition. Teofilo F. Ruiz.
© 2018 John Wiley & Sons, Ltd. Published 2018 by John Wiley & Sons, Ltd.

Figure 11.1 The Strait of Messina. Source: Courtesy of Scarlett Freund.

seems to me that to write a history that takes these unique islands and towns – Sicily, Majorca, Barcelona, Tunis, or Marseille – as representative of the civilization of the sea as a whole is a terrible mistake. The sinews of Mediterranean life can also be found in small islands and towns. They formed a network of places connected always by sea routes and coastal sailing. They may not have had a past that included Arabic and Jewish settlements. Most of them had no medinas dating to the first centuries of the Arab invasion. They enjoyed no pride of place as trading or cultural centers; yet, they were essential to the life of the sea and to its development over time. Here, therefore, I turn to those neglected places, their history often unknown or set aside by the history of larger and more influential locations.

SMALL ISLANDS ON THE SEA

Montecristo

Let us begin with islands. Although all these islands also had (sometimes) towns of their own, it is their size – some large, others small – and their role in the life of the sea that reveal important points about trading networks, places of memory, and the unglamorous (or very glamorous) life of the Mediterranean. As you may expect, judging from the preceding chapters, for me there is no better place to begin this inquiry than with the island of Montecristo, or Isola de Montecristo. There was, of course, no actual Count of Monte Cristo, or certainly not the fictional character created by Dumas's fertile imagination, but there is certainly an island of Montecristo, even though its description as an island, considering its size, may be a stretch.

Located in the Tyrrhenian Sea and part of the so-called Tuscan Archipelago, the island of Montecristo is part of a series of small islands that run in a slight arc roughly north-south. The northernmost island is Gorgona (even smaller than Montecristo), due west from the port of Livorno. The southernmost and smallest of the islands is that of Giannutri. It is also the one closest to the coast, lying north of Civitavecchia. The largest of the islands comprising the Tuscan Archipelago is the island of Elba, but Montecristo, because of its literary fame, claims equal recognition. Significantly, although both islands had, as shall be seen, histories of their own, both were also deeply associated with France. Elba was briefly Napoleon I's abode and kingdom following his resignation from the throne and exile in 1814 until just before his dramatic return to France to reclaim his throne. Montecristo's association is due to Dumas's novel. Other islands in the Tuscan Archipelago are Capraia, Pianosa, and Giglio.

Lying east of Corsica, with which it shares some topographical features, the island of Montecristo is very small with probably barely over four square miles of surface. It is also very rugged, and Dumas's descriptions of Montecristo are quite accurate. One could easily see why he chose the island – as mysterious and uninhabited as one could find in the nineteenth- or twenty-first-century Mediterranean – for the abode of the mysterious count, or Sinbad, as he called himself while living in his mysterious cave. It is also easy to see why we first meet the island as a stopping place for smugglers and other outlaws plying the waters of the western sea. Today the island is uninhabited and part of a natural preserve. But it has had a long and complicated history. It has not been a site of encounters, as conquerors and settlers have come in small numbers and only in successive waves. It suffers (or it suffered until very recently) from flora and fauna infestations: black rats had been a serious problem for many years, as have been plants introduced into the island that compete with the local flora.

The island has been witness to repeated efforts to exploit its limited natural resources or to benefit from its isolation in spite of being on well-traveled sea lanes. The Etruscans, Greeks, and Romans came to the island to carry away its oak trees, mine its quarries for building stones, and claim a presence there, as ephemeral as it proved to be. By the fifth century, as Rome collapsed and some Christians found the Church's growing power and involvement with the world intolerable, Christian hermits sought the refuge of the island's caves as a place of solitude and an escape from the sins of the world. These hermits gave a new name to the island, Mons Christi. Some of these communities, founded in imitation of the eremite communities of the Sinai, became organized under a monastic rule by the late sixth century. In spite of their isolation, the few inhabitants of the island did not escape some of the Germanic raids plaguing Italy. Pisa also claimed jurisdiction over the island, since it enjoyed an important geographical position for Pisan trade. Yet, its religious community, said to be fabulously rich (hence Dumas's invention of the treasure hidden on the island), did not endure into the present. Although the monastery founded under Gregory I's papacy lasted almost a millennium, it was sacked by Ottoman corsairs and was briefly in Ottoman hands in the late sixteenth century, when the island, no longer with a monastic community present, became uninhabited again.

The Spaniards, with their long-term interest in Italy and in permanent struggle with Ottoman corsairs and naval forces for control of the Mediterranean, reclaimed the island and kept it, either directly or through the agency of some of its vassal states, until Napoleon conquered most of Italy in the early nineteenth century. Little did Napoleon know that his first exile would take place in that Tuscan Archipelago, which must have been but an afterthought in his long-term imperial plans. But the island of Montecristo and the other islands in the archipelago had also a connection to Corsica, a place always close to Bonaparte's heart and political aims. Throughout the nineteenth century, many attempted to settle the island, use it as a game preserve, or profitably farm or exploit its meager natural resources. Every one of these attempts failed until the Italian government purchased Montecristo and, eventually, declared it a natural preserve with limited access to its shores. Today, a few buildings, most notably the remains of the sixth-century monastery, mark the island's connections to the social and cultural history of the western Mediterranean.[1]

Beyond this brief synthesis of the island's long history, what do that these fragmentary details tell us about the place of the island of Montecristo in the life of the sea as a whole? Montecristo is one of the smallest of the over many islands that dot the entire Mediterranean. In a list of islands ranked by size, it appears as number 155 out of 159. Its population is limited to the two caretakers that patrol and maintain the natural reserve. Nonetheless, Montecristo is representative of a large number of small islands that, often as part of archipelagos either close to the mainland or to other islands, can be found between Sicily and the Straits of Gibraltar. Most of these small islands, though now sparsely populated or, like Montecristo, often designated as natural reserves, have a long history of human habitation and attempts to exploit their natural resources, often going back to the Paleolithic period. Most of the time, they were also safe places away from the wars and conflicts sweeping the mainland.

These small islands reveal to us a very different face of the Mediterranean. Unless they were located close to the coast or in strategic locations, as is the case with Ischia (across from the Bay of Naples) or Djerba, they only played a minor role in the larger history of the western sea. Yet, the patterns of life and historical developments in most of these little islands, their history of occupation by the large maritime powers battling for control of the sea, their role as strategic lookouts over sea lanes and trade routes, and their experiences with successive masters provide a lens through which to view the larger history of the western Mediterranean, the political conflicts, the linguistic connections with the mainland, and a host of other factors that complicate and expand the history of the western sea.

I would need many pages simply to list all of these small islands dotting the western sea or to provide the briefest of accounts. It may suffice to look at two additional small islands, before considering a large one that did not play a role as a site of encounter such as that played, for example, by Sicily or Majorca. One peculiar fact is that while these small islands proliferate along the coasts of Italy,

France, and Spain, few can be found off the coast of Africa. Only five islands lay off the coast of present-day Tunisia. One of them is Djerba, which was discussed in an earlier chapter and which played a significant economic role in Mediterranean trade and social history. The others are very small islands or rocky high promontories: Chergui, Gharbi, the Galite Islands, and Zembra. Neither Algeria nor Morocco has islands near their shores on the western Mediterranean besides the ones discussed briefly below.

Tabarka

In that sense, and for geographical reasons that had to do with volcanic activity and the meeting of the African and European continental plates, the African Mediterranean coast is quite distinct from its European counterpart, above all, around Italy and Sicily. One may wonder on the protection that these small islands provided for the European mainland. They were points from which attacks could be detected or where naval bases could be built. The contrary is, of course, also true. Corsairs and smugglers sought these islands as places from which they could carry out their attacks and business with some impunity. In the first case, small islands, though often uninhabited or unexploited, provided a first line of defense from maritime surprise attacks and were important parts of the connectivity of the western sea. Or second, as was the case with the Genoese settlements on the island of Tabarka, they served as a launching point for trade and political designs. Tabarka is a very good example of the complex histories of some of these islands.

Located at a very short distance from the town of the same name, and close to the border between Algeria and Tunisia today, the island of Tabarka, with its Numidian and Roman historical roots, became successively a short-lived Spanish presidio and a Genoese concession for the exploitation of coral. Coral was fished off Tabarka's coast by the Genoese and shipped to Genoa, Livorno, and elsewhere to be turned into jewelry and art objects. For almost two centuries between the 1540s and 1740s, the Genoese held the island and maintained a garrison right within "a rifle shot" of the mainland. By the mid-eighteenth century, the Genoese relinquished the island into the hands of the Bey of Tunisia, the Ottoman representative in the region. The entire population of Genoese descendants was relocated. Some went to Sardinia and some to Tunis. In both locations they preserved their Genoese dialect until recent times. Tabarka, then, unlike the island of Montecristo and other locations examined in these pages, had more of a cosmopolitan feel and more experiences of encounter. Yet, the island, for all its complex history, did not generate new and hybrid cultural forms.

Another island by the same name, known also as New Tabarca (Nova Tabarca), off the coast of Spain close to Alicante, was also populated by the Genoese exiled from the Tunisian Tabarka. There they also preserved their Genoese identity and speech. Both small islands, the Tunisian Tabarka and the Spanish one, are reminders of the close connection between coastal islets and the nearby ports to which they are connected by an almost symbiotic relationship. This is also clearly the case with the Château d'If and Marseille. Yet, the short distance separating the islands from the mainland made the world of difference.

Lucette Valensi pointed out to me not long ago that many of these islands served as prisons or places of exile. They were convenient locations to which to remove troublesome political enemies. The French exiled Bourguiba, the eventual president of a free Tunisia, to the island of Tabarka. Illegal immigrants today are housed in the island of Lampedusa and the Sicilian town of Mineo, as already noted in an earlier chapter. The Château d'If is, of course, the best example of a prison, made all the more secure by being surrounded by the sea. Even until recently that pattern has held. The infamous island of Alcatraz in San Francisco Bay serves as an example of islands turned into prisons or places of exile. As to the latter category, no other small island has had as fertile a history in that sense than Elba.[2]

Elba

In Dumas's *The Count of Monte Cristo*, Edmund Dantès, saddled with the responsibility of guiding the ship back to Marseille, stops, as commanded by his dying captain, briefly at Elba. There he sees the exiled emperor and collects a package that will prove his undoing. Elba is, of course, closely associated with Napoleon, as the place of his first exile before his final defeat at Waterloo and imprisonment in Saint Helena – yet another island prison but this time in the middle of the Atlantic Ocean. Located in the Tyrrhenian Sea and part of the Tuscan Archipelago of which the island of Montecristo also forms a part, Elba is a large island by the standard of the small islands in the western Mediterranean. It is ideally located between the Italian coast of Tuscany and Corsica, separated from the mainland by around 20 kilometers and from Corsica by 50 kilometers or less. As is true of all the islands in the Tuscan Archipelago or in the western Mediterranean, Elba has a high mountain and a fairly rugged topography with some plains where human inhabitation prospered. From Antiquity, Elba was famous for its iron ore deposit, and ancient people, even before the Etruscans came to the island, mined Elba's iron.

Historically, the island was a microcosm of the political ebb and flow so peculiar to the western Mediterranean. Under Etruscan and Roman rule, successively, Elba became part of the Republic of Pisa during the Middle Ages, just before Pisa lost its access to the sea. The Dukes of Milan and the rulers of Florence held the island between the Renaissance and the late sixteenth century, when Elba, as was the case with other western Mediterranean islands and lands, came under Spanish domination. As such, the island became part of the Spanish strategy to control the western Mediterranean and to fend off corsair activity from North Africa. In 1802, with the ascendance of France and the Napoleonic conquest of Italy, the island became a French possession and a convenient outpost for keeping the Tuscan coast under surveillance or a stopping station for ships sailing around Corsica and Sardinia on their way to the French coast. Little could Napoleon imagine that Elba, a very small pawn in his political calculations in the early 1800s, would eventually become his realm after his 1814 defeat at the Battle of the Nations, or Battle of Leipzig, and his abdication as France's emperor. In Emil Ludwig's romantic and dated biography of Napoleon, we see the deposed emperor actively reforming the island, developing its economy, and improving its infrastructure. His rule lasted only for a few months before his bold return to France, to power, and to eventual defeat at Waterloo, but the emperor's presence marked Elba's history and makes it one of the best-known small islands in the Mediterranean.

After Napoleon's defeat in 1815 and his exile to Saint Helena in the middle of the Atlantic, Elba reverted to the Duchy of Tuscany before becoming part of a united Italy in 1860. Connected to the Italian mainland by frequent ferries and by air (Piombino is a few minutes away and there is even a ferry connection to Capri), Elba shares with Djerba, Tabarka, the islet of If, and other similar small islands in the western Mediterranean a close relationship with the mainland. It profits from this proximity by being a favorite destination for tourists, whether historical buffs in search of traces of Napoleon's presence in the island, or those seeking the beauty of Elba's beaches and topography. The island's many lives and faces – an important source for iron in Antiquity, a strategic location for Pisan and Tuscan commerce in the Middle Ages, a military base for Spain in the early modern period, a French possession and place of exile for a French emperor, a tourist destination – are representative of the role that these small islands played and still play in the larger history of the sea.

A Large, Neglected, and yet Important Island: Sardinia

Long contested by western Mediterranean maritime powers vying for control of the sea, Sardinia, the second-largest island in the western Mediterranean (after Sicily), has a long and checkered history. Lying very close to Corsica (north of Sardinia) and almost the same distance from the Italian and French mainland as it is from Tunisia, Sardinia has, as is the case with most of the Mediterranean islands on the European coast, a rugged topography. Some mountain peaks, such as Punta La Marmora, rise to an altitude of over 6,000 feet. Because the high mountain chains run north-south for almost the whole length of the island, Sardinia is in fact divided into two distinct cultural and geographical zones. The region lying east of the mountain range looks towards Italy. The region west of the mountains looks towards the westernmost part of the Mediterranean and what in the Middle Ages would have been the Crown of Aragon. Cagliari, the present capital, is on the southeast coast of the island in a gulf or large bay. It faces both the Italian mainland and North Africa, directly north of Tunisia. On the western part of the island, the natural bay on the Gulf of Oristano opens in the direction of the Balearic Islands and the medieval lands of the Crown of Aragon, with which it had long-lasting ties in the Middle Ages.

In fact, Sardinia, because of its checkered history and the successive waves of settlers and conquerors, still remains a multilingual society. A local dialect or language (it is officially recognized as one of the languages of the island) is

Sardinian, a romance language that developed in the relative isolation of the island after the waning of Roman power in the West. Sassarese, spoken in the north of the island, adjacent to Corsica, is a mixture of Sardinian, Corsican, and other forms of speech coming from mainland Italy, mostly the Genoese dialect (the language of Christopher Columbus). Gallurese is also a dialect spoken in the northern part of the island and closely associated with Sassarese, while Algherese, or Catalan Algherese, reflects the settlements of Catalan speakers in the northwest part of the island, the region of Alghero. It is still an official or semi-official language in the island. Tabarchino, a form of Ligurian or Genoese dialect, is also spoken in the island.

Sardinia's linguistic variety alerts us to one Mediterranean reality, that is, the multilingual character of the region. Sardinia, because of its rugged topography and relative isolation, is an ideal example of how different linguistic groups may share an island and, despite political change, preserve these linguistic and cultural differences until today. Although Sardinia has fared well economically in recent times, enjoying the highest per capita income in the *mezzogiorno*, it was not always so. Its pre-modern economy depended on livestock (mostly sheep, still an important part of the Sardinian economy) and crops. The latter was typical of the Mediterranean: wine, olive oil, and wheat as the main staples. Today the island benefits from fiscal exemptions, abundant sources of electrical power, and increased tourism. But it is the history of Sardinia and of its successive masters that is somewhat similar to those of other large islands in the western Mediterranean, most strikingly Sicily, the Balearic Islands, and even nearby Corsica, but also quite different because of its different historical development.

As was the case elsewhere in the western Mediterranean, Sardinia already had inhabitants from the Paleolithic period onwards. Successive waves of settlers from the European mainland, mainly via Corsica, populated the island. Impressive archeological sites and ruins attest to the importance of Sardinia before Etruria and Rome came into the picture as rulers of the island. Today, some of these pre-Greek and pre-Roman archeological sites are the destination of many tourists. The vast Nuragic architectural complex at Muraghe Su Nuraxi, near Barumini, is close to 3,500 years old, and is juxtaposed to an ancient village also dating back three millennia. Other archeological sites, at Tiscali and Nuraghe Mannu, long pre-date the Phoenician, Greek, and Roman settlements. Although the provenance of these settlers is not always clear, there are indications that some of them may have belonged to the people who have been described as "the sea people," whose invasion of the eastern Mediterranean greatly disrupted the established civilizations of the ancient world, including the Hittite Empire.

As was also a commonplace in the western sea, the Phoenicians, and later the Carthaginians, settled first along the coast, establishing convenient way stations for their expansive trade routes into the western Mediterranean, and then slowly came to control significant parts of the island's interior, attracted by its important mineral resources. After the defeat of Carthage in the First Punic War, Sardinia became a Roman province in 238 BCE. For the next 600 years, the island was in the orbit of Rome. It became, as was the case with

Sicily, an important supplier of grain to the endless and voracious needs of the citizens of Rome. But, as in Iberia and North Africa, Roman influence did not extend fully into the mountainous areas. And, although Roman ruins can still be seen throughout the island, it is clear that Sardinia did not benefit from the Roman civilizing influence as much as Sicily or coastal North Africa did.

By the mid-fifth century, Sardinia had fallen to the Vandals, one of the Germanic groups that had settled in North Africa. Vandal rule (as their name, but only because of modern and unhistorical usage, implies), consisted mostly of corsair activity in the western Mediterranean and of frequent raids on the European mainland. As in North Africa, the Vandals had little impact. In many respects, it is historically significant and related to the island's later history that the Vandals, with their power base on coastal North Africa and having little impact on local culture, held the island as opposed to other Germanic groups that became, in time, highly Romanized. By the mid-sixth century, the Justinian-led reconquest of the West brought Sardinia under partial Byzantine rule. As a far-flung and fairly isolated province of the eastern Roman Empire, Sardinia did not enjoy the full impact of a Byzantine presence, as occurred in Sicily, Ravenna, or even early medieval Rome, nor did the Byzantine presence and/or evangelization program fully succeed in the island's mountainous area. It is precisely this incomplete colonization of the island, its century-long occupation by the Vandals, and the eventual demise of a Byzantine presence that explains the different political paths followed by Sardinia, as opposed to those of Sicily.

When, early in the eighth century, Muslim raiders from North Africa began to probe Sardinia's shore, the inhabitants of the island found themselves in a situation not uncommon in the Mediterranean. They became caught between the retreating power of Byzantium and the growing power of Islam. Unlike Sicily or Majorca, where Islam was eventually triumphant, in Sardinia the Muslim raids never succeeded in establishing control of the island. This had important consequences for Sardinia. The inability of Islam to capture the island meant that Sardinia was not fully connected to the commercial networks that linked Dar al-Islam with the European West. Although not completely excluded from the growing commercial life of the western Mediterranean, Sardinia never became the vibrant place for commercial exchanges that Sicily and Majorca would become by the eleventh and twelfth centuries. Not unlike Corsica, its close northern neighbor, Sardinia would not keep pace with the "commercial revolution" that swept most of the western sea.

In terms of political development, Sardinia also took a different course from that of Sicily, missing out those Islamic or Norman interludes that the latter island experienced. Instead, the inhabitants of Sardinia were able to develop their own political and administrative structures. Their institutions differed from those of nearby islands and from the mainland, reflecting the very different paths that other western Mediterranean polities took in their transition from Christian to Islamic domination. In that respect, the absence of an Islamic presence was crucial for Sardinia's development. In the vacuum created by the demise of Byzantine power in the West and the failure of Islam to capture the island, Sardinians developed a system of judgeships or *Giudicati*. The island became fragmented (following along the island's geographical contours) into five, and eventually four, semi-autonomous areas, each presided over by a lord or noble family. Although, in the eleventh and twelfth centuries, the republics of Pisa and Genoa extended their influence throughout the island – as part of the expansionist thrust of Italian polities into the western Mediterranean – the Giudicati preserved their own fragile independence. By the late thirteenth and early fourteenth century, Sardinia had fallen victim to the upheaval created in the western Mediterranean by the event known as the Sicilian Vespers (see Chapter 3).

A confusing period, marked by the struggles of the Crown of Aragon against France and Italian polities for control of Sicily and the profitable Mediterranean trade, led to papal attempts to establish Sardinia and Corsica as a separate kingdom. In a sense, it was a very early and failed attempt to establish a realm within historic Italy. Yet, by some strange historical coincidence, Italian unification is closely related to both the Piedmont and Sardinia in the nineteenth century. Of note, and the object of great pride for Sardinian historians, is the proclamation of the so-called *Carta de Logu* (Charter of the Land), a set of laws that regulated everyday life and material transactions throughout the land in the first half of the fourteenth century. Although quite late when in comparison to other such charters throughout the western Mediterranean, as, for example, the *Ustages* of Barcelona, the *Siete Partidas* in Castile, or Frederick II's famous proclamations in Amalfi, the Carta de Logu, as was the case with most Mediterranean law codes, provided the citizens of the Giudicati with some political and property rights. Along the lines of similar Mediterranean legal codes, it protected women's rights over property. The most remarkable aspect of the Carta de Logu was not its content – in that sense it was in line with other earlier law codes elsewhere in the Mediterranean region – but that it was composed in Sardinian. While the use of the vernacular for law codes was also common elsewhere in Mediterranean society, the use of the vernacular further separated Sardinia from its neighboring Sicily and continental Italy.

By the fourteenth century, and most decidedly by the early fifteenth century, Sardinia had come under the orbit of the Crown of Aragon and, by the sixteenth century, under the firm control of the Spanish Habsburgs. As such, the island became part of the broader conflict for control of the western Mediterranean between Spain and the Sublime Porte. Sardinia experienced numerous raids – some of them as late as the eighteenth century – by the North African or Barbary corsairs operating out of Tunis and other North African ports. This prompted the construction of a system of fortifications to guard not only the island but also the maritime routes between the eastern shores of Sardinia and the Italian mainland. But Sardinia was never a central lynchpin in Spain's Mediterranean strategy. More than four centuries of Spanish rule did not leave a powerful imprint on the island, except for the presence of Catalans in the western parts of Sardinia and some folkloric and festive traditions. By the early eighteenth century and after the War of Spanish

Succession (1701–1714), the island had passed first into the hands of the Austrian Habsburgs and then into those of the rulers of Savoy. Their new title, kings of Savoy (or Piedmont) and Sardinia, spoke of the strange combination of an inland power with ties to France and Northern Europe and a neglected Mediterranean island. Nonetheless, Savoy-Sardinia, in one of those frequent ironies of history, would become the foundations for the unification of Italy (see Chapter 4).

From Italian unification to the present, Sardinia's path has been an uneven one. Separatist movements, not unlike those of Corsica, massive migration out of, and into, the island, a remaking of its economic structure, the phasing out of its agricultural base, the beginning of a tourist boom, and, most of all, integration into the European community have shaped the island into something very different and distinct from its earlier historical manifestations. The autonomous nature of the island and the recognition of diverse Sardinian native languages as official administrative languages are clear indications of the distinctive character of the island in relation to other regions of Italy, as evident in its linguistic developments, culinary traditions, and political structures. In addition, if throughout this brief discussion of Sardinia I have continuously placed it in comparison to Sicily and other western Mediterranean islands, it is to emphasize, once again, the myriad possibilities that existed, and still exist, to develop along diverse paths. There is no Monreale, no Cappella Palatina, and there are no great Greek and Roman ruins in Sardinia as is the case in Sicily and, to a lesser extent, Majorca. There were no sites of encounter in Sardinia or, if there were, they did not rise to the level of those I have described in the previous chapter. This was the outcome of geography and the long history of settlements, of the absence of Islam and Norman conquerors, and of the relatively small imprint of Jews on the island, much more so after their expulsion in 1492 by the Spanish decree of expulsion.

There is another aspect of Sardinia's history, also replicated in Sicily, which I have not given the consideration it deserves because of the limitations of space. Specific topographies on the islands of the Mediterranean or in the mountainous areas around the western sea often led to widespread banditry. Even if, as Braudel famously argued, they were not always forms of resistance to the state, banditry, almost endemic in Sicily and Sardinia late into the twentieth century, emerged from complex social and geographical factors that shaped the peculiar histories of these areas. Highly romanticized at times – I vividly remember my fascination with Salvatore Giuliano, a kind of Robin Hood in 1940s Sicily – banditry and rural (as well as urban) violence marked areas of these islands and mountain regions as being apart from the normative discourse of state formation, order, and control that defined the reception of modernity in the western Mediterranean. Thus, Sardinia provides us with a template that emphasizes differences in the Mediterranean of large islands and the distinct paths that each of these societies took during the long history from the unity of the Mediterranean under Rome to the political fragmentation that followed Rome's collapse in the fifth century and to the present world of nations.[3]

TOWNS AND VILLAGES ON THE SHORES OF THE WESTERN SEA

True to the agenda I set in the introduction to this chapter, I turn here to those small villages and towns – some as ancient as the earliest human settlements in the Mediterranean, others of recent provenance – that, in many ways, are far more representative of Mediterranean life than the better known great cities we have glossed in earlier chapters. There is no Palermo, Tunis, Marseille, or Barcelona to be found in these pages, but places, often times, neglected by history, even though in this age of global tourism few of them escape the crunching presence of cruise tours, organized groups, and independent travelers. Below I offer a few examples from different parts of the Mediterranean, both middle-sized towns and small villages. I hope to draw small vignettes from both sides of the sea, though the European side provides the documentary evidence that makes the task easier. The order of selection is arbitrary, guided more by my own taste and personal experiences of these places than by any rational organizing principle. That is why I begin with the small towns along the so-called Cinque Terre region on the western Mediterranean coast of Italy.

Cinque Terre and Vernazza

From late spring to late fall, tour buses and trains (mostly from Livorno or La Spezia) disgorge groups of tourists, most of them, though not all, senior citizens enjoying the pleasures of retirement and wealth. The buses cannot access the towns on the Cinque Terre national park directly. Guides lead groups on foot from the high hills into the town and eventually to the sea. Others come directly by a train service that conveniently stops in the center of most of the towns. Others, more fortunate ones, approach one or two of the towns by small boats and then take the long walk from town to town along the seashore. Hardier souls trek from one town to another on trails built high in the mountains that abut the settlements of the Cinque Terre.

The Cinque Terre is located on rugged slopes, now a national park and UNESCO World Heritage Site, on the Ligurian coast of Italy. Five small towns can be found in the region, fairly well connected today, as I note above, by hiking trails, a railroad, and, of course, the sea. One of Italy's autostrade, or major highways, links the towns, though it must lead high up in the surrounding mountains to do so, to the rest of Liguria and Tuscany. The towns are Monterosso al Mare, Vernazza, Corniglia, Manarola, and Riomaggiore. Four of the towns hug the coast of the Mediterranean. Only Corniglia stands on a high promontory overlooking the sea. They are, notwithstanding the press of tourists, wondrous places to behold, especially if approaching the region from the sea.

They are, in many respects, not very different from other towns on the Amalfi coast (see below) or the Italian Riviera. Yet, the relative isolation of these towns and the colors of their buildings as they contrast with the green terraced mountains that surround them and the blue of the Mediterranean Sea make

Figure 11.2 View of Manarola from the Mediterranean Sea. Source: Courtesy of Scarlett Freund.

these towns such an aesthetic experience that only by seeing them can one capture their transcendental beauty.

The four towns that face the sea have no attractive or useful harbors. At most, there are small coves that permit the mooring of very small boats. In a sense, the absence of sufficient places to land must have been an added benefit to the settlers of these towns, for it made invasions from the sea as difficult as invasions from the mountains behind. All the towns, with exception of Corniglia, which although facing the sea is perched on a high hill, slope down to meet the water. The backs of the buildings are to the mountains and rugged hills that surround them. Yet, the land behind the towns was and remains essential, even if by now most of the income earned by the inhabitants of the Cinque Terre comes from tourists. In carefully terraced hillsides, the work of many centuries, vineyards and other crops are lovingly tended. Yet, the mountains are also places of danger. When torrential rains come down, landslides, such as the one that recently destroyed a great deal of Vernazza, present a continuous threat. And the sea is not forgiving either. Storms, the eternal pounding of the waves, and high winds imperil these communities as well.

Vernazza. It may be useful to turn to one of these five Cinque Terre communities to see what it may tell us about the life and history of these small towns along the coast of the western Mediterranean. While four of the five towns, excluding Corniglia, share the same economic patterns of agricultural and fishing – although now focusing mostly on tending to avid tourists – each one is distinct. Although I have chosen Vernazza as a case study because it is my favorite town among the five settlements in the Cinque Terre and because its medieval church has very attractive architectural features, any of the other four would do as well. Corniglia, with little or no access to the sea, may stand for other types of towns on the shores of the Mediterranean and is an exception in the Cinque Terre region. Essentially what one says about Vernazza could be said about Monterosso al Mare, Manarola, and Riomaggiore as well.

Although the village of Vernazza today has barely more than 1,000 permanent inhabitants – a population tripled or quadrupled during the tourist season – its medieval, early modern, and modern populations before the tourist boom were even smaller. Vernazza's history, as is the case with many small settlements along the Mediterranean coast, was closely tied to corsair activity. This corsair activity came mostly from North Africa (and was at its height in the sixteenth century), but Vernazza was also affected by the endless struggles for control of the western Mediterranean between North African powers, Italian communes, and the Crown of Aragon. Its very small cove, even after the construction of a sea wall in the mid-seventeenth century, however, barely allowed for an important strategic presence. It is impossible to imagine Vernazza, in spite of assertions to the contrary by patriotic local historians, as an important maritime outpost. Nonetheless, Vernazza and other Ligurian towns lived by and from the sea. One could imagine periodic raids from the sea, as corsairs and others naval forces came looking for people to enslave or treasures to rob. The earlier textual evidence for the town, dating from the eleventh century, describes it as a fortified place. Stronger walls and fortifications were built in the fifteenth century at a time when corsair activity began to climb to its high point in the sixteenth.

Figure 11.3 View of Vernazza from the Mediterranean Sea. Source: Courtesy of Scarlett Freund.

Vernazza was, as were the other four villages in Cinque Terre, fairly isolated from the rest of Liguria and Italy. (For a color aerial photograph of Vernazza, see the front cover of this book.) Land communications were minimal until the building of a railroad connection to La Spezia or the construction of the autostrada east of the coast. These were villages that depended on limited agricultural production and, with the exception of Corniglia, fishing. Wine and olive oil, as mentioned before, are still produced in the area. Vineyards and olive groves, the quintessential Mediterranean staples, hug the mountainside, growing in terraced soil that dates back to the Middle Ages. Today, the vineyards in the region produce a white wine highly praised by the locals but of rather pedestrian quality. It does not travel well. The olive oil is famous for its quality, as are the olives. Yet, as was the case for many other Mediterranean towns and villages, the sea was the most important source of food and income. It provided protection from invaders, but it was also the place from where attacks could come unexpectedly. Politically, Vernazza and the entire region were in the orbit of Genoa. As such, they shared in the Genoese expansion into the western and eastern Mediterranean, suffered the same threats from North Africa and from Genoa's traditional rivals in the Central Middle Ages – Pisa, the Crown of Aragon, and others – and came to be, though in a very minor role, part of the Spanish-Genoese alliance vying for control of the western Mediterranean and in direct opposition to French and North African incursions by the fifteenth century and into the early modern period.

Vernazza, devastated by flooding and a mudslide in 2011, and now mostly restored to its pristine glory (I was there in 2013 and saw how far advanced the restoration efforts were), has one significant building that bespeaks of the improbable manner in which Mediterranean societies were able to construct places of great charm and artistic value even in isolated villages. Although the houses, the new port, the fifteenth-century Doria Castle (a testimony to the Genoese connection), the main square of the village, and other architectural elements are particularly charming, it is the church of Santa Margherita d'Antiochia that is quite unique to Vernazza. Already the selection of Santa Margherita (St Margaret) of Antioch as a patron saint is a bit odd. She was one of those early medieval eastern saints who, as shown by Maya Maskarinec,[4] made their way to Rome in the seventh and eighth centuries and was appropriated by the papacy for the construction of their religious authority in the West. Expelled from her home by her father – who opposed her embracing of Christianity – she became a shepherdess, repelled the advances of a Roman official, was taken prisoner, was tempted by the devil, survived execution by fire and water, and was then beheaded and martyred for her beliefs. Also known as Marina, she is the patroness of childbirth and her feast day is, conveniently for the tourist season, on July 20.

How she ended up as patroness of Vernazza and other localities in the West (there is a church dedicated to her in New Jersey, USA, another in Kent, England, and there are others in myriad other places) is a mystery, perhaps having to do with the slow but decisive integration of eastern saints into the liturgical calendar of the West. Her church at Vernazza, dating from the early fourteenth century, is, however, a truly special site showing the possibilities for even small villages to acquire an important saint and a very attractive church.

The story is that one of Saint Margaret's fingers washed ashore at Vernazza, and the church is, in many respects, a reliquary for one of the saint's body parts. Built in a Romanesque-Genoese style and very different from the churches built around Tuscany and Umbria, Santa Margherita's church is also located in an impressive setting. It faces today a little cove, the result of the sea wall built later in the Middle Ages and reworked in the modern period. It is also adjacent to the town's main square, the Piazza Marconi, the only area of the town not on an incline. Behind and to the left of the church, as one exits its portal, is Vernazza, rising gradually against the mountainside. The church's portal faces east, and because of Vernazza's isolation and decline during the early modern period it has not undergone radical transformations. In many respects, most of its charm resides in the fact that the structure and interior, despite the ghastly mudslide in 2011, remain quite faithful to the original plan. Nothing that I can write would capture Vernazza and the other Cinque Terre villages' unique aesthetic appeal. It must be seen to grasp what it may have been like to live there in the Central Middle Ages or early modern period, or indeed, allowing for the flood of tourists, what it may be like to live there even today.[5]

Amalfi and the Amalfi Coast

We ought not leave the Italian Mediterranean coast without a brief glance at Amalfi and the coastal towns generally identified as part of the Amalfi coast. Strategically located on Italy's western shores, in the region of Campania (province of Salerno), Amalfi is not too distant from the Strait of Messina and has convenient access to Sicily (with which its history is closely bound) and

Figure 11.4 Church of Santa Margherita in Vernazza. Source: Courtesy of Scarlett Freund.

the eastern Mediterranean. In the Central Middle Ages, Amalfi was an important seafaring and trading town. Today, Amalfi, Salerno, Positano, Ravello (high in the mountains overlooking Amalfi), and other towns are, above all, a destination for tourists and for cruise ships' daily visits. The town of Amalfi hugs the rugged mountains that rise sharply barely a kilometer outside its main square, serving as an impressive backdrop to Amalfi's beautiful cathedral and charming setting. The town, though quite small, exudes a sense of wealth with its elegant late early modern and nineteenth-century buildings. But to really appreciate Amalfi one must approach it from the sea and then, after seeing it on foot (for it is quite small), take the bus to Ravello, a quaint little town in the mountains. Climbing on a steep and curvy road, the views of Amalfi and of the sea are impressive indeed.

Amalfi and the Amalfi coast played a significant role in the history of southern Italy and Sicily, in the events of the Norman and Hohenstaufen period, and in the accomplishments of the rulers of the so-called Kingdom of the Two Sicilies. This was most surely the case with Frederick II (1212–1250), an effective and cunning ruler. Later history included Amalfi's role in the expansive Crown of Aragon, in Spain's time as a player in early modern Italy, and then in its final integration into the nascent Italian state in the second half of the nineteenth century. An independent polity until the 1070s, when the city and its hinterland fell to the Normans, Amalfi's precocious development in the ninth and tenth centuries allowed it to dominate a great deal of the trade with the eastern Mediterranean, to mint gold coins (far before the extent to which other Italian communes did), and to developed a code of maritime laws and customs used throughout most of the western Mediterranean. Conquered by

Figure 11.5 View of the Mediterranean from the hill road between Amalfi and Ravello. Source: Courtesy of Scarlett Freund.

Figure 11.6 View of Amalfi from the Mediterranean Sea. Source: Courtesy of Scarlett Freund.

the Pisans, the city was destroyed by a tsunami in 1343, relegating the town to a minor role in seafaring and politics to this day.

It is in Amalfi's beautiful cathedral and its multivalent architectural and decorative themes that one may capture the importance of the town from the eleventh to the thirteenth century before the tragic tsunami hit the city. The cathedral's location, rising from the central square of the town up long and steep stairways, its evocation of Byzantine, Norman, and other styles, plus the objects, chapels, and devotions are a historical roadmap to Amalfi's long history. The cathedral's origins go as far back as the ninth century, when the first basilica was built in the Arab-Norman-Byzantine style we have already seen in Palermo and elsewhere throughout the western Mediterranean. According to tradition, the cathedral became the repository of an important relic, the body of Saint Andrew. Pillaged from Constantinople in the aftermath of the sacking of the city during the Fourth Crusade (1204), the relic served as a centerpiece for the continuous rebuilding of the church. Throughout the centuries new architectural features were added that did not occlude the old design. The result is quite striking, not just because of the perspective (one looks at the church from below as it rises with its distinctive striped Arab-Norman features and its impressive campanile), but also because of the intense blue skies that serve as a frame for the building.

The cathedral is a complex architectural site that has been the subject of many learned studies. Here, I would like to emphasize two of the elements that provide clues to the history of the town and its place in the overall history of the western Mediterranean. Beyond the façade of the cathedral (rebuilt in the nineteenth century), the cloister, or so-called "cloister of paradise," is a thirteenth-century jewel, reminding the viewer of the importance of Islamic culture throughout the Mediterranean, but also that the combination of styles

Figure 11.7 Façade of the Cathedral of Amalfi. Source: Courtesy of Scarlett Freund.

(Romanesque, Norman, Byzantine, Islamic) can create new architectural vocabularies of beauty. The second feature may not have the architectural heritage of the first, but it is nonetheless quite impressive. The Spanish chapel in the crypt of the cathedral has an elaborate baroque ceiling and a shrine where the body of Saint Andrew is supposed to rest. Endowed by Philip III of Spain and built in the 1600s, the chapel adds one more architectural style to the mélange of styles present in the medieval cathedral. It is also a testimony to the presence of Spain in the western Mediterranean and its ties to Italy (and to Amalfi) during the early modern period. But it is time now to return to other areas of the Mediterranean.

Sète

Much larger than Vernazza and other towns around the Mediterranean, Sète (known as Cette until the nineteenth century), on the Mediterranean coast of the southern French region of Languedoc-Roussillon, has a long history associated with the sea. Today it is connected to Tangier by a ferry, and it is one of the ports that witnesses migrants returning home during their summer vacation. For reasons that are unclear, Sète also had a large Italian migration. From the end of the early modern period, and coinciding with Louis XIV and his *intendant* Colbert's desire to establish a presence in the Mediterranean, Sète has officially existed as an established commune. The town, originally an island and then turned by human labor into part of the mainland, was linked to the rest of France by the Rhône canal, an extension of the ancient Canal du Midi built in the seventeenth century. Today, it has a well-protected port, located between the sea and a salt lagoon, the Thau Lagoon (*Étang de Thau*), not unlike the one that separates Tunis from La Goulette. A solitary mountain, Mont St-Clair, dominates the landscape. In the Late Middle Ages and early modern period it was a place of refuge for corsairs and other people in trouble with the law.

Although Sète, and the area around the present town, has been inhabited since pre-history, there is little textual evidence for its pre-modern history. Neolithic ruins and Greek and Roman remains attest to its strategic location and ancient origins. The town is, after all, one of the few good ports on the French Mediterranean coast west of Marseille. Thus, Sète (or Cette) had Roman and later early medieval settlements. Since most western Mediterranean sailing was usually, and remains, coastal sailing, Sète was a convenient stop for sailors making their way between Sicily, Naples, Genoa, or Marseille and ports west of the town, such as Barcelona.

Politically, Sète was fully a part of the Languedoc region's perennial conflicts. The latter was a turbulent area in the Middle Ages and contested by its lords, the counts of Toulouse, the French Crown (after the beginning of the thirteenth century), and the Crown of Aragon, or, to be more exact, the kings of Majorca, ruling from Perpignan (see Chapter 3). Sète was an attractive location to local rulers, not only because of its harbor and access to the sea, but also because its topographical features created an important point of reference for Mediterranean voyagers. Mont St-Clair was an easy reference point for vessels sailing past the troublesome Gulf of Lion and, thus, an important landmark for navigation. One of the captains making a "protest against the sea" in the nineteenth century refers to Sète (or Mont St-Clair) as an easy reference to locate his position at sea (see Chapter 2).

Today, besides being an active port, Sète attracts tourists to its August feasts of marine jousting, a re-creation – most likely a mostly invented medieval tradition – of supposedly medieval jousting at sea. The town also attracts tourists avoiding the more expensive towns and beaches of the French Riviera. It has also, as do most coastal towns, a growing immigrant population. But the scant information about Sète summarized here reflect that it is a Mediterranean port that differs markedly from the experiences of Tunis, Marseille, Palermo, or Barcelona. Unlike those leading Mediterranean towns, none of Sète's complex ancient and medieval history can be unearthed. None of the dynamics associated with sites of encounter, where different religious and ethnic groups commingled, can be fully documented, although there is evidence that there was substantial heretical activity in the area in the twelfth century and early thirteenth. Even today, while its beaches attract many tourists, a good number of them from France itself, Sète remains a fishing port. I lingered in a bar by the port many years ago as I traveled from Arles to Barcelona. The bay was filled with small vessels, a good number of them not fancy pleasure boats but fishing ones. And then, of course, Sète was the birthplace of some important French literary and artistic figures, most significantly, Paul Valéry.

And yet, Sète, like other towns and islands in this section, was part of the network of maritime locations that connected different areas of the Mediterranean into one variegated whole. Below we will have the opportunity to examine other southern French towns left behind and away from the sea by the silting of the marshes around them, but now we should sail across the western Mediterranean to the coast of North Africa.[6]

Oran

Unlike those towns and islands that we have toured above, Oran, although not fully a site of encounter such as Sicily or Palermo, was (and is) a location "betwixt and between." Its long history, dating from the tenth century, reflects the successive passage of different people and accompanying religious and political contestations. Yet, because it lacked throughout the Middle Ages and the early modern period an adequate port for large ships, and because, while facing the Mediterranean on the north side of the town, expansion southward was, and is, limited by a large lagoon – it is yet another of these Mediterranean shore locations with a lagoon either separating it from the sea, as is the case with Tunis, or blocking access to the interior, as is the case with Sète – Oran developed in ways quite different from those of other North African and Western European Mediterranean cities. Today's good port facilities exist because of modern-built and very substantial jetties that protect the piers along the city's seafront from unexpected weather from the Mediterranean. These protecting sea walls, a noticeable feature of Oran's maritime structures, allow for large facilities and the mooring of large ships. In the sixteenth century, as can be seen on a map from the period, the Spanish fortifications and remaking of the city's port facilities, as well as the building close by of the fort of Mers el-Kébir (today an Algerian naval base also made possible by an imposing sea wall), created a narrow and protected channel. It led from the Mediterranean to the old heart of the city or Vieux Port, now no longer on the waterfront.

Located on the coast of modern-day Algeria, west of the city of Algiers, and close to the border with Morocco, Oran is the second-largest city in the country with almost three quarters of a million people. It is fairly close to inland Tlemcen, the center for one of the North African political realms in the Middle Ages, to which it had served as a commercial link and outlet to western Mediterranean trade and as a base for raids along the shores of the Middle Sea. Today, ferries ply the sea between Oran and ports in Iberia, such as Almería and Alicante. But Oran is also well within the reach of both Cartagena and the area around Granada and its main port, Málaga, something that, to a large extent, shaped the history of the city in the Late Middle Ages and the early modern period. Its is indeed this enduring connection to the Spanish coast, once part of the sprawling North African empires (mostly Almoravid and Almohad), and Oran's long history as a Spanish military enclave in North Africa that serve as reminders of the political and strategic "connectivity" of the western Mediterranean, regardless of political and religious circumstances.

Throughout its more than a millennium of history, Oran has seen and suffered many different phases of occupation. The traditional narrative is that the city was founded or re-founded by Andalusi traders, establishing a foothold in North Africa for the profitable trade with al-Andalus. As such, the city changed hands in the strife that was part and parcel of North Africa's political life. It was, at first, part of the expansive Spanish Umayyad Caliphate or

Caliphate of Córdoba. Then it came into the possession of the rising Fatimids in Egypt and Ifriqiya (or the region of Tunis). It changed hands with the rise of the Almoravids, a Berber dynasty that controlled most of the coast of North Africa west of Oran in the eleventh century. These new masters brought with them not only more exacting forms of religious practices and spirituality, but also the widespread use of Berber as an administrative language. Because of the Almoravid control of most of southern or Mediterranean Spain, Oran played a significant role in providing access to Spanish western Mediterranean ports besides that given by North African sea outlets at Tangier (on the Atlantic), Tétouan (close to the Straits of Gibraltar on the Mediterranean side), and modern Béjaïa, or, as it was known in the Middle Ages, Bougie (east of Oran).

By the mid-twelfth century, Oran had come under the Almohads. As we have seen in other chapters, the Almohads were a dynamic and expansive power. Not only did they hold control of most of the western Mediterranean until the early thirteenth century, they also supported the building of significant religious and secular buildings, as we have seen in the example of Seville (see Figure 11.7). The great Ibn Khaldûn, though praising Oran in some sections of *The Muqaddimah*, nonetheless establishes a very clear hierarchy of Maghribi cities in the Middle Ages. Fez was the standard by which other cities were to be judged. Tlemcen came next, with Oran and Bougie afterwards. As he writes: "This can be exemplified by the condition of the poor and the beggars. A beggar in Fez is better off than a beggar in Tlemcen or Oran."[7]

The demise of the Almohads led to an almost 300-year interlude in which Oran came under the power of the kings ruling from Tlemcen. During the Late Middle Ages, Oran benefitted from growing commercial ties to Italy. It also had a substantial Jewish community engaged in trade and as interlocutors between North African and European commerce. The significant date in Oran's history, however, is its capture by Spanish forces in 1509. As were other Spanish military outposts in North Africa, such as Ceuta, Melilla, and others, Oran was unique. Its institutions, population, and administrative practices differed radically from those of the metropole and provide significant evidence of what European presence on the coast of North Africa was like previous to the great period of European colonization in the late nineteenth century.

Oran and other Spanish maritime bases on the Mediterranean shores of North Africa were a poor substitute for the grand plan of the Catholic Monarchs, Ferdinand and Isabella, in the late fifteenth and early sixteenth century. Their grand strategy was to conquer most of the North African coast and make the western Mediterranean into a Spanish lake. Those plans, as we have seen, were wrecked by religious wars in Europe and by Spain's ultramarine conquests in the New World. Thus, Oran, ruled by the Spaniards from 1509 to 1708 and then again during another short interlude between 1732 and 1792, was, in many respects, a continuation of the Spanish Reconquest and of the successful occupation of Granada in 1492, marking the end of Islamic power in Iberia. But Spanish Oran, though it engaged in alliances or armed conflicts with local powers, never turned into a successful beachhead from which to expand into the interior of Africa or to gain control of the trade routes that linked the Mediterranean coast of North Africa to sub-Saharan markets. Oran, as was the

Figure 11.8 The Almohad-styled minaret of the Pasha Mosque in Oran.
Source: Courtesy of Brian McMorrow.

case with Ceuta and other Spanish enclaves on the Mediterranean coast of North Africa, was a military outpost and organized as a presidio, that is, as a fortified military base used to keep an eye on natives, enemies, and the like. As such, Oran's presidio was replicated in the New World and throughout Spain's imperial possessions. But because of Oran's geographical location, its relative proximity to Spain, and the conflict between North African corsairs and Spain, Oran remains a very interesting case study of institutions and quotidian practices that developed from specific circumstances.

As Yuen-Gen Liang has shown in a superb study of the relationship between noble families and the administration of the Spanish Empire, the captain general of Oran was often a member of the great noble family of Fernández de Córdoba throughout the sixteenth century. Unlike viceroys elsewhere throughout the empire, the captain general of Oran was always someone with vast military expertise and familiarity with frontier warfare and diplomacy.[8] The Spaniards at Oran engaged in the construction of elaborate defense works, fortifications, and walls to protect the city. Yet, Oran was always in a precarious situation. It had to be supplied from Spain and, as Yuen-Gen Liang shows, while sometimes the trip could take only 16 hours of sailing from Cartagena, adverse weather conditions (quite common in the western Mediterranean) could make the voyage endless. Moreover, once the supply ships arrived at Oran, they could not moor at Oran proper but had to land their merchandise at Mers el-Kébir and be taken to the city overland. Oran was not the easiest or most profitable of possessions, but it allowed the Spaniards to keep a watch on the movement of Ottoman and North African corsairs.

There is another way in which Oran was unique. Its vulnerable location during its Spanish period demanded new ways of administering the presidio. As Claire Gilbert, Yuen-Gen Liang, and others have noted, Oran had a pluralistic religious and linguistic society. At a time when the Spanish monarchs had already expelled Jews from most Spanish territories and, through the Inquisition, fiercely monitored the activities of those suspected of conducting Jewish practices in secret, Oran welcomed Jewish exiles and allowed them to live fairly peacefully, to practice their faith openly, and to play a key role in the administrative practices of the city as late as the second half of the seventeenth century. As Claire Gilbert shows in her excellent dissertation (already mentioned in Chapter 7), specific Jewish families, the Cansinos and the Sasportas, almost monopolized the positions of translator (or *trujumán*) and administrator in Oran. They did so with royal sanction and for more than a century. As interlocutors between the Spanish administration and the Muslim (Arabic-speaking) population in Oran and surrounding areas, these Jewish translators (there were some Christian translators as well) served a unique role in support of a Spanish presence on an isolated outpost on the North Africa coast. The Jews remained in Oran until 1669 when they were exiled to Livorno and other European Mediterranean cities. From Livorno, they continued to play, as shown magisterially by Francesca Trivellato, a significant role in western Mediterranean trade.[9]

Many of Oran's Jews, however, would return home, even if not to stay permanently. In 1792, the Ottoman rulers sponsored a renewal of the Jewish presence in the city. The sumptuous Great Synagogue of Oran is a testimony to the community's prosperity until 1962 when the wave of decolonization and the passions and political strife created by the Palestinian question led to the expulsion of Jews from Oran and from all of Algeria. The Great Synagogue of Oran was turned into a mosque, following the old Mediterranean tradition of turning the sacred places of rival religions into your own place of worship. It is proper to note here that many of the Algerian Jews, especially those living on the coast, as opposed to those inhabiting the Sahara, enjoyed the benefits of French citizenship. After the expulsion of 1962, many of the former ended up in France. As noted elsewhere in this book, their exile to France, mostly to Paris, transformed Jewish religiosity in the French capital. Their presence can still be seen in some of the outer arrondissements, such as the 19th and the 20th, as well as in the area around the rue des Rosiers in the Parisian neighborhood of the Marais.

Spanish colonial rule also welcomed Andalusi Muslims returning to North Africa after the fall of Granada and their forced conversion in the early sixteenth century. Oran also became a refuge (even under Spanish rule) for the Moriscos expelled from Spain in the early seventeenth century. It is a paradox that those who were forbidden to practice their religion in Iberia or to speak Arabic would find a new Spanish home in Oran, Melilla, Ceuta, and other small Spanish outposts on the North Africa coast. Beyond Oran's multilingual and religious atmosphere, the city did not generate the kind of cultural products we have seen in Seville, Palermo, and elsewhere. The Jewish and Muslim presence was a factor of Spanish administrative needs and of their attempt to link with Oran's hinterland. Yet, as Spanish power ebbed in Western Europe, so Oran faded. It became a neglected part of the Spanish monarchy. Although the Spanish, after losing the city to the Bey of Algeria (an Ottoman client), made an effort to resettle their colony there, the terrible earthquake of 1790 that devastated the city and its main fortification convinced the Spanish authorities that Oran was a lost cause.

That same year the Ottomans established their rule over the city. For the next 40 years, Oran was under the Bey of Algeria or Ottoman rule. The city recovered most of its vitality, became a capital for the Bey, saw its Jewish community restored, and gained a number of substantial new buildings. These included the Bey Othmane Mosque with its traditional minaret redolent with references to the great Almohad buildings of the twelfth century (see Seville and Tunis). The Ottoman connection allowed Oran what it had never had under Spanish rule: the opportunity to enter fully into the sprawling commercial and cultural networks that joined the eastern Mediterranean, the North African coast, and the African interior. Alas! It did not last long. By 1830, a French invading army had taken Mers el-Kébir, rendering Oran vulnerable to French attacks. The city fell and became part of the French colonial empire until the Algerian revolution in the late 1950s and early 1960s, decolonization, and its eventual independence as one of the most important cities in Algeria.

Under the French, the city's population grew apace, as did a series of French colonial administrative, cultural, and administrative buildings. In that respect, Oran replicates the experiences of Tunis, Algiers, and other French colonial cities in North Africa. The Cathedral of the Sacré Coeur (yet another Sacred Heart!) was consecrated in 1913, and the Great Synagogue opened to worshipers in 1918. Theaters, trams, and other symbols of modernity made Oran one of the hubs of French presence in North Africa. The artificially protected naval base at Mers el-Kébir became one of the most important sites for the French maritime presence in the western Mediterranean. Oran suffered during World War II, surrendering to Allied Forces in 1942. In the 1950s, as the city, Algeria as a whole, and North Africa rose against French colonization, Oran was witness to some of the most violent conflicts between native Algerians, French settlers, the *pieds noirs* resisting Algerian independence, and the French forces. Although the action was set in Algiers and not in Oran, as already mentioned, Gillo Pontecorvo's iconic film *The Battle of Algiers* brilliantly captures the essence of the violent tactics used by the French colonial administration and French settlers in an effort to retain French control over most of North Africa, and by Algerian nationalists in their struggle to gain independence. Oran was also the site of a great demonstration and acts of violence in 1962. That year the leader of the OAS (Organisation de l'armée secrète), Edmond Jouhaud, was arrested. Once free, he torched the port area where thousands of gallons of fuel were stored. The Algerian reaction, also known as the Oran massacre of 1962, brought a swift end to French occupation of the city and of Algeria. After more than 500 years of foreign domination, the city and the country were finally free.

After 1962, Algeria became an independent country. Rich in oil and gas, most of it exported to Europe via the port of Oran, Algeria had seen major upheavals and political strife – some of these violent upheavals coming close to a civil war. Both Oran specifically and Algeria in general had large numbers of settlers even after independence. Oran itself had almost a majority of Spanish descendants (Moriscos) in its population. However, the situation was very different for Oran's Jews. They had prospered in Oran, but, as noted above, were expelled in the wake of the Israeli–Palestinian conflict. For me, Oran has always been a place in the mind. Albert Camus, the great French writer and one of my favorite authors, was born in Oran (Algeria), yet, he was a descendant of *pieds noirs*, and also an opponent of Algeria's independence. He chose the city as the site for his novel *The Plague* (1947), as he chose North Africa and the shores of the Mediterranean for the locale of *The Stranger*. Here, again, we have the conundrum of a great French intellectual, born in North Africa, writing novels that closely capture what it was to live in Oran in the midst of a plague or to question the meaning of life as one gazes on the blue waters of the Middle Sea. Just as Camus's beloved Saint Augustine (another North African) would have done more than a millennium and a half before, Camus would have reflected on the world, God (or in Camus's case, the absence of God), and meaning by the shores of the Mediterranean.[10]

TOWNS OF SILT, SEA, AND LAND

Oran, Vernazza, and other of the islands and towns described here, while not hubs for exchange (though Oran comes close to being in that category), were places with direct access to the coast or to some modicum of trade and had the ability to exploit the resources of the sea. The western Mediterranean shows us, however, a variety of land and seascapes. They yield yet another Mediterranean. Environmental forces transformed the historical development and realities of many of the localities around the Middle Sea. I have already noted how Pisa was left inland by the slow transformation of its surrounding landscape, or how Seville's access to the Atlantic became limited to only small vessels by the early seventeenth century because of the silting of the Guadalquivir River. The enduring impact of long-term ecological transformations altered the very nature of settlements on the shores of the sea and led these communities down very different paths of historical development. Human activity or greed also created communities where none existed before. Here I wish to provide a brief look at three specific communities around the Rhône delta and at the effects that ecology and human efforts have produced. As it approaches the Mediterranean the Rhône fans out. My interest lies in the western part of the Rhône delta, the region of the Camargue itself and the area west of the Camargue from Saintes-Maries-de-la-Mer to La Grande Motte, including Aigues-Mortes.

The Rhône delta is one of the most peculiar ecological niches of the western Mediterranean. Nothing in western North Africa comes close to it, nor can anything similar be found on the western Mediterranean European coast. The Nile delta, though much larger than that of the Rhône, is the only real parallel example for delta societies and economies in the Mediterranean basin, but with some significant differences. The delta of the Nile has long supported important and profitable agricultural production. Moreover, the geographical features of northern Egypt allowed for a great port, that of Alexandria, to flourish. That certainly was not, and it is not, the case in the Camargue. Similar to the Nile delta, the Rhône delta, and above all the region of the Camargue, supports a flora and fauna fairly distinct from areas around it. It is also the location for peculiar towns that constitute yet another different face of the Mediterranean.

From Saintes-Maries-de-la-Mer to La Grande Motte by way of Aigues-Mortes

Saintes-Maries-de-la-Mer, located deep in the heart of the Camargue region and its regional capital, is perhaps the region's most representative town. Close to the sea but not directly on the shore of the Mediterranean, Saintes-Maries-de-la-Mer (a name that dates only from the nineteenth century, even though the town is ancient) is located on the Rhône delta on a marshy and silted area. Lagoons, or *étangs*, so predominant along some coastal areas of the Mediterranean (we have seen them in Tunis, Oran, and elsewhere), dot Saintes-Maries-de-la-Mer's hinterland. The town has barely more than 2,000 inhabitants today, though its population increases to over 50,000 in the summer. Tourism, as is the case throughout most of the western Mediterranean, has mostly replaced millennia-old fishing and herding activities. The symbiotic relationship of shore dwellers with the sea and their unique ecological niche has also been replaced by the artificiality of modern tourism.

Unlike La Grande Motte, which has a very recent provenance, and Aigues-Mortes, which has medieval roots, Saintes-Maries-de-la-Mer's origins hark back to Antiquity – it is mentioned in a fourth-century CE geographical work. Dependent on Arles's ecclesiastical jurisdiction, the village or small town did not play an important historical role. Its development and history remained tied to the ebb and flow first of Roman and later of lordly and ecclesiastical jurisdiction in the area. In many respects, the marshes of the Camargue protected the town somewhat from the turbulence that swept southern France after the demise of Rome. Its awkward relation to the sea and the geographical constraints to direct access to the shore, except for very small boats, also provided some relief from the corsair activities carried out from North African shores against the European coastal towns. In that sense, unlike other great cities on the shores or near the shores of the western sea, Saintes-Maries-de-la-Mer shared its centuries of relative obscurity and isolation with other small localities, such as the villages along the Cinque Terre. Like them, however, Saintes-Maries-de-la-Mer and most of these remote and geographically fairly inaccessible villages and towns have become magnets for modern tourism precisely because of their quaint buildings and lifestyle preserved by centuries of neglect. Saintes-Maries-de-la-Mer does, however, have other traditions that make it distinct from the many other villages on the shores of the Mediterranean.

For many years now, the Roma people have undertaken a pilgrimage to worship the dark image of Sainte Sara (Sarah) kept in the ninth- or tenth-century central church of Sainte Marie de la Mer (the name, as noted earlier, was changed in the nineteenth century, as was that of the town, to the designation of Saintes Maries, or three Maries). Many legends surround the image of Sainte Sara and local lore traces the pilgrimage of the Roma people to the location on May 24–25 back to the Middle Ages. This is rather doubtful since the Roma or Gypsies did not arrive in Western Europe until probably the fourteenth or fifteenth century, and only as small waves of immigrants from India, Eastern Europe, and the eastern Mediterranean. Since Saintes-Maries-de-la-Mer was also a stopping point for pilgrims on the well-established route from Arles, Saint-Gilles, and other points in southern France to Saint James the Apostle's tomb at Santiago de Compostela, one can easily see the medieval origins of these pilgrimages. Whatever the origins of the Roma pilgrimage and the worship of Sainte Sara were, the reality is that in the modern period and, even more so today, thousands upon thousands of Roma people descend upon Saintes-Maries-de-la-Mer every year. Gypsy caravans cover the countryside. Different Roma dialects are heard on the crowded streets of the town, music is everywhere, as are songs – Spanish, French, Eastern European – and haunting Gypsy music: what in Spain is called the *cante jondo* or deep song. Those plaintive melodies are vivid reminders of the persecutions and massacres that the Gypsies have experienced, and still experience, through their stateless lives in Europe. The western Mediterranean was also (and remains) a place of celebrations – and those of May 24–25 in the Camargue are unforgettable experiences – but the Mediterranean has been, and still is, a place of persecution, discrimination, and death.[11]

Aigues-Mortes. Although not unlike almost every town on the western Mediterranean that claims ancient origins, Aigues-Mortes (Dead Waters) was neither very ancient, like Saintes-Maries-de-la-Mer, or very modern, like la Grande Motte. Because the medieval French monarchy did not control Marseille or any of the other significant Mediterranean harbors on what is today the coast of France until the sixteenth century, Aigues-Mortes is, in many respects, the relic of the misplaced and failed attempts by the French kings to built a port on the Mediterranean as the launching point for Louis IX's (Saint Louis, 1226–1270) unfortunate Crusades and later expedition to North Africa.

Located west of Saintes-Maries-de-la-Mer and barely over 50 miles from Marseille, Aigues-Mortes is a living testimony to the obvious constraints that geography and topography presented to many of the towns on the shores of the western Mediterranean. Its history, from the Middle Ages onward, has been a struggle between the desire to have direct access to the sea, a desire often thwarted by the silting of the canals that led to the sea, and ecological constraints. It is not as if Aigues-Mortes had been, or is now, completely isolated and removed from maritime access to the Mediterranean. The problem has been that the marshy area and the silting of the canals and waterways that led to the shore have always deeply impacted the history of the town. Today a branch of the Rhône canal connects the town to Sète, but the canal is neither deep nor wide enough to allow anything other than small vessels. As was the case for settlements in the main Camargue region slightly to the east of Aigues-Mortes, lagoons, marshes, and canals surround and traverse the town.

Once connected to the sea directly by a port at Le Grau-du-Roi (the only settlement and usable harbor in the Gard district directly fronting the sea), Aigues-Mortes, notwithstanding its small population (barely over 2,000 inhabitants), remains an impressive place, redolent of its medieval connections and the tragedy of the town's many efforts to reach the sea. It sits alone on the plain and marshes of La Petite Camargue. No settlements are visible outside its well-preserved medieval walls. It is built almost on a square pattern with its symmetrical gates leading into the center of the town. When I visited in 2005, it had few if any tourists. Being there felt almost as if one was walking back in time to a different and less complicated age. That different age was the thirteenth century, when, as already noted, Aigues-Mortes was rebuilt to fit the strategic and pious needs of the French king, Louis IX. As William C. Jordan showed magisterially many years ago, building Aigues-Mortes as a French royal port, granting the only access to the Mediterranean, and as a launching point for Louis IX's crusades in 1248 and 1270, required a great deal more than constructing channels or walls.[12]

Thus, Aigues-Mortes's development and subsequent history depended on a series of strategic factors that yielded specific outcomes and that shaped the future history of the town itself and the region. Because of Louis IX's desires to be independent from Italian naval forces, his conflict and rivalry with the kings of the Crown of Aragon and the lords of nearby Montpellier, and his inability to access Marseille (not part of the French realms until the second half of the fifteenth century), the saintly king desperately wished to build a French port on the Mediterranean. This meant, as Jordan has described it, "restructuring the trade in and around Aigues-Mortes." A far more important effort was that of securing a flow of supplies for his armies in 1248 and 1270. Everything, from wood to food supplies and even salt, had to come from outside. The rights to the town and to the lands surrounding the town had to be purchased. Local loyalties had to be gained through tax rebates and fiscal exemptions. Thus, medieval Aigues-Mortes was born out of the exigencies of economic factors and the politics of sanctity. Yet, Louis IX's great crusading plans came to naught. As has been seen in the discussion of Tunis in Chapter 10, his second crusade into North Africa, launched from Aigues-Mortes in 1270, ended in the king's death abroad. Aigues-Mortes was left behind by the silting canals, its population meager, until all of its commercial importance disappeared with the integration of the great port of Marseille into the French kingdom. It remains a testimony to a bygone era, a reflection of the failed struggle of men against the imperatives of geography and ecology. It is a place worth visiting for the portrait that it provides of the world as it may have been centuries ago and of the possible lived experiences of a Mediterranean settlement.

La Grande Motte. If Saintes-Maries-de-la-Mer and Aigues-Mortes invite us to reflect on a long bygone past, La Grande Motte, a planned beach community built between the early 1960s and the second half of the 1970s along modern architectural lines, invites us to think of what modern architecture and homogeneous urban landscapes mean to the visitor and to permanent residents. For reasons having to do with the possibility of obtaining good and not too expensive accommodation, I, together with 36 undergraduates, spent five days in La Grande Motte in the summer of 2005. We used it as our base to explore medieval sites in Occitania, including Aigues-Mortes, Saint-Gilles, and Arles. It was the height of the summer and the beaches and restaurants were often crowded. While La Grande Motte has a permanent population of around 10,000 people, during the summer as many as 2 million visitors come to the town.

A wise reader commented on what may be regarded as an error in including La Grande Motte, so ugly and pedestrian, in this chapter. And it is precisely because it is perhaps so unattractive that it is important to note that the Mediterranean also has such places. There is nothing here that reminds one of the vacation spots and towns on the Côte d'Azur or the Italian Riviera, with their quaint buildings that reach back into the past and exist in conversation with the new. Nice is a very good example of this type of town, with its ancient fishermen's village and the fashionable nineteenth-century buildings on the Promenade des Anglais, as is Sestri Levante, with its old part situated adjacent to the new town. Yet, while these locations attract an international clientele, most of the summer visitors to La Grande Motte are French and, overwhelmingly, from the ranks of the lower bourgeoisie. What is striking in such an invented and artificial town is the modernist architecture. There are no references to the past, and there is no historicizing, even fictitious, of the region. I am quite fond of modern architecture, but La Grande Motte shares with La Défense (across the Seine from Paris on the western border of the city) the same kind of cold and sterile feeling. With few aesthetic or architectural attributes, it is a town firmly grounded on its functionality, that is, how to accommodate and feed as many people as possible at low cost and for the greatest profit. And yet, to be frank, my students loved the beach and the placid family-oriented climate of the town, while it still had enough nightspots and clubs to provide a frisson for the young. In many respects, La Grande Motte is not unique, reminding us of many new communities built by the sea along the Costa Brava or the Costa del Sol. Many of them are abodes for the rich, others, even more modest than La Grande Motte, for low-income retirees from Nordic climes.

CONCLUSION

We have journeyed around the western Mediterranean looking at some of its islands and small towns (with the exception of Oran). The emphasis here has been on the European shores. This choice is due in part to the paucity of islands off the coast of Africa, as opposed to the many archipelagos that dot the coasts of Italy and France. Unlike Chapter 10, where I explore sites of encounter and/or places of convergence, these locations – though some of them witnessed large influxes of immigrants and violent conflict, such as the massacre of Italian immigrants in Aigues-Mortes in the very late nineteenth century – represent, as noted above, yet another face of the Mediterranean. They range from small isolated islands like Montecristo, turned by new ecological awareness into natural preserves, to modern towns built for the specific purpose of serving the needs of modern tourism, as exemplified by La Grande Motte, a kind of lesser Cancun of Europe.

Some of the towns chosen here, such as Oran, had checkered histories of colonial domination, or had diverse populations of Jews, Christians, and Muslims that commingled to serve the needs of foreign masters, whether Spanish or French. Yet, although Oran shared many of the conditions for a site of encounter so easily discernable in Palermo, Tunis, or Seville, no real new dynamic cultural products emerged from the experiences of almost 300 years of Spanish occupation. In the end, what the brief and impressionistic portraits of these locations tell us about the western Mediterranean concerns the diversity of lived experiences by the side of the sea. These examples also tell us about the ecological niches – small areas, such as the Camargue and the entire Rhône delta, where different social and economic patterns emerged over time, making the writing of a total history of the area impossible and raising significant methodological questions as to how to write a history of the whole sea, as opposed to a series of vignettes.

If, as Marc Bloch is supposed to have said, the history of the Middle Ages is the history of localities, then the history of the western Mediterranean is also the history of all the myriad small places (as Richard Kagan argued), inhabited by very few people who, nonetheless, are as representative of the Mediterranean as are the citizens of Marseille or Barcelona. Thus, here I have sought to capture briefly the "small" histories of places – an idea for which I am, once again, most grateful to Richard Kagan – that may not mean much to the modern reader but which were and are, for those who lived and live there, the centers of a world that revolved (and revolves) around a blue sea. They were and are places of memory and longing, such as Oran was for Camus, that have endured the passing of years, the silting of canals, and even, as is the case of the island of Montecristo, the absence of people and the presence of rats.

NOTES

1 There is a vast literature on the Tuscan Archipelago's botanical and geological history, but, with the exception of Elba, the history of the small islands, including Montecristo, has to be garnered from a variety of sources, often guide books and

Italian history surveys. See Averil Mackenzie-Grieve, *Aspects of Elba and the Other Islands of the Tuscan Archipelago* (London: Jonathan Cape, 1964). Also see Sylvie Hogg *Frommer's Italian Islands* (Hoboken, NJ: Wiley, 2011); chapter 7 deals with the Tuscan Archipelago with two pages of description of Montecristo.

2   Philippe Gourdin, *Tabarka: histoire et archéologie d'un préside espagnol et d'un comptoir génois en terre africaine (XVe–XVIIIe siècle)*, with a contribution by Monique Longerstay (Rome: Institut National du Patrimoine de Tunis: Ecole Française de Rome, 2008).

3   Pietro Marongiu, *Teoria e storia del banditismo sociale in Sardegna* (Cagliari: Edizione Della Torre, 1981). There is an abundant bibliography on Sardinia's different histories; see, for example, *Storia dei Sardi e della Sardegna*, ed. Massimo Guidetti, 3 vols (Milan: Jaca, 1987 and 1988). Also Geoffrey Symcox, *Victor Amadeus II: Absolutism in the Savoyard State, 1675–1730* (Berkeley: University of California Press, 1983).

4   Maya Maskarinec, *Building Rome Saint by Saint in the Early Middle Ages* (Philadelphia: University of Pennsylvania Press, 2017).

5   Elena Manara, *S. Margherita di Vernazza: una chiesa, un borgo, una storia* (Genova: Edizioni Culturali Internazionali Genova, 1990).

6   Jean Sagnes, *Histoire de Sète* (Toulouse: private printing, 1987); Jean Rieucau, *Les gens de mer: Sète en Languedoc* (Paris: L'Harmattan, 1990).

7   Ibn Khaldûn, *The Muqaddimah. An Introduction to History*, trans. Franz Rosenthal (Princeton: Princeton University Press, 1989), 274–275.

8   Yuen-Gen Liang, *Family and Empire. The Fernández de Córdoba and the Spanish Realm* (Philadelphia: University of California Press, 2011), 139–170.

9   See the brilliant books by Jean-Frédérick Schaub, *Les juifs du roi d'Espagne* (Paris: Hachette, 1999), and Francesca Trivellato, *The Familiarity of Strangers: The Sephardic Diaspora, Livorno, and Cross-Cultural Trade in the Early Modern Period* (New Haven: Yale University Press, 2009).

10 See in general Julia Clancy-Smith, ed., *North Africa, Islam and the Mediterranean World: From the Almoravids to the Algerian War* (London: Frank Cass Publications, 2001).

11 Eric Wiley, "Romani Performance and Heritage Tourism: The Pilgrimage of the Gypsies at Les Saintes-Maries-de-la-Mer," *The Drama Review*, 49, 2 (2005), 135–158.

12 William C. Jordan, "Supplying Aigues-Mortes for the Crusade of 1248: The Problem of Restructuring Trade," in William C. Jordan, Bruce McNab, and Teofilo F. Ruiz, eds. *Order and Innovation in the Middle Ages. Essays in Honor of Joseph R. Strayer* (Princeton: Princeton University Press, 1976), 165–172. For a bibliography of works related to Aigues-Mortes and the restructuring of trade, see Jordan, notes to chapter 11 in *Order and Innovation in the Middle Ages*. Above all, see Augustin Fliche, *Aigues Mortes et St. Gilles*, 2nd ed. (Paris, 1950).

[12] EPILOGUE: THE WESTERN MEDITERRANEAN AND THE WORLD

As I attempt to bring to a conclusion our long journey across the western Mediterranean, I would like to provide two different vignettes of the western sea at specific moments in time. Throughout most of its long history, the Mediterranean served as a center for western societies. Its decline, signaled by the fall of Rome in the West (and the shift to northern Frankish lands as the center of European civilization), was soon remedied by the rise of Mediterranean commerce led by Genoa and by the slow withdrawal of Islam from the northern shores of the western sea. If this book is intended to be a vision of the western Mediterranean through the lens of world history and to assess the place of the sea in the development of a global society, there are two specific developments that are crucial to our understanding of the sea and its links to other parts of the world.

The first is that extended moment in time when political turmoil in Italy and elsewhere in the western Mediterranean led to the opening of the Atlantic at the end of the Middle Ages and throughout the early modern period. That led to the eventual demise of the western Mediterranean as central to European and Islamic civilizations. Yet, this demise in the face of Atlantic and Asian expansion also led to the transmission of Mediterranean culture(s), politics, religions, and languages throughout the known world. The second moment has been underway for the last few years and is, at the writing of this book, reaching unprecedented centrality in the history of the contemporary world. Propelled by climatic changes, food and water crises, and political strife, millions of people are on the move, seeking refuge in Europe. The Mediterranean has become the most important site for the migration crisis. Once again, the great human tragedy of immigration – a topic that has underlain most of this book – is played again with the Mediterranean as a whole (not just its western part) as the setting for these tragic events. The outcome of this great crisis lies in the future. Historians are notoriously bad forecasters of the future, but everything seems to indicate that the outcome will not be a rosy one. Below I seek to draw a portrait

The Western Mediterranean and the World: 400 CE to the Present, First Edition. Teofilo F. Ruiz.
© 2018 John Wiley & Sons, Ltd. Published 2018 by John Wiley & Sons, Ltd.

of these two periods in which the Middle Sea lost its centrality and then regained it, not necessarily for benign reasons.

THE MEDITERRANEAN, THE ATLANTIC, AND THE WORLD

Several times in the course of this book I have described the western Mediterranean today as a sea teeming with luxury cruises and pleasure yachts. Although the Suez Canal does not accommodate those very large tankers and container ships that now rule the world's oceans, the reality is that seafaring still has a home in the waters of the western Mediterranean. Anyone sailing from the Atlantic into the Middle Sea through the Straits of Gibraltar will notice the heavy traffic going in both directions. Ports such as Livorno, Civitavecchia, La Spezia, Marseille, Genoa, Barcelona, Tunis, and others are crowded with ships, large and small, that carry in their holds products from every corner of the world. Smaller ships go out to fish daily from small coves and artificial ports in locations such as the towns of the Cinque Terre, Sète, Rosas, and other small settlements on both shores of the western sea, as they have done since time immemorial. Trade still moves between the great Mediterranean ports. But the Mediterranean no longer enjoys the economic and strategic role that it once did in western history in relation to the world at large.

As we come to the end of this long journey in the waters of the western Mediterranean and the lands that encircle the sea, it may be a good idea to pinpoint the moment in which, as outlined in the introductory paragraphs of this chapter, the western Mediterranean, a sea that had held a central place in the affairs of the known world or certainly in western historiography, ceased to do so. From the rise of Carthaginian trade and settlements (or going back even earlier to the Phoenicians and Greeks) on the shores of North Africa, Iberia, and Sicily to the long Roman control of both shores of the sea, the Islamic conquests, again on both shores of the sea, and finally the rise of Italian polities and the Crown of Aragon, the western Mediterranean had been linked to a wider world. Trade routes connected it to sub-Saharan Africa. Other such routes reached into Northern Europe, while goods coming from Asia and the Spice Islands reached the shores of the western Mediterranean through the expansive trade routes that via the Silk Road and the Indian Ocean connected the Far East with the eastern Mediterranean and beyond. Surely, China, India, Mali, the Mongol Empire, and other polities had similar claims to primacy, but in the West, the civilizations that rose and were in turn replaced by others were centered on the Mediterranean.

To when, then, may one trace that moment in time when the Mediterranean lost its centrality in the western world? When did the western Mediterranean become connected to larger global networks of trade and politics not as the main player but as a secondary one? The Mediterranean has, of course, always been a place of "connectivity" – to use, once again, Horden and Purcell's term. That connectivity always transcended the shores of the Mediterranean.

Whether linked to sub-Saharan Africa by ancient caravans traversing the desert, ports in North Africa, and sailors crossing the sea to European shores, or to the East by the Silk Road and the maritime routes that crisscrossed the Indian Ocean, the western Mediterranean has always been open to a wider world. Notwithstanding Henri Pirenne's arguments for the shift of the Mediterranean's commercial and political hegemony to Northern Europe, the Middle Sea remained a site of encounter between different religions, commercial networks, and cultures. While it remains so into the twenty-first century, it does so now as part of a global world, the centers of which are in America, Northern Europe, and Asia.

By the end of the Middle Ages, the time was coming when the western Mediterranean would languish badly compared to the dynamic commercial, cultural, and political life of new Northern European powers – England, France, the Dutch Republic, and others. These polities were growing ever more powerful. Their economic and political power flourished along the shores of different oceans (the Atlantic, the Pacific, the Indian Ocean). The hegemony of Northern Europe can be dated to the early modern period, and the consequences of the rise of these new colonial powers still shape the history of the Mediterranean today. From having been the epicenter for commercial innovation, banking, and cultural production throughout the Middle Ages and into the early modern period, the European western Mediterranean has become a destination for others.

First, it became (above all, Italy) a significant stage in the Grand Tour. Then it became the locale for romantic musings or the orientalizing of the Mediterranean. Nowadays, millions of tourists descend upon Mediterranean shores in search of pleasure, shopping, and, yes, even a glimpse at the enduring monuments of Mediterranean culture. This applies as much to Florence and Cinque Terre as it does to Fez and Marrakesh. So, once again, when did the Mediterranean become marginal in the large-scale development of rising European powers? Paradoxically, in terms of the world economy, the western Mediterranean was diminished, its light burning less bright, with the dawn of a new age – the age of exploration.

THE DEMISE OF THE WESTERN MEDITERRANEAN IN THE AGE OF EXPLORATION

Christopher Columbus's voyage across the Ocean Sea (the Atlantic) and his unexpected encounter with a New World in 1492 – he was engaged in pursuing the ill-conceived idea that he could easily reach the Indies by sailing westward – has long been considered one of the chronological watersheds in Western European and world history. A traditional historiography has focused on 1492, together with the fall of Constantinople in 1453 and the invention of printing in the West in the 1460s, as historical turning points, dividing the Middle Ages from the early modern period. Not unlike the claim made in Henri Pirenne's famous thesis on the shift from the Mediterranean world to Frankish Northern Europe as the new center of

Western European civilization, Columbus's momentous voyage has been seen as signaling the demise of the Mediterranean and the rise of the Atlantic in world history. Nothing, of course, could be farther from the truth.[1]

Commercial exchanges and the movement of people between the Atlantic coast (Spain, Africa, and Northern Europe) and the Mediterranean, a movement that flowed in both directions, have had a long history, pre-dating Columbus by more than a millennium. The encounter between the Old World and the New in 1492 and in the decades following Columbus's landing in the Caribbean – in Mexico in the 1520s and Peru in the 1530s – did not lead directly or immediately to the collapse of the Mediterranean as one of the foci of western history; nor were the opening of Atlantic trade or the establishment of far-flung Portuguese and Spanish imperial ventures beyond the Ocean Sea the sole causes of the geopolitical reshaping of the western world. After all, bankers in Mediterranean Italy benefitted immensely from these new opportunities, as did scholars in the service of the Spanish monarchy. In this concluding chapter, I seek to illustrate briefly the nature of Mediterranean-Atlantic contacts and to explore the changing relationships between these two intertwined worlds. In fact, Claire Gilbert has already pointed out the importance of this Atlantic Mediterranean, exemplified, most of all, by the diplomatic and commercial exchanges between Morocco (the only North African kingdom with an Atlantic coastline) and the Iberian Peninsula in the early modern period.[2] Below I briefly sketch the prelude to this flow from the Mediterranean to the Atlantic and, before turning to the issue of migration, give a few additional concluding comments on the nature and transformation of these relations. My emphasis here is on the late medieval and very early modern period, when voyages of exploration increased and slowly but inexorably brought about changes in the western parts of the Middle Sea, leading, in turn, to the waning of Mediterranean societies and the rise of Atlantic ones.

PRELUDES

As we have already seen in an earlier chapter, toward the conclusion of Alexander Dumas's *The Count of Monte Cristo*, one of the quintessential novels about the Mediterranean, Dumas describes the sea as a "huge lake that extends from Gibraltar to the Dardanelles and from Tunis to Venice."[3] Although the Mediterranean is certainly not a lake, Dumas's words convey the author's sense of, and his characters' intimacy with, the Middle Sea. They also express how the Mediterranean linked together all the lands bounding the sea on the four points of the compass. That sense of the distinctiveness of the Mediterranean, clearly present in Dumas's novel, has also been one of the many issues animating long and vigorous historiographical debates about the Mediterranean since the publication of Fernand Braudel's paradigmatic *The Mediterranean* in 1949. It is important to note that, ironically, Braudel chose to study the Mediterranean precisely in the period in which the Middle Sea was, as I argue here, losing its relevance.[4]

Of these many historiographical questions or problems, I would like to focus briefly on just one specific issue: What were the historical reasons for the demise of the Mediterranean as the center of European economic, cultural, and political life and the rise of the Atlantic world in the Late Middle Ages and early modern period? Although there were several factors leading to this shift, the process began in earnest with the Portuguese and Castilian maritime incursions into the Atlantic from the fourteenth century onwards. These were soon followed by the European exploration of, and settlements in, Africa, Asia, and the New World, over the next two centuries. There were, of course, many earlier precedents. The connections between the two seas are as old as mankind itself. Yet, even if from the eighteenth century onwards a neglected Mediterranean was reinserted into a growing world economy as new seafaring technologies allowed for easier sailing in and out of the Middle Sea (see Chapter 9), these increased links between the Mediterranean and the Atlantic did not mark a return to a hegemonic role for the former. In the Late Middle Ages and in early modern Europe, the fate of the Middle Sea was fixed on particular historical paths.

THE MEDITERRANEAN AND THE ATLANTIC

If Dumas imagined the Mediterranean as a lake, his vision was based upon very real geographical factors. Nowadays, the Straits of Gibraltar do not offer the obstacles to navigation that they did until very recently. Huge cruise and cargo ships, propelled by powerful engines, sail in and out of the Mediterranean without great difficulty. Corsairs do not wait on either the European or the North African coast to pounce on vessels slowly laboring from the Mediterranean into the Atlantic. Travelers sailing into the Mediterranean – as I did a few years ago – barely notice the transition from one body of water and the next. For earlier voyagers it was not so simple. As we have seen (Chapter 2), sailing out of the Mediterranean into the Atlantic has never been easy. An upper current flowing from the Atlantic inwards (on top of another current which flows outwards) often made the transit from the Mediterranean to the Atlantic an ordeal. As already mentioned, even as late as the nineteenth century, ships waited for favorable winds in Algeciras for weeks and months.[5] Storms were also quite common in the area of the Straits, as the "protests against the sea" accumulated at the Archive of the Crown of Aragon for the late eighteenth and early nineteenth century dramatically show (see Chapter 2). In addition, in the Middle Ages and as late as the nineteenth century, corsair activity operating from both Muslim and Christian ports near the Straits added to the difficulties in navigating out of the Mediterranean into the Atlantic or vice versa. And corsair activity was not limited to the strategic entrance at Gibraltar; corsairs sailed from North African and European Atlantic ports hoping to make a profit around the troubled Atlantic waters off the Straits as well.

Mediterranean-Atlantic Contacts before 1300

In spite of the difficulties of sailing out of the Mediterranean, there has long been a history of contact between the two seas. Phoenicians, Greeks, and

Romans ventured out of the Mediterranean into the Atlantic despite the difficulties created by adverse currents and winds. Phoenician and Carthaginian merchants and sailors sought new markets for their expansive commercial empires, settling a Phoenician/Carthaginian colony at Mogador (a Portuguese name given in the sixteenth century to the settlement now known by its Berber name of Essaouira) on Africa's Atlantic coast. From there the Carthaginians probably explored the Canary Islands, the Fortunate Islands of Antiquity, and the coast of Africa. The voyages of Hanno the Navigator (king of Carthage ca. fifth century BCE) along the coast of Africa show the extensive knowledge that Carthaginians and Greeks had of the Atlantic. Phoenician and Carthaginian sailors also traveled along the Atlantic coast of Iberia before the Common Era. The Greeks – commercial rivals and eventual successors to the Phoenicians, and who also translated the account of Hanno's voyages – also ventured into the Atlantic. This was so in spite of the designation of the Straits of Gibraltar as the Pillars of Hercules's, marking the end of the world.[6] For the Greeks, one piece of evidence suffices. Focusing on the Greeks' search for tin in the Atlantic world, Max Cary's almost century-old article shows the manner in which the Greeks sailed to Brittany, Cornwall, and elsewhere in the northern Atlantic, searching for that commodity. Even though the Carthaginians were able to partially block Greek merchants from sailing into the Atlantic through the Straits of Gibraltar until the Romans dealt a deathblow to Carthaginian hegemony, Greek traders still maintained a trade route between Hellenistic Alexandria and the Atlantic. A Greek trade network linked both the eastern and the western Mediterranean with the North Atlantic. Sailing along the coast of the western Mediterranean from their outposts in Sicily, Marseille, and on the African coast, Greeks (as well as Carthaginians) sailed out of the Mediterranean to such Atlantic sites as Cádiz (Gades) and modern Tangier. One could see the advantages of having recourse to bases just at the entrance (or exit) of the Mediterranean before embarking on long and perilous voyages into the North Atlantic. And tin was not the only commodity that traveled from the Atlantic into the ancient Mediterranean. Just as the Phoenicians had done, the Greeks are said to have ventured into the open Atlantic, reaching the Canary Islands. All this information seems to contradict my earlier statements about the difficulties of sailing out of the Mediterranean. These examples do not necessarily dismiss my earlier observations. They serve only to point out that, in spite of the difficulties, the lure of trade and of particular commodities made ancient, medieval, and early modern merchants and sailors risk the challenges of the Straits of Gibraltar. Moreover, as noted in Chapter 10, there were ways to access the Guadalquivir by a land route that followed river valleys to the river proper, from where it was possible to sail south to Cádiz.

The rise of Rome as the premiere western Mediterranean power marked the demise of the Carthaginian and Greek presence in Atlantic Mediterranean commercial exchanges. Although the Romans maintained an active naval traffic between Egypt (one of the empire's most important suppliers of grain and papyrus), Sicily, and North Africa (also suppliers of grain and fish sauce), Rome was not an aggressive commercial empire. Nonetheless, the Romans had substantial interests in Atlantic Spain, the Atlantic coast of what is today southwest France, and, of course, England. In spite of the difficulties of sailing out of the Mediterranean, well-established maritime trade routes linked the city of Rome (through its port at Ostia) to Barcelona, its great colony of Gades (Cádiz) in Atlantic Spain, and England. That well-regulated and frequent traffic through the Straits of Gibraltar was disrupted after the waning of Roman power in the West and the establishment of Germanic kingdoms on the Mediterranean and Atlantic coasts of Iberia, as well as in France and England.

By 711, the Mediterranean, in Pirenne's formulation, had almost become a Muslim lake. From its Mediterranean bases in North Africa, Iberia, southern France, and Sicily, the Muslims had a stranglehold on the western Mediterranean. Even though Islamic powers in North Africa did not promote extensive explorations into the Atlantic, Muslim ports on what is today Atlantic Morocco (at Salé, Mogador, and Tangier, the latter just at the western side of the Straits of Gibraltar) allowed for a permanent contact between the two seas. In the ninth and tenth centuries, the Vikings raided the Atlantic coast of Iberia. In 844, they sailed up the Guadalquivir River, sacked Seville, and held it against Muslim counterattacks for more than a month. By the ninth century, they had entered the Mediterranean as part of their bold moves (there was also intense Viking activity through the Russian fluvial networks and through land and sea routes into the eastern Mediterranean) to reach Byzantium. Vikings raided the Muslim coast of North Africa and threatened Corsica and Sardinia. In the eleventh century, Normans established their rule in Sicily. Trade also existed between Scandinavia and the Muslim western Mediterranean, attesting to the double character of Viking expansion: as both traders and raiders. But the Vikings often came to stay. It was mostly a one-way traffic, bringing northern people and Atlantic cultures into the Mediterranean world. Getting out was more difficult after the collapse of Rome, and not fully underway until the Late Middle Ages.

THE TWO SEAS IN THE LATE MIDDLE AGES AND THE EARLY MODERN PERIOD

The eventual demise of the western Mediterranean and the rise of the Atlantic in world history was a long-term development, coming to a high point only after the sixteenth century. The reasons for this shift from one sea to the other were not just the outcome of voyages of exploration and settlement in the New World from 1492 onwards or of the Portuguese's exploration of the coast of Africa and their epic voyage to India in the fifteenth century. Many other factors came into the equation. And it was the sum total of these factors that tolled the death knell for the centrality of the western Mediterranean in Western European history. Below, I try to examine some of these factors in a succinct fashion. Please note that although these different explanations for the eventual demise of the western Mediterranean are examined individually, they constituted an overlapping pattern of historical developments.

The Impact of War and Trade before Columbus

In 1212, a large international Christian army defeated the Almohads at the battle of Las Navas de Tolosa. The crushing defeat of the Almohads (a North African Berber dynasty that had invaded southern Spain in the twelfth century and pushed back Castilian and Arago-Catalan advances on the frontier) was swiftly followed by Christian conquests throughout most of Mediterranean and Atlantic Iberia. Ferdinand III, king of Castile and León (1217–1252), conquered Córdoba in 1236 and Seville in 1248. His son, Alfonso X (1252–1284), took Cádiz and Puerto de Santa María (both on the Atlantic) and Murcia (on the Mediterranean) in the first decade of his rule. Jaume I (1213–1276), king of the Crown of Aragon, gained the great city of Valencia and its eponymous kingdom in 1238, marking the eastern kingdom's last serious participation in the work of the reconquest and the beginning in earnest of its Mediterranean expansion.[7]

By 1300, Muslim presence on the peninsula had been limited to the kingdom of Granada, though Muslim powers in North Africa held on precariously to Gibraltar and Algeciras in western Andalusia. This would come to an end, at least for the first two locations, in the mid-fourteenth century when Alfonso XI of Castile (1312–1350) won an impressive battle at Salado River, the high point of a series of energetic campaigns to recover the Spanish region around the Straits of Gibraltar. These political changes and the wane of Muslim power on the European shores of the Mediterranean and the Atlantic adjacent to the Straits of Gibraltar had important consequences for trade and navigation between the two regions in the Late Middle Ages and afterwards. This is not to say, of course, that Christian control of one shore of the Straits was the sole reason for the increase in trade. It was not. Even before the conquest of Seville in 1248 a large number of Genoese merchants and bankers had settled in the city. The Christian victories led to the formalization of trade routes between Northern Europe and Italy. And the Genoese were not the only Italian merchants involved in the Atlantic-Mediterranean connection. Merchants from Pisa, Florence, and even Venice benefitted from the new opportunities to sail across the Straits and, far more important, from having secure ports on the European Atlantic side of the Straits. These ports provided the facilities to refurbish their ships and served as launching points toward northern waters and markets.

Shortly after 1300, the traffic between the Mediterranean and the Atlantic began to increase dramatically. But the impetus for this increase in commerce between the two seas was not a sudden one. These mercantile links had been in the making for a while. The rise of textile manufacturing in Italy, to rival that of Flanders, increased the need for wool and other commodities. Mediterranean merchants, mostly Italians from Genoa, Piacenza, and other points on Italy's western coast, maintained permanent trade routes into the Atlantic, establishing commercial links with England, Atlantic Spain, and Flanders. The Genoese, who, as we have seen above, had settled an important mercantile and banking outpost in Seville, became important players in the trade that linked Iberia and the Mediterranean to the North Atlantic.[8]

As a result of complex geopolitical factors at work towards the end of the Middle Ages, there was already in the making a noticeable shift from the Mediterranean to the Atlantic as the focus of Western European commercial life. This shift was not immediate, nor was it perhaps even fully noticed by those most affected by this transformation. Braudel's influential book, after all, still places the Mediterranean at the heart of Europe. He describes Mediterranean trade as an expansive commercial world that reached, though a series of roads and fluvial networks, Northern Europe.

The nature of the Atlantic-Mediterranean trade was a complicated one, having its roots in previous medieval political and economic changes. The connections may not always be obvious, but they were there. For example, Ferdinand III's conquest of Seville had depended, to a large extent, on Ramón Bonifaz's naval expertise. Bonifaz was a merchant of Burgos (a trading city in the center of Castile) engaged in trade with Northern Europe. At the command of the king, he organized a fleet in the Bay of Biscay area (composed mostly of ships from an area long engaged in trade with Flanders and England) and sailed around the Iberian Peninsula to the mouth of the Guadalquivir River, leading to Seville. There he defeated a combined North African and Andalusi fleet, besieged the city from the river, and played a crucial role in the surrender of Seville. Many years ago, Robert S. Lopez, the great economic historian who coined the phrase "the commercial revolution," argued that Ramón Bonifaz had Genoese origins. Whether he did or not, the links between the Bay of Biscay Castilian ports, Northern Europe, Seville (or Cádiz), and the Mediterranean Italian manufacturing centers became a reality. Before Columbus, there were Genoese merchants already actively engaged in the opening of the Atlantic trade or as interlocutors for a complex web of trading and sailing that brought the Mediterranean and the Atlantic into enduring economic exchanges. Moreover, as Olivia R. Constable has persuasively shown, this was precisely the period in which Iberian trade experienced a dramatic repositioning, shifting away from being part of the commercial networks that linked Spain and the western Mediterranean to Dar al-Islam into a pattern of economic exchanges that connected southern Iberia to the North.[9]

Castilian merchants from Cantabrian and Basque ports carried luxury Italian cloth, such as purple cloth from Venice and gold brocade from Lucca, as well as textiles from Montpellier, to Castile's southern Atlantic ports for distribution by land throughout the kingdom. Castilian merchants also carried wool, on behalf of the Bardi and Peruzzi banking houses, from England to the Italian textile centers in the first half of the fifteenth century. In 1338, John Bussyns, a merchant of Piacenza, received safe conduct from the English monarch, Edward III, to go to Wynchelse (modern-day Winchelsea) "to recover goods and merchandise lately put on board a ship of Spain (by which they meant Castile) which had been carried away by men of Wynchelsea." Similar grants were issued to merchants of Chieri (or Cheiri), Piacenza, and Asti. Diagus (Diego) Lopes de Arbo Lanchia, Lopes Sanches de Bassurco, and other merchants of Bilbao received royal protection from the English Crown in 1337 to "trade in Gascony, Brabant, Ireland and other lands friendly to England, and passing to and from Lombardy and their own ports." On

November 20, 1337, Sebastian of Nordyncho of San Sebastián on the Basque coast hired his ship *la Seint John* to merchants of the Bardi society to carry 600 sacks of wool to Lombardy. A ship from Bermeo (on the Cantabrian coast of Castile) also carried wool to Italy that year for the Bardi, while a ship from Santander did the same for the Peruzzi in 1338. Genoese merchants, not just from Florence's great trading and banking houses, also took an important role in this Mediterranean-Atlantic trade. Ships sailed out of the Mediterranean carrying Italian goods, stopped in Seville or Cádiz, made their way to Gascony, England, and Flanders, and came back following the same route in reverse.[10]

The beginning of the Hundred Years War brought greater opportunities for merchants, as well as added risks. Although war and plague eventually led to the English defaulting on their debt to Italian banks, signaling the collapse of the powerful Bardi and Peruzzi societies, war also offered the opportunity for profit. While supplying France would have often been done through the roads that led along the Rhône River valley from the Mediterranean to Flanders or to the ancient fairs at Champagne, England and Gascony had to be reached by sea. Shifting alliances during the war – Castile, for example, supported England from the 1340s to 1360s and then shifted its support to France in 1365 with the advent of a new dynasty – and increased confrontation along the sea routes from the Straits into the English Chanel affected the volume and frequency of exchanges between the two seas. But war and trade were not the only agents for the shift to the Atlantic. Other factors came to the forefront toward the end of the Middle Ages that led to a veritable revolution in the relationship between the two seas.

RELIGION, CONFLICT, AND NEW TECHNOLOGIES OF SEAFARING AND CARTOGRAPHY

Although not all the new techniques of chart making, naval know-how, and seafaring technology originated in the Mediterranean world, a good number of these new ways of navigating the oceans came from there. As these new technologies were exported to the Atlantic and were improved and altered, they also contributed to the slow demise of the Mediterranean. In addition, by the beginning of the fifteenth century, the rivalry between Christendom and Islam had taken a sharp turn. Ottoman successes in the eastern Mediterranean reanimated the Christian search for the mythical kingdom of Prester John (a mythical Christian king who ruled over a kingdom – located in a diversity of geographical areas, depending on the period – engaged in confrontation with Islam) as an ally in the struggle against the Muslims. As will be seen below, Ottoman victories also had important economic consequences. Italian merchants, mostly Venetians, were now challenged for their almost sole access to goods coming into the eastern Mediterranean from Asia. The trade did not stop, but the price for spices and luxury goods rose steeply under Ottoman control of the region. It would take many decades for the Venetians to be fully dislodged from their trading stations and colonies in Crete, Cyprus, and elsewhere, but dislodged they would be. In this sense, the Portuguese capture of Ceuta in 1415 marked the opening of one front in the West as a response to the increased Ottoman control of the eastern seas.

Geography and Seafaring

Cardinal Pierre d'Ailly's publication of his treatise *Imago Mundi* (*Image of the World*) in 1410 provided a wealth of new geographical information, collecting Greek, Latin, and Arabic lore about the shape of the world. A highly influential book, *Imago Mundi* presented a description of the world that transcended the narrow confines of the Mediterranean Sea. So did, for that matter, the travel accounts of Marco Polo, the fictional narrative of John of Mandeville, and other European medieval travel literature. The problem, of course, now that one had that knowledge, was how to sail into an open ocean and how to locate one's position at sea accurately with no sight of land. In the Mediterranean, most sailing remained coastal sailing. It was quite easy to determine one's location by observing land features along the coast. Catalan and Italian hydrographers (makers of sea charts) had begun to map out the coast of the European Mediterranean. The Portuguese would do the same for most of the coast of western Africa. But new astronomical knowledge and the use of compasses would allow sailors and merchant captains to determine their latitude in the open sea.

The North Star (or Pole Star) helped sailors with no immediate landmasses in sight to determine where they where in terms of latitude. But while the use of the North Star, compasses, and new ship technology (see below) greatly facilitated sailing into the Atlantic, these advantages partly disappeared once one sailed south of the Equator, as the Portuguese began to do by the mid-fifteenth century. Astrolabes had been known in the West since the Middle Ages, but determining your latitude using careful sightings of the sun at midday was never a very easy thing to do, often requiring landing to allow an accurate observation. By the 1470s, thanks to Abraham Zacuto's work, these difficulties were partially overcome. Zacuto was born in Salamanca in 1452 and studied and taught astronomy there and elsewhere. Fleeing Spain after the Edict of Expulsion of the Jews in 1492, Zacuto went to Portugal. There he received a warm welcome from the Portuguese court and saw his most influential work, the *Almanach perpetuum*, translated into Portuguese. His development of a new astrolabe and charting of the sun's declination allowed for a more accurate fixing of one's position even south of the equatorial line. Vasco da Gama carried both Zacuto's more efficient astrolabe and the tables on his voyage to India. As a kind of denouement to this story, Zacuto went, once again, into exile after the forced conversion of Portuguese Jews, traveled to North Africa (Tunis), and died in or near Jerusalem, a remarkable example of the connections and contacts between the Mediterranean and the Atlantic.[11]

Ships

It is a commonplace to posit Mediterranean ships as mostly heavy galleys powered by oars under the harsh conditions endured by enslaved rowers. Galleys did ply the waters of the Mediterranean, mostly engaged in naval warfare, but most Mediterranean navigation was done by sail, undertaken by small vessels (barques, caravels) engaged in coastal sailing, and connecting the different regions or "micro-economies' of the Mediterranean (see Chapter 9). Yet, cogs, for example, a type of ship developed in the Atlantic and the Baltic Sea that could be rowed but depended mostly on sail power, appeared in Mediterranean sources only by the fourteenth century, coinciding with the opening of the Straits to navigation and confirming the importance of that event in the late medieval and early modern history of the Mediterranean. Hulks, also of northern provenance, made their way into the Mediterranean in the Late Middle Ages. Clearly, ship design and ship construction resulted from the wedding of seafaring technologies from both the North Atlantic and the Christian and Islamic Mediterranean.

In the opening of the Atlantic to exploration, no other development would be as important as the combining by the Portuguese of types of ships designed for Atlantic sailing with the lateen sail of Mediterranean origin. The caravels that crossed the Atlantic and reached India combined aspects of northern ship technology with Mediterranean rigging. In this and many other developments, the Portuguese led the way. The caravel deployed the lateen sail, allowing for easier tacking to the wind and freeing the ships from a dependency on oars as the main source of power. Whether the *caravela redonda*, combining square with lateen sails, or the *caravela latina*, depending exclusively on lateen sails, these types of ships, followed by carracks and galleons, would dominate the Atlantic. These technological advances propelled the Portuguese and, eventually, the Castilians to gain a short-lived hegemony in the Atlantic and the Indian Ocean. Together with the Portuguese introduction of broadside artillery, that is, the use of artillery on board the ships (probably in the 1470s), these technical innovations led to the rise of Atlantic powers that had now a much easier access to the fabulous fortunes to be made in the spice trade and, eventually, in the silver mines of Mexico and Peru.

THE RISE OF THE ATLANTIC AND THE DECLINE OF THE MEDITERRANEAN

The reasons for Mediterranean decline were manifold and not all of them related to Prince Henry the Navigator's (1394–1460) sponsorship of Atlantic explorations, to Portuguese access to Indian markets, or to the Castilian encounter with the New World. The point here is that the rise of Atlantic realms to a hegemonic position paralleled chronologically a series of political, economic, and religious developments that would have affected the western Mediterranean economy and the region's political role even without the developments in the Atlantic and Africa.[12] What were these economic and political changes?

The Rise of the Ottomans

The rise of the Sublime Porte, highlighted by the fall of Constantinople in 1453, represented a direct threat to western powers by land and sea. Ottoman armies marched to the gates of Vienna in the early sixteenth century. Ottoman ships and Ottoman-sponsored corsairs, the fabled Barbarossa brothers above all, threatened the shores of Christian nations even long after the great Christian naval victory at Lepanto in 1571. Lepanto was a great symbolic moment in the confrontation between Islam and Christianity, but it had little long-term impact on Mediterranean politics. These conflicts disrupted trade in the Mediterranean, made eastern goods more expensive, and rendered the coasts of the western Mediterranean unsafe.

As I noted in Chapter 9, one significant consequence of the rise of the Ottoman Empire and of corsair activity in the western Mediterranean – a corsair presence that would remain a threat into the nineteenth century – was to dry up a great deal of the trade between Mediterranean Europe and Mediterranean Africa. In the Middle Ages, the capture of enemies at sea, ransoming of slaves, and raids on each other's coasts were part and parcel of broader patterns of exchange. It was not, however, all antagonism. Majorca, to give one single example, had important commercial ties – mostly carried out by Jews and later by conversos – with North Africa. Trade and exchange relationships, as threatened as they were by new developments, prevented the complete isolation of one shore of the Mediterranean from the other. Gradually, as the Ottomans expanded their sphere of influence into North Africa and sanctioned corsair operations from North African ports, commercial relations diminished or, in some cases, vanished. One should note that these corsairs, operating from both shores of the Middle Sea, were often renegades, bringing to their activities an added sectarian dimension. The European Christian outposts on the Mediterranean – Ceuta after1415 and Oran, conquered by Spain in the sixteenth century – did not provide an entry point into the interior of Africa, nor did they become commercial entrepôts. Between the Ottomans, the Spanish Mediterranean fleet, the Italian Republics' navies, and corsairs from both religions, western Mediterranean trade was, for all practical purposes, asphyxiated. Italy and western Mediterranean islands, such as Majorca and Sicily, suffered most of all. In many respects, these changes were not directly related to the rise of Atlantic trade; yet, they further benefitted Atlantic ventures.

Spain and France

The rise of Spain and France as dominant Western European powers in the late fifteenth and early sixteenth century had a considerable impact on Italy. Italian urban centers, Florence, Venice, Genoa, Naples, and others, had been dominant either as cultural or as economic centers. In the case of Florence, Venice, and Naples, they had been both. By 1494, Italy had become a battlefield for France and Spain until the Battle of Pavia (1525) gave Charles V, Holy Roman emperor (1519–1556) and king of the diverse Spanish kingdoms (from 1516), the upper hand. Most of Italy came to be either directly ruled by Spain or under its heavy-handed protectorate. Italy's vaunted local independence and its cultural Renaissance waned markedly by the mid-1550s. Culture and trade did not vanish from the Mediterranean, they just found better homes elsewhere. If Italian bankers and merchants profited from the Atlantic trade they did so either as part of the far-flung Spanish administration or as faithful allies, as was the case of the Genoese whose fortunes rose and fell with those of Spain.

With Italy the launching point for Spanish armies on the fabled Spanish Road to Flanders, and its citizens either beholden to or cowed by the Spanish presence there, a great deal of the dynamism shown by Italian bankers and merchants in the Late Middle Ages and on the eve of the opening of the Atlantic waned. Italy ceased to play a significant role in European affairs. Cultural centers moved elsewhere – to France, Spain, the Low Countries, and England. So, with some notable exceptions, did financial ones. The Spaniards were not easy masters. The sack of Rome by Charles V's German and Spanish troops in 1527 was a reminder that to oppose Spain, or to form alliances with Spain's enemies, as the papacy had done, would bring frightful consequences. France, the great rival of Spain in the sixteenth century, had no significant ports on the Mediterranean besides Marseille, nor did it have a notable naval presence there. It could not compete in the Atlantic either, but France sponsored corsair and piratical activities on both seas. They were significant enough that Cervantes, in one of his stories within the larger story of *Don Quixote*, tells us of a Spanish captive and his friends fleeing the slave prison in Algiers (the *banhos* in Argel). As they sailed toward Majorca from the North African coast, they ran into a French pirate that took all their possessions but spared their lives. They eventually made it to the southern coast of Spain, near Málaga, alive and free but without a penny.

Religion

In addition to the armed conflicts affecting the western Mediterranean because of the rivalry between the Sublime Porte and western naval powers led by Spain, the Protestant Reformation, beginning with Luther's challenges to Catholic orthodoxy in 1521, also severed, in many respects, the Mediterranean world, mostly Catholic, from a Protestant North. The horrific religious wars that followed (and that remained fairly unresolved until the treaty of Westphalia in 1648) wrecked most of Central Europe and eventually turned Spain into a third-rate power. The energy and funds that were to be deployed in the great plans of Ferdinand and Isabella and, later, their grandchild, Charles V, to conquer all of North Africa and turn the western Mediterranean into a Spanish lake were wasted in useless sectarian struggles in Central Europe. And the economic consequences were long felt as well, with European commercial ventures redirected into Atlantic, African, and Asian markets.

The Mediterranean that Braudel envisions in his great book extended into the Baltic, the North Sea, and the Atlantic. The reality was not as promising. Although religious conflicts did not bring trade and cultural exchanges to a standstill, they made relations between the Catholic Mediterranean and the Protestant North less vibrant and frequent. Northern Europe no longer had to depend on Italian merchants as intermediaries between Asia, the eastern Mediterranean, and the world north of the Alps. Spanish wool that had been exported to Flanders in large quantities from the 1300s onwards became a less profitable commodity as the Low Countries became the site for fierce conflict between the Spanish Catholic overlords and the Protestants in the Northern Provinces, or Holland. I often tend to discount religion to my own loss, but religion mattered. It affected patterns of trade and relations. Italy, the kingpin of the western Mediterranean, became less relevant. Even Italian artists and philosophers began to go abroad in search of patrons, as Leonardo did to France or Giordano Bruno to England and France.

The Triumph of the Atlantic

While all these developments affected the history of the Mediterranean and the sea's place in European affairs, the reality was that Portugal and Castile had long been involved in the Atlantic. Even without war, the Protestant Reformation, and the Ottoman threat, the Mediterranean's central role in Europe's economy and culture may have declined. Felipe Fernández-Armesto's *Before Columbus* traced this flow from the Mediterranean to the Atlantic.[13] Here it is important to emphasize, once again, the symbiotic relationship between the two seas. A great deal of the technical know-how and administrative practices that would allow for conquest and settlement in the Atlantic world had already been tried out in Sicily, Majorca, and southern Spain. Earlier, we saw how the development over time of new technologies of seafaring, shipbuilding, broadside artillery, and the like (a good number of them originating in the Mediterranean) made possible the bold voyages of Portuguese and Castilian seamen down the coast of Africa, to Asia, and to the New World. Mediterranean Sea charts, geographical treatises, and the revival of ancient classical sources, most of these developments taking place in Italy, underpinned and deeply influenced new Atlantic expansion. In the early Atlantic crossing and settlements in the New World, the cultural narratives were often provided by Italians serving the Castilian Crown. Columbus was, after all, from Genoa. And he had sailed the Atlantic to Iceland, to the Canary Islands, and down the coast of Africa long before 1492.

Long before the Spanish invasion of Italy in response to French military incursions in the peninsula in 1494, the Portuguese (an Atlantic maritime power) had begun their expeditions along the coast of Africa to the Cape of Good Hope and, eventually, to India and the fabulous profits to be found there. These voyages would have been impossible without new types of sailing vessels (the *caravela redonda*), or without the astrolabe, compass, and sea charts. Propelled by these new seafaring technologies, the dates of Portuguese progress southwards along the coast of Africa read like a clear guide book to the eventual demise of the Mediterranean.

Conquering Ceuta in 1415, the Portuguese established a foothold in Africa at the opening of the Straits of Gibraltar. The Madeira Islands and the Azores fell into Portuguese hands by 1418 and 1427–1431, respectively. The islands of Cape Verde were reached in the 1450s. Bartolomeu Dias rounded the Cape of Good Hope in 1487–1488 while other Portuguese explorers reached as far inland as fabled Timbuktu, sailing up the Congo River deep into the heart of sub-Saharan Africa. Vasco da Gama's historic expedition to India (1497–1499) and his return to Lisbon in a ship laden with spices marked, far more than

Columbus's earlier voyages into the Atlantic, a real shift in the late medieval and early modern economy. But it also altered the geographical centrality of the Mediterranean in a global context.[14]

The relationship between the Mediterranean and the Atlantic, one so dramatically represented in the natural and human deterrents (currents and corsairs) that made sailing out of the Mediterranean so difficult, shifted after the European expansion into the Atlantic world and Asian markets. Northern and Atlantic ports no longer needed access to the Mediterranean for the lifeblood of their respective economies. Although the Mediterranean would eventually be linked to this new world economy, the Middle Sea lost its centrality as the privileged site of European culture and commerce. What Pirenne, in his great book, had mistakenly claimed had taken place with the coming of Islam into the western Mediterranean in the seventh and eighth centuries really took place in the early modern period. The opening of Atlantic, African, and Asian markets represented a watershed in Mediterranean history, as the sea and the lands around the western sea would not begin to play a significant role in world affairs again until the present period.

AFTERMATH: FROM THE ATLANTIC TO THE MEDITERRANEAN

In the centuries following the slow decline of western Mediterranean trade and its centrality in European life, the Ottoman power also began to wane. Religious wars came to an end in the mid-seventeenth century, although other types of conflict did not. Spain's military hegemony was shattered at the Battle of Rocroi in 1643. New powers rose to prominence. They were all Atlantic powers – England, France, the Dutch Republic – even if their interests were essentially global. Italy became the destination for eager visitors in search of antiquities and curiosities. It became an impoverished land. Spain came under Bourbon rule in 1715 and firmly in the orbit of France. Although Spain was able to preserve most of its colonial empire until 1821, the Iberian Peninsula lost a great deal of its importance in European and global affairs. Portugal came under England's political and economic influence. Yet, by the late eighteenth and for most of the nineteenth century (and even before), Atlantic goods, that is, Northern European manufactured goods and wood and agricultural products from Scandinavia and the Americas, began to flow back into the Mediterranean. Braudel has provided us, as he did for the Mediterranean Sea, with a bird's eye view of the transformation of the world economy and the new place of the Mediterranean in those commercial transactions.[15]

As we have seen in Chapter 9, where I examine the protests against the sea kept at the Archive of the Crown of Aragon, seeking to ferret out what they tell us about commerce, trade with countries on the Atlantic Ocean began to play a significant role in the Mediterranean economy during the modern period. The protests against the sea are formulaic depositions by merchant sea captains complaining of bad weather and damage to their cargo. There are more than

25,000 such depositions for the period between 1766 and 1868. These protests show unequivocally the growing trade from Atlantic and Northern European locations into the Mediterranean. Wood from Scandinavia, machinery from England, sugar from Pernambuco (Brazil) or Cuba, and cotton from the southern United States flowed into Barcelona, a pattern of trade probably replicated for other Mediterranean ports. And yet, the most revealing evidence in all the documentation is the paucity of references to North African ports. Not only were the trade and economy of western Mediterranean Sea overtaken by the rise of the Atlantic, they were also mostly severed from its North African counterpart until the beginnings of the European colonial projects there. But, it is time to turn to a matter that has underlain the entire thrust of this book, and that has become an issue of great concern for Western Europeans and for the world. It may, in time, transform the very structures of European life (and those of the entire world). This is, of course, the question of immigration.

TWENTIETH- AND TWENTY-FIRST-CENTURY IMMIGRATION

As I revise the final pages of this book, the news from Europe, the United States, and other parts of the world tells us in grim detail of the massive movement of people from their homelands in the Middle East, Africa, and Latin America to Western Europe and the United States. Propelled by climatic changes (with their concomitant impact on supplies of food and water), scarcity, endemic violence, and war, millions of people, often at the risk of their lives, seek a refuge in Western Europe or the United States. In the case of Europe, the Mediterranean is the locus for these new migratory patterns. As it did in Antiquity, crossing the sea in search of a new home has become the norm for the early decades of the twenty-first century. It is not exaggeration to argue that immigration, legal and illegal, is the central social, cultural, and political issue of our times. What the outcome of this present crisis will be is hard to tell, as the anti-migratory rhetoric rises in volume and in vitriolic content. With some notable exceptions, after welcoming fleeing immigrants, Europe (and the United States as well) has moved to curtail their movement and to deny immigrants access to a new life. This is, first and foremost, a Mediterranean story.

Immigration or, at least, the widespread movement of people from depressed, unjustly ruled, or turbulent areas of the world to advanced or "First World" societies is an important historical issue with significant historical consequences. Europe experienced one fairly large movement of people coinciding with the waning of the Roman Empire in the West. That was, of course, the widespread movement of Germanic people into the different regions of the Roman Empire. Two other less convincing examples come to mind. The Muslim expansion of the seventh century does not qualify as a large migratory event since the Arabs were few in number and depended on the conversion of local people to establish their rule. The Northmen, or Normans (Vikings), were also small in number, relative to the areas they placed under their rule. These two were armed invasions, but they were followed probably by large movements of people across the Mediterranean. The later assertion is, of course, almost impossible to measure or to quantify. The reality is that substantial movement of people from one shore to another has always characterized the western Mediterranean. This movement goes in two directions: from outside the region into the area under study, and from the western Mediterranean into the world at large. In a pre-modern world, a world without secure borders and passports, the movement of people is difficult to document. Even today, illegal immigration masks the real volume of population exchanges in the region.

Large migration in the nineteenth and early twentieth century involved the relocation of large numbers of Mediterranean people: Spaniards, Italians, Greeks, Jews, and Armenians from the Ottoman lands into the New World (Italians also migrated to North Africa, as French did to Algeria). Germans and Scandinavians had also migrated in large numbers in the mid-eighteenth century and in the succeeding century, and so had Jews and Poles from areas in western Russia, and English people to America, Australia, and elsewhere. The Irish, their migration triggered by the infamous potato famine, traveled in large numbers to the United States in the mid-nineteenth century.

All these migrations, however, went to countries or regions that either were not densely populated (the Midwest and West in North America, the pampas in Argentina), where they could replace or remove the native populations by force, or had growing cities with flowering industrial development (New York, Chicago, Boston, and other industrial centers in the United States). These migrations were profoundly different from present-day migratory patterns. In the nineteenth century, most immigrants severed ties with their family and country of origin. Today's immigrants go back and forth between the two different worlds they inhabit. It is ironic that many of the countries which today pass draconian measures against immigrants (who are often Muslims or ethnically different) benefitted immensely by shipping their own surplus population to other parts of the world. European and western Mediterranean history, if nothing else, is the history of migration.

While in previous chapters we were able to glance briefly at the experiences and alienation of present-day immigrants in Western Europe, here I wish to focus on the demographic (and religious) impact of massive immigration from North Africa, sub-Saharan Africa, and Eastern Europe into the West. In the case of Spain, Latin America has also been an important source of migrants because of the historical ties between Spain and the New World. Of course, internal immigration within Western Europe (from the South to the North) has also been a common pattern throughout the last century, counterbalanced to an extent by retirees migrating to the Mediterranean from Northern Europe. Spain and Portugal sent thousands of immigrants to France, Germany, and the Low Countries during the industrial recovery of Europe after World War II. As I note earlier, some of the same people who now lament the influx of North Africans or sub-Saharan Africans themselves benefitted from the opportunity to migrate to countries enjoying better economic conditions than their own. Sicilians, Sardinians, and people from the perennially depressed *mezzogiorno* flocked to the Italian manufacturing centers in Bologna, Turin, and Milan in the 1960s and 1970s. They also traveled to Switzerland, a country not ever known for being receptive to immigrants, and to Scandinavian countries. A poignant Italian film, *Bread and Chocolate* (*Pane e cioccolata*), directed by Franco Brusati in 1974, traces the adventures and misadventures of a southern Italian illegal immigrant to Switzerland. Though intended as a comedy, the film's depiction of the tragic life of an illegal immigrant is replicated today in much grimmer terms all over Europe.

The experiences of modern immigrants – the Roma people above all (entire families sleep on the sidewalks of Paris) – are a harsh reminder of the politics and economics of migration, not just from the southern shores of the Mediter-ranean, but also from the underdeveloped world to the developed one. Such terms as "developed" and "underdeveloped" belong, of course, to dated discourses identifying relations of subordination. In every country in the world today, including the United States and the countries of Western Europe, there are classic examples of people living in "First World" and "Third World" conditions existing side by side. By definition, of course, this includes the countries from which the immigrants themselves hail. There the upper classes share a culture, material and otherwise, with their counterparts in the more developed world. The global reach of English and US material culture has had a homogenizing impact on the world's economic elites.

But what does this growth in number of immigrants into Europe and into the European Mediterranean mean for the immediate present and, far more important, for the future? What are the reasons for such a dramatic increase in the number of people fleeing their countries? As I indicated above, there is a link between migration and climatic changes, overfishing, reduction in the availability of food supplies, and violence. Scholars have argued that the long-term drought affecting Syria and other regions of the Middle East is crucial for the understanding of the mechanism that triggered the civil war there. As farmers saw their lands dry up and become barren, they sought refuge in Syrian cities, Damascus and Aleppo first of all. In the face of their government's inability to address their needs, civil strife erupted, with the horrific conse-quences we have witnessed for the last five years or more. Of course, climatic change is only one factor in what is a very complex situation involving ethnic and religious strife, a harsh dictatorship, and the general breakdown of civil society in the region.

The rising temperatures in the Middle East, the result of long-term global warming, have also had a deleterious impact on food production. In August 2015, the *New York Times* reported riots in Iraq triggered by the inability of the government to provide enough electricity to run air conditioners. It is clear that life may not be sustainable in many parts of the world in the near future because of the probably irreversible impact of rising temperatures on the world's climate. This affects all nations of the world, but underdeveloped societies in the Middle East most of all. Along these lines, the Sahara Desert has been growing, as have other deserts throughout the world, and this has had a serious impact on agriculture. Africa has experienced severe famines over the last few decades, and it is now, in 2017, in the midst of another dramatic one. Famines are often accompanied by tribal violence as people struggle for diminishing resources. But it is not just climate change that is causing these problems. Overfishing of the coast of West Africa has sent numerous fishermen in the region on their way to Europe. The subsistence fishing common to the region has, for all practical purposes, become untenable.

The incompetence of western powers, the United States above all, and in particular the Bush government's imprudent intervention in Iraq and attempts at nation-building in the region, have unveiled the deep divisions that existed (and exist) in those places: Iraq, Syria, Afghanistan, Lebanon, and others. These countries suffer from the powder keg inherited from colonial powers whose arbitrary organization of nations reflected their scant understanding of the deep religious divides or enduring tribal traditions that were present in these regions. This, of course, applies to Africa as well. These nations remained at peace only under the rule of brutal dictatorships that kept warring factions (Shi'a/Sunni, tribal divisions, etc.) under control by the repression of one group by the other – Saddam Hussein being just one example. It is very clear that western interventions have unraveled these failed states and triggered great conflicts in the regions. Having caused the problems, or allowed (as in the case of the Syrian crisis) violence and despair to continue, these same western powers now refuse to admit the throngs of immigrants fleeing the conditions the West helped to create.

These dramatic population movements are reflected both in the sheer number of immigrants and in the transformations that have followed from such an influx of people. When set in contrast with the extraordinarily low fertility rates of Western Europe's native population (or that of the United States for that matter), the issue becomes even more relevant. While every country in Western Europe has experienced an influx of newcomers, those around the western Mediterranean have been most affected. And this is particularly poignant when one considers that the countries on the shores of the European western Mediterranean have not recovered from the great economic crisis of 2007–2008, and that the immigrants are entering an already depressed economy.

But what does the growing number of immigrants coming into Europe and the European Mediterranean mean for the future? An editorial in the *New York Times* on February 1, 2014, signaled the nature of the immigration problem facing Western Europe and, most of all, the European shores of the western Mediterranean – the entry point for the wave of immigrants trying to enter Europe illegally. While correctly identifying turmoil in Syria and Libya as one of the reasons for the sharp increase in migrants, and lamenting the loss of immigrant's lives as they attempt to reach Western Europe by sea, the figures given in the editorial are a sobering reminder of the new realities of immigration. One thousand immigrants are calculated to have made the illegal crossing of the Straits of Gibraltar during a 48-hour period in August 2014. Spain blames Morocco, but the latter "is reeling from its role as a staging ground for people attempting to reach Europe . . . Italy is at a breaking point. More than 100,000 people have arrived in Italy from North Africa since the beginning of this year (2014) . . . 4,000 migrants [were rescued] over one weekend in

August alone."[16] And this has only grown worse with the flood of immigrants from Syria, Iraq, Libya, and elsewhere.

In France, immigrants and their children born there represent close to 19% of the population. Four million people from the Maghreb or of Maghrebi descent live in France now. A further million come from sub-Saharan Africa. Twenty-four per cent of the entire population of France has at least one parent not born in Europe, as a Museum of Immigration poster proudly reported in a Metro advertisement. In Italy and Spain, 7.5% and 12%, respectively, of the population are foreign born. When one thinks of melting pots, one tends to think of the United States with its long history of migration, but Europe now confronts critical challenges to its traditional imagining of self-identity and religious homogeneity. Living in Paris in 2014, I could tell – as the World Cup played out in the bars and cafes outside my window – that Algeria had as much support as the French national team, at least in the arrondissement where I was living. Losses or gains by the Algerian national team led to waves of violence. Many French complained bitterly. Yet, the French national team, as I remarked in another chapter, is a good example of this ethnic, religious, and cultural mélange that is so typical of France today. Many of its members were either born abroad or are the children of those who came from outside, but that is often forgotten in the euphoria of national celebration after every victory.

France and other Western European societies have cherished the idea (as illusory as it may actually have been) of being ethnically, religiously, and socially homogeneous societies. The "imagining" of their communities came from very deliberate efforts in the nineteenth century to create nations. Centralized public education, growing secularization, and the exaltation of the fatherland or motherland shaped people and fostered communal bonds of national solidarity. This was certainly the case in France. Spanish unity was brought about through harsh measures to repress local identities, languages, and aspirations of nation-hood. Italy's national ideals only date to the second half of the nineteenth century, and then these ideas were mostly the monopoly of intellectuals and scholars. The social, political, and cultural implications of racism, xenophobia, and the rise of the right throughout Europe since World War II (or the United States throughout most of 2016 in the grips of a rabid xenophobic political campaign among the Republicans and under a nativist administration since 2017) are themes for a different kind of book. We see some of these feelings already noted in Theroux's account from the 1990s and in the ever-present pejorative representations of Algerians in French popular discourse. These representations are still with us, together with those of the Roma, sub-Saharan people, and many others. Here, we should simply note how the immigration patterns of the last 25 years – not all of it from the southern shores of the Mediterranean but mostly from North Africa – represent different kinds of encounters. These encounters lead to strife, sharp social differences, and religious conflicts. But one must hope against dwindling hope that, as it was once before the waning of Rome, the western Mediterranean will become a place where people on both shores are united by their common Mediterranean identities, or, as the song by Serrat cited at the beginning of this book says, united because almost all of them were "born in the Mediterranean."

It often takes a lifetime to become integrated into another culture. Sometimes, it doesn't happen at all. In that sense, such crossings in the past, when national identities were not yet fully formed, represented far less of a challenge than leaving behind one's own country and building a life in another place where customs, food, and identity are different from one's own. There was, after all – and this is an important point made in this book – a rough western Mediterranean culture formed by the flow of trade, conversions, culinary traditions, and warfare between the two shores of the Mediterranean. And this was so in spite of linguistic, religious, and cultural differences. Movement and migration across the western Mediterranean also represented, and represent, an uneasy transition for those who were, and are, the hosts, often unwilling to accept the presence of immigrants into their carefully protected and ordered world. In this sense, culinary practices, one of the most resilient cultural traits of all, remain a touchstone of difference to this very day. We may become acculturated in many different ways, but what we eat at feasts or special celebrations tells a great deal about our identity, even in the twenty-first century. But the issue, becoming more critical with every passing day, is not about food, but about the movement of people in the modern western Mediterranean.

Nothing brings this problem as forcefully to our awareness as a series of connected events of late March 2014. Towards the middle of the month, over 1,000 people of sub-Saharan origin, after their long trek across the desert, hid in the woods near Melilla's border with Morocco (Melilla is a Spanish enclave on the Mediterranean coast of Morocco). At a predetermined moment, these refugees rushed the metal fence that protects Melilla from not only outsiders but also from Moroccans. Climbing the fence in a frenzy of desperation, almost half of the invaders (who were often beaten or repelled by the small number of guards patrolling the fence) were able to get inside. Even though they were detained, many of these new arrivals kissed the ground, chanted "Victory!" and felt as if they had completed the first and most significant leg of their long journey from sub-Saharan Africa to an outpost of the European community. It did not matter than many of these sub-Saharan people (mostly males from Mali and Senegal) would never cross the Mediterranean and enter Europe legally. For them, driven by unemployment, inequality, hunger, and political repression, reaching Melilla was already a victory indeed. George R.R. Martin, the author of the popular series "Game of Thrones," has a constant refrain: "winter is coming." Well, the immigrants are coming and, it does not matter how many fences we build, how well we patrol what once were open borders or the tunnels connecting the continent to England. The immigrants are coming, and we should deal with this in the most compassionate and enlightened way we can. We are, after all, in one way or another, all immigrants – I as much as anyone.

These recent immigrant journeys (from sub-Saharan Africa to the shores of the western Mediterranean) parallel earlier travel that linked sub-Saharan Africa with the North African coast. If, in the Middle Ages and in the early modern period, Mali functioned as a site of encounters and as a commercial hub, connecting the movement of southern African products and raw materials to the North African Mediterranean coast, now Mali, Senegal, and other countries in southern West Africa (south of the desert) look to Western Europe as a refuge from their unbearable conditions. A similar story was played out, and continues to play out, in Sicily. There hundreds of illegal immigrants from Albania and other eastern Mediterranean locations (and more recently from the Middle East) have sought to enter the European Union, but they end up as detainees, as has already been seen, at the little island of Lampedusa or at Mineo. The almost universal response to the flood of illegal immigrants has been either to vote for extreme right parties, or to enact repressive legislation or voice harsh opinions against these waves of people seeking refuge in the West. Well-educated and kind people with progressive ideas nonetheless bitterly oppose the flow of immigrants into their country at a time of a severe recession. Even Germany, which has fared best in the enduring economic crisis and which at the beginning of the crisis took exemplary steps to admit Syrians, will extradite all those without employment after six months. In the United States, in spite of Obama, a centrist-liberal Democrat, being at the helm, the number of illegal immigrants returned to their countries of origin reached unprecedented levels. The anti-migratory position of almost all the Republican candidates to the US presidency in 2016 reached vitriolic levels before the candidacy was eventually won by the most vitriolic of all, Trump. It was ironic that two of the candidates proudly disputing which of them had the most extreme repressive views on illegal immigrants were themselves the children of immigrants.

The problem of accommodating people from impoverished areas in affluent societies is a worldwide phenomenon. The pressure of migration, whether in the present Mediterranean or in the United States, is the legacy of the nineteenth-century colonial projects. There is obvious and growing inequality between different regions of the world: Europe and Africa, Western and Eastern Europe, the United States and Latin America. It was not always so before the early modern period. Addressing conditions in the regions from where the immigrants come is a rational first step towards normalizing the movement of people.

CONCLUSION

Throughout the chapters above, I have attempted to provide a sense, a "feel," for what it was to live in the western Mediterranean at different points in its long history: from the fall of Rome in the West to the present-day immigration crisis. My emphasis has been to capture what it was like, to cite Serrat's recurring sentence in the song that opens this book, to "be born (and to live) in the Mediterranean." Besides the geographical and historical contexts, this book has focused on religion, language, immigration, and those locations along the shores of the Middle Sea where new cultures were forged by the encounters of different people. But I am also concerned with those small islands and towns where not much happened yet where Mediterranean quotidian experiences were as deeply felt as those in the hubs of trade and encounter that we saw in Chapter 10.

Finally, this chapter provides a brief introduction to a much larger and intractable question. That question is immigration. It affects the western world, including the United States, in profound ways. The enduring legacies of colonialism and the workings of modern capital investment, it is social inequality and civil strife within the immigrants' homelands, economic exploitation, and real inequality of education and wealth between these nations and the West that have left hundreds of thousands with little choice but to seek to escape there. Immigration will undoubtedly reshape the nature of politics and culture in the United States and Western Europe. How that reshaping will take place is difficult to predict. But changes are coming, as profound and dramatic as those that transformed the ancient world and the western Mediterranean in its transition to the Middle Ages.

Finally, the opening of the Atlantic world (Africa and the Americas) to conquest and trade signaled an important change in Mediterranean history. By the sixteenth century, the slow demise of Italian political autonomy and the commercial shift to an Atlantic economy transformed western Mediterranean life and initiated a period of decline for the entire region that has in many ways lasted until today. The problem of the "South," or *mezzogiorno* – which also includes, from a whole series of social and economic perspectives, Africa's northern coast – remains an important issue today. The migration of North Africans across the Mediterranean into Western Europe provides yet another opportunity to study the Middle Sea as a laboratory in which diverse people encounter each other and are dramatically transformed by their location in those points of convergence. But this is an old story, a Mediterranean story that was carried out through the Straits of Gibraltar into the open waters of the Atlantic Ocean and on to new settlements across the world.

NOTES

1 A section of this chapter has been published in a different form as "The Mediterranean and the Atlantic," in *A Companion to Mediterranean History*, eds. Peregrine Horden and Sharon Kinoshita (Oxford: Wiley-Blackwell, 2014), 411–424. See also William D. Phillips Jr and Carla Rahn Phillips, *The Worlds of Christopher Columbus* (Cambridge: Cambridge University Press, 1992), 3–36; Henri Pirenne, *Mohammed and Charlemagne*, trans. Bernard Miall (New York: Meridian Books, 1960, originally published in 1937).

2 Claire Gilbert, "The Politics of Language in the Western Mediterranean c.1492–c.1669: Multilingual Institutions and the Status of Arabic in Early Modern Spain." PhD diss., University of California, Los Angeles, 2014.

3 Alexander Dumas, *The Count of Monte Cristo*, trans Robin Buss (London: Penguin, 2003), 1230.

4 Fernand Braudel, *The Mediterranean and the Mediterranean World in the Age of Philip II*, 2 vols, trans. Siân Reynolds (Berkeley and Los Angeles: University of California Press, 1995); Peregrine Horden and Nicholas Purcell, *The Corrupting Sea. A Study of Mediterranean History* (Oxford: Blackwell. 2000); David Abulafia, *The Great Sea. A Human History of the Mediterranean* (Oxford: Oxford University Press, 2011); Jessica Goldberg, *Trade and Institutions in the Medieval Mediterranean: The Geniza Merchants and their Business World* (Cambridge & New York: Cambridge University Press, 2012).

5   Archibald S. Lewis, "Northern European Sea Power and the Straits of Gibraltar, 1031–1350 A.D.," in *Order and Innovation in the Middle Ages. Essays in Honor of Joseph R. Strayer*, edited by William C. Jordan, Bruce McNab, and Teofilo F. Ruiz (Princeton: Princeton University Press, 1976), 139–164.

6   See Max Cary, *The Ancient Explorers* (Baltimore: Penguin, 1963); and his older piece "The Greeks and Ancient Trade with the Atlantic." *Journal of Hellenistic Studies*, 44, 2 (1924), 166–179. See also J.O. Thomson, *History of Ancient Geography* (Cambridge: Cambridge University Press, 1965).

7   Joseph F. O'Callaghan, *A History of Medieval Spain* (Ithaca, NY: Cornell University Press, 1975), 331–427; Angus MacKay, *Spain in the Middle Ages. From Frontier to Empire, 1000–1500* (London: Macmillan, 1977).

8   Antonio Collantes de Terán, *Sevilla en la Baja Edad Media* (Sevilla: Ayuntamiento de Sevilla, 1977).

9   Olivia R. Constable, *Trade and Traders in Muslim Spain: The Commercial Realignment of the Iberian Peninsula, 900–1500* (Cambridge & New York: Cambridge University Press, 1994). See also Teofilo F. Ruiz, "Two Patrician Families in Late Medieval Burgos: The Sarracín and the Bonifaz," in Ruiz, *The City and the Realm: Burgos and Castile, 1080–1492* (Aldershot, UK: Variorum, 1992).

10 See Teofilo F. Ruiz, *Order and Continuity. Land and Town in Late Medieval Castile* (Philadelphia: University of Pennsylvania Press, 1994), 196–215.

11 Francisco Cantera Burgos, *El judio Salmantino Abraham Zacut. Notas para la historia de la astronomía en la España medieval* (Madrid: C. Bermejo, impresor, 1931).

12 Peter E. Russell, *Prince Henry "the Navigator": A Life* (New Haven & London: Yale Nota Bene, 2001).

13 Felipe Fernández-Armesto, *Before Columbus: Exploration and Colonisation from the Mediterranean to the Atlantic, 1229–1492* (Basingstoke, UK: Macmillan Education, 1987).

14 Sanjay Subrahmanyam, *The Career and Legend of Vasco da Gama* (Cambridge & New York: Cambridge University Press, 1997).

15 Fernand Braudel, *Capitalism and Material Life, 1400–1800*, trans. Miriam Kochan (New York: Harper Colophon, 1975).

16 *New York Times*, September 1, (2014), A16.

BIBLIOGRAPHY

PRIMARY SOURCES

Achard, Paul. *La vie extraordinaire des frères Barberousse, corsaires et rois d'Alger*. Paris: Les Éditions de France, 1939.

Al-Idrīsī, Abu ʿAbdallāh Muḥammad. *Description de l'Afrique et de l'Espaqne*. Translated by R. Dozy and M.J. de Goeje. Leyden: Brill, 1866.

Alighieri, Dante. *De vulgari eloquentia*. Edited by Steven Botterill. New York: Cambridge University Press, 1996.

Archivo de la Corona de Aragón (ACA) *Indice de los registros de protestas de mar (1766–1868)* and *Registros de protestas de mar. 1766–1868* in 33 vols. Barcelona: ACA Real Audiencia. Consulado de Mar. Serie 4. IRPM.

Brown, Irving Henry. *Nights and Days on the Gypsy Trail through Andalusia and on other Mediterranean Shores*. New York & London: Harper & Brothers, 1922.

Calvete de Estrella, Juan Cristóbal. *El felicísimo viaje del muy alto y poderoso Príncipe Don Felipe . . . desde España a sus tierras de la Baja Alemania*. 2 vols. Antwerp, 1562; Madrid: Sociedad de Bibliófilos Españoles, 1930.

Cervantes y Saavedra, Miguel de. *Don Quixote de la Mancha*. Edited by Martín de Riquer. 2 vols. Barcelona: Editorial Juventud, 1995.

Cook, Miriam, Erdağ M. Göknar, and Grant Richard Parker. *Mediterranean Passages: Readings from Dido to Derrida*. Chapel Hill: University of North Carolina Press, 2008.

de Haedo, Diego. *Topografía e historia general de Argel*. 3 vols. Madrid: Sociedad de Bibliófilos Españoles, 1927–1929.

Dpir Lehatsʿi, Simēon, and George A. Bournoutian. *The Travel Accounts of Simēon of Poland*. Costa Mesa, CA: Mazda Publishers, 2007.

Dumas, Alexander. *The Count of Monte Cristo*. New York: Penguin, 2003.

Eberhardt, Isabelle, and Victor Barrucant. *Dans l'ombre chaude de l'Islam*. Paris: Librairie Charpentier et Fasquelle, 1906.

Géographes et voyageurs au Moyen Âge. Edited by Henri Bresc and Emmanuelle Tixier du Mesnil. Nanterre: Presses Universitaires de Paris Ouest, 2010.

Hennen, John. *Sketches of the Medical Topography of the Mediterranean; Comprising an Account of Gibraltar, the Ionian Islands, and Malta; to which is Prefixed, a Sketch of a Plan for Memoirs on Medical Topography*. London: Underwood, 1830.

Itinerary from Bordeaux to Jerusalem. The Bordeaux Pilgrim (333 A.D.). Translated by Aubrey Stewart. London: Palestine Pilgrims' Text Society, 1887.

Jackson, James Grey. *An Account of Timbuctoo and Housa, Territories in the Interior of Africa, by El Hage Abd Salam Shabeeny . . .* London: Longman, Hurst, Rees, Orme and Brown, 1820.

Khaldûn, Ibn. *The Mugaddimah. An Introduction to History.* Translated by Franz Rosenthal, edited and abridged by N.J. Dawood. Princeton: Princeton University Press, 1967.

Longino, Michèle. *French Travel Writing in the Ottoman Empire: Marseilles to Constantinople, 1650–1700.* New York: Routledge, 2015.

Matar, Nabil. *An Arab Ambassador in the Mediterranean World: The Travels of Muḥammad Ibn 'Uthmān al-Miknāsī, 1779–1788.* New York: Routledge, 2015.

Mistral, Frédéric. *Mirèio. A Provençal Poem.* Translated by Harriet W. Preston. Boston: Roberts Brothers, 1872.

Montefiore, Lady Judith Cohen, and Louis Loewe. *Notes from a Private Journal of a Visit to Egypt and Palestine, by way of Italy and the Mediterranean.* London: Wertheimer, Lea, & Co., 1885.

R.E. Lewis, *An Account of Spain; Being a New Description of that Country and People; and of the Sea Ports along the Mediterranean: of Ceuta, Tangier &c.* London: Printed for Joseph Wilde, 1700.

Sillitoe, Alan. *Leading the Blind: A Century of Guide Book Travel.* New York: Open Road Media, 2016.

Sultana, Donald. *The Siege of Malta Rediscovered: An Account of Sir Walter Scott's Mediterranean Journey and His Last Novel.* Edinburgh: Scottish Academic Press, 1977.

The History and Description of Africa and of the Notable Things Therein . . . . Translated by John Pory. Edited by Robert Brown. 3 vols. London: Hakluyt Society, 1896.

The Itinerary of Benjamin of Tudela. Edited and translated by Marcus Nathan Adler. New York: Philipp Feldheim, first edition, 1907.

The Travels of Ibn Battūta, A.D. 1325–1354. Translated by H.A.R. Gibb. Cambridge: Cambridge University Press, 1958.

The Travels of Ibn Jubayr. Translated by R.J.C. Broadhurst. London: Jonathan Cape, 1952.

Theroux, Paul. *The Pillars of Hercules: A Grand Tour of the Mediterranean.* New York: G. P. Putnam's Sons, 1995.

Viajes de Ali Bey el Abbassi por Africa y Asia durante los años 1803,1804, 1805, 1806, 1807. Translated by P.P. Volume 1. Valencia: Librería de Mallén y Sobrinos, 1836.

GENERAL HISTORIES OF THE MEDITERRANEAN AND WESTERN MEDITERRANEAN COUNTRIES

Abulafia, David. *The Mediterranean in History.* Los Angeles: J. Paul Getty Museum, 2003.

Abulafia, David. *The Great Sea: A Human History of the Mediterranean.* New York: Oxford University Press, 2011.

Abun-Nasr, Jamil M. *A History of the Maghrib.* New York: Cambridge University Press, 1971.

Al-Baghdādī, Ibn Ṭāhir. *Al-Farq Bain al-Firak (Moslem Schisms and Sects).* Translated by Kate C. Seelye. 2 vols. New York: AMS Press, 1966.

Allen, Harriet D. *Mediterranean Ecogeography.* New York: Prentice Hall, 2001.

Ames, Christine C. *Medieval Heresies: Christianity, Judaism, and Islam.* New York: Cambridge University Press, 2015.

Bergin, Joseph. *A History of France*. London: Palgrave, 2015.

Braudel, Fernand. *The Mediterranean and the Mediterranean World in the Age of Philip II*. Translated by Siân Reynolds. 2 vols. Berkeley and Los Angeles: University of California Press, 1995.

Braudel, Fernand. *Les mémoires de la Méditerranée: préhistoire et antiquité*. Edited by Roselyne de Ayala and Paule Braudel. Preface and notes by Jean Guilaine and Pierre Rouillard. Paris: Editions de Fallois, 1998.

Broodbank, Cyprian. *The Making of the Middle Sea: A History of the Mediterranean from the Beginning to the Emergence of the Classical World*. Oxford: Oxford University Press, 2013.

Brummett, Palmira Johnson. *Mapping the Ottomans: Sovereignty, Territory, and Identity in the Early Modern Mediterranean*. New York: Cambridge University Press, 2015.

Castro, Américo. *The Structure of Spanish History*. Princeton: Princeton University Press, 1954.

Clancy-Smith, Julia Ann. *North Africa, Islam, and the Mediterranean World: From the Almoravids to the Algerian War*. Portland: Frank Cass, 2001.

Clark, Michael K. *Algeria in Turmoil: A History of the Rebellion*. New York: Praeger, 1959.

Daniel, Glyn, and J.D. Evans. *The Western Mediterranean*. London: Cambridge University Press, 1967.

Faguet, Émile. *A Literary History of France*. New York: C. Scribner's Sons, 1907.

Freeman, Edward A. *The History of Sicily from the Earliest Times*. Oxford: At the Clarendon Press, 1891–1894.

Frost, Honor. *Under the Mediterranean: Marine Antiquities*. London: Honor Frost Foundation, 1963.

Goitein, Shelomo D. *A Mediterranean Society: The Jewish Communities of the Arab World as Portrayed in the Documents of the Cairo Geniza*. 6 vols. Berkeley: University of California Press, 1967–1993.

Haine, W. Scott. *The History of France*. Westport: Greenwood Press, 2000.

Harris, W.V., ed. *Rethinking the Mediterranean*. Oxford: Oxford University Press, 2005.

Hoffmann, Eleanor. *Realm of the Evening Star: A History of Morocco and the Lands of the Moors*. Philadelphia: Chilton Books, 1965.

Horden, Peregrine, and Nicholas Purcell. *The Corrupting Sea: A Study of Mediterranean History*. Oxford: Blackwell, 2000.

Julien, Charles André. *History of North Africa: Tunisia, Algeria, Morocco. From the Arab Conquest to 1830*. New York: Praeger, 1970.

Kenney, Jeffrey T. *Muslim Rebels: Kharijites and the Politics of Extremism in Egypt*. New York: Oxford University Press, 2006.

Luzzatto, Gino. *An Economic History of Italy: From the Fall of the Roman Empire to the Beginning of the Sixteenth Century*. London: Routledge and Kegan Paul, 1961.

Matthew, Donald. *The Norman Kingdom of Sicily*. Cambridge: Cambridge University Press, 1992.

McPhee, Peter. *A Social History of France, 1780–1880*. London: Routledge, 1992.

McKendrick, Melveena. *A Concise History of Spain*. London: Cassell, 1972.

Norwich, John Julian. *The Middle Sea: A History of the Mediterranean*. New York: Doubleday, 2006.

Pasamar, Gonzalo. *Apologia and Criticism: Historians and the History of Spain, 1500–2000*. New York: Peter Lang, 2010.

Perkins, Kenneth J. *A History of Modern Tunisia*. New York: Cambridge University Press, 2004.

Porch, Douglas. *The Conquest of Morocco*. New York: A.A. Knopf, 1983.

Riall, Lucy. *Risorgimento: The History of Italy from Napoleon to Nation State*. New York: Palgrave Macmillan, 2009.

Smith, Denis Mack. *A History of Sicily: Medieval Sicily, 800–1713*. London: Chatto & Windus, 1980.

Tartakoff, Paola. *Between Christian and Jew: Conversion and Inquisition in the Crown of Aragon, 1250–1391*. Philadelphia: University of Pennsylvania Press, 2012.

Zamagni, Vera. *The Economic History of Italy, 1860–1990*. Oxford: Oxford University Press, 1993.

OTHER SECONDARY WORKS

Abulafia, David. *Italy, Sicily, and the Mediterranean, 1100–1400*. London: Variorum Reprints, 1987.

Abulafia, David. *Frederick II. A Medieval Emperor*. London: Penguin, 1988.

Abulafia, David. *Commerce and Conquest in the Mediterranean*. Aldershot, UK: Variorum, 1993.

Abulafia, David. *A Mediterranean Emporium: The Catalan Kingdom of Majorca*. Cambridge: Cambridge University Press, 1994.

Abulafia, David. *Mediterranean Encounters, Economic, Religious, Political, 1100–1550*. London: Routledge, 2000.

Abulafia, David, ed. *The Mediterranean in History*. London: Thames & Hudson, 2003.

Almarcegui, Patricia. *Ali Bey y los viajeros europeos a Oriente*. Barcelona: Bellaterra, 2007.

Andaloro, Maria, ed. *The Royal Palace of Palermo*. Modena, Italy: Franco Cosimi Panini, 2011.

Antier, Jean Jacques. *Marins de Provence et du Languedoc: Vingt-cinq siècles d'histoire du littoral français méditerranéen*. Avignon: Aubanel, 1977.

Arendt, Erich. *Art and Architecture on the Mediterranean Islands*. London: Abelard-Schuman, 1968.

Attenborough, David. *The First Eden: The Mediterranean World and Man*. Boston: Little, Brown, 1987.

Aurell, Jaume. *Authoring the Past: History, Autobiography, and Politics in Medieval Catalonia*. Chicago: University of Chicago Press, 2012.

Bachvarova, Mary R., Dorota Dutsch, and Ann Suter. *The Fall of Cities in the Mediterranean: Commemoration in Literature, Folk Song, and Liturgy*. Cambridge: Cambridge University Press, 2016.

Baer, Yitzhak. *A History of the Jews in Christian Spain*. 2 vols. Philadelphia: The Jewish Publication Society of America, 1966.

Baldoli, Claudia. *A History of Italy*. New York: Palgrave Macmillan, 2009.

BBC. "Mapping Mediterranean Migration." http://www.bbc.com/news/world-europe-24521614 (accessed March 31, 2017).

Bennassar, Bartolomé, and Lucile Bennassar. *Les Chrétiens d'Allah: L'histoire extraordinaire des renégats, XVIe et XVIIe siècles*. Paris: Perrin, 1989.

Bennassar, Bartolomé. *Les tribulations de Mustafa des Six-Fours*. Paris: Criterion, 1995.

Berque, Jacques. *Ulémas, fondateurs, insurgés du Maghreb: XVIIe siècle*. Paris: Sindbad, 1982.

Berque, Jacques. *Ibn 'Askar, Muhammad ibn 'Ali, The Sheikhs of Morocco in the XVIth Century*. Translated by T.H. Weir. Edinburgh: G.A. Morton, 1904.

Bevan, Andrew, and James Connolly. *Mediterranean Islands, Fragile Communities and Persistent Landscapes: Antikythera in Long-Term Perspective.* Cambridge: Cambridge University Press, 2013.

Bradford, Ernle Dusgate Selb. *The Sultan's Admiral: The Life of Barbarossa.* London: Hodder & Stoughton, 1969.

Braudel, Fernand. *Capitalism and Material life, 1400–1800.* Translated by Miriam Kochan. New York: Harper Colophon, 1975.

Braudel, Fernand. *Memory and the Mediterranean.* Edited by Roselyne de Ayala and Paule Braudel. Translated by Siân Reynolds. New York: A.A. Knopf, 2001.

Brenan, Gerald. *The Spanish Labyrinth: An Account of the Social and Political Background of the Civil War.* Cambridge: Cambridge University Press, 1950.

Brett, Michael. *Ibn Khaldun and the Medieval Maghrib.* Aldershot, UK: Ashgate Variorum, 1999.

Brown, Carl L. *The Tunisia of Ahmad Bey, 1837–1855.* Princeton: Princeton University Press, 1974.

Brown, Peter. *The World of Late Antiquity, AD 150–750.* New York: Harcourt Brace Jovanovich, 1971.

Brown, Peter. *Augustine of Hippo: A Biography.* London: Faber and Faber, 2000.

Brown, Peter. *Through the Eye of a Needle: Wealth, the Fall of Rome, and the Making of Christianity in the West, 350–550 AD.* Princeton: Princeton University Press, 2012.

Brown, Peter. *The Rise of Western Christendom: Triumph and Diversity, A.D. 200–1000.* Revised edition. Oxford: Wiley-Blackwell, 2013.

Burke, Peter. *Languages and Communities in Early Modern Europe.* Cambridge: Cambridge University Press, 2004.

Burns, Robert I. *The Crusader Kingdom of Valencia (1238–1276): A Study in the Organization of the Medieval Frontier.* Baltimore: Johns Hopkins University Press, 1958.

Buttigieg, Emanuel, and Simon Phillips. *Islands and Military Orders, c.1291–c.1768.* Burlington: Ashgate, 2013.

Caldwell Ames, Christine. *Medieval Heresies: Christianity, Judaism, and Islam.* New York: Cambridge University Press, 2015.

Cantera Burgos, Francisco. *Alvar García de Santa María. Historia de la Judería de Burgos y de sus conversos más egregios.* Madrid: Instituto Arias Montano, 1952.

Cantera Burgos, Francisco. *El judío Salmantino Abraham Zacut. Notas para la historia de la astronomía en la España medieval.* Madrid: C. Bermejo, Impresor, 1931.

Carboni, Stefano. *Venice and the Islamic World, 828–1797.* New Haven: Yale University Press, 2007.

Carr, Raymond. *Spain:1808-1939.* Oxford: Clarendon Press, 1966.

Carrington, Richard. *The Mediterranean: Cradle of Western Culture.* New York: Viking Press, 1971.

Cary, Max. *The Ancient Explorers.* Baltimore: Penguin, 1963.

Cary, Max. "The Greeks and Ancient Trade with the Atlantic." *Journal of Hellenistic Studies,* 44 (1924): 166–179.

Catlos, Brian A. *Infidel Kings and Unholy Warriors: Faith, Power, and Violence in the Age of Crusade and Jihad.* New York: Farrar, Straus and Giroux, 2014.

Catlos, Brian A. *Muslims of Medieval Latin Christendom, c. 1050–1614.* Cambridge: Cambridge University Press, 2014.

Catlos, Brian A. "Accursed, Superior Men: Ethnoreligious Minorities and Politics in the Medieval Mediterranean." Forthcoming in *Comparative Studies in Society and History,* 56, 4 (2014): 844–869.

Çaykent, Özlem, and Luca Zavagno, eds. *Islands of the Eastern Mediterranean: A History of Cross-Cultural Encounters*. London: I.B. Tauris, 2014.

Chaker, Salem. *Berbères aujourd'hui*. Paris: L'Harmattan, 1989.

Chaker, Salem. *Manuel de linguistique Berbère*. 2 vols. Algiers: Ed. Bouchène, 1991.

Chemla, Jacques, Monique Goffard, and Lucette Valensi. *Un siècle de céramique d'art en Tunisie. Les fils de J. Chemla, Tunis*. Tunis: Éditions Déméter, 2015.

Cherif, Mohamed-Hédi. *Pouvoir et société dans la Tunisie de H'usayn bin 'Ali: 1705–1740*. Tunis: Université de Tunis, 1986.

Christie, Neil, and S.T. Loseby, eds. *Towns in Transition: Urban Evolution in Late Antiquity and the Early Middle Ages*. Brookfield: Scolar Press, 1996.

Clancy-Smith, Julia Ann. *Rebel and Saint: Muslim Notables, Populist Protest, Colonial Encounters (Algeria and Tunisia, 1800–1904)*. Berkeley: University of California Press, 1994.

Clark, Peter. *European Cities and Towns: 400–2000*. Oxford: Oxford University Press, 2009.

Cochrane, Eric. *Florence in the Forgotten Centuries, 1527–1800: A History of Florence and the Florentines in the Age of the Grand Dukes*. Chicago: University of Chicago Press, 1973.

Collantes de Terán, Antonio. *Sevilla en la Baja Edad Media*. Sevilla: Ayuntamiento de Sevilla, 1977.

Collins, Roger. *Visigothic Spain, 409–711*. Oxford: Blackwell, 2004.

Cómez, Rafael. *El alcázar del rey Don Pedro*. Sevilla: Diputación de Sevilla, 2006.

Constable, Olivia Remie. *Trade and Traders in Muslim Spain: The Commercial Realignment of the Iberian Peninsula, 900–1500*. New York: Cambridge University Press, 1994.

Constable, Olivia Remie. *Housing the Stranger in the Mediterranean World: Lodging, Trade, and Travel in Late Antiquity and the Middle Ages*. New York: Cambridge University Press, 2003.

Cowan, Alexander. *Mediterranean Urban Culture, 1400–1700*. Exeter: University of Exeter Press, 2000.

Crackanthorpe, David. *Marseille*. Oxford: Signal Books, 2012.

Crowley, Roger. *Empires of the Sea: The Siege of Malta, the Battle of Lepanto, and the Contest for the Center of the World*. New York: Random House, 2008.

Curtius, Ernst Robert. *European Literature and the Latin Middle Ages*. Princeton: Princeton University Press, 1953.

D'Amico, Stefano. *Spanish Milan: A City within the Empire, 1535–1706*. New York: Palgrave Macmillan, 2012.

Davis, Natalie Zemon. *Trickster Travels: A Sixteenth-Century Muslim Between Worlds*. New York: Hill and Wang, 2006.

de Certeau, Michel. "Walking in the City." In *The Practice of Everyday Life, 91–110*. Berkeley: University of California Press, 1984.

de Certau, Michel. *The Writing of History*. Translated by Tom Conley. New York: Columbia University Press, 1988.

de Pallejá, Don Cavetano, trans. *Consulado del mar de Barcelona: Nuevamente traducido de cathalan en castellano*. Barcelona: J. Piferrer, 1732.

Dietz, Maribel. *Wandering Monks, Virgins, and Pilgrims*. State College: Penn State University Press, 2005.

Dunn, Ross. *The Adventures of Ibn Battuta: A Muslim Traveler of the 14th Century*. London: Croom Helm, 1986.

Edwards, John. "Religious Faith and Doubt in Late Medieval Spain: Soria, circa 1450–1500." *Past & Present: A Journal of Historical Studies*, 128 (1990): 152–161.

Ellenblum, Roni. *The Collapse of the Eastern Mediterranean: Climate Change and the Decline of the East, 950–1072*. Cambridge: Cambridge University Press, 2012.

Elliott, John H. *Imperial Spain, 1469–1716*. New York: St Martin's Press, 1964.

Elliott, John H. *The Count-Duke of Olivares. The Statesman in an Age of Decline*. New Haven: Yale University Press, 1986.

Epstein, Steven. *Genoa and the Genoese, 958–1528*. Chapel Hill: University of North Carolina Press, 1996.

Erlanger, Steven. "Melting Pot of Melodrama Enthralls French Nightly." *New York Times*. http://www.nytimes.com/2009/03/03/world/europe/03marseille.html?pagewanted=all&_r=0 (accessed March 31, 2017).

Espuny Tomás, José María. "El Real Consulado de Comercio del Principado de Cataluña (1758–1829)." PhD diss., Universitat Autònoma de Barcelona, 1992.

Euben, Roxanne Leslie. *Journeys to the Other Shore: Muslim and Western Travelers in Search of Knowledge*. Princeton: Princeton University Press, 2006.

Fancy, Hussein. *The Mercenary Mediterranean: Sovereignty, Religion, and Violence in the Medieval Crown of Aragon*. Chicago: University of Chicago Press, 2016.

Fernández-Armesto, Felipe. *Before Columbus: Exploration and Colonisation from the Mediterranean to the Atlantic, 1229–1492*. Basingstoke, UK: Macmillan Education, 1987.

Finley, M.I., Denis M. Smith, and Christopher Duggan. *A History of Sicily*. London: Chatto & Windus, 1986.

Fliche, Augustin. *Aigues-Mortes et Saint-Gilles*. Second edition. Paris: H. Laurens, 1950.

Fontes, Torres. *Repartimiento de la huerta y campo de Murcia en el siglo XIII*. Murcia: Consejo Superior de Investigaciones Científicas, 1971.

Fox, Robert. *The Inner Sea: The Mediterranean and its People*. New York: A.A. Knopf, 1993.

Freedman, Paul H. *The Origins of Peasant Servitude in Medieval Catalonia*. Cambridge: Cambridge University Press, 1991.

García Arenal, Mercedes. *Ahmad al-Mansur: The Beginnings of Modern Morocco*. Oxford: OneWorld, 2009.

García Arenal, Mercedes. *La diáspora de los Andalusíes*. Barcelona: Icaria Editorial, 2003.

Geary, Patrick J. *The Myth of Nations: The Medieval Origins of Europe*. Princeton: Princeton University Press, 2002.

Gilbert, Claire. "The Politics of Language in the Western Mediterranean c. 1492–1669: Multilingual Institutions and the Status of Arabic in Early Modern Spain." PhD diss., UCLA, 2014.

Gilbertson, Nicole. "Sites of Encounter in World History." *Perspectives on History*, 50 (2012): 32–33.

Ginzburg, Carlo. *Night Battles: Witchcraft and Agrarian Cults in the Sixteenth and Seventeenth Centuries*. Baltimore: Johns Hopkins University Press, 1983.

Gladstone, Rick. "Stepping Over the Dead on a Migrant Boat." *New York Times*. https://www.nytimes.com/2016/10/06/world/europe/migrants-mediterranean.html (accessed March 31, 2017).

Glick, Thomas F. *Islamic and Christian Spain in the Early Middle Ages: Comparative Perspectives on Social and Cultural Formation*. Princeton: Princeton University Press, 1979.

Goldberg, Jessica. *Trade and Institutions in the Medieval Mediterranean: The Geniza Merchants and their Business World*. New York: Cambridge University Press, 2012.

Goldberg, Jessica. "Choosing and Enforcing Business Relationships in the Eleventh-Century Mediterranean: Reassessing the Maghribi Traders." *Past & Present*, 216 (2012): 3–40.

Gourdin, Philippe. *Tabarka: histoire et archéologie d'un préside espagnol et d'un comptoir génois en terre africaine (XVe–XVIIIe siècle)*. Rome: Institut National du Patrimoine de Tunis: Ecole Française de Rome, 2008.

Gu, Sharron. *A Cultural History of the Arabic Language*. Jefferson, NC: McFarland & Company, 2014.

Guidetti, Massimo, ed. *Storia dei Sardi e della Sardegna*. 2 vols. Milan: Jaca, 1987–1988.

Herlihy, David. *Pisa in the Early Renaissance: A Study of Urban Growth*. New Haven: Yale University Press, 1958.

Henning, Joachim. *Post-Roman Towns, Trade, and Settlement in Europe and Byzantium. Vol. 2, Byznantium, Pliska, and the Balkans*. Berlin: W. de Gruyter, 2007.

Herzfeld, Michael. "Practical Mediterreanism: Excuses for Everything, from Epistemology to Eating." In *Rethinking the Mediterranean*, edited by W.V. Harris, 45–63. Oxford: Oxford University Press, 2005.

Hodges, Richard. *Towns and Trade in the Age of Charlemagne*. London: Duckworth, 2000.

Hogg, Sylvie. *Frommer's Italian Islands*. Hoboken, NJ: Wiley, 2011.

Horden, Peregrine. "Travel Sickness: Medicine and Mobility in the Mediterranean from Antiquity to the Renaissance." In *Rethinking the Mediterranean*, edited by W.V. Harris, 179–200. Oxford: Oxford University Press, 2005.

Horden, Peregrine, and Sharon Kinoshita. *A Companion to Mediterranean History*. Oxford: Wiley-Blackwell, 2014.

Houston, James M. *The Western Mediterranean World: An Introduction to its Regional Landscapes*. Especially sections by J. Roglic and J.I. Clarke. New York: Praeger, 1967.

Human Rights Watch. "The Mediterranean Migration Crisis: Why People Flee, What the EU Should Do." https://www.hrw.org/report/2015/06/19/mediterranean-migration-crisis/why-people-flee-what-eu-should-do (accessed March 31, 2017).

Jacobshagen, Voleker H., ed. *The Atlas System of Morocco: Studies on its Geodynamic Evolution*. Berlin: Springer-Verlag, 1988.

Jados, Stanley S. *Consolat de Mar, and Related Documents*. Tuscaloosa: University of Alabama Press, 1975.

Jehel, Georges. *Aigues-Mortes, un port pour un roi: Les capétiens et la Méditerranée*. Roanne: Horvath, 1985.

Jensen, Kurt Villads, Kirsi Salonen, and Helle Vogt. *Cultural Encounters during the Crusades*. Odense: University Press of Southern Denmark, 2013.

Jones, Prudence, and Nigel Pennick. *A History of Pagan Europe*. New York: Routledge Press, 1995.

Jordan, William C. "Supplying Aigues-Mortes for the Crusade of 1248: The Problem of Restructuring Trade." In *Order and Innovation in the Middle Ages: Essays in Honor of Joseph R. Strayer*, edited by William C. Jordan, Bruce McNab, and Teofilo F. Ruiz, 165–172. Princeton: Princeton University Press, 1976.

Kantorowicz, Ernst. *Frederick the Second, 1194–1250*. London: Constable & Co., 1931.

King, Russell. *The Mediterranean Passage: Migration and New Cultural Encounters in Southern Europe*. Liverpool: Liverpool University Press, 2001.

King, Russell, Pauloa de Mas, and J. Mansvelt-Beck. *Geography, Environment, and Development in the Mediterranean*. Brighton: Sussex Academic Press, 2001.

Kippenberg, Hans G., and Guy G. Stroumsa. *Secrecy and Concealment: Studies in the History of Mediterranean and Near Eastern Religions*. New York: Brill, 1995.

Kraemer, Ross Shepard. *Unreliable Witnesses: Religion, Gender, and History in the Greco-Roman Mediterranean*. New York: Oxford University Press, 2011.

Langevin, Philippe, and Jean-Claude Juan, eds. *Marseille: une métropole entre Europe et Méditerranée.* Paris: La Documentation Française, 2007.

Levack, Brian P. *The Witch-Hunt in Early Modern Europe.* Third edition. Harlow: Pearson-Longman, 2006.

Lewis, Archibald R. "Northern European Sea Power and the Straits of Gibraltar, 1031–1350 A.D." In *Order and Innovation in the Middle Ages: Essays in Honor of Joseph R. Strayer,* edited by William C. Jordan, Bruce McNab, and Teofilo F. Ruiz, 139–164. Princeton: Princeton University Press, 1976.

Liang, Yuen-Gen. *Family and Empire. The Fernández de Córdoba and the Spanish Realm.* Philadelphia: University of California Press, 2011.

Liedl, Gottfried *Mediterraner Islam.* Wien: Turia & Kant, 2007.

MacKay, Angus. *Spain in the Middle Ages: From Frontier to Empire, 1000–1500.* London: Macmillan, 1977.

Mackenzie-Grieve, Averil. *Aspects of Elba and the other Islands of the Tuscan Archipelago.* London: Jonathan Cape, 1964.

Manara, Elena. *S. Margherita di Vernazza: Una chiesa, un borgo, una storia.* Genoa: Edizioni Culturali Internazionali Genova, 1990.

Marino, John A., ed. *Early Modern Italy, 1550–1796.* Oxford: Oxford University Press, 2002.

Marino, John A. *Pastoral Economics in the Kingdom of Naples.* Baltimore: Johns Hopkins University Press, 1988.

Marongiu, Pietro. *Teoria e storia del banditismo sociale in Sardegna.* Cagliari: Edizione Della Torre, 1981.

Maskarinec, Maya. *Building Rome Saint by Saint in the Early Middle Ages.* Philadelphia: University of Pennsylvania Press, 2017.

Metcalfe, Alex. *The Muslims of Medieval Italy.* Edinburgh: Edinburgh University Press, 2009.

Migliorini, Bruno, and T. Gwynfor Griffith. *The Italian Language.* London & Boston: Faber and Faber, 1984.

Mokhbery, Susan. "France and Persia in the Age of Absolutism." PhD diss., UCLA, 2010.

Montaner, M. Carmen, and Anna María Casassas. "Between Science and Spying: Maps of the Northern Africa and the Near East in the Works of Ali Bey el-Abassi (1766–1818)." *Eastern Mediterranean Cartographies,* 25/26 (2004): 181–196.

Montoto, Santiago. *La catedral y el alcázar de Sevilla.* Second edition. Madrid: Editorial Plus Ultra, 1951.

Moore, R.I. *The War on Heresy: Faith and Power in Medieval Europe.* London: Profile, 2012.

Nef, Annliese, and Martin Thom. *A Companion to Medieval Palermo: The History of a Mediterranean City from 600–1500.* Boston: Brill, 2013.

Nercessian, Nora Nouritza. "The Cappella Palatina of Roger II: The Relationship of its Imagery to its Political Function." PhD diss., UCLA, 1981.

Nirenberg, David. *Neighboring Faiths: Christianity, Islam, and Judaism in the Middle Ages and Today.* Chicago: University of Chicago Press, 2014.

O'Callaghan, Joseph F. *A History of Medieval Spain.* Ithaca: Cornell University Press, 1975.

Owens, Jonathan. *A Linguistic History of Arabic.* New York: Oxford University Press, 2006.

Paine, Lincoln P. *The Sea and Civilization: A Maritime History of the World.* New York: A. A. Knopf, 2013.

Pascual, Pere. *Agricultura i industrialització a la Catalunya del segle XIX: Formació i desestructuració d'un sistema econòmic*. Barcelona: Crítica, 1990.

Phillips, William D. Jr, and Carla Rahn Phillips. *The Worlds of Christopher Columbus*. Cambridge: Cambridge University Press, 1992.

Piña Homs, Román. *El Consolat de Mar, Mallorca, 1326–1800*. Palma de Mallorca: Institut d'Estudis Baleàrics, 1985.

Pirenne, Henri. *Mohammed and Charlemagne*. Translated by Bernard Miall. New York: Meridian, 1960.

Piterberg, Gabriel, Teofilo F. Ruiz, and Geoffrey Symcox. *Braudel Revisited: The Mediterranean World 1600–1800*. Toronto: University of Toronto Press, 2010.

Pratt, Mary Louise. *Imperial Eyes: Travel Writing and Transculturation*. London: Routledge, 1992.

Purcell, Nicholas. "The Ancient Mediterranean: The View from the Customs House." In *Rethinking the Mediterranean*, edited by W.V. Harris, 200–232. Oxford: Oxford University Press, 2005.

Remensnyder, Amy. *La Conquistadora: The Virgin Mary at War and Peace in the Old and New World*. New York: Oxford University Press, 2014.

Reyerson, Katheryn, and John Drendel, eds. *Urban and Rural Communities in Medieval France: Provence and Languedoc, 1000–1500*. Boston: Brill, 1998.

Reyes Morales, Hevia, and Ana Marcos Alvarez, eds. *El conjunto histórico de Sevilla. Rehabilitación singular*. Sevilla: Ayuntamiento de Sevilla, Gerencia Municipal de Urbanismo, 1996.

Reynier, Christine. *Cross-Cultural Encounters between the Mediterranean and the English-Speaking Worlds*. New York: Peter Lang, 2011.

Reynolds, Paul. *Trade in the Western Mediterranean, AD 400–700: The Ceramic Evidence*. Oxford: Tempus Reparatum, 1995.

Rieucau, Jean. *Les gens de mer: Sète en Languedoc*. Paris: L'Harmattan, 1990.

Rivera-Cordero, Victoria. "Spatializing Illness: Embodied Deafness in Teresa de Cartagena's *Arboleda de los enfermos*," *La Corónica: A Journal of Medieval Hispanic Languages, Literatures, and Cultures*, 32 (2009): 61–77.

Roberts, Sean E. *Printing a Mediterranean World: Florence, Constantinople, and the Renaissance of Geography*. Cambridge: Harvard University Press, 2013.

Robinson, Andrew. *Lost Languages: The Enigma of the World's Undeciphered Scripts*. New York: McGraw-Hill, 2002.

Robinson, Cynthia. *Imagining the Passion in a Multiconfessional Castile: The Virgin, Christ, Devotions, and Images in the Fourteenth and Fifteenth Centuries*. State College: Penn State University Press, 2013.

Rodgers, Alan. *The Industrial Geography of the Port of Genova*. Chicago: University of Chicago Press, 1960.

Rodriguez, Jarbel. *Captives and Their Saviors in the Medieval Crown of Aragon*. Washington, DC: Catholic University of America Press, 2007.

Rubin, Miri. *Mother of God: A History of the Virgin Mary*. New Haven: Yale University Press, 2009.

Ruiz, Teofilo F. "The Holy Office in Medieval France and in Late Medieval Castile: Origins and Contrast." In *The Spanish Inquisition and the Inquisitorial Mind*, edited by Angel Alcalá, 33–51. New York: Columbia University Press, 1987.

Ruiz, Teofilo F. "Two Patrician Families in Late Medieval Burgos: The Sarracín and the Bonifaz." In *The City and the Realm: Burgos and Castile, 1080–1492*, by Teofilo F. Ruiz. Aldershot, UK: Variorum, 1992.

Ruiz, Teofilo F. *Order and Continuity. Land and Town in Late Medieval Castile*. Philadelphia: University of Pennsylvania Press, 1994.

Ruiz, Teofilo F. "The Peasantries of Iberia, 1400–1800." In *The Peasantries of Europe: From the Fourteenth to the Eighteenth Centuries*, edited by Tom Scott, 49–73. Longman: London, 1998.

Ruiz, Teofilo F. *Spanish Society, 1400–1600.* Harlow: Longman, 2001.

Ruiz, Teofilo F. "Trading with the 'Other': Economic Exchanges between Jews, Muslims, and Christians in Late Medieval Castile." In *Medieval Spain: Culture, Conflict, and Coexistence: Studies in Honour of Angus MacKay*, edited by Roger Collins and Andrew Goodman, 53–78. Basingstoke, UK: Palgrave Macmillan, 2002.

Ruiz, Teofilo F. *From Heaven to Earth. The Reordering of Castilian Society, 1150–1350.* Princeton: Princeton University Press, 2004.

Ruiz, Teofilo F. *Spain's Centuries of Crisis: 1300–1474.* Oxford: Blackwell, 2007.

Ruiz, Teofilo F. "Sites of Encounters and Cultural Production: An AHA Initiative for an Action Thématique." *Perspectives on History* (2007). http://www.historians.org/perspectives/issues/2007/0712/0712vic1.cfm (accessed March 31, 2017).

Ruiz, Teofilo F. *A King Travels. Festive Traditions in Late Medieval and Early Modern Spain.* Princeton: Princeton University Press, 2012.

Russell, Peter E. *Prince Henry 'the Navigator': A Life.* New Haven: Yale Nota Bene, 2001.

Sagnes, Jean. *Histoire de Sète.* Toulouse: private printing, 1987.

Schaub, Jean-Frédérick. *Les juifs du roi d'Espagne.* Paris: Hachette, 1999.

Schwarts, Stuart B. *All Can Be Saved: Religious Tolerance and Salvation in the Iberian Atlantic World.* New Haven: Yale University Press, 2008.

Signoles, Pierre. *L'espace Tunisien: capitale et etat-région.* 2 vols. Tours: Laboratoire Urbama, Institut de Geographie, 1985.

Signoles, Pierre, A. Belhedi, J.M. Miossec, and H. Dlala. *Tunis: évolution et fonctionnement de l'espace urbain.* Tours: Centre Interuniversitaire d'Études Méditerranéennes, 1987.

Silleras Fernández, Núria. *Chariots of Ladies: Francesc Eiximenis and the Court Culture of Medieval and Early Modern Iberia.* Ithaca: Cornell University Press, 2015.

Simon, Larry J., and Robert Burns. *Iberia and the Mediterranean World of the Middle Ages: Studies in Honor of Robert I. Burns.* New York: Brill, 1995–1996.

Sirat, Colette, Lenn J. Schramm, and W.C. Watt. *Writing as Handwork: A History of Handwriting in Mediterranean and Western Culture.* Turnhout, Belgium: Brepols, 2006.

Slim, Hédi, Ammar Mahjoubi, Khaled Belkhodja, and Abdelmajid Ennabli. *Histoire générale de la Tunisie*, 3 vols. Tunis: Sud Éditions, 2003–2007.

Smail, Daniel. *On Deep History and the Brain.* Berkeley: University of California Press, 2008.

Straka, Georges. *Les dialectes de France au Moyen Age et aujourd'hui: domaines d'oïl et domaine Franco-Provençal.* Paris: Klincksieck, 1972.

Subrahmanyam, Sanjay. *The Career and Legend of Vasco da Gama.* New York: Cambridge University Press, 1997.

Subrahmanyam, Sanjay. *Three Ways to be Alien: Travails and Encounters in the Early Modern World.* Waltham, MA: Brandeis University Press, 2011.

Symcox, Geoffrey. *Victor Amadeus II: Absolutism in the Savoyard State, 1675–1730.* Berkeley: University of California Press, 1983.

Szpiech, Ryan. *Conversion and Narrative. Reading and Religious Authority in Medieval Polemic.* Philadelphia: University of Pennsylvania Press, 2013.

Tabak, Faruk. *The Waning of the Mediterranean, 1550–1870: A Geohistorical Approach.* Baltimore: Johns Hopkins University Press, 2008.

Takeda, Junko Thérèse. *Between Crown and Commerce: Marseille and the Early Modern Mediterranean.* Baltimore: Johns Hopkins University Press, 2011.

Talbert, Charles H. *Reading Luke-Acts in its Mediterranean Milieu.* Leiden: Brill, 2003.

Thomas, Hugh. *The Spanish Civil War.* New York: Harper & Brothers, 1961.

Thomson, J.O. *History of Ancient Geography*. Cambridge: Cambridge University Press, 1965.

Thouzellier, Christine. *Catharisme et valdéisme en Languedoc à la fin du XIIe et au début du XIIIe siècle: politique pontificale-controverses*. Marseille: Laffitte Reprints, 1982.

Torres Fontes, Juan. *Repartimiento de la huerta y campo de Murcia en el siglo XIII*. Murcia: Consejo Superior de Investigaciones Científicas, 1971.

Trivellato, Francesca. *The Familiarity of Strangers: The Sephardic Diaspora, Livorno, and Cross-Cultural Trade in the Early Modern Period*. New Haven: Yale University Press, 2009.

UNHCR (UN Refugee Agency). "Refugees/Migrants Response – Mediterranean." http://data.unhcr.org/mediterranean/regional.php (accessed March 31, 2017).

Valensi, Lucette. *Le Maghreb avant la Prise d'Alger, 1790–1830*. Paris: Flammarion, 1969.

Valensi, Lucette. *Tunisian Peasants in the Eighteenth and Nineteenth Centuries*. Translated by Beth Archer. New York: Cambridge University Press, 1985.

Valensi, Lucette. *Fables de la mémoire: La glorieuse bataille des trois Rois*. Paris: Seuil, 1992.

Valensi, Lucette. "The problem of Unbelief in Braudel's *Mediterranean*." In *Braudel Revisited: The Mediterranean World 1600–1800*, edited by Gabriel Piterberg, Teofilo F. Ruiz, and Geoffrey Symcox, 17–34. Toronto: University of Toronto Press, 2010.

Valensi, Lucette. *Ces étranger familiers. Musulmans en Europe (XVIe–XVIIIe siècles)*. Paris: Éditions Payot et Rivages, 2012.

Vilar, Pierre, Ernest Lluch, Núria Sales et al. *La formació de la Catalunya moderna*. Esplugues de Llobregat: Ariel, 1970.

Vitaglione, Daniel. *The Literature of Provence: An Introduction*. London: McFarland, 2000.

Wachtel, Nathan. *The Faith of Remembrance: Marrano Labyrinths*. Translated by Nikki Halpern. Philadelphia: University of Pennsylvania Press, 2013.

Webb, Diana. *Pilgrims and Pilgrimage in the Medieval West*. London: I.B. Tauris, 2001.

Wickham, Chris. *Framing the Early Middle Ages: Europe and the Mediterranean 400–800*. New York: Oxford University Press, 2005.

Wiley, Eric. "Romani Performance and Heritage Tourism: The Pilgrimage of the Gypsies at Les Saintes-Maries-de-la-Mer." *The Drama Review*, 49 (2005): 135–158.

Winks, Robin W., and Teofilo F. Ruiz. *Medieval Europe and the World*. New York: Oxford University Press, 2005.

Wolf, Eric R. *Religion, Power, and Protest in Local Communities: The Northern Shore of the Mediterranean*. Berlin: Mouton, 1984.

Yaghmaian, Behzad. *Embracing the Infidel: Stories of Muslim Migrants on the Journey West*. New York: Delacorte Press, 2005.

Yardley, Jim, and Gaia Pianigiani. "Three Days, 700 Deaths on Mediterranean as Migrant Crisis Flares." *New York Times*, May 29, 2016. https://www.nytimes.com/2016/05/30/world/europe/migrants-deaths-mediterranean-libya-italy.html (accessed March 31, 2017).

Zaldivar, Antonio. "Language and Power in the Medieval Crown of Aragon: The Rise of Vernacular Writing and Codeswitching Strategies in the Thirteenth-Century Royal Chancery." PhD diss., UCLA, 2014.

INDEX

The Western Mediterranean and the World: 400 CE to the Present, First Edition. Teofilo F. Ruiz.
© 2018 John Wiley & Sons, Ltd. Published 2018 by John Wiley & Sons, Ltd.